Bentham, Byron, and Greece

BENTHAM, BYRON, AND GREECE

Constitutionalism, Nationalism, and Early Liberal Political Thought

F. ROSEN

CLARENDON PRESS · OXFORD
1992

Oxford University Press, Walton Street, Oxford OX2 6DP

Oxford New York Toronto
Delhi Bombay Calcutta Madras Karachi
Petaling Jaya Singapore Hong Kong Tokyo
Nairobi Dar es Salaam Cape Town
Melbourne Auckland

and associated companies in
Berlin Ibadan

Oxford is a trade mark of Oxford University Press

Published in the United States
by Oxford University Press, New York

British Library Cataloguing in Publication Data
Data available

Library of Congress Cataloging in Publication Data
Rosen. F.
Bentham, Byron, and Greece: constitutionalism, nationalism, and
early liberal political thought/F. Rosen.
p. cm.
Includes bibliographical references and index.
1. Bentham, Jeremy, 1748–1832—Contributions in political science.
2. Byron, George Gordon Byron, Baron, 1788–1824—Contributions in
political science. 3. Liberalism—Great Britain—History—19th
century. 4. Political science—Great Britain—History—19th
century. 5. Greece—Constitutional history. 6. Greece—Politics
and government—1821–1832. I. Title.
JC223.B5R67   1992
3205'13'0941—dc20   91–26451
ISBN 0–19–820078–1

Typeset by Cambrian Typesetters, Frimley, Surrey
Printed and bound in
Great Britain by Bookcraft Ltd,
Midsomer Norton, Bath

For the Bentham Project 1983–1990:
SC, TV, PS, RH, CA, CC, MM, PK, CB, JH,
and AH—with affection and thanks.

Preface

In preparing the new edition of Jeremy Bentham's *Constitutional Code*, I became aware of Bentham's involvement in the Greek struggle for independence in the 1820s, during which time he sent (among other books and papers) an early draft of his *Code* to the new Greek government. During the search for this document (which, alas, has not yet been recovered), I spent some time working through the relatively unknown archive of the London Greek Committee which had also been presented to the Greek government, though a century later in 1924, by the grandson of the Honorary Secretary of the Committee, John Bowring. The study of this archive led me to puzzle over the relationships between Bentham's constitutional theory, the activities of the Committee (especially the presence of Lord Byron as its agent in Greece), and the bloody struggle between Greeks and Turks in which few prisoners were taken and humanitarian actions were rare. Though highly indebted to studies of philhellenism and Byron (students of Bentham and utilitarianism have neglected this aspect of Bentham's life and thought), I found myself at odds with numerous interpretations found in these studies, largely because I took more seriously than other scholars in this field the role of ideas in general and particularly those of Bentham and his so-called disciples. I was thus stimulated to write this book, and it is hoped that students of political ideas as well as historians of the period will find material of interest in it.

I am indebted to STICERD (Suntory-Toyota International Centre for Economics and Related Disciplines) for a grant which enabled me to make several journeys to Greece to inspect various archives, and especially that of the London Greek Committee in the National Library of Greece. I also received a Hayter travel award to cover part of the cost of one journey. The task of exploring various archives in Greece has been eased considerably by the assistance and warm hospitality of Mrs Loukia Droulia, Director of the Centre for Neo-Hellenic Research in Athens, whose knowledge of both archives and philhellenism is unrivalled. Her numerous suggestions ensured that my visits to Athens were always fruitful, and I am grateful both to her and to her staff for their assistance. Thanks are also due to the Director of the National Library, Mr P. Nikolopoulos, and to the staff of the Manuscript Library, especially to Miss Catherine Cordouli, who enabled me to proceed quickly and efficiently with my research. Professor Paschalis Kitromilides, University of Athens, who has studied Greek political ideas in this period, has been generous with his advice and assistance in numerous ways.

The chapters on Bentham's constitutional theory are based on research currently being carried out at the Bentham Project, generously funded by the British Academy and the Economic and Social Research Council. The ESRC has made it possible for Dr Philip Schofield to edit a series of volumes in the *Collected Works* on Bentham's theory of constitutional law and government, the first two of which have been extensively used here. I am indebted to Dr Schofield for his assistance on several aspects of this book. The whole of the manuscript has been read by Dr Stephen Conway, University College London, who made many suggestions for improvement, virtually all of which have been adopted. His advice and encouragement have been invaluable, though he bears no responsibility for the ideas and arguments developed here.

For permission to quote from manuscripts and for other valuable assistance, I wish to thank the directors, librarians, and archivists of the following repositories: Aberdeen University Library (Gordon papers), Benaki Museum (Mavrokordatos papers and general archive), Bibliothèque Publique et Universitaire, Geneva (Dumont papers), Bodleian Library (Barker papers), British Library (Bentham, Broughton, and Place papers), British School of Archaeology at Athens (Finlay and Hastings papers), Centre for Neo-Hellenic Research, Athens (Louriottis papers), ELIA Foundation, Athens (Tricoupi papers), General State Archives, Athens (Mavrokordatos papers, Orlandos and Louriottis copybooks, Stanhope papers, and general archive), John Murray Ltd. (Byron papers), Kent County Archives (Lord Guilford papers), National Library of Greece (London Greek Committee papers), Public Record Office (Colonial Office papers), University College London (Bentham and Brougham papers).

Several articles based on research for this volume have been published, and I am grateful to the editors and publishers for permission to reprint parts of the following: 'Bentham's Constitutional Theory and the Greek Constitution of 1822', *Balkan Studies*, 25 (1984), 31–54 (in Chapter 5); 'The Origin of Liberal Utilitarianism: Jeremy Bentham and Liberty', in R. Bellamy (ed.), *Victorian Liberalism* (London, 1990), 58–70 (in Chapters 2 and 3); 'Majorities and Minorities: A Classical Utilitarian View', in J. W. Chapman and A. Wertheimer (eds.), *Majorities and Minorities: Nomos XXXII* (Yearbook of the American Society for Political and Legal Philosophy) (New York, 1990), 24–43 (in Chapters 4 and 5).

I have received assistance and advice from a large number of colleagues and friends, only a few of whom can be mentioned here: Dr Ivon Asquith, Dr Cyprian Blamires, Professor J. H. Burns, Professor M. Cranston, Mrs Claire Gobbi Daunton, Professor Martin Daunton, the late Professor J. R. Dinwiddy, Dr Allison Dube, Ms Gill Furlong, Professor William Gwyn, Mrs Haireti, Professor Joseph Hamburger, Mr D. Haritatos, Miss Jane Haville, Dr M. H. James, Dr Dorothy Johnston, Dr Paul Kelly, Professor Douglas Long, Mrs Virginia Murray, Mrs Janet Percival, Professor J. M. Robson, Mr William St Clair, Dr Martin Smith, Mrs Lydia Tricha, and Professor W. L. Twining. Mrs Rosamine Hayeem typed the whole text and notes, and Mrs Angela Hesselgren typed several revised chapters.

To my wife Maria, and to my sons Gregory and Alexander, I owe a great debt for allowing me the time both to do the research and to write the book. I hope that the result is some recompense for the sacrifices that have had to be made. As Jeremy Bentham is now a familiar figure in our household, I need not apologize for yet another book on him; and Byron has become a welcome addition. Much of the book has been written during holidays spent in the Dartmoor village of Peter Tavy. I am grateful to my neighbours in the Coombe (and especially to all of the Collinses, the Whites, and the Walkers) for cheerfully tolerating and even encouraging a project so apparently remote from the rugged beauty of Dartmoor. Finally, my debt to the members of the Bentham Project over the years I have served as General Editor is so great that I wish to dedicate this book to them.

A note on the transliteration of Greek words: early nineteenth-century practice used Anglicized or Latinized versions of Greek names, while current practice attempts to link transliterated Greek words more closely with the Greek alphabet. Hence, the Greek leader Mavrokordatos appears in this form when I discuss him, but as Mavrocordato when quoted from nineteenth-century texts. Although consistency in the presentation of Greek names and titles of books has eluded me, it is hoped that no great confusion has resulted.

F. R.

University College London
30 July 1990

Contents

List of Abbreviations

Bowring   *The Works of Jeremy Bentham*, ed. J. Bowring, 11 vols.
           (Edinburgh, 1838–43).

CW   *The Collected Works of Jeremy Bentham*, ed. J. H. Burns, J. R.
           Dinwiddy, and F. Rosen (London and Oxford, 1968–).

LGC   London Greek Committee papers, National Library, Athens.

UC   Bentham MSS, University College London.

I

INTRODUCTION

1. A Brief Summary

This book is a study of British political ideas in the early nineteenth century. It deals specifically with the British involvement in the Greek struggle for independence roughly between 1821 and 1827. The ideas are examined, however, in a number of larger contexts such as the evolution of constitutional thought from Montesquieu, the emergence of liberalism as a political ideology against a background of Whig and radical political ideas, and the response in Britain to movements towards national independence in the Mediterranean basin.

Some of the characters that appear here, like Jeremy Bentham (1748–1832) and Lord Byron (1788–1824), will be familiar, though they will not be presented in familiar ways. Others, like Edward Blaquiere and Leicester Stanhope,[1] will be virtually unknown, and their importance to this study will surprise some readers. Still other members of the dramatis personae, like John Bowring, Joseph Hume, and John Cam Hobhouse,[2] will be well known to historians of nineteenth-century movements for reform. Although they will appear here in familiar roles on this 'different' stage, their contributions will be assessed in different ways.

The account of the British involvement in Greece has been told in several distinguished studies of philhellenism and in biographical

---

[1] Edward Blaquiere (1778–1832), former Royal Navy lieutenant, and subsequently author and propagandist in the Greek 'cause'. See below, Ch. 7. Leicester Stanhope (1784–1862), later 5th earl of Harrington, soldier and leader of expedition to Greece with Byron in 1823–4. See below, Ch. 8.

[2] Sir John Bowring (1792–1872), Bentham's literary executor, first editor of the *Westminster Review*, radical MP and diplomat, and Secretary of the London Greek Committee; Joseph Hume (1777–1855), MP and reformer, and leading figure in the London Greek Committee; John Cam Hobhouse (1786–1869), later Baron Broughton, radical MP, friend of Byron, and, like Hume, a leading figure in the London Greek Committee.

works of Byron,[3] but none of these has seriously examined the contribution of Bentham and his so-called disciples.[4] This omission reflects a widely held assumption which this book in part has been written to challenge—that the involvement of Bentham and those associated with him in one way or another was foreign to philhellenism, which was supposedly based more on an admiration of Greek culture and classical civilization. In this view, Bentham and Byron stand poles apart with authenticity resting with Byron and not with Bentham.

The assessment of Bentham's contribution to philhellenism forms a small, though important, part of this study and will correct some deficient accounts that have been written in the past. But the book has not been written just as a contribution to the history of philhellenism. It began as an attempt to understand the relationship between Bentham's theory of constitutional democracy, as elaborated in his *Constitutional Code*, the early draft of which he sent to Greece with the expedition led by Stanhope and Byron, and the concrete events of the Greek struggle for independence.[5] The exploration of this relationship has proved to be highly complex, requiring not only a fresh account of the development of Bentham's constitutional theory[6] but also a critical discussion of the

---

[3] On philhellenism, see e.g. D. Dakin, *British and American Philhellenes during the War of Greek Independence 1821–1833* (Thessaloniki, 1955); C. M. Woodhouse, *The Philhellenes* (London, 1969); William St Clair, *That Greece Might Still Be Free: The Philhellenes in the War of Independence* (London, 1972); Alexis Dimaras, 'The Other British Philhellenes', in Richard Clogg (ed.), *The Struggle for Greek Independence* (London, 1973), 200–23; Dimaras, 'Foreign, and Particularly English, Influences on Educational Policies in Greece during the War of Independence and Their Development under Capodistrias, 1821–31' (Ph.D. thesis, London University, 1973); Anastasiou D. Lignadē, *To Proton Daneion tēs Anexartēsias* [The First Loan of Independence] (Athens, 1970). On Byron and Greece, see *'For Freedom's battle'*, vol. xi (1823–4) of *Byron's Letters and Journals*, ed. Leslie A. Marchand (London, 1981); Marchand, *Byron: A Biography*, 3 vols. (London, 1957); Marchand, *Byron: A Portrait* (London, 1971); Doris Langley Moore, *The Late Lord Byron: Posthumous Dramas* (London, 1961); Moore, *Lord Byron: Accounts Rendered* (London, 1974).

[4] Some exceptions are Dimaras, 'The Other British Philhellenes', 204 ff.; P. Kitromilides, 'Jeremy Bentham and Adamantios Korais', and F. Rosen, 'A Note on Bentham and Korais', *Bentham Newsletter*, 9 (1985), 34–48, 49–50.

[5] See *Constitutional Code*, i. ed. F. Rosen and J. H. Burns (Oxford, 1983), (*CW*), pp. xvi ff. See also F. Rosen, 'Bentham's Letters and Manuscripts in Greece', *Bentham Newsletter*, 5 (1981), 55–8.

[6] It is important to distinguish Bentham's constitutional theory from his theory of democracy, even though the final development of his constitutional theory takes the form of a constitutional democracy. Nevertheless, the development of Bentham's constitutional ideas precedes the commitment to democracy and is based

ideological context against which that theory has in the past been interpreted. To understand the evolution of his theory, it has been necessary to start with his idea of constitutional liberty from the period when he first began to develop it at the time of the struggle for American independence and its evolution from the debate with Blackstone in *A Fragment on Government*, through the French Revolution to the 1820s and its application to Greece. This material constitutes Part I of the book and forms a self-contained study of Bentham's constitutional theory.

In so far as he was creating a philosophical theory (despite the fact that it often appeared as practical commentaries on laws and codes), Bentham's aim was to develop coherent and comprehensive ideas that could stand up to critical scrutiny and meet the test of utility as he conceived it. His theory followed in the larger tradition of philosophical politics, and he readily acknowledged its roots in such writers as Locke, Montesquieu, and Hume.[7] Yet the status of his theory and his objects in advancing it have often been misconstrued. Elie Halévy's important study of Bentham and Philosophic Radicalism has been responsible for much confusion by measuring Bentham's theory against an ideological conception of liberalism.[8] According to Halévy, Bentham's adherence to the principle of utility and his rejection of the constitutional doctrines of Montesquieu led him to adopt an authoritarian brand of liberalism. 'Bentham', he wrote, 'had never been a liberal; always impatient of philanthropic reforms, he merely passed from a monarchic authoritarianism to a democratic authoritarianism, without pausing at the intermediary position, which is the position of Anglo-Saxon liberalism.'[9] Halévy confused the role of liberty in Bentham's theory with a conception of Whig/liberal ideology which he used as the intellectual context to interpret his theory. According to Halévy, liberalism meant a devotion to liberty, that is

on different premises. For an account of Bentham's democratic theory, see F. Rosen, *Jeremy Bentham and Representative Democracy: A Study of the Constitutional Code* (Oxford, 1983).

[7] See below, Chs. 2 and 3.

[8] E. Halévy, *La Formation du Radicalisme Philosophique*, 3 vols. (Paris, 1901–4, trans (though without the extensive annotation) by Mary Morris as *The Growth of Philosophic Radicalism* (London, 1928). See F. Rosen, 'Elie Halévy and Bentham's Authoritarian Liberalism', *Enlightenment and Dissent*, 6 (1987), 59–76.

[9] Halévy, *The Growth of Philosophic Radicalism*, 375–6. See the use made of Halévy's interpretation in Eric Stokes, *The English Utilitarians and India* (Oxford, 1959), 72 ff., 324.

to say, liberty *as opposed to* utility, and, in addition, the acceptance of certain Whig doctrines like the social contract, separation of powers, the British judicial system, and, generally, that conception of the British constitution as presented by Montesquieu and Delolme. In so far as Bentham rejected these ideas, he is believed to have rejected both liberalism and a belief in liberty.

As for the opposition between liberty and utility in Bentham's theory, much recent work on Bentham's principle of utility has tended to conclude that liberty and utility do not in any sense stand in opposition to each other.[10] To see them as opposing terms neglects the importance Bentham gave to security and especially to security of expectation in his account of civil and political liberty.[11] The utilitarian legislator does not rule like a Hobbesian sovereign, issuing commands and compelling obedience. He rules indirectly in establishing a basic security that enables individuals to develop their own projects with the expectation that they will not be interfered with by others and that they will be secure additionally against the misuse of power by government. In moving from liberty to security Bentham acknowledged the logical difference between liberty as acting as one pleases, and civil and political liberty as security, requiring restraints on one's actions so that others are free to act. Liberty, as security, is none the less still liberty, and liberty thus remains the key component of Bentham's utilitarianism.[12]

This study of Bentham's constitutional theory will show historically that his idea of constitutional liberty was derived largely from Montesquieu and that this notion of liberty (as security) is at the heart of his constitutional theory. Again, this interpretation will be seen to contradict that of Halévy who saw

[10] See F. Rosen, *Jeremy Bentham and Representative Democracy*, 55–75; 'Bentham and Mill on Liberty and Justice', in G. Feaver and F. Rosen (eds.), *Lives, Liberties, and the Public Good* (London, 1987), 121–38; P. J. Kelly, *Utilitarianism and Distributive Justice: Jeremy Bentham and the Civil Law* (Oxford, 1990), 71–103; D. A. Dube, 'The Theme of Acquisitiveness in Bentham's Political Thought', (Ph.D. thesis, London University, 1989).

[11] See Kelly, *Utilitarianism and Distributive Justice*, 141 ff.; R. Harrison, *Bentham* (The Arguments of the Philosophers) (London, 1983), 250 ff.; G. J. Postema, *Bentham and the Common Law Tradition* (Oxford, 1986), 147 ff.

[12] Not all interpreters of Bentham's thought would agree with this estimation of Bentham's devotion to liberty. See e.g. Douglas G. Long, *Bentham on Liberty: Jeremy Bentham's Idea of Liberty in Relation to His Utilitarianism* (Toronto, 1977); C. F. Bahmueller, *The National Charity Company: Jeremy Bentham's Silent Revolution* (Berkeley, Calif., 1981).

Bentham's authoritarianism emerging precisely because he rejected Montesquieu. Halévy made this error because he wrongly conflated Bentham's theory with a so-called liberal ideology that he associated with Montesquieu. At the level of theory, Bentham followed Montesquieu in his analysis of civil and political liberty in terms of security, and if he rejected Montesquieu's admiration for the British constitution, he clearly did so because by the 1770s both the extravagant Lockean formulation of constitutional liberty in the form of Richard Price's theory and the confused combination of Locke and Montesquieu in the writing of Blackstone had rendered it imperative to reconsider the idea of constitutional liberty from first principles. Bentham's theory is a response to this need, a response that was completed only with the evolution of his mature theory in the 1820s. In this context, Bentham's theory represents a development from that of Montesquieu.

The idea of liberalism that Halévy used to argue that Bentham rejected liberty in his system is equally confused. If Halévy was referring to the emergence of liberalism as a political ideology linked closely to practice, such an ideology did not begin to emerge much before the 1820s, and even then, as we shall see, it is somewhat anachronistic to speak of liberalism as an ideology exhibiting widespread support and providing a political programme. If Halévy meant by liberalism the Whig tradition of the social contract, division of power, limited government, and a defence of traditional English liberties, as interpreted via Montesquieu, Delolme, Blackstone, and Burke, he seriously underestimated the complexity of the transformation which took place in the early nineteenth century, involving Whig and radical ideas, in relation to the emergence of liberalism as an ideology. This transformation is only now receiving serious study, and clearly, it cannot be assumed that the emergence of liberalism as a political doctrine simply reflects or is reflected in the earlier thinkers Halévy admired. Halévy confuses the philosophical politics of Locke, Montesquieu, Hume, Bentham, and J. S. Mill with the ideological politics of Whigs, radicals, and liberals.[13]

In distinguishing between theory and ideology, this study rejects the view that the London Greek Committee either followed

[13] Cf. J. W. Burrow, *Whigs and Liberals: Continuity and Change in English Political Thought* (Oxford, 1988), where philosophical politics and ideological politics also tend to be merged, but here in a concept of 'political culture'.

Bentham's ideas or attempted to apply them to Greece. The ideas
of Blaquiere, Stanhope, and others have been examined here in
their own right, as they developed in their respective writings.
From research on this material, the connections between various
ideas of Whigs and radicals and emerging liberalism are presented
not as ones of continuity and change within a single political
culture, but as part of a vast market-place of ideas competing for
acceptance at various layers of political culture and related to action
in different ways. In Part II of the book, concerned with ideology,
these ideas are discussed on several different levels. At one level,
within the London Greek Committee, liberalism is portrayed as an
emerging doctrine which takes two conflicting forms, the first
accommodating nationalism and the second, influenced by conceptions of empire, rejecting it. At this level, liberalism, though
obviously new and dynamic as a guide to action, lacked much
widespread support within society at large. On the larger stage, the
main political division was the traditional one between Tories and
Whigs, and this division determined the broad pattern of support
for the Greek 'cause', with the Whigs showing the most and the
Tories, after some initial enthusiasm, the least. The London Greek
Committee drew support from some Tories and numerous Whigs,
but was not especially animated by ideas of radical reform. Noted
radicals, such as Francis Place and James Mill, as well as figures like
William Cobbett and 'Orator' Hunt, were conspicuously absent
from the ranks of the Committee. What separated the Whigs and
many radicals in the 1820s was the preoccupation of the latter with
parliamentary reform, and the cause of Greece was not directly part
of this debate.

Although the very 'foreignness' of Greece enabled Whigs and
some radicals to come together in the London Greek Committee,
the ideas that animated their support for Greece were neither
distinctly Whig nor radical, yet could conceivably be supported by
both. Opposition to the politics of the Holy Alliance, support for
free trade, for republican government in Greece (if not in Britain),
for the liberty of the Greeks to be self-governing and to develop a
free press, educational system, and other institutions could excite
people across a wide band in a Whig/radical political spectrum and
even include many Tories.

Within the London Greek Committee, therefore, one is aware of
an emerging liberalism, divided within itself, though directly

related to practice. One is also aware of liberalism as influencing a synthesis of Whig and radical ideas more generally in society by providing a stage on which some people from each side might come together. At still another level, Bentham and Byron appear as liberal 'icons', as major cultural figures on the European stage, to be invoked in support of Greece. This appearance as icons had little to do with what they were saying or doing, but much more with how they were perceived by others. Finally, numerous myths, affecting perceptions of liberalism at this time and later, were generated, and these myths have encouraged different interpretations of the development of liberalism in the nineteenth and twentieth centuries.

In the world of Tories, Whigs, and radical reformers, emerging liberalism is far removed from the world of the philosophical politics of Bentham's constitutional theory. By drawing a clear distinction between these two worlds, one can understand each on its own terms without confusing the two (as Halévy did). It will be possible to see how Bentham's philosophical ideas had little or no direct influence on the Greek struggle for independence while at the same time acknowledging that Bentham had an enormous influence as an icon of the European Enlightenment used for ideological purposes. It will also be possible to understand how so-called disciples of Bentham advanced doctrines foreign to his ideas while, at the same time, invoking his name in their support. Bentham, it will be seen, belongs to the two worlds of philosophical politics and ideology but in different ways. The world of philosophical politics is concerned with the truth, coherence, and consistency of ideas and not necessarily with their influence; that of ideology with the application of ideas, however confused, incomplete, and contradictory, to practice. Thus Part I explores Bentham's constitutional theory and Part II is devoted to ideology.

Part I begins by establishing in Chapter 2 that Bentham gave liberty a central place in his political theory. At the time of the debate in Britain over support for American independence in 1776, he formulated conceptions of individual and civil liberty in opposition to the Lockean ideas of Richard Price and the utilitarianism of Richard Hey. He followed Montesquieu in linking civil liberty with the concept of security, and he began at this time to extend his conception of civil liberty to embrace political and constitutional liberty.

Chapter 3 shows how Bentham moved towards a theory of constitutional liberty in *A Fragment on Government*, and examines his rejection of the doctrines of the mixed constitution and the separation of powers as the basis of such a theory. The ideas of Montesquieu and Delolme are also examined in so far as they are the figures Bentham most admired and against whom he developed his own ideas. This chapter also considers Bentham's writings at the time of the French Revolution when he both developed his own theory of constitutional democracy and then apparently abandoned it as the Revolution turned against liberty.

The fourth chapter takes up Bentham's mature constitutional writings of the 1820s and attempts to examine them as constitutional theory, beginning with his critique of monarchy and moving to the development of a positive theory based on the identification of individual interests with the public interest. A key feature of this chapter is its account of how Bentham changed his position from the view that minimum power in the hands of government was the best security for good government to the view that, without 'power maximized', securities for good government would not be effective. This change in orientation became an important feature of his democratic theory in *Constitutional Code* where the institutions of government were granted sufficient power to act in the public interest with an indirect, though effective, system of control built into the system. Bentham came to fear inefficient and incompetent government more than a government with powers that were more extensive than had previously been the practice.

In Chapters 5 and 6, Bentham's involvement with Greece is examined firstly in a study of his commentary on the first Greek constitution and secondly by examining his involvement as mediator in an important dispute over the terms of the first Greek loan.[14] In Bentham's commentary and in his role as mediator it is possible to see best his attempts, and the limits of these attempts, to translate philosophical theory into practice. The 'Observations'

---

[14] Bentham had been associated with Greece from 1821 when he was first visited by Pikkolos, an emissary from Adamantios Korais, the classical scholar and thinker who resided in Paris. See Kitromilides, 'Jeremy Bentham and Adamantios Korais', 34–48. Both Korais and Bentham wrote commentaries on the first Greek constitution. See Korais, *Sēmeiōsis eis to prosōrinon politeuma tēs Ellados tou 1822 etous*, ed. Th. P. Volides (Athens, 1933). See also Kitromilides, 'Tradition, Enlightenment, and Revolution: Ideological Change in Eighteenth and Nineteenth Century Greece' (Ph.D. thesis, Harvard University, 1978), 228–70.

(discussed in Chapter 5) might be interpreted as a commentary on a constitution that existed only on paper, and thus Bentham might be regarded as standing twice removed from political reality in trying to argue for reforms of institutions that did not in fact exist. It is shown, however, that this view underestimates the importance of constitutions in the 1820s, especially in new states, where they provided important signals about political aspirations if not about political reality. Bentham's response to these aspirations was warmly welcomed by the Greeks because they regarded it as part of an important process of the legitimization of Greece as an independent, European state. We see in this chapter Bentham's inventive mind at work as he attempted to improve the constitutional arrangements made hastily by the Greeks themselves.

Bentham's embroilment in the dispute over the first Greek loan (discussed in Chapter 6) also reveals his practical inventiveness in using philosophical concepts to resolve important conflicts of practice. Here he was called upon by Ioannis Orlandos and Andreas Louriottis (the two Greek Deputies who came to London to negotiate the first Greek loan) to assist them in their dealings with Bowring to save the 'honour' of Greece. In both of these practical interventions, Bentham failed in what he set out to achieve. Nevertheless, such failure has not been used here as evidence of the absurdity of his position, but it is seen in the larger context of philosophical politics where failure in practice is not the same as failure in theory. Without denying that there was failure in what Bentham attempted to achieve, it is argued that these practical engagements simply mark the boundaries and limits of theoretical politics. Like his constitutional theory, Bentham's position in relation to practice then allows us to see more clearly those practical ideologies which do *not* depend on theory.

Part II begins with Chapters 7 to 9, devoted to an examination of the opinions regarding Greece that were expressed in books, articles, and correspondence by two major figures in the London Greek Committee, Blaquiere and Stanhope. Both are depicted as liberal ideologues, with Blaquiere committed to Greek nationalism and Stanhope to an authoritarianism acquired largely from his experience in India. Once freed from their accustomed role as misguided disciples of Bentham, their own views and the conflict between them become more important in understanding the British involvement in the struggle for Greek independence. Here

we see ideas that were never part of Bentham's theory, developed
in relation to practice, and it is argued that Blaquiere and Stanhope,
rather than Bentham and Byron, formed the ideological polarities
in Greece.

In Chapter 10, the source of the myth of Stanhope, the disciple of
Bentham, and Byron standing opposed on principle and doctrine in
Greece is examined in considerable detail. Its origin in William
Parry's *The Last Days of Lord Byron* is considered along with the
trial for libel between Parry and John Hunt of the *Examiner* in 1827.
Parry was not only responsible for establishing the myth of the
opposition between Bentham (through Stanhope) and Byron, but
also for creating the myth of his own close relationship with
Byron. The chapter explores both the sources of these myths and
their persistence in recent scholarship, particularly in the writing of
Doris Langley Moore.[15] Having uncovered the central ideological
dispute within liberalism, expressed by Blaquiere and Stanhope, it
is possible to see these various other interpretations of the opposing
forces at work in the context of Greece as mythical and largely as
projections of the views of recent authors on to their accounts of
philhellenism. The exploration of these myths is based on a
distinction between theory and ideology. Because the study of
ideology has here been closely linked with practice and concrete
events, it is largely an empirical study. As such, the examination of
ideology allows us to discern as mythical, accounts of these events
that can be described variously as Romantic, Byronic, Marxist, and
so on.

The final chapter in the section devoted to ideology moves
beyond liberalism to consider another division within British
society—between Whigs and Tories—that directly influenced the
broader pattern of British support for Greece. At one level the
chapter provides an account of the subscriptions and other attempts
at fund-raising that, apart from the Greek loan, preceded and
followed the expedition to Greece under Stanhope and Byron. But
in writing this account, it soon became evident that what halted the
growth of philhellenism in Britain was opposition from the
government, and what hampered efforts at fund-raising was the
reluctance of the Tories, taking their cue from the government, to
support the cause. Thus, what started as a study of the formation of

---

[15] See Moore, *The Late Lord Byron* and *Lord Byron*.

the Greek Committee and fund-raising for Greece became a chapter on the significance of the division between Whigs and Tories to these various efforts. Although Whigs and Tories may not have differed over Greece on doctrinal grounds, they had by the 1820s emerged as doctrinally distinct parties. At times the pattern of support for Greece among Whigs and Tories seemed based more on interest than on an articulate set of principles directing action. Nevertheless, as an underlying division in society, the distinction was an important factor determining the generation of support for Greece: hence, the inclusion of the chapter in the section on ideology.

The final part of the book bears the heading 'Interest' and contains two chapters which, on the face of it, seem to have little in common. The first (Chapter 12) challenges the view that the expedition funded by the Greek Committee failed due to its doctrinaire attempt to impose Bentham's ideas in Greece. It is argued instead that Bowring and the Committee relied heavily on the advice and planning of one of the few military officers with actual experience in Greece, Thomas Gordon of Cairness. In spite of proposing the expedition and recommending some of the key personnel, Gordon himself withdrew at the last minute but did so in a way that ensured that the expedition would go ahead without him. Gordon was not willing to return to Greece at this time unless conditions were favourable to his own advancement, and his withdrawal sealed the fate of the expedition.

The second of the two chapters (Chapter 13) does not look for interest where others have seen ideology but argues that even where blatant self-interest is revealed to have been rampant, as in the Greek loan scandal of 1826, the actions of the main characters, like Hume and Bowring, cannot be understood fully without taking into account ideological considerations as well as self-interest. In both of these chapters (as well as in earlier ones) it is emphasized that motivation is highly complex, and no simple distinction between ideology and interest can usually be made.[16] The distinctions employed in the various parts of this book are used to insist not that one aspect of thought or motivation is the deciding one, but that attempts to simplify our understanding of complex events by ascribing motivation (say) to ideology or to interest alone

[16] See the useful discussion in H. T. Dickinson, *Liberty and Property: Political Ideology in Eighteenth-Century Britain* (London, 1977), 1–10.

are misleading and inevitably present a false view of these events. This book is critical of numerous simplifications of this nature, especially those that link Bentham and his disciples to a doctrinaire and authoritarian ideology opposed to the development of liberalism, an ideology that was supposedly applied to Greece where it failed abysmally. The book concludes in Chapter 14 with brief discussions of liberalism, nationalism, and the place of both Bentham and Byron in the growth of these 'isms' in the early nineteenth century.

2. Some Notes on Method

Throughout the composition of this book, I have been conscious of the efforts of distinguished scholars since the 1960s to establish the study of the history of political ideas and intellectual history generally on firmer methodological foundations.[17] This has followed a perceived need to rescue this essentially historical field of study from various ahistorical uses to which it has been put. Nevertheless, while obviously indebted to this body of work, this book will be seen to depart from it at a number of points, and, if these are not indicated, some readers will accuse the author of a more naïve approach to his subject than may be deserved.

1. Perhaps of greatest importance will be the reluctance to employ consciously in this study an appropriate method, paradigm, matrix, milieu, model, language, or idiom. The research began more directly (and perhaps less reflectively) with a series of problems which took the form of questions: why was Bentham involved in the bloody struggle for independence taking place in Greece? In what senses could Blaquiere and Stanhope be considered disciples of Bentham? Why did much of the recent literature on Byron and philhellenism either ignore or criticize Bentham and his followers? Was there any connection between Bentham and Byron and their joint involvement in Greece? Why did the expedition to Greece and the Greek loans fail? What was the political significance

[17] For recent assessments of these achievements see J. G. A. Pocock, 'Introduction: The State of the Art', *Virtue, Commerce, and History: Essays on Political Thought and History, Chiefly in the Eighteenth Century* (Cambridge, 1985), 1–34: and the papers collected in J. Tully (ed.), *Meaning and Context: Quentin Skinner and His Critics* (Cambridge, 1988).

of the Greek loan scandal? In attempting to answer these questions (and there were numerous related ones following from them) a number of more general problems arose in the form of further questions: how was Bentham's theory different from the doctrines advanced by Blaquiere and Stanhope in Greece? Was it appropriate to discuss these doctrines in terms of early liberalism? Was it appropriate to discuss these doctrines as part of an ideology? To what extent were ideological considerations important in determining the course of events? What role did other divisions in society play in determining support for Greece? These secondary questions are perhaps closest to what might be considered as raising methodological issues, but they were not conceived primarily as raising problems of the construction and application of a *general* method. These questions were seen instead as requiring specific answers which would determine how the text of the study would be presented. As a result, I proceeded to arrange the various chapters under the three headings of 'Theory', 'Ideology', and 'Interest', and, within the chapters, highlighted and discussed the relationships of philosophical theory and practice, of ideology and political action, of myth and reality, and of ideology and interest. None of these relationships were discussed generally or abstractly as problems of method, but more concretely as problems of understanding specific ideas and events.

2. As this book is primarily concerned with explaining historical events, it does not, as does recent scholarship, focus on the more limited problems associated with text and context. This concentration on events has led to an emphasis on different problems—relating theory to practice, ideology to interest, and theory to ideology. The exploration of these relationships has enabled me to reach important conclusions about Bentham's theory, early liberalism, and the character of ideological politics in the early nineteenth century. I have not puzzled over the problems of the 'meaning' of a particular text, even though part of the book is devoted to the study of a series of texts (published and unpublished) from which Bentham's constitutional theory has been extracted. In this material I have perhaps explored the philosophical context of Bentham's writings most explicitly in discussing their evolution from Montesquieu, but even here, context plays only a limited role in providing an account of a text or the level on which it should be read. I have been impressed by the way in which Bentham's

writing *both* drew upon earlier writers *and* created a new context by
the way he used their ideas. Locke, Montesquieu, Hey, Paley,
Delolme, Blackstone, Hume, and others were used by Bentham to
construct his theory, but the theory he constructed cannot be
understood simply in terms of the way he used or abused the
traditions of writing (and especially ideological traditions) about
constitutions which he inherited. In his hands constitutional theory
became something different—at once more theoretical and related
to practice in a different manner. It might even be argued that
Bentham invented constitutional theory out of various writings
about liberty and constitutionalism that preceded him. It is not
claimed here that Bentham invented philosophical politics: in this
he was preceded by Hobbes and Hume, to name just two. But he
did invent constitutional theory as a rigorous and disciplined study
of constitutional government from first principles. And his efforts
to relate this theory to practice are also distinctive and unique.
Bentham's conception of his role as a philosopher and jurist seems
as important to this creative process as are the immediate contexts
on which he drew to construct his theory.

3. This book pays more attention to the problem of influence
than seems to appear in the methodological writings noted above.
While accepting the view of Skinner that the concept of influence
provides a highly elusive model for a history of political thought,[18]
it is fair to say that influence is none the less an important part of
most accounts of human relationships, including the transmission
of ideas from one person to another. The problem with the
employment of influence in intellectual history is that it is often
used in a simplistic manner. Some measure influence by simply
noting a loose affinity of ideas or the citation of one thinker in the
work of another. While these approaches need not be misleading,
they are somewhat superficial when one considers the diverse ways
that people influence each other, or that ideas can influence action.
Consider, for example, the debates over Bentham's influence on
the Philosophic Radicals and on the Victorian revolution in
government. Either one reads of the all-pervasive influence of
Bentham or that he had little or no influence at all.[19] If one

[18] See Q. Skinner, 'Meaning and Understanding in the History of Ideas', in Tully
(ed.), *Meaning and Context*, 45–6, 297.
[19] For the debate over Bentham's influence on the Victorian revolution in
government, see the references in Rosen, *Jeremy Bentham and Representative*

conceives of a single programme of reform set forth by the Philosophic Radicals as a derivation from the greatest happiness principle, as Sabine did (following Halévy), it is not difficult to refute this view of Bentham's influence by simply pointing out that the Philosophic Radicals did not in fact make such a derivation.[20] The obvious conclusion then would be that Bentham had little direct influence on these reformers; but such a conclusion would ignore the numerous and complex ways that one thinker can influence another.

As this book attempts no general innovation of method, no *model* of influence will be found here. Nevertheless, the problem of assessing influence arises at a number of points, and it has played an important role in this study. In the first place I was struck by the failure of Bentham's philosophical theory to influence political action. Neither he nor his friends could take his ideas on the level he wrote them and put them into practice. In the distinction between theory and ideology this is revealed most fully. In exploring this distinction it is also argued that both Bentham and Byron had enormous influence in Europe and Greece as liberal icons, admired, revered, quoted, but not studied for the ideas or poetic insights they were attempting to set forth. That these figures took an interest in Greece and sought to assist the Greeks in their struggle played an important role in legitimizing that struggle. This legitimizing role belongs to the realm of ideology, to the task of translating political ideas into action, and, by making the distinction between theory and ideology, it is possible to dissolve what is apparently a paradox of one's ideas having great influence at one level and no influence at another.

In the second place, the theme of influence enters into the account of Bentham's relationships with his so-called disciples. Again we shall encounter paradox in so far as Blaquiere and Stanhope, both of whom claimed to have been advancing Bentham's ideas in Greece, are found not to have been true disciples, but were mainly using Bentham for their own purposes.

Democracy, 9 n.–10 n. For the most recent contribution, see S. R. Conway, 'Bentham and the Nineteenth Century Revolution in Government', in R. Bellamy (ed.), *Victorian Liberalism* (London, 1990), 71–90. On the Philosophic Radicals, see William Thomas, *The Philosophic Radicals: Nine Studies in Theory and Practice, 1817–1841* (Oxford, 1979), esp. 1–13.

[20] See G. H. Sabine, *A History of Political Theory* (3rd edn., London, 1963), 674–5.

At the level of ideology, we shall also find Blaquiere and Stanhope bitterly opposed over ideas and policies even though both are supposedly disciples of Bentham. No simple conception of influence will resolve these paradoxes, and such a resolution will require an account that takes into consideration the problem of influence on several levels.

Unlike the work of Skinner and Pocock, which tends to emphasize the persistence and alteration of languages 'horizontally' through time, this study is equally concerned with the way ideas pass 'vertically' through various layers of thought. Here we shall meet philosophical theory, explicit ideology, underlying expressions of ideology, public and private expressions of opinion in books, pamphlets, journals, newspapers, and private correspondence, with attention especially paid to the way ideas pass between these various strata and forms of communication. This approach attempts to avoid the common mistake of using arguments and ideas from one level to explain ideas and events on another. For example, the idea of the Philosophic Radicals, each of whom is not only active in politics but also highly individual and lively in his own thinking, rigidly deriving plans of reform from something so abstract as the greatest happiness principle is so improbable as to strike most readers as absurd. Nevertheless, it is not considered absurd by a number of historians because they have confused a philosophical method with a position in ideological politics. This confusion then makes Bentham seem absurd, as he is seen as the *deus ex machina*, providing the first principles for everyone else's thought. This is an inaccurate picture both of Bentham's philosophical method and of the way those who were associated with him were or were not influenced by him. As I have suggested, this very conception of Bentham and his influence invites refutation.

In this book one finds little direct influence of Bentham either on other thinkers or on events in Greece. Yet, like Byron, he is continually cited and revered, just as John Locke, Adam Smith, and J. S. Mill are treated as great 'liberal' figures today. In this latter sense, he exerted great influence over the movement in support of Greek independence in Britain. Nevertheless, this kind of influence is often confused with his influence as a philosopher or with a kind of direct influence on particular disciples which was often more limited and specialized. To see Bentham as directly providing the animating spirit of the London Greek Committee through men like

Bowring, Blaquiere, Stanhope, and Hume overestimates his influence at one level and underestimates it at several others.

4. This study exhibits a willingness to accept a degree of anachronism as inevitable in intellectual history. Pure chronology is certainly possible, but it usually makes dull history. In so far as one is conscious of history as making an enquiry from the present into the past as opposed to providing purely a chronicle of past events, anachronism is bound to enter the account, if not in the substance, then in the method, model, or paradigm. It might also be argued that the very nature of historical evidence in the form of materials that have managed to survive to the present day renders most historical studies to a degree anachronistic. One anachronism employed in the book is the use of the terms 'liberalism' and 'liberal' in assessing political ideas in the 1820s. This is justified in part by referring to uses of the term at this time and its use by other historians in similar contexts.[21] Nevertheless, there was no established liberal ideology in the 1820s and it can only be seen to be so in retrospect several decades later. If we scrupulously avoided using the terms 'liberal' and 'liberalism' here, it might be thought that there was little point in examining the ideas in the first place. It is precisely because the ideas are important in the development of liberalism that they are carefully examined in this book. Not to employ the terms might be considered overly fastidious.

Another anachronism is the use of the term 'ideology' to indicate a type of discourse closely linked to political action.[22] This use of the word is clearly one devised in the twentieth century, and, indeed, in the latter part of it. For some time, I resisted the use of the term and planned to refer to the distinction between theory and ideology in terms of the ancient Greek words *epistemē* and *doxa* ('knowledge' and 'opinion'). *Doxa* possessed that element of half-truth commonly associated with the thinking closely linked to political action and debate. This conception was eventually abandoned, for however inadequate such doctrines appeared from the perspective of theory, there was a coherence and direction in them that might be overlooked if they were conceived simply as *doxai* or 'opinions'. Hence, the anachronistic use of the term 'ideology' was reluctantly adopted to link the doctrines advanced by Blaquiere and Stanhope with what has come to be called

[21] See the discussion of liberalism in Ch. 14 below.
[22] The use of 'ideology' in this fashion is discussed in Ch. 14 below.

'ideology' more than 100 years later. In adopting the term, there is
of course an awareness that further confusion might be caused by
the link with what we now call 'ideologies'.

3. Byron and Bentham

It should now be obvious that no equivalent examination of
Byron's poetry is presented here to complement the study of
Bentham's constitutional theory. Such an investigation is beyond
the scope of the book and probably beyond the capacity of the
author. There is some justification for not presenting here a study
of Byron's poetry in that he wrote very little poetry during the last
period of his life in Greece. His correspondence for this period has
been extensively used. Nevertheless, Byron plays an important role
in this book, if not as the romantic hero, then as liberal icon and
ultimately as the victim of an ill-conceived plan that led him to go
to Missolonghi as the agent of the London Greek Committee.
Byron is not usually presented as a victim and a passive one at that.
If his decision to go to Greece represented a heroic gesture, his
behaviour once he arrived did not. The contrast, however, between
his actual conduct in Greece and his posthumous reputation is
striking and is one of the themes investigated here.

This is not the first book to compare Byron and Bentham. Louis
Crompton's recent study of Byron's homosexuality successfully
uses Bentham's unpublished manuscripts on sexuality to compare
the responses of the two writers to the growing homophobia in
Britain during this period.[23] The most important aspect of
Crompton's book for our purposes is his tendency to examine the
two writers as moving in the same direction as opposed to their
being represented in terms of polarities of thought and doctrine.
Once it is grasped that the utilitarian philosopher and the romantic
poet were not opposed on many issues, the explanation of their
joint involvement in Greece raises numerous interesting questions.
For example, neither Byron nor Bentham actually subscribed to the
strong nationalist views expressed by the Greeks and some of their
admirers. Both supported the use of British Commissioners to
control the loan and to keep it in British hands. Furthermore, if

---

[23] *Byron and Greek Love: Homophobia in 19th-Century England* (London, 1985).

there was a romantic hero in Greece representing the London Greek Committee, it was surely Leicester Stanhope, generally despised by students of Byron as a follower of Bentham.[24] And both Byron and Bentham were, for the most part, moderate in the views they expressed regarding Greece and its future. The enthusiasm of Blaquiere and others cannot be found in either writer.

The parallels can be taken further. Both writers were despised and scorned by certain sections of British society, while vigorously defended by others. Both seemed to be admired more abroad than at home and such admiration was not necessarily for anything they actually wrote or did. And both have been considered in retrospect as the most influential figures of this period. If Byron does not receive equal treatment with Bentham, the presence of his name in the title of this book may be justified in part by the emphasis placed on seeing the two as moving along parallel lines in the same direction in their political thought. As philosopher and poet, as reformers, as sharing a taste for the unusual and exotic, both Bentham and Byron may profit from being studied together.[25]

4. The London Greek Committee Archive

A considerable stimulus to attempt this study was provided by an examination of the little-known archive of the London Greek

[24] In *Byron: The Years of Fame* (Harmondsworth, 1954), 190–1, Peter Quennell observed: 'One has sometimes heard it suggested that the utilitarian spirit of the new age was largely responsible for the rapid and appalling decay of aesthetic intelligence which culminated in the Great Exhibition of 1851. It is curious fact, however, that the ills with which the Victorian age was chiefly afflicted were caused by the very excess of Romanticism, and by the Victorian susceptibility to exotic influences.' In 1851, within weeks of succeeding to the title of the earl of Harrington, Stanhope designed a new house to be built on vacant land on the east side of Kensington Palace Gardens. Although most of the houses were in the Italianate style, Stanhope's was 'Gothic' in design. The style was widely criticized and one writer in the *Builder* said of the windows: 'Instead of "repose" we have actual torture—the very thumbscrew of design.' Stanhope eventually died in Harrington House in 1862, and the house has since become the embassy of the Soviet Union in London. See F. H. W. Sheppard (ed.), *Survey of London*, xxxvii (London, 1973), 171–3.

[25] The same parallel movement may also be seen in the political thought of Bentham and Dickens. Although they are usually contrasted due to Dickens's comments about the excesses of utilitarianism in *Hard Times*, one can see many similarities, from their attitudes towards revolution and violent change (see *Barnaby Rudge* and *A Tale of Two Cities*) to their belief in the importance of legal reform, especially of the Court of Chancery (see e.g. *Bleak House*) and the reform of prisons (see *Great Expectations* and *Little Dorrit*).

Committee which had been presented to the Greek government in
1924 by a grandson of John Bowring, and has been deposited in the
National Library of Greece in Athens.[26] The archive consists of ten
volumes of minutes, documents, correspondence, and a collection
of the issues of the newspapers begun in Greece under the
Committee's auspices by Leicester Stanhope.[27] Few studies of the
period or of philhellenism in English have made extensive use of
it.[28] Anastasiou Lignadē's book in Greek on the first Greek loan is
the only study to have worked through the archive as a whole.[29]
But Lignadē did not concentrate on ideas and was not particularly
sensitive to the implications of both ideas and events in the context
of British political thought. Nevertheless, he has been the first
writer to appreciate the significance of the quarrel between
Blaquiere and Stanhope and to assess Stanhope's role in preventing
the payment of the proceeds of the first loan to the Greek
government.

The London Greek Committee archive has enabled me to present
in detail an account of how a pressure group in the 1820s, barely
tolerated by the government of the day, was formed, raised
subscriptions, called public meetings, influenced public opinion,
and eventually organized an expedition to Greece and floated a
major loan. The archive has also enabled me to present the first full
account of the clash of ideas and personalities which animated its
meetings and the correspondence between the major figures in it.
Few studies in the history of political ideas make extensive use of
archives and private correspondence.[30] This is partly due to a

[26] See E. S. De Beer and Walter Seton, 'Byroniana: The Archives of the London
Greek Committee', *Nineteenth Century*, 100 (1926), 396–412.

[27] Besides this material, there is an additional volume of manuscripts connected
with Bowring's later career in the Far East which seems to have been inadvertently
included in the archive.

[28] The first scholar to use the archive was Virginia Penn. See 'Philhellenism in
England (1821–1827)', *Slavonic Review*, 14 (1935–6), 363–71, 647–60; 'Philhellenism
in Europe, 1821–1828', *Slavonic Review*, 16 (1937–8), 638–53. Others, like Leslie
Marchand (*Byron: A Biography*) have used the archive for specific purposes, e.g. for
the Byron material. But Dakin (*British and American Philhellenes*) drew heavily on the
important collection of intercepted letters in the Colonial Office Records in the
Public Record Office (see esp. CO 136) rather than on the London Greek
Committee archive. St Clair (*That Greece Might Still Be Free*, 380–1) was aware of
the archive but did not make systematic use of it. Nor did Woodhouse in *The
Philhellenes*.

[29] *To Proton Daneion tēs Anexartēsias* (1970).

[30] The notable exceptions in the period covered by this book are, of course, those
written by J. H. Burns, John Dinwiddy, Joseph Hamburger, and William Thomas.

preoccupation with major published texts and their contexts and partly to the influence of research on earlier periods where comparable archives are not available. There may also be a seldom-stated premiss in some recent work that (following Wittgenstein's theory of language) one concentrates on public culture and ideas rather than on its more private manifestations. In this respect it is worth noting that much of the important correspondence in the archive, and especially that of Stanhope, Blaquiere, and Bentham, though private in form, quickly achieved a public status either in being published or in being copied and widely circulated.[31] But private correspondence not intended for publication has been especially useful in clearly establishing the objects and intentions of key figures in the Committee. One often finds in this material a franker communication of beliefs than is contained in more prudent public declarations. The correspondence in the London Greek Committee archive has revealed, for example, estimations of conditions in Greece and relations with the Greek Deputies considerably different from those which appeared in print under its name.

5. Constitutional Theory and the Bentham Edition

Most scholars will find in the section on Bentham's constitutional theory not only a new approach to his thought but also new material on which this approach is based. This new material has been brought to light as part of research for volumes in the new edition of the *Collected Works of Jeremy Bentham*.[32] Much of the material discussed here is part of a sub-project on Bentham's theory of constitutional government, directed by T. P. Schofield and funded by the Economic and Social Research Council and the British Academy. The account of Bentham's mature constitutional theory in Chapter 4 is taken from manuscripts that appear in *First*

---

[31] See e.g. L. Stanhope, *Greece, in 1823 and 1824; being a Series of Letters, and other Documents, on the Greek Revolution, Written during a Visit to that Country* (new edn., London, 1825) and E. Blaquiere, *Narrative of a Second Visit to Greece* (London, 1825). Numerous copies of Bentham's correspondence with Orlandos and Louriottis were made and circulated. See below, Ch. 6.

[32] *The Collected Works of Jeremy Bentham*, ed. J. H. Burns (1961–79), J. R. Dinwiddy (1977–83), F. Rosen (1983–).

Principles Preparatory to Constitutional Code, and the discussion of
Bentham's writings for Greece is based on materials published in
*Securities against Misrule and Other Constitutional Writings for Tripoli
and Greece*.[33] In addition, Bentham's experience of the French
Revolution, discussed in Chapter 3, is based on a volume nearing
completion, containing Bentham's writings during this period.[34]
Mention should also be made here of the use of Bentham's
Correspondence in several chapters. Although the volumes for the
period covered by most of this study have not yet been edited, the
transcripts which are available have proved invaluable in this
research. When published, the later volumes of Bentham's *Correspondence* will provide an important guide to his numerous activities
in the Mediterranean basin and elsewhere throughout the 1820s.[35]

As the research for this book progressed in parallel with the
editorial work on these volumes in the *Collected Works*, the
references are at times to the volumes as published and, at other
times, to the manuscripts that were used in the construction of the
published texts. Footnotes in each chapter will easily connect the
manuscripts and published works for which they were intended.
Like much of Bentham's work, his writings for Greece and his
contributions to a theory of constitutional government either were
unpublished, or, if published, were not widely circulated. The new
edition of the *Collected Works* will make these texts widely available
and for the first time allow a full assessment of this aspect of his
work. This book is intended as a contribution to this assessment.

---

[33] *First Principles Preparatory to Constitutional Code*, ed. T. P. Schofield (Oxford,
1989); *Securities against Misrule and Other Constitutional Writings for Tripoli and Greece*,
ed. T. P. Schofield (Oxford, 1990).

[34] Tentatively entitled *Essays on French and British Political Reform, 1788–95*, ed.
M. James and C. P. Blamires.

[35] *The Correspondence of Jeremy Bentham* is now under the direction of Dr S. R.
Conway and should be completed in 14 vols. Bentham's involvement in the Greek
struggle for independence will begin in vol. x (1820–1), forthcoming from Oxford
University Press.

PART I

THEORY

. . . would he not provoke laughter, and would it not be said of him that he had returned from his journey aloft with his eyes ruined and that it was not worth while even to attempt the ascent?

(Plato, *Republic*, 7. 517a (trans. Paul Shorey))

Bentham, who lived in Queen Square Place, Westminster, took his utilitarian walks with [Francis] Place, and accompanied him on his business calls to take orders from his customers, or deliver the garments he had made for them. While Place was engaged within, Bentham would walk outside until his friend emerged again, when they would continue their walks and their political conversation.

One day when Place was detained longer than usual with a customer difficult to please, Bentham sat down on the step, leaning his head upon his hand, probably meditating some constitution for the government of New Brazil, when there came under his eye an open palm with a shilling in it. The sight aroused him from his reverie, and, on raising his head, he found a gentleman, who hastily withdrew his hand and begged pardon. He had mistaken Bentham for a person in distress needing assistance. But on Bentham looking up with his bright glance, refined expression, and white flowing locks, he saw he was a gentleman. The hand was instantly withdrawn with apologies. Bentham told Place of his adventure with expressions of respect for his kindly intending friend.

(George Jacob Holyoake, *Sixty Years of an Agitator's Life*)

2
Liberty and Constitutional Theory

'The Definition of Liberty', wrote Jeremy Bentham in 1776, 'is one
of the corner stones of my system: and one that I know not how to
do without.'[1] When he wrote these words, he was assisting his
friend John Lind in the latter's critique of Richard Price's influential
pamphlet *Observations on the Nature of Civil Liberty* (1776).[2] His
role was mainly one of supplying Lind with numerous characteristic ideas which Lind employed with considerable rhetorical effect
in articles and pamphlets directed against Price's conception of
liberty and support for American independence.[3] Bentham's most
important contribution was his clarification of the concept of
liberty, and it was at this time that he developed important ideas
about liberty which were to have a lasting influence on his
constitutional theory.

1. Locke and Price on Liberty

The conception of liberty which Bentham opposed in Price's
theory might best be described as Lockean. Locke conceived
individual liberty as 'a power in any agent to do or forbear any
particular action', and he linked liberty, defined in terms of power,
with both reason and law.[4] Locke's conception was both negative
and positive. On the one hand liberty was conceived as the absence
of constraint and was in this sense negative; but in being conceived

---

[1] *Correspondence*, i, ed. T. L. S. Sprigge (London, 1968) (*CW*), 311.
[2] The full title of Price's pamphlet is *Observations on the Nature of Civil Liberty, The
Principles of Government, and the Justice and Policy of the War with America* (London,
1776).
[3] For an account of Bentham's relationship with John Lind and the debate with
Price, see H. L. A. Hart, *Essays on Bentham: Studies in Jurisprudence and Political
Theory* (Oxford, 1982), 53 ff.
[4] J. Locke, *An Essay Concerning Human Understanding*, ed. A. C. Fraser, 2 vols.
(New York, 1959), II. xxi. 8. See also: II. xxi. 15, 51.

as a power, it also contained a positive element. The absence of constraint included that constraint derived from 'Absolute, Arbitrary Power' and one's power extended to the active preservation of one's life and property.[5] Locke also stressed the importance of law: the free man required, in nature, the law of nature to guide him, and in civil society, 'to have a standing Rule to live by, common to every one of that Society, and made by the Legislative Power erected in it'.[6] '*The end of Law*', he noted, 'is not to abolish or restrain, but to *preserve and enlarge Freedom*,' for '*where there is no Law, there is no Freedom*'.[7]

Price approached the theme of liberty by considering it under four headings: physical, moral, religious, and civil.[8] Under each of these headings he recognized both negative and positive dimensions. Physical liberty was defined as a 'principle of *Spontaneity*, or *Self-determination*, which constitutes us *Agents*; or which gives us a command over our actions, rendering them properly *ours*, and not the effects of the operation of any foreign cause'.[9] Moral liberty was 'the power of following in all circumstances, our sense of right and wrong; or of acting in conformity to our reflecting and moral principles, without being controuled by any contrary principles'.[10] Religious liberty was 'the power of exercising, without molestation, that mode of religion which we think best; or of making the decisions of our own consciences, respecting religious truth, the rule of our conduct, and not any of the decisions of others'.[11] Finally, civil liberty was 'the power of a *Civil Society* or *State* to govern itself by its own discretion; or by laws of its own making, without being subject to any foreign discretion, or to the impositions of any extraneous will or power'.[12] The main theme, as Price acknowledged, in these various conceptions was that of 'self-direction' or 'self-government', and the line between liberty and slavery was marked by the imposition of restraints on self-government.[13]

Although Price followed Locke in recognizing positive and

---

[5] See J. Locke, *Two Treatises of Government*, ed. P. Laslett (Cambridge, 1963), II. 23.   [6] Ibid. II. 22.   [7] Ibid. II. 57.

[8] Price, *Observations*, 2. In his *Additional Observations on the Nature and Value of Civil Liberty* (London, 1777), 13–14, Price also distinguished between the liberty of the citizen, government, and community. See D. O. Thomas, *The Honest Mind: The Thought and Work of Richard Price* (Oxford, 1977), 187–8.

[9] Price, *Observations*, 3.   [10] Ibid.   [11] Ibid.
[12] Ibid.   [13] Ibid. 3, 5.

negative aspects of liberty and, like Locke, he stressed the
importance of reason, there were important differences between
the two thinkers. As D. O. Thomas has noted, Price replaced
Locke's doctrine of consent with an emphasis on the continuous
participation of the people in government and the more democratic
belief that all men should have the right to participate.[14] Price's
more radical doctrine seems to have envisaged wide-scale change;
according to his conception of liberty, most people lacked self-
government and could be considered political slaves.[15] He also
abandoned the framework of natural law, which Locke used both
to link individual and civil liberty in a coherent doctrine and to
emphasize moderate conceptions of change and preservation. Price
used the idea of self-government to provide the link between
individual and civil liberty. Despite some ambiguity arising from
the attempt to apply the complex notion of liberty to the four
categories of liberty, his conception was especially useful (as was
Locke's) in linking in a coherent way individual and civil liberty.
What so alarmed Price's readers and led to widespread controversy
was the radical nature of his almost Rousseauian belief in self-
government and participation. Even though he accepted the use of
representation to extend self-government to large states and he
believed that self-government was compatible with a 'hereditary
council' and a 'supreme executive magistrate',[16] the implications of
his doctrine, in a world where representative democracy had yet to
be widely established, were abundantly clear:

In general, to be *free* is to be guided by one's own will; and to be guided by
the will of another is the characteristic of *Servitude*. This is particularly
applicable to Political Liberty. That state . . . is *free*, which is guided by its
own will; or, (which comes to the same) by the will of an assembly of
representatives appointed by itself and accountable to itself. And every
state that is not so governed; or in which a body of men representing the
people make not an essential part of the Legislature, is in *slavery*.[17]

Price saw the importance of active consent through participation
and self-government in so strong a manner that he was led to
suggest that in a free state: 'every man is his own Legislator. All
taxes are free-gifts for public services. All *laws* are particular

---

[14] Thomas, *The Honest Mind*, 193–4.
[15] Ibid. 193. See Price, *Observations*, 5.
[16] Price, *Observations*, 12.   [17] Ibid. 11.

provisions or regulations established by *Common Consent* for gaining protection and safety. And all *Magistrates* are Trustees or Deputies for 'carrying these regulations into execution.'[18] It was remarks like these which aroused such controversy when the pamphlet was published, especially when set against the background of the American struggle for independence whose cause Price so energetically advanced.

2. Liberty as a Negative Idea

In the letter from Bentham to John Lind with which this chapter began, Bentham referred to 'a kind of discovery' which he believed he had made, namely, 'that the idea of Liberty, imported nothing in it that was positive: that it was merely a negative one: and that accordingly I defined it "*the absence of restraint*" '.[19] In the context of the dispute with Price, Bentham's insight was an important one, but given Hobbes's discussion of liberty in *Leviathan*, he might have hesitated to emphasize its originality.[20] And yet, Hobbes did not say precisely that liberty was merely something negative, although he defined it in negative terms as the 'absence of opposition'.[21] Furthermore, the conception of liberty as the absence of restraint had been adopted by some of Bentham's contemporaries, especially those, like Richard Hey and William Paley, who employed utilitarian conceptions of civil and political liberty.[22]

Bentham's 'originality' lay in the critical use to which he put his conception of liberty as an entirely negative notion, and in this respect Hobbes might be considered only as an important precursor. Nevertheless, Bentham himself soon rejected the notion of liberty as the 'absence of restraint' when he realized that this conception was too narrow and would not include the more positive notion of constraint. For this reason, he adopted the definition of liberty as the 'absence of coercion' which, while still wholly negative, embraced both constraint and restraint and

---

[18] Price, *Observations*, 6–7.   [19] *Correspondence*, i (*CW*), 310.
[20] See T. Hobbes, *Leviathan* (Oxford, 1962), ch. 21.   [21] Ibid.
[22] See R. Hey, *Observations on the Nature of Civil Liberty, and the Principles of Government* (London, 1776), and W. Paley, *The Principles of Moral and Political Philosophy* (London, 1785).

seemed to him more in accordance with the common understanding of liberty. In making this move he criticized Richard Hey who was so concerned to keep liberty as a wholly negative notion that even the absence of constraint seemed too positive for his system. Bentham argued:

If the word Liberty does not signify in any case the absence of constraint, I should be glad to be informed what other word there is that does? I for my part know of none. Were I obliged, were I constrained to walk 20 miles every day whether I would or no, although I were restrained in no one single aspect of my conduct further than was necessary to my walking of the twenty miles, although I might choose the time, the place, the company, I must confess I could not help looking upon myself as very far from being at perfect liberty. I should be very apt to complain in this behalf of a want of that valuable blessing: Nor should I have any suspicion that in doing so I was advancing any thing inconsistent with common notions, or offending in any respect against the propriety of language. [A]nd should any one set about maintaining to me that my stock of liberty was no ways impaired or diminished by such coercion, I should rather think it was he who was offending against the propriety of language.[23]

The reason that Hey rejected Bentham's formulation of liberty as the absence of coercion was not entirely clear even though he devoted a footnote to it in his pamphlet.[24] But there he simply argued that common language would not see the positive coercion involved in constraint as an abridgement of liberty. It seems probable that Hey insisted on the narrower construction of liberty as the absence of restraint because it was more compatible with the constraints imposed by law and fitted more easily into a utilitarian theory. In imposing duties the law imposed constraints in the form of numerous obligations, for example, in the obligation to pay taxes. For Hey, an obligation would represent no violation of liberty as it did not place anyone under restraint, except in the few cases where such restraint was necessary as punishment. Thus, liberty, as the absence of restraint, would be compatible with most of the operations of government. Furthermore, the notion of individual liberty as the absence of restraint was generally

[23] UC lxix. 58. I am grateful to Professor Douglas Long for encouraging me to examine Bentham's early writings on liberty. See also D. Long, *Bentham on Liberty* (Toronto, 1977), esp. 45–83.

[24] See Hey, *Observations*, 9 n. See also *Happiness and Rights: A Dissertation upon Several Subjects Relative to the Rights of Man and His Happiness* (York, 1792), 156.

compatible with a conception of civil liberty in which negative duties would secure rights to person and property. By restraining the 'violent and unprincipled', the peaceable citizen would find his own liberty enhanced.[25]

Bentham believed that the notion of liberty as the absence of coercion was not only a more accurate conception of liberty but also equally suitable in Hey's system. Furthermore, he thought that it would make more sense in giving an account of the deprivation of liberty involved in slavery. In Hey's view, the slave who was constrained to labour was still at liberty so long as he was not restrained by chains or imprisonment. But Bentham regarded such a view of liberty as contrary to common understanding: 'If speaking of a Slave, any one to say that he had regained his Liberty, what is the notion that would be most forward to offer itself to our minds? The notion, I should suppose, of his being no longer forced, no longer constrained to work.'[26]

Bentham then distinguished between positive and negative duties, and expressed the view that in states like Great Britain, negative duties tended to predominate, and it made more sense to conceive of liberty in terms of the absence of restraint. It was on these negative duties, in which others refrained from interfering with one's property, that the individual's liberty with regard to his property was based. Individuals were seen as best able to look after themselves and any restraint on their liberty to do so was especially opposed. However, in states where slavery was common, positive duties to constrain people to work were perhaps stronger than negative duties. In these states, he argued, the absence of constraint as well as restraint would be regarded as a condition of liberty.[27]

3. Individual and Civil Liberty

Besides seeking a more accurate conception of liberty, Bentham went further to question the way in which individual liberty could be coherently related to civil liberty, and it was here that his idea of liberty as wholly negative was most usefully applied. For Locke, individual and civil liberty were closely related through the

[25] See Hey, *Observations*, 56.   [26] UC lxix. 59.   [27] Ibid.

doctrine of natural law. Less successful, perhaps, though still intelligible, was Price's notion of self-government which linked individual and civil liberty, though, for Price, there was some confusion between what was called civil liberty (embracing rights to person and property) and political liberty. Price overcame this confusion to a degree by arguing that in a self-governing state the individual was more likely to possess securely his rights and property.

Bentham, as we have seen, took the view that liberty was wholly a negative idea (the absence of coercion) and that legal and political systems could only be understood as being opposed to liberty. Although Lind in his critique of Price attempted to fashion a notion of civil liberty based on restraint applied to everyone else in a particular group, the argument was not convincing.[28] Bentham himself at this time continuously emphasized the opposition between liberty and law:

Liberty then is neither more nor less than the absence of coercion. This is the genuine, original and proper sense of the word Liberty. The idea of it is an idea purely negative. It is not any thing that is produced by positive Law. It exists without Law, and not by means of Law.[29]

From this perspective, Bentham could see that the notions of civil and political liberty would be difficult to explain, as they were, at one level, self-contradictory. Simply put, the law that supposedly created civil and political liberty was itself hostile to liberty in so far as law operated by coercion or the threat of coercion. Bentham was not tempted by the utilitarian argument he found in Hey's pamphlet. Hey argued that civil liberty could be conceived as the absence of civil restraints, and as a medium between tyranny on the one hand (too much restraint) and licentiousness on the other (too little). Lest it immediately become apparent that 'licentiousness' might be defined as 'the absence of restraint', and hence be seen as productive of civil liberty, Hey proceeded to justify the curb placed on the licentious as being productive of liberty:

But a law may, by tying up the hands of the violent and unprincipled, contribute more to the liberty of the peaceable citizen than it takes away from his liberty by the new restraint which it does itself impose. So that,

[28] See J. Lind, *Three Letters to Dr. Price* . . . (London, 1776), 67.
[29] UC lxix. 44.

on the whole, he becomes freer to follow his own will, and is less controuled in his actions than he was before.[30]

Hey continued by depicting a perfect condition of civil liberty in the following terms:

It is the nature of Society, that each member of it can only be allowed to pursue his own happiness in a manner consistent with that of the other members; or we may say, that he ought to procure his private Good through the Medium (as it were) of the public Good. Wherever that does not require him to be curbed, our Principle would leave him as free as he himself can wish or conceive. If he is ambitious of being more free than the public Good will allow, he forgets surely that he is a member of Civil Society.[31]

While Bentham might not disagree with Hey's attempt to link private and public interest, he would insist that it had little to do with liberty and much more with utility. The argument advanced several years later by William Paley was similar in attempting a utilitarian account of civil liberty. Like Hey, Paley defined liberty as the absence of restraint, and civil liberty as '*not being restrained by any law, but what conduces in a greater degree to the public welfare*'.[32] All that civil liberty required was that restraints were justified by providing more good than the evil they caused. Nevertheless, Paley's account simply amounted to liberty becoming confused with utility. At one point, Paley was led by his argument to the position that if one was imprisoned under a law which brought great benefits to society, the person may have lost his personal liberty but not his civil liberty.[33]

In attempting to devise a coherent utilitarian account of civil liberty, based on the conception of liberty as the absence of restraint, both Hey and Paley explicitly rejected the influential definition of political liberty adopted by Montesquieu: 'The political liberty of a citizen is a tranquillity of mind arising from the opinion each person has of his safety [sûreté]. In order to have this liberty, it is necessary that the government be so constituted that a citizen need not fear another citizen.'[34]

For Hey, Montesquieu's conception confused liberty first with a

---

[30] Hey, *Observations*, 55.   [31] Ibid. 56.
[32] Paley, *The Principles of Moral and Political Philosophy*, in *The Works of William Paley, D.D.*, 5 vols. (London, 1819), i. 392.   [33] Ibid. i. 394.
[34] Montesquieu, *De l'esprit des lois*, in *Œuvres complètes* (Paris, 1964), xi. 6.

right to liberty and then with its effects, namely security and tranquillity of mind.[35] Paley referred to the idea of civil liberty as security as 'neither so simple nor so accurate' as his own account, though he admitted that it was closer to 'common discourse'.[36] He also believed that it encompassed too many and different ideas of civil liberty to be worth using. In his critique of Richard Price, Lind wrote of both 'civil and political liberty' and 'civil and political security' and cited Montesquieu as the source of the latter notion.[37] But by 1776, Bentham had moved beyond this confusion. His view that liberty must be wholly a negative idea and that liberty could not be produced by the action of law led him to see no logical connection between individual liberty on the one hand and civil and political liberty on the other. He also rejected the utilitarian account of civil liberty, as restraints justified by reference to the common good, as found in Hey and Paley.

4. Liberty as Security

'That which under the name of Liberty is so much magnified, as the invaluable, the unrivalled work of Law, is not *Liberty*', wrote Bentham, 'but *Security*', and he clearly adopted Montesquieu's approach to civil and political liberty.[38] When Paley considered liberty as security, he listed a number of different notions of civil liberty related to security, including: (1) laws based on actual consent; (2) laws based on indirect and virtual consent; (3) the separation of the legislative and executive offices of government; (4) laws established, known in advance, with inflexible rules of action and adjudication; (5) the right of the people to tax themselves by their own representatives; (6) freedom of election of representatives by the people; and (7) control over the military establishment by the people.[39] Paley also thought that these notions described 'not so much liberty itself, as the safeguards and preservatives of liberty' and that all sorts of similar ideas might be advanced under the heading of security.[40] If Paley rejected the conception of liberty

[35] Hey, *Observations*, 35.
[36] Paley, *Principles*, 395.
[37] Lind, *Three Letters*, 74 ff., 87–8.
[38] UC lxix. 44.
[39] Paley, *Principles*, 396–7.
[40] Ibid. 397. I am indebted to Professor W. B. Gwyn, Tulane University, for first suggesting that I examine Paley's writings on security and liberty.

as security, Bentham, nevertheless, found in the term a more accurate way of expressing ideas which were often used in a confused fashion under the headings of civil and political liberty.[41]

In the context of law and politics security had two characteristics which Bentham was quick to notice. Firstly, security is often conceived as being *against* something. Security against intruders is established by locks and alarms; and security against invasion, by a military force. What provide security are the instruments of security (that is to say, the locks and alarms). Bentham concentrated on the development of such instruments of security across a wide spectrum of law and policy, from constitutional law (security against misrule) to civil procedure (security against delay, vexation, and expense) and to liberty of the press (security to make known complaints and remonstrances). These instruments could be clearly stated and their utility assessed more directly and easily by seeing them as part of security rather than as embedded in the traditional rhetoric of liberty. Secondly, security *against* marks off a framework within which one can locate liberty. The house with adequate locks and alarms will be free of intruders. In this fairly definite sense, security can be seen as creating freedom. This approach to liberty also allows liberty to be seen as a more limited notion than some of the rhetoric associated with various claims and conceptions of liberty has tended to suggest. It is possible to be secure in one sense but not in another. The man who is secure behind his locks and bolts might not possess the keys to get out. If he is free from intruders, he might not be free to leave the premises. Nevertheless, such problems would necessarily be commonplace and no confusion need arise so long as security is seen as providing freedom which is appropriate to the context of the security. To be free from interference by intruders does not in itself give one freedom from confinement by these same instruments of security.

Bentham also appreciated that security was oriented not simply towards immediate constraints but also towards future threats and dangers.[42] For example, like Hume, he believed that the Statute of Proclamations of 1539 (31 Hen. VIII, c.8) which gave the proclamations of Henry VIII the force of law was a grave threat to liberty not because any immediate constraints followed the passage

[41] Consider e.g. the distinction between civil and political liberty in J. Priestley, *An Essay on the First Principles of Government; and on the Nature of Political, Civil, and Religious Liberty* (London, 1768), 12 ff.   [42] See Paley, *Principles*, 395.

of the law, but because the law posed a grave danger to the security of the subject which had been established by the constitution.[43] 'The constitution was actually destroyed', wrote Bentham, echoing Hume who had written: 'The parliament, having thus resigned all their religious liberties, proceeded to an entire surrender of their civil; and without scruple or deliberation they made by one act a total subversion of the English constitution.'[44] In encompassing more than immediate constraints, the notion of security provided a broader foundation for political liberty.

That Bentham rejected the move to conceive of civil and political liberty in terms of the simple calculation of utility and, in addition, that he found the emphasis on security was rejected by some contemporary utilitarians is of some importance in understanding the significance of liberty in his utilitarian system. As security, liberty played the most fundamental role as the main end of legislation and as a component of the principle of utility itself. Security established the framework within which each person could set out to realize his happiness. Security pointed to the pains against which every human being sought protection. It was a main constituent of happiness and closely related to the relief of pain.[45] Security was also fundamental in that without security, and especially security of expectation, on which the continued existence of the individual's hopes and projects depended, there could be little pleasure and even less happiness.[46] For without security of expectation few of the pleasures of civilized life could be enjoyed and those of a simpler existence would be fleeting and always under threat.

The legislator, for Bentham, could not maximize the pleasures of each individual in a society or even respond to each person's wishes and desires. He could not possibly know what gave each person pleasure, and if he did, he would not have the resources to satisfy

---

[43] *A Comment on the Commentaries and A Fragment on Government*, ed. J. H. Burns and H. L. A. Hart (London, 1977) (*CW*), 56–7.

[44] Ibid. 56. D. Hume, *The History of England from the Invasion of Julius Caesar to the Revolution in 1688*, 6 vols. (Liberty Classics Edition) (Indianapolis, 1983), iii. 266.

[45] See *An Introduction to the Principles of Morals and Legislation*, ed. J. H. Burns and H. L. A. Hart (London, 1970), III. 1 (*CW*), p. 34.

[46] See the excellent discussions of security of expectation in G. J. Postema, *Bentham and the Common Law Tradition* (Oxford, 1986), 147 ff.; and P. J. Kelly, *Utilitarianism and Distributive Justice: Jeremy Bentham and the Civil Law* (Oxford, 1990), 71 ff.

everyone. What he could do, however, was to provide for their basic security so that they were able to maximize their own choice of pleasures and to establish a way of life which brought them happiness. Even though Bentham characteristically listed four ends of legislation—security, subsistence, abundance, and equality—the latter three ends were regarded both as additional ends and as part of security. For example, abundance was an end people sought beyond subsistence for their own happiness, but it was also a means to security as future subsistence. Even equality was interpreted not only as an end in itself, but also as part of security. Without increasing equality of wealth in society, for example, the security of both rich and poor would be under threat. The rich would suffer from the threat of civil strife, and the poor from the threat of starvation. Without entering here into the complexities of Bentham's utilitarian theory, it is important to see how security provided the framework within which each individual lived. That framework might be called a framework of civil and political liberty.

It is important to appreciate that Bentham eschewed simple consequentialism in approaching the complex problems of law and politics. The legislator acted indirectly; he established the framework of security through law and public opinion, a framework whose value was judged initially by the liberty each person had to pursue his own pleasures so long as he did not cause harm to the interests of others. At the level of the civil law, the legislator was to secure rights to property, prevent interference, simplify titles and judicial proceedings, and enhance competitiveness in commercial transactions. At the level of the criminal law, he secured the individual against crime with a rational criminal code and a strong and effective system of police and judiciary. At the level of constitutional law, the legislator aimed to provide security against misrule.

Bentham also followed Montesquieu in seeing a close link between political liberty and constitutionalism, and in doing so turned Locke's argument upside down. In place of Locke's primary emphasis on individual liberty with civil liberty arising to protect the individual, Montesquieu first conceived political liberty in terms of constitutional arrangements with individual liberty developed within this framework. At this time (around 1776) Bentham believed that the British constitution was 'found by experience to possess a greater degree of expedience, to be more highly conducive to the happiness of those who live under it than any other yet exemplified'.[47] Nevertheless, Bentham's critical, analytical mind was not satisfied (as was Blackstone's) simply to praise the British constitution. If Bentham followed Montesquieu in the shift from Lockean liberty to that of *L'Esprit des lois*, he soon left far behind this eighteenth-century preoccupation with small republics, constitutional monarchies, and absolute monarchies. Bentham attempted nothing less than a complete re-examination of constitutional ideas which began with *A Fragment on Government* and continued, with a lengthy interruption following the French Revolution, into the 1830s. Yet, he brought to this study a preoccupation with liberty, now seen as security, which remained at the heart of his system.

5. Constitutional Liberty

Just as with the notions of liberty and security, a good deal of Bentham's attention in his earliest constitutional writings was devoted to determining the truth of commonly held doctrines. One such doctrine, which he criticized, was entitled 'The more Law, the more Liberty'. Beginning with his conception of liberty, he posed the problem in the following manner: 'It is the Characteristic of Law to produce restraint. Liberty is the absence of restraint. How should Law then produce Liberty? How should the quantity of Liberty be in proportion to the quantity of Law?'[48]

Bentham argued that only in constitutional law where complex regulations were needed to confer powers and to prescribe limits to the powers did the maxim seem to apply. The despotic Turkish pasha operated with far fewer laws and was 'sooner instructed' than the Governor of Jamaica or a Chief Justice of the King's Bench at Westminster. But constitutional law was only a small portion of the total mass of laws, and to most of this mass the maxim did not apply. Liberty actually had been increased in the law of property with the simplification and reduction of feudal laws. The multiplicity of conditions affecting tenure had especially had this effect.

[47] *Comment/Fragment (CW)*, 56.
[48] UC lxix. 148.

He also pointed to laws regarding taxation and the laws of excise and custom and expressed doubt that the maxim could apply in these areas. As though to clinch his argument, he pointed to France 'where they have so much less liberty than we have' but 'they have much more law'.[49]

Another notion concerning liberty which Bentham criticized was the tendency to have a confused idea of 'free government' and to confuse it with 'popular government'. Nearly every government was in some sense free in so far as it was all-powerful in a territory. But one often spoke of a free government when referring to a popular one in which the number of people participating in government was large in proportion to the population of the state.[50] Nevertheless, the real meaning of 'free government', he believed, was that the people enjoyed political security. They knew in advance the rules of conduct they would have to observe, and their interests would be similar to those of their governors.

In numerous manuscript passages written at this time Bentham analysed and criticized aspects of the notion of the separation of powers. At one point, for example, he saw its use in a positive light in preventing partiality in government. Ideally, the legislature could not be partial towards particular people, because its laws were framed in a general way. Even though it dealt more with individuals, the executive could not easily be partial, because the people with whom it dealt were marked out in general terms by the legislature. Thus, the separation of powers helped to prevent the enactment of laws directed unfairly against particular people.[51]

In another passage Bentham puzzled over the notion that the power of the supreme legislature was superior to the power of the supreme executive. He thought that this formulation did not make sense in so far as it was the executive and not the legislature which for the most part actually exercised power. The legislature could only direct and point out general objects for punishment. It was the executive that actually punished.[52] Similarly, he questioned the separation of functions which supposedly was part of the separation of powers. Instead of the neat separation suggested by some writers, he found: 'The Legislature exercises the executive function in many instances, as well judiciary as dispensational. The King makes Laws. And Judges too make laws.'[53] At another point, he

[49] UC lxix. 148.   [50] UC lxix. 153.   [51] UC lxix. 186-7.
[52] UC lxix. 155.   [53] UC lxix. 155-6.

took up the view in England of Parliament as the supreme legislative power and the king as the supreme executive power. As Parliament was considered the supreme power in the country, and since it too performed executive functions, then Parliament and not the king might be regarded as the supreme executive.[54] Or, at still another point, he noted that as the military power exercised by officers under the king included legislative, executive, and judicial powers, it might be argued that the king possessed these three powers.[55]

As he developed these points in numerous sketches of arguments, it was clear that Bentham was not about to become an advocate of any existing constitutional theory. Although he held Montesquieu and his follower Jean Delolme in high regard, and was indebted to Montesquieu for his emphasis on security and the link between security and liberty, he could see grave difficulties in the doctrine of the separation of powers as the basis of a system of constitutional liberty. Bentham's most important writing on government at this time was *A Fragment on Government*, which has been characterized as an essay on sovereignty; but such a characterization is not wholly satisfactory.[56] From the argument of this chapter, one might call the *Fragment* an essay on liberty in which the author was determined not to misuse the term. Put more generally, it might be called an essay on constitutional liberty in which many of the questions Bentham had been putting to himself in his various unpublished manuscripts were now put for the first time publicly to his life-long adversary William Blackstone.

[54] UC lxix. 156.   [55] Ibid.
[56] See L. J. Hume, *Bentham and Bureaucracy* (Cambridge, 1981), 62, who quotes from F. C. Montague's edition of the *Fragment on Government* (Oxford, 1891), 59.

3

Constitutional Theory I: From the *Fragment* to the French Revolution

In the *Fragment on Government* Bentham posed the general question of how free and despotic governments differed. The answer, he suggested, was not that rulers in a despotic state had more power than those in a free state, but that the distinction 'turns upon circumstances of a very different complexion'.[1] He then listed these 'circumstances' on which free government rested as follows:

on the *manner* in which that whole mass of power, which, taken together, is supreme, is, in a free state, *distributed* among the several ranks of persons that are sharers in it:—on the *source* from whence their titles to it are successively derived:—on the frequent and easy *changes* of condition between govern*ors* and govern*ed*; whereby the interests of one class are more or less indistinguishably blended with those of the other:—on the *responsibility* of the governors; or the right which a subject has of having the reasons publicly assigned and canvassed of every act of power that is exerted over him:—on the *liberty of the press*; or the security with which every man, be he of the one class or the other, may make known his complaints and remonstrances to the whole community:—on the *liberty of public association*; or the security with which malecontents may communicate their sentiments, concert their plans, and practise every mode of opposition short of actual revolt, before the executive power can be legally justified in disturbing them.[2]

Bentham's list is important for our purposes in two respects. Firstly, in the last two 'circumstances', liberty of the press and public association, he clearly linked security with liberty and used this formulation to define an extensive framework for constitutional liberty. Secondly, in concentrating on general 'circumstances', Bentham established that he was not looking at particular institutions, such as the British constitution, as the source of liberty but

---

[1] *A Comment on the Commentaries and A Fragment on Government*, ed. J. H. Burns and H. L. A. Hart (London, 1977) (*CW*), 485. [2] Ibid.

more broadly to general principles. In this respect, he was beginning to move away from the focus on the British constitution as the embodiment of constitutional liberty which Blackstone had adopted from Montesquieu, though without necessarily giving up the principles to which those writers had subscribed. Although he could accept at this time that the British constitution was 'the finest and most excellent with all its imperfections of any the world ever yet saw',[3] his orientation was more towards general theory than towards the praise or defence of particular institutions.

Nevertheless, it is not entirely clear what status Bentham intended these 'circumstances' to have. They seem more suggestive than exhaustive and are not formulated in a way which would enable them to be interpreted as necessary or sufficient conditions for free government. On David Hume's criteria, in so far as Bentham's formulation was 'free from party-rage, and party-prejudices', he might be said to have been engaged in cultivating 'a science, which, of all others, contributes most to public utility'.[4] Perhaps Bentham also thought, as Hume did, that 'the world is still too young to fix many general truths in politics'.[5] To understand the development of Bentham's idea of constitutional liberty, however, it will be best to look at Bentham's critique of Blackstone's own account of the British constitution where current ideas of constitutional liberty might be found.

1. The Incoherence of Blackstone

Thus much for the British Constitution; and for the grounds of that pre-eminence which it boasts, I trust, indeed, not without reason above all others that are known: Such is the idea our Author gives us of those grounds.—'You are not satisfied with it then', says some one.—Not perfectly.—'What is then your own?'—In truth this is more than I have yet quite settled. I may have settled it with myself, and not think it worth the giving: but if ever I do think it worth the giving, it will hardly be in the form of a comment on a digression stuffed into the belly of a definition. At

---

[3] Ibid. 220–1. See also 56–7.

[4] D. Hume, *Essays: Moral, Political, and Literary*, ed. E. F. Miller (Liberty Classics Edition) (Indianapolis, 1985), pt. I, essay 12, 'Of Civil Liberty', 87.

[5] Ibid. See also pt. I, essay 4, 'Of the Origin of Government', 40–1, where Hume depicts free government.

any rate it is not likely to be much wished for, by those, who have read what has been given us on this subject by an ingenious foreigner: since it is to a foreigner we were destined to owe the best idea that has yet been given of a subject so much our own. Our Author has copied: but Mr. De L'olme has thought.[6]

With these words Bentham began his concluding remarks to the chapter on the British constitution. Full of allusion and suggestion, it is nevertheless not an easy passage to understand. It shows clearly Bentham's reticence to set forth his own account of the British constitution. He suggested that he had not yet worked out his ideas, but he also intimated that he had a good idea of how he might do so. Where he noted that these ideas might not be 'worth the giving', he was probably not engaging in uncharacteristic modesty but reflecting his own commitment to exploring these problems on a theoretical level rather than in a polemic against Blackstone.[7]

He did provide a hint of his own position by suggesting that his ideas would not be welcomed by those who had read sympathetically Jean Delolme's study of the British constitution.[8] But he immediately shrouded his comment in paradox. On the one hand, Delolme had written a better book than Blackstone, but on the other hand Bentham felt that he must criticize Blackstone, even though he might better argue with Delolme. Bentham's position becomes clearer when we consider the quotation from Montesquieu which appeared on the title-page of both the 1776 and 1823 editions, and which may be translated: 'Nothing is a greater obstacle to our progress in knowledge than a bad work of a celebrated author; because before we instruct, we must begin by undeceiving.'[9] Montesquieu was referring to his colleague the

---

[6] *Comment/Fragment (CW)*, 472–3. On Bentham and Blackstone, see J. H. Burns, 'Bentham and Blackstone: A Lifetime's Dialectic', *Utilitas*, 1 (1989), 22–40. See also David Lieberman, *The Province of Legislation Determined: Legal Theory in Eighteenth-Century Britain* (Cambridge, 1989), 31–67, 219–90.

[7] The tension between theory and polemic which characterizes the *Fragment on Government* perhaps reveals Bentham's 'strategy' more clearly than that suggested by C. D. Tarlton, 'The Overlooked Strategy of Bentham's *Fragment on Government*', *Political Studies*, 20 (1972), 397–406.

[8] Jean Louis Delolme, *La Constitution de l'Angleterre* (1771). The English version is used here: *The Constitution of England; or, An Account of the English Government* (London, 1775).

[9] See *Comment/Fragment (CW)*, 391–2. The reference is to *L'Esprit des lois*, xxx. 15.

Abbé Dubos, whose *Histoire critique de l'établissement de la monarchie française dans les Gaules* (1743) was used to enhance the claims of French kings to absolute power and which Montesquieu criticized in book xxx of *L'Esprit des lois*.[10] Bentham was presumably identifying with Montesquieu on the need at times to criticize an influential bad book rather than, as also might be necessary, an influential good book. That Bentham had Montesquieu in mind when he alluded to Delolme was evident from the fact that elsewhere he used the same phrase to compare Montesquieu with Blackstone, for example, 'the Englishman copied: but the Frenchman thought'.[11]

Blackstone has been regarded as a follower of Montesquieu and his account of the British constitution has been treated as an inferior replica.[12] But all that they seem to have in common at the level of constitutional theory is their admiration of the British constitution. Blackstone, for example, seems to have confused the notion of the mixed constitution, with its long pedigree from Polybius and Cicero, with the more modern idea of the separation or division of powers, suggested by Locke but developed by Montesquieu. Though these ideas were occasionally conflated, there was a clear difference between the two that Blackstone ignored. The view that mixed government, the combination of monarchy, aristocracy, and democracy in the institutions of king, Lords and Commons, was able to combine the virtues of each form of government without any of the vices, was not one especially favoured by Montesquieu and was easily ridiculed by Bentham. When, for example, Blackstone referred to 'the Lords Spiritual and Temporal, which is an aristocratical assembly of persons selected for their piety, their birth, their wisdom, their valour, or their property',[13] Bentham noted that Blackstone had derived the virtues of the Lords from their titles and in the process confused what ought to be the case with what was the case. It was one thing to say that the bishops ought to be pious, but quite another to say, as Blackstone did, that they were pious by virtue of being bishops.[14] Such criticisms led

---

[10] See R. Shackleton, *Montesquieu* (Oxford, 1961), 330 ff.
[11] *Comment/Fragment* (*CW*), 278 n.
[12] See F. T. H. Fletcher, *Montesquieu and English Politics* (London, 1939), 121.
[13] Quoted from Blackstone, *Commentaries on the Laws of England*, 4 vols. (Oxford, 1765–9), i. 50–1, quoted in *Comment/Fragment* (*CW*), 461.
[14] *Comment/Fragment* (*CW*), 464–5.

Bentham to conclude that all that remained of Blackstone's conceptions of monarchy, aristocracy, and democracy were the various numbers (one, few, and many) of which they were composed. In a well-known passage he then used Blackstone's 'mathematics' to devise a theorem to prove that the British constitution was all-perfect, and by the same manner '*all-weak, all-foolish, and all-knavish*'.[15]

The doctrine of the mixed constitution was traditionally concerned with the division of sovereign legislative power. Blackstone, however, shifted somewhat abruptly in the midst of his argument to refer to another problem, that of 'executive power'—'lodged in a single person' and having 'all the advantages of strength and dispatch that are to be found in the most absolute monarchy'.[16] The switch from one doctrine to the other, from the notion of mixed government to the separation of powers, was shown by Bentham to be even more confused. As for the latter doctrine, he proceeded to raise a number of questions as to what was meant by 'executive power'. He wondered if the king really possessed it or if he was merely said to possess it. He asked if executive power included judicial power and, if so, if it included the power of making '*general, permanent, spontaneous* regulations of procedure' (as some judges made) as well as particular decisions. If this was the case, executive power would include legislative power. He asked if executive power included supreme military power during war and peace. Did it include, he asked, the power to declare war and to end a state of war? Did it include the supreme fiscal power or the power (called 'dispensatorial') over items of public property, the power to grant patents and charters of incorporation, the power to make treaties with foreign nations and to deliver over subjects to foreign countries? Bentham did not attempt to answer these questions but simply observed: 'He that would understand . . . let him *think of these things*.'[17]

Bentham was not criticizing Blackstone for being ignorant of who in the British constitution had the power to conclude treaties, declare war, or grant patents. In Bentham's eyes, Blackstone had failed to consider in any depth the very distinction between

[15] *Comment/Fragment* (*CW*), 472.

[16] Blackstone, *Commentaries*, i. 50, quoted in *Comment/Fragment*, 461.

[17] *Comment/Fragment* (*CW*), 462–4. Besides the allusion to Phil. 4:8, Bentham is also referring to Delolme and Montesquieu. See nn. 6 and 11 above.

legislative and executive power. As noted in Chapter 2, Bentham
could see in military service the exercise not only of executive
power but also of legislative and judicial power so that simply
calling the power to direct the armed forces 'executive power'
would raise more questions than it would answer. Blackstone had
not even considered a problem like this. Nor had he taken up the
problem of the separation of powers as a theory of political liberty.
For an account of the *theory* that Bentham would eventually
oppose, it will be more useful to examine that theory in the work of
the writer he did admire, Jean Delolme.

2. The Theory of Montesquieu and Delolme

Even though the widely read *Constitution de l'Angleterre* was also
indebted to Montesquieu, Delolme seemed to use the debt more
creatively than Blackstone to produce a philosophical study of the
British constitution.[18] As befitted a citizen of Geneva and a student
of Rousseau, Delolme was concerned with the way in which liberty
had been sacrificed in republican governments, where the people,
though ostensibly in power, became the slaves of unscrupulous
politicians. Delolme believed that the inadequacies of republican
government could be overcome by an appreciation of the complex
and subtle structure of the British constitution.

Of the themes which Delolme developed throughout his book
none was given greater attention than that of executive power.
Throughout his discussion, one feels the strong influence of
Montesquieu's examination of the same problem.[19] For
Montesquieu, to preserve liberty executive power, separate from
legislative power, should rest in the hands of a single monarch, not
subject to impeachment or trial by the legislature, and with the
power to call and prorogue the legislative bodies. The executive
should have the power to participate positively in the legislative
process or, at least, to participate in debates. The legislature, in
turn, while possessing no authority to interfere in the execution of
the laws, would control funds for the executive, would have the
power to examine generally how the laws were executed, and

[18] Cf. Fletcher, *Montesquieu*, 130 ff., who finds the work lifeless and mechanical.
[19] See *L'Esprit des lois*, xi. 6.

could impeach ministers of the Crown, though not the monarch, in the House of Lords. In defining the parameters of legislative and executive power, Montesquieu, like Delolme to follow, was preoccupied with the theme of liberty and the way the structure of the British constitution prevented, at least for the present, its loss. In this respect, he found the British constitution far superior to those of the less stable ancient republics.

Montesquieu's discussion was brief, highly compressed, and not clear in several respects. For example, he did not provide a clear definition of the executive or of executive power. At one point, he seemed to conceive of the judiciary as a branch of the executive, while at other points he clearly distinguished between them. As for executive power, he was content to say that the prince 'makes peace or war, sends or receives embassies, establishes security and provides against invasions'.[20] This part of executive power was concerned with the 'law of nations'; while the other, dealing with the punishment of criminals and the settlement of disputes, which he later called judicial power, was based on the civil law. While Montesquieu was more concerned to establish the constitutional status of executive power in relation to liberty rather than to define the functions of a chief executive, he left his fundamental concepts without a clear definition. Nevertheless, he was one of the first writers to use 'executive' in a modern sense and to juxtapose it with 'legislative' and 'judicial'.[21]

Delolme went beyond Montesquieu in attempting to provide a more detailed account of the scope of the king's executive power which he placed under seven headings.[22] He then used this

---

[20] See *L'Esprit des lois*, xi. 6.

[21] See M. J. C. Vile, *Constitutionalism and the Separation of Powers* (Oxford, 1967), 96.

[22] In the *Constitution of England*, 81–3, these are summarized as follows: Firstly, the king is responsible for the administration of justice, as chief magistrate. He is the source of judicial power; judgements are made with his seal and executed by his officers. He is directly concerned in all offences and prosecutions are carried out in his name in courts of law. He has the power to pardon offences. Secondly, he can distribute titles, make peers of the realm, and give various offices to whomsoever he wishes. Thirdly, he is 'the superintendent of Commerce' and in this he regulates weights and measures and alone has the power to coin money. Fourthly, he is supreme head of the Church, has the power to appoint bishops and archbishops, and convenes the assembly of the clergy. He must assent to its acts and the king can prorogue or dissolve the Convocation. Fifthly, he is commander-in-chief of all military forces and can alone levy troops, equip fleets and armies, build fortresses, and fill all the positions in the armed forces. Sixthly, in relation to foreign countries,

catalogue of powers to establish more directly than Montesquieu the way in which these extensive powers in the hands of one man were arranged to maximize political liberty rather than lead to tyranny. This was due to the important fact that, despite his extensive powers, the king still depended upon legislative power to fund his various activities, and without such funds he was unable to exercise these powers. For Delolme, executive and legislative power were not directly antagonistic, but were so organized as to have to co-operate to support the constitution. And the very power of the king and his position above the law restrained the legislature from attempting to carry out its own laws. Furthermore, due to the location of this enormous power in one man, there was an interest among all other members of society not to usurp his powers but to combine to confine them.[23]

Delolme's account of the scope of executive power would answer some of the questions Bentham asked of Blackstone's use of the notion. It would reveal more clearly than Blackstone, or indeed Montesquieu himself, how such a concentration of political power was none the less crucial to the establishment of a regime embodying political liberty. But it would not answer the most important questions Bentham asked, such as that concerning the nature of executive power and how it might be distinguished from legislative power beyond the observation that the objects of legislative power were general and those of executive power, particular. Bentham was probably the first thinker to point out that a good deal of what was considered the exercise of executive power or administration was hardly distinguishable from legislation except in its source, and the catalogue of Delolme revealed just how extensive the scope for 'executive' legislation might be.

In approving the special status of the British monarch and his distinctive place in the constitution, Delolme feared that he would be interpreted as being partial to all monarchies and hostile to republics.[24] In denying this position, he frequently dwelled on the role of the people in the British constitution, as in the following passage:

he represents the nation and has the power to send and receive ambassadors, make and break alliances, declare war, and make peace. Finally, in all of these activities and in carrying out the various laws, the king is above the reach of the courts and his person is 'sacred and inviolable'.

[23] Ibid. 194 and n.   [24] Ibid. 388.

If we consider the great advantages to public liberty which result from the
institution of the Trial by Jury, and from the Liberty of the press, we shall
find England to be in reality a much more Democratical State than any
other we are acquainted with. The Judicial power, and the Censorial
power, are vested in the People.[25]

Several chapters were devoted to the two institutions just
mentioned: trial by jury and the press. As for the first, Delolme was
especially concerned that judicial power was exercised in a manner
which would be neither arbitrary nor tyrannical. In a phrase which
Bentham would have approved, Delolme wrote that 'all judicial
power is an evil, though a necessary one'.[26] To reduce and contain
this evil, Delolme thought it necessary that judicial power should
not be part of executive power but that it should also not be
exercised by an independent body. In an absolute monarchy, an
independent judiciary might effect some restraint in the government, but in a limited monarchy or other form of government it
might also become a dangerous influence in the constitution. In the
jury system, albeit in a highly selective view of it, Delolme found
the institution which took ultimate judicial authority out of the
hands of the executive and the judges. For Delolme 'the Trial by
Jury is that point of their liberty to which the people of England are
most thoroughly and universally wedded'.[27] Delolme examined
numerous aspects of the English judicial system, from the use of
Counsel in one's defence, the practice of challenging jurors, to the
use of Habeas Corpus, all of which enhanced the liberty of the
subject, and he found in the jury system the most important of
these numerous securities. Judicial punishment depended on this
institution, which brought a humanitarian element into the judicial
process. In addition, no one need live in fear of particular
individuals who had the power of inflicting judicial punishments.
If trial by jury placed in the hands of the people judicial power,
the institution of a free press placed in their hands 'censorial
power'.[28] The people had the right to present petitions to the king
and to both Houses of Parliament. They could also lay their
complaints before the public by means of a free press. If they
violated laws in doing so, they must be tried by the jury system
which might very well not convict them of the offences. Their

[25] *Constitution of England*, 408 n.   [26] Ibid. 140.
[27] Ibid. 161.   [28] Ibid. 280.

representatives in Parliament could also speak with immunity from all prosecution. But Delolme especially regarded the free press as 'a formidable right . . . which, continually dispelling the cloud of majesty by which they are surrounded, brings them [rulers] to a level with the rest of Mankind, and strikes at the very being of their authority'.[29] He criticized Montesquieu and Rousseau for praising the Roman Censorial Tribunal without appreciating the great and, indeed, arbitrary power it placed in the hands of particular magistrates. 'Though I have been called by some an advocate for Power', he wrote, 'I have carried my ideas of Liberty farther than many Writers who have mentioned that word with much enthusiasm.'[30] For Delolme, under the British constitution the people themselves operated a great censorial tribunal without a threat to their liberty.

The jury system and liberty of the press were two important 'democratic' institutions which also preserved and enhanced civil liberty. A third was the right of election and the system of representation in the House of Commons. Even allowing for the very narrow franchise which existed at the time Delolme was writing, the very existence of the House of Commons was widely regarded as the 'democratical' element in the constitution.

A fourth institution which in Delolme's view enhanced the power and security of the people was the concentration of the executive power in the hands of the king. The separation of executive from legislative power prevented the legislature from ceasing to represent the people by self-aggrandizement. 'It is the Throne above all,' wrote Delolme, 'it is this jealous Power, that makes the People sure that its Representatives never will be any thing more than its Representatives.'[31] A constant theme in his book was concerned with the way the people in ancient republics, though they had a greater direct involvement in government, were betrayed by their magistrates. In Britain, because they were unable to obtain the power possessed by the king, representatives were presumably more content to remain representatives of the people. They would be less inclined to betray the people, and the rich to betray the poor:

Leaving to the rich no other security for his palace, than what the peasant has for his cottage, has united his cause to that of the latter;—the cause of

---

[29] Ibid. 280–1.   [30] Ibid. 279 n.   [31] Ibid. 273.

the powerful to that of the helpless;—the cause of the Man of extensive influence and connections, to that of him who is without friends.[32]

When Bentham wrote that Delolme, unlike Blackstone, 'thought', he was probably referring both to the way Delolme attempted a more detailed and comprehensive view of the subject (as in his account of executive power) and to the way he systematically linked the various institutions and practices of the British constitution to conceptions of liberty and democracy. Delolme looked beneath the surface of institutions which seemed to possess enormous power over the people to see that power controlled and confined to benefit the people. Beneath appearance was a different reality, and a reality which could be grasped by theory. The theory enabled Delolme to mount a telling critique of both European monarchies and traditional republics. Though he voiced sentiments which were often similar to those of Delolme, Blackstone's *Commentaries* lacked this critical dimension.

3. Bentham's Theory and the French Revolution

It was not until the period of the French Revolution that Bentham was tempted to construct a theory of constitutional liberty. Prior to that time, he was apparently content to expand and refine the sort of list which he employed in distinguishing between free and despotic government in the earlier *Fragment*. In material written in 1782 for his 'Essay on Indirect Legislation' he discussed fifteen securities against misrule, many of which would have been familiar to readers of the *Fragment*, while others would be eventually rejected or used in other contexts.[33] Furthermore, as late as 1788, even though he became sympathetic to major reform in France and wrote a number of essays in favour of reform there, he initially argued that he was content with the British constitution.[34] Late in 1789 and during 1790, however, he began to develop his ideas in favour of a democratic constitution for Britain.[35]

Clearly events in France had stimulated Bentham to consider the

---

[32] *Constitution of England*, 273.   [33] See UC lxxxvii. 102–27.
[34] See H. L. A. Hart, *Essays on Bentham* (Oxford, 1982), 66–8. See also J. H. Burns, 'Bentham and the French Revolution', *Transactions of the Royal Historical Society*, 5th Series, 16 (1966), 95–114.
[35] Bentham's writings on reform at this time will be published in a volume in the *Collected Works* entitled *Essays on French and British Political Reform, 1788–95*, ed.

theoretical basis of the best constitution. In doing so, he did not wholly neglect the British constitution but simply saw it in a different light: 'though good in comparison of absolute monarchy, or absolute aristocracy, [it] is perhaps equally bad in comparison of a well-organized commonwealth.'[36] In one of the essays, entitled 'British Parliamentary Reform', he developed a critique of the existing franchise for election to the House of Commons and set forth an outline of a constitutional democracy. The critique of the franchise was at one level an implicit critique of Delolme who, throughout his study of the British constitution, treated the House of Commons as being based on a democratic franchise. For Bentham, the franchise was too small; the right to vote was based on a property qualification which aggravated the importance of wealth, though only one kind of wealth, freehold property, was acceptable. 'Though wealth is the only test of fitness', he wrote, 'men overflowing in wealth are rejected while beggars are received.'[37] Electoral districts were too large, making it difficult to exercise the right to vote, and the inequality between the numbers of voters in various districts was enormous. The qualifications for office as representatives were also unsatisfactory and were used by the nobility to exclude 'the vulgar herd all such as have neither wealth [n]or birth to boast of', those 'who wish to serve their country and know how' as opposed to 'young noblemen and gentlemen' 'who have all the wants of the opulent without any of the means: men who are too proud to work and too poor to live without working'.[38]

After a complex and subtle analysis of the mischievous consequences of the electoral system in Britain, one which emphasized the unsuitableness of both elections and representatives, and the tendency for the latter to enlarge their power at the expense of the poor, Bentham eventually turned to his proposals for reform. It is significant that the manuscript for this part of the essay had originally been prepared as part of his proposals for the French which he now simply transferred to Britain.[39] He proposed annual

M. H. James and C. P. Blamires. I am indebted to Dr James for the use of his transcripts for the material presented here. See also M. H. James, 'Bentham's Democratic Theory at the Time of the French Revolution', *Bentham Newsletter*, 10 (1986), 5–16.

[36] UC cxxvii. 7.   [37] Ibid.   [38] UC clxx. 169.
[39] See UC cxxvii. 8.

elections, a large number of equal electoral districts, secret ballot, and that all citizens, male or female, who were of full age, sound mind, and able to read, should have the right to vote. Citizenship was easily obtained if not acquired at birth. Everyone was eligible for office, though a Deputy, once elected, could not hold another office unless he already held it when he was elected. Deputies could be removed from office by petition and a new election. Bentham also favoured a unicameral legislature.[40]

Although the essay on the reform of representation revealed the sort of system Bentham would introduce and some reasons for his dissatisfaction with the existing one, it did not attempt to present a theory of constitutional liberty. This was attempted in another essay, 'False Principle Division of Power', where Bentham dealt directly with the theory advanced and justified by Delolme, Blackstone, and Montesquieu:

The true and efficient cause and measure of constitutional liberty or rather security is the dependence of the possessors of efficient power upon the originative power of the body of the people.

A spurious efficient cause and measure that has been hitherto commonly substituted to the one above mentioned is the division of the mass of political power by the allotment of different branches of it to different hands.[41]

Bentham presented three main arguments against dividing power in government. Firstly, if rulers were already accountable to the people, no additional security was gained by dividing power.[42] Indeed, where historically the division of power had been useful, it was because the different parties in conflict had appealed to the

---

[40] See UC cxxvii. 8.

[41] UC cxxvi. 8. Later in the *Constitutional Code*, Bentham replaced 'efficient' and 'originative' with 'operative' and 'constitutive'. See *Constitutional Code*, i, ed. F. Rosen and J. H. Burns (Oxford, 1983), ch. 4, art. 6 (*CW*), p. 27. Note that Bentham distinguished between the more conservative doctrine of mixed government (which emphasized the division of legislative power between King, Lords, and Commons) and the doctrine emphasized by both Montesquieu and Delolme, the separation of powers between legislative, executive, and judicial branches of government. In one passage he declared that the doctrine of the separation of powers was actually more pernicious in its effects than the division of legislative power. 'If the division . . . is confined only in the legislative branch,' he wrote, 'the business of government may yet go on.' To which he added: 'Place the disagreement between two of those branches, the legislative and the judicial, every thing is in confusion. What the one commands the other forbids. The citizen knows not whom to obey, nor what to do to be at peace.' UC cxxvi. 9.   [42] UC cxxvi. 8.

people generally for help in their struggle. 'As they quarrelled they appealed to the people: as the appeal spread and the people availed themselves of it, the people gained liberty.'[43] Thus, the division of power did not in itself establish constitutional liberty, but where there was conflict, the people were able to benefit from existing divisions to enhance their liberty. However, once accountable government was established, no such division would be necessary. Secondly, with the division of power there was a likely substitution of minority for majority rule. This development might not be immediately apparent, as one justification for the division of power was that it required a broader consensus for agreement than a simple majority. But Bentham argued that the division gave minorities a veto on legislation and, by virtue of this power, the minorities could secure what they wanted against the wishes of the majority of the people. Bentham did not believe that the sacrifice of majority to minority rule was necessarily a characteristic of good government, and nearly always saw in it mischievous effects. Thirdly, he argued that when there was no opposition among those who possessed divided power, the system was entirely without effect. Any measure might be adopted unless there was some popular accountability, and it was the accountability to the people and not the division of power which had the greater effect.

When Bentham turned more specifically to the separation of powers between legislative, executive, and judicial branches of government, he found additional problems. He believed that the notion was confused in its very conception, and he emphasized the ambiguity about the status of judicial power and its relation to the executive:

All power comes under one or other of two or three branches; for such is the confusion at the very outset: legislative and executive: or legislative judicial and executive. Judicial power is and is not a branch of the executive. This much however is agreed that whatever is not legislative is either executive or else either judicial or executive.[44]

He then argued that the separation of powers into three branches with a total separation of both function and personnel had been repeatedly violated in the French constitution where this separation was instituted, and without such violation it would have been impossible for the government to function. No government could

---

[43] UC cxxvi. 11.   [44] UC cxxvii. 4.

function successfully, he argued, under a strict separation of powers, and most modern constitutional theorists would tend to agree, although it is true to say that few advocates of the separation of powers originally proposed its institution in so extreme a form.[45]

Bentham advocated the reconsideration of constitutional theory from new premises and completely abandoned the doctrine of the division of power (in all its forms) as its basis. Bentham's theory, as we have seen, was founded on the dependence of all branches of government, directly or indirectly, on the people with sovereign power placed in a supreme legislature chosen and dismissible by the people. This sovereign power was to include legislative, judicial, and executive power, for part of making laws was seeing that they were obeyed. Sovereign power need not, however, include *all* legislative power as there could be 'local legislatures' which enacted laws without the consent of the sovereign legislature though under its control.

Neither a king nor any body not directly accountable to the people was to have a share in legislative power, although a king might play a useful role in the orderly succession of parliaments. Nor was he to have a role in judicial or executive power. Bentham, as might be expected from the *Fragment*, paused over the notion of executive power, and defined it in a manner which gave it a minor role in government. If judicial power was designed to ensure obedience to the laws, executive power was appropriately exercised when others failed in their obedience. In this conception, executive power, instead of being, for Delolme, the power of the king and the key to understanding liberty in the British constitution, became subordinate to judicial power and no business of the king. Nevertheless, Bentham did not become wholly a republican, as he termed 'administrative' power what Delolme called 'executive' and suggested that a hereditary monarch might, under the control of the legislature, command the military and dispose generally of public property. Although the king might not be removable from office, none of his acts were valid unless performed with the agreement of someone who was accountable and removable.

In a series of notes written at this time Bentham further

---

[45] See e.g. Vile, *Constitutionalism and the Separation of Powers*, and A. Hamilton, J. Jay, and J. Madison, *The Federalist* (New York, n.d.) (The Modern Library Edition), no. 47, pp. 312–20.

elaborated this discussion of constitutional organization first set out in the essay.[46] Here he used the notion of sovereignty in two respects, referring to the 'sovereign constituent and disconstituent power' in the hands of the people and the 'sovereign efficient power' in the legislative assembly. The legislature also possessed judicial power—to alter the judgements of the supreme judicial body, to collect evidence, to remove obstructions to the actions of the legislature, and to regulate the activities of members during sittings. The administrative power was clearly subordinate to the legislative. It might be lodged in a king who had 'constituent power' in appointing ministers but no 'efficient power'. The 'efficient power' was exercised by ministers who were fully responsible to the legislature, and who had a seat there but not a vote. The king, through his ministers, might thus propose legislation. Bentham added a cautionary note about minimizing the influence on the assembly by the king and his ministers as much as possible. As for judges, the local ones were appointed by the district assemblies and superior ones presumably by the legislature.

There were clearly great differences between Bentham's system and that of Delolme. Bentham had swept away the pretence that there was a 'democratic' component in the legislature in the British constitution, by favouring a single assembly directly elected by the people by universal suffrage. He had also limited the power of the king to one of appointing ministers and to some control over the military forces. Delolme's notion of a powerful and independent executive to prevent usurpation by the legislature was clearly rejected.

Furthermore, Delolme's idea of constitutional liberty was more concerned with curbing the exercise of *arbitrary* power which was best limited by the separation of legislative, executive, and judicial power. He also linked the exercise of arbitrary power with notions of tyranny and usurpation. Bentham attacked this position in the following passage:

When the three branches of power, the legislative, the executive and the judicial, are united in the same hands, arbitrary power, say the partizans of the balancing system, takes place: in other words the mass of power, take it all together, is arbitrary. This ill name thus bestowed, the proposition in question is supposed to be demonstrated and the business done. But what

[46] UC clxx. 47.

is meant by arbitrary? *Arbitrium* means decision, will. What then is the grievance? that questions relative to the exercise of power should be decided in the first instance by the will of those invested with it? But this is neither more nor less than what the case must always be.[47]

Bentham argued that the exercise of all political power required the exercise of will and decision, and that to call 'undivided' or 'unseparated' power arbitrary made no sense. Either the person acted according to the law or he did not. What was especially important was the way Bentham severed the link between so-called 'arbitrary' power and tyrannical power, and in doing so raised questions about the coherence of the doctrine of the separation of powers.

Nevertheless, we might wonder why, in this theoretical study, Bentham did not have the legislature appoint ministers and propose a Prime Minister appointed by the legislature, who was com-mander-in-chief of the armed forces, as later appeared in the *Constitutional Code* in the 1820s.[48] In spite of all of his criticisms of an independent executive power, he hesitated to do away with its last vestiges. It is possible that Bentham was merely prudent, and working within the system as then established, or was genuinely looking for a role for a monarch, but it is hard not to see traces of influence of Montesquieu and Delolme in the way Bentham set out his conception of adminstrative power.

Furthermore, like Delolme, though more strongly, Bentham linked 'democratic' practices in constitutional theory with consti-tutional liberty. He expressed the link almost in terms of a mathematical proportion: 'Constitutional liberty depends upon and is proportioned to the dependence of the possessors of efficient public power upon the will of the body of the people, in virtue of the originative power they possess.'[49] The dependence would be achieved in proportion to 'the degree of facility which the will of the people has of manifesting itself'.[50] The conditions for such manifestation were freedom of speech, assembly, writing and printing, and communication (including the use of the post office). Full publicity must be given to the acts of government officials and to all related documents. In these remarks Bentham, like Delolme,

---

[47] UC cxxvi. 10.
[48] See *Constitutional Code*, vol. i, ch. 8, § 1–9 (*CW*), pp. 147–59.
[49] UC clxx. 168.   [50] Ibid.

but also like other writers of the time, saw great virtue in the liberty of the press and related freedoms.

If the division of power was considered so deficient as the basis of liberty, one wonders why philosophers and politicians have devoted so much time and attention to its justification. How could Bentham see that it was absurd, when so many writers would have disagreed? The problem with the doctrine of the division of power was that it lacked intelligibility. There was no way of ascertaining the character of the division or the amount of division which would establish constitutional liberty. Once it was shown to be unintelligible another theory had to replace it. Bentham could see an important role for himself in constitutional theory, and he was just beginning to explore it, when events in France led to an abandonment of constitutional theory, which was not undertaken again in any systematic manner for approximately thirty years. In reading the notes Bentham wrote between 1792 and 1795, the psychological shock he must have received can still be felt.

The British constitution in 1793 assumed in his writings a permanence and utility it had not enjoyed earlier ('inestimable advantage of a formed constitution such as the British'[51]) and republicanism took on a sinister, destructive dimension: 'The Euthanasia of the British Constitution is a Republic. The French in forming a Republic are sacrificing the happiness of the present generation to that of the future.'[52] And in a personal passage, Bentham declared his belief that the British constitution should not change:

No man in the three kingdoms has a fuller comprehension of the imperfections of the law: no man a more painful and indignant sense of them: no man has been more assiduous in investigating them, nor more successful in discovering them: no man more sensible, no man less sanguine in his expectations of seeing them voluntarily amended. It is with this body of grievances before my eyes that I say notwithstanding—no change in Constitution—no reform of Parliament.[53]

These were not merely prudential remarks, but reflected a fundamental change in Bentham's position. He turned against majority rule.[54] He argued that the king 'ought to have the habitual initiative in legislation' and that the House of Lords was necessary

[51] UC clxx. 175.   [52] UC clxx. 51.   [53] UC clxx. 173.
[54] UC clxx. 177.

'to give elevation to the King, their superior and creator'.[55] Some of the comments became so extreme as to be nearly unintelligible: for example, 'truer to say the Americans have no Constitution than that the English have none'; and 'the more perfect the constitution in point of equality of right of suffrage, the less valuable the right of suffrage, the less being the effect and value of each man's vote'.[56]

The reader of these notes can virtually feel Bentham struggling to make sense of his recent steps in constitutional theory in light of the disastrous developments in France. Although he had returned in dramatic fashion to his attachment to the British constitution, he still hoped none the less that he had done so from reason rather than from prejudice.[57]

He saw developments in France with despair:

All France is become a great *Arena*—to exterminate or be exterminated is the question. To exterminate is at once the business and the amusement of life—Feigned tragedies are become insipid and produce no sensation—they must have real ones. All virtue is swallowed up in ferocity. The social virtues are become infamous.[58]

As for the detailed proposals for the reform of representation and the critique of the division of power in the British constitution, Bentham's writings represented a massive retreat with the weapons and equipment of his earlier arguments cast aside. Only his commitment to rational argument seemed to remain, though even here it survived more as an article of faith than as a guide to practice. In a revealing passage, he attempted to fly the flag of reason against both the democrats and Edmund Burke:

The system of the democrats is absurd, and dangerous: for it subjugates the well-informed to the ill-informed *classes* of mankind. Mr. Burke's system though diametrically opposite, is absurd and mischievous for a similar reason, it subjugates the well-informed to the ill-informed *ages*.[59]

[55] UC clxx. 173. [56] UC clxx. 178. [57] UC clxx. 176.
[58] UC xliv. 2. [59] UC xliv. 5.

4
Constitutional Theory II: The Mature Theory of the 1820s

When Bentham returned to constitutional theory in the early 1820s, as part of his great project of drafting the *Constitutional Code*, he had already developed many of his characteristic ideas in earlier writings on parliamentary reform and public finance.[1] Although these writings provided much of the material he would need, he still had to develop a framework of appropriate concepts for understanding the role of constitutions in political life.

The idea of the social contract (as, for example, in Hobbes and Locke) had shifted the focus of attention from the problem of the merits of different constitutions to an account of the origins of civil society. This move placed the question of the forms of government in a subordinate position. If the heart of Aristotle's *Politics* consisted of the analysis of six constitutions and their various forms, Hobbes, after placing his emphasis on the formation of the Commonwealth, reduced the constitutions to three with the differences between them merely a difference of numbers.[2] Montesquieu revived the importance of different constitutions, and, under his influence and especially that of Blackstone and Delolme, Bentham was stimulated, as we have seen, to take up constitutional problems in the early *Fragment*. But Montesquieu's approach to constitutional theory, including the emphasis he placed on constitutional monarchy in the British context, was regarded by Bentham as fundamentally misconceived, if not incoherent. If, for Aristotle, there was a major distinction between monarchy and tyranny in that in one there was rule for the common good but not in the other, and for Hobbes there was only a difference in name between monarchy and tyranny, Bentham took the argument in a new

---

[1] See the account of this development in L. J. Hume, *Bentham and Bureaucracy* (Cambridge, 1981), 165 ff.
[2] See Aristotle, *Politics*, bks. 4–6, and T. Hobbes, *Leviathan*, ch. 19.

direction by arguing that in effect monarchy was tyranny. He saw
one critical task of constitutional theory to explore this assertion.

1. Monarchy as Tyranny

To argue that monarchy was, in effect, a tyrannical regime, even
where the powers of the monarch were limited and shared by
representative institutions, Bentham must deal with some obvious
objections derived especially from the considerable experience of
constitutional monarchy in Britain. Consider, for example, the
criticisms made later in the decade by T. B. Macaulay of a more
limited critique of monarchy by James Mill, as Macaulay's
arguments will also be applicable to Bentham's position.[3] Macaulay
contended that the desires of a monarch and an aristocracy were
fairly limited and easily satisfied. Very few monarchies, he
observed, had in fact plundered their subjects and left them at the
level of bare subsistence.[4] 'It is clear', he argued, 'that a king or an
aristocracy may be supplied to satiety with mere corporal pleasures,
at an expense which the rudest and poorest community would
scarcely feel.'[5] Beyond the satisfaction of these desires, he continued, a monarch, like most men, would desire the 'good opinion
of others'. No one, and especially a ruler, wished to be subject to
the 'hatred and contempt of the public', and the desire for
posthumous fame was a powerful motive among most men, and
not least among most rulers.[6] Thus, the monarch would have every
incentive to work for the good of the community.

Bentham's response to Macaulay's defence of monarchy would
have consisted of several related arguments. He could accept that it
was not necessarily in the interest of a monarch to leave his subjects
at the level of subsistence, even though the monarch's interest was
implacably opposed to those of the people. Where the prosperity of
the people enhanced that of the monarch, he favoured it. He also
favoured the enhancement of the general security of the people, so
long as no security was established that would represent a serious
curb on his own power over them.[7] Nevertheless, Bentham would

---

[3] See the useful collection of essays which comprised this debate in J. Lively and
J. Rees (eds.), *Utilitarian Logic and Politics* (Oxford, 1978).

[4] Ibid. 104.   [5] Ibid. 105.   [6] Ibid.

[7] 'Supreme Operative' in *First Principles Preparatory to Constitutional Code*, ed.
T. P. Schofield (Oxford, 1989), § 3 (*CW*), pp. 152–5.

regard the belief that the monarch easily satisfied his own desires and often sought the good opinion of his subjects as naïve. He did not deny that the monarch often appeared to rule for the good of his subjects and, especially, that the subjects themselves *believed* that he was doing so. Bentham pointed to a problem of false consciousness created by the monarch in so far as he was able to secure his own 'sinister interest' behind a façade of advancing the public good. But even here, the monarch's 'real' interest was scarcely veiled. The 'community of interest' between monarch and subjects was like that between masters and tame animals:

A community of interest (it may be said) has place between a Monarch and his subjects: and this community of interest will suffice for securing them against ill treatment at his hands: nay: for securing to them the best treatment in his power. True. There is a community of interest between a Post-master and his Post-horses: but this community of interest suffices not to save them from an untimely death at the end of a life of torment. The interest which a Monarch has in common with his subjects is not sufficient to render him in general so well disposed towards his subjects as a Post-master is to his Post-horses. By the horses nothing is usually done by which irritation and hatred towards them are produced in the breast of the Master. By the subjects much is constantly done by which hatred and continually renewed irritation is produced in the breast of the Monarch.[8]

At another point he noted that 'the best that can happen to them [the subjects] in the hands of the best-tempered Monarch is to be treated upon as good a footing as cattle are treated upon by a good tempered Master'.[9]

Bentham's account of the manner in which the sinister interest of the ruler was veiled and made compatible with a façade of commitment to the welfare of the ruled did not explain why the people, when his sinister interest was revealed, did not resist, and, indeed, often willingly sacrificed their own interests to his. Bentham dealt with this problem under the heading of 'interest-begotten prejudice'. 'Notorious are the instances,' he wrote, 'in which, by thousands and ten thousands, by prejudice in its various modes, men have been led to sacrifice each of them his own unquestionable interest while contributing to the sacrifice of the universal interest at the alter of monarchical and aristocratical

---

[8] Ibid. § 4, pp. 155–6.   [9] Ibid. § 5, p. 161.

despotism.'[10] These bitter words were used in an attempt to explain why men in their thousands were willing to give life and limb in wars, for example, which brought them no benefit and which had often been started to satisfy the whims of rulers. Bentham fully recognized that the people tended to sacrifice their interests on a grand scale 'without resistance or discontent'.[11]

For Bentham, the monarch's 'sinister interest' arose and developed because his interests were inevitably and continually opposed to those of the people. But the existence of sinister interest was largely connected with the development of 'interest-begotten prejudice'—a far more powerful and invidious force in politics than 'sinister interest' itself. To appreciate the depth and power of 'prejudice' one must also appreciate that by monarchy Bentham did not refer simply to the rule of one person. The monarch ruled with a supporting cast in the aristocracy and with the further support of clergy, lawyers, politicians, and the military. The maintenance of this establishment was a major task of monarchical rule involving patronage, corruption, and exploitation. This great machine was kept well oiled by a wide range of beliefs which the people had long been conditioned to accept. These beliefs were not simply about monarchy; they extended to basic conceptions of knowledge and time. For example, beliefs about change and the preservation of institutions might be formed by sinister interest operating through prejudice:

Though the absurd institution or arrangement is not productive of any immediate advantage to yourself', says the modern Machiavel to his patron, 'preserve it notwithstanding: for though the existence of it does not serve, the abolition of it would disserve, your own particular interest: to justify the abolition it would be necessary to bring into action some position, conformable to reason and subordinate and subservient, bearing a reference more or less obvious, to the all-comprehensive and universally applying principle—the greatest happiness principle.[12]

As for the relationship between 'sinister interest' and 'interest-begotten prejudice', the former, as we have seen, begot the latter, but the latter became more powerful than the former. There were limits to the number of people who could directly benefit from

---

[10] 'Supreme Operative' in *First Principles Preparatory to Constitutional Code*, ed. T. P. Schofield (Oxford, 1989), § 1 (*CW*), p. 152.

[11] Ibid. § 3, p. 154.   [12] Ibid. § 8, p. 176.

sinister interest, with the limit set by the number of people who participated directly or indirectly in the activities of the ruling class. But there was no limit to those who were gripped by prejudice which took a firmer hold on the mind (and was less subject to rational calculation), and might even persist when the interests were no longer operative. At one point, Bentham distinguished between knaves and dupes, with the knaves controlled by interest, 'bandied about from side to side', while the dupes, ruled by prejudice, 'kept steady all the while in a uniform and consistent, howsoever erroneous and pernicious, course: steadily engaged in giving their support to the sinister sacrifice'.[13] Where Macaulay argued that rulers were deterred from oppressing their subjects by their fear of resistance,[14] it might also be argued, as Bentham did, that rulers were able to oppress their subjects with considerable impunity because of the operation of prejudice. Although Bentham believed that popular resistance was an important ultimate check on the abuse of power by rulers, it seldom developed due to the operation of prejudice and was often discounted by rulers themselves.

One possible objection to Bentham's account of monarchy is that it failed to take into account the decline of the power of monarchy in Britain, and the growth of other opposing institutions such as the House of Commons. Bentham seemed at times to see the monarch as the *deus ex machina*, operating the complex machinery of government, establishment, and wider organs of 'prejudice' like a master puppeteer. At the same time, however, he argued that monarchs were often ignorant and lacked much incentive to participate in public life. He even contended that most monarchs were unfit to rule and pointed to evidence of 'mental derangement' in royal families in eleven of fourteen European monarchies.[15] Furthermore, the education of a monarch was planned in such a way that he soon saw himself as having interests opposed to those of the community. In Bentham's view, the monarch's contempt for the people soon turned to a hatred of them, a hatred which gave him a natural though a somewhat perverse pleasure.[16] The monarch also necessarily lacked aptitude because, whatever his

[13] Ibid. § 9, p. 182.
[14] See *Utilitarian Logic and Politics*, 115–16.
[15] 'Supreme Operative', § 7 (*CW*), pp. 170–1 n.
[16] Ibid., see § 6, pp. 165–7.

native ability, it was seldom developed and directed to benefit the community as a whole. As Bentham argued on numerous occasions, intellectual aptitude was useless unless directed towards the public good by moral aptitude. But if the monarch lacked aptitude, or if his aptitude was misdirected, why did Bentham consider him so important? The answer which he gave was that the monarch was not the same as the monarchy. The operation of sinister interest was perfectly compatible with a declining role for the monarch himself. As he wrote:

Arch-forciant—Arch terrorist—Arch-corrupter—Arch-Deluder—this he is by the mere virtue of his situation, without need of action on his part, without need of so much as *volition* on his part, without any such interruption to his ease: they in their several situations Sub-forciant, Sub-terrorist, Sub-Corrupter, Sub-Deluder.[17]

Those in the subordinate positions, the soldiers, lawyers, and clergy, depended on the monarch for status, pay, and honours, but they did not require an active monarch to carry on their activities. The direct exercise of power by the monarch was seldom necessary, and his only major concern was with the generation and maintenance of the myths of the importance of monarchy, or what Bentham called the 'delusive influence' of this institution.

One might wonder how Bentham could argue that on the one hand the people were the best judges of their own interests and capable of establishing a representative democracy, while on the other hand, they were victims of interest-begotten prejudice and delusion to such an extent that they would tolerate the worst abuses by rulers. Bentham's account of this deep and pervasive 'false consciousness' might lead one thinker, such as Plato, to more pessimistic conclusions about the possibilities of constitutional change, or another, such as Marx, to seek a remedy in violent revolution. Bentham believed that each person could best calculate his own interests partly because the human condition itself—the human need for security and subsistence—provided motives for such calculation and partly because no other person was better able to make these calculations. But any political society, even the most democratic, was continually at risk from the operation of sinister interest, prejudice, and delusion, and a major task of a democratic politics was to prevent their influence from becoming pervasive.

[17] 'Supreme Operative', § 10, p. 183.

As for confidence in political change, Bentham only favoured gradual change, unless there was a need to resist oppression. But the change he envisaged was meant to be fundamental and increasingly in his later years he conceived his constitutional code as a utopian creation which might not be adopted for at least a hundred years after his death.[18]

2. Operative and Constitutive Power

Bentham analysed constitutional government in terms of two kinds of power: operative and constitutive. Operative power is the power of government in all of its forms: legislative, executive, and judicial. Constitutive power is 'the power of determining at each point of time in the hands of what individual functionary or individual functionaries the correspondent operative power shall at that time be lodged'.[19] At one point, he called constitutive power a 'power of patronage'.[20] It was neither the power to draft constitutions nor did it owe its active power to a constitution. As Bentham explained in the following passage, constitutive power was derived only from the operative power of government:

The operative power is the power by which every thing that is done in the way of government is done. . . . Take away all operative power, you take away all constitutive power: No constitutive power has any subject matter to operate upon.

Of the nature and magnitude of Constitutive power no conception therefore can be formed but in so far as a conception is formed and entertained of the nature of the correspondent operative power.[21]

As Bentham rejected the doctrine of the social contract and an initial foundation for civil society, he turned instead to find the origin of constitutive power in the operative power of government itself. Even where a new constitution was being adopted, say by

[18] See Bowring, v. 278.
[19] UC cxiii. 6. The material in this section has been based on manuscripts written for Bentham's essays 'Economy as Applied to Office' and 'Identification of Interests' which have been published for the first time in First Principles Preparatory to Constitutional Code (CW), 3–147.
[20] UC cxiii. 4.
[21] UC cxiii. 6; see also UC cxiii. 9. In MS original, operative power is called 'the necessary basis of the Constitution' (UC cxiii. 6).

constitutional convention or by the whole people acting together, the decision to vest constitutive power, for example, in the people would be regarded by Bentham as an act of operative power. If one tried to trace an original constitutive power to its source, he noted, 'a sort of cloud hangs over the operation at the spot in which that source is looked for'.[22] The relationship between operative and constitutive power was a complex one. On the one hand, the holders of operative power might easily destroy constitutive power and thereby destroy constitutional rule in the process. On the other hand, constitutive power could only be enhanced by variations in the arrangements of operative power. In principle, operative power, the power of government, was unlimited. But it was necessarily limited by a constitution and the way it was organized as, for example, in the distinct arrangements for a legislature, executive, and judiciary. In the process of limiting and organizing operative power, constitutive power would be increased or diminished. Nevertheless, what was ultimately important was not only the amounts of power possessed by the two forms but also the way they functioned together. Bentham explored this relationship at one point in terms of the analogy between the main spring and regulator of a traditional watch.

> In the construction of this part of the machine, the first mentioned power performs the office of the main spring in a watch; the other that of the regulator in a watch. Without the regulator the main spring would do too much: without the main spring the regulator would do nothing . . . in so far as they are aptly proportioned to each other, they will do that which is required.[23]

Operative power is the main spring of the watch and, as such, is the driving force of government. Constitutive power 'regulates' operative power, but if the exercise of constitutive power consists only of 'the power of patronage', this regulative role would not be entirely clear. It is, of course, true that the regulator simply ensures the steady and regular unwinding of the main spring, and in terms of constitutive power this might be seen as the appointment and dismissal of government functionaries who went beyond or abused such 'regulation'. Furthermore, the function of the regulator could be seen more broadly in terms of a counterforce to the main spring,

---

[22] UC cxiii. 21.
[23] *First Principles Preparatory to Constitutional Code (CW)*, 135.

which was exercised by constitutive power. The 'apt proportion' in the relationship between the main spring (operative power) and the regulator (the counterforce in constitutive power) was the arrangement of the master watchmaker, or, in the language of the period, the legislator.

Bentham's theory was undoubtedly novel. He seemed to sever the connections, established in constitutionalism from antiquity (and present to an extent even in so modern a writer as Montesquieu), between constitutions, citizenship, and virtue. Nevertheless, constitutional government did have a special status in Bentham's thought, and in this important sense the link with ancient thought was partially retained. Constitutional government was clearly different from and superior to other forms of government, because it provided the means by which power might be exercised in the public interest.

It might be argued that Bentham's account of constitutional government as the offspring of operative *power* suffers from the same defects which H. L. A. Hart found in the Austinian account of law conceived in terms of orders backed by threats.[24] Nevertheless, it is immediately obvious that, for Bentham, the relationship between constitutive and operative power was not a simple vertical one between sovereign and subject. Indeed, the notion of a sovereign power outside the law is not part of Bentham's account. While the holders of operative power might place themselves above the law (as might the holders of constitutive power), this is not a necessary characteristic of Bentham's model as it is, for example, for the sovereign in Hobbes's theory. Furthermore, Bentham's theory, unlike the Austinian theory criticized by Hart, provides the basis for an account of continuity between succeeding sovereigns. The kinds of power to which Bentham referred are not external to the system but internal and dependent upon the various operations of constitutional government. The interaction of constitutive and operative power is based on rules and generates further rules as to the arrangements for appointing and dismissing holders of operative power. Bentham's account not only provides for the continuity of sovereign power but also for continuing change and variation in the exercise of that power.

The notion employed by Hart which is closest to what Bentham

---

[24] See H. L. A. Hart, *The Concept of Law* (Oxford, 1961), chs. 2–4, pp. 18–76.

meant by the interaction of constitutive and operative power is the 'rule of recognition'. This rule (viewed from the inside) provides empirical answers to questions about the validity of laws and is often identified by Hart as the constitution itself or various constitutional arrangements.[25] It is of interest that Bentham did not identify the exercise of constitutive power with a constitution. He did not do so partly because he was attempting to answer a different question, that is, one about the nature of a constitutional system rather than one about a legal system. Bentham was sufficiently realistic not to argue that it was the constitution itself which defined the constitutional system. While not denying that a constitution provided answers to questions about the validity of laws, Bentham would argue that this was neither its most important function nor its most characteristic one. Constitutions, for Bentham, were concerned primarily with offices and power and with the principles which governed their distribution. In the interaction between constitutive and operative power one sees the dynamic operation of a constitutional system.

One might note that Bentham's view of constitutionalism as being concerned with offices and power was a somewhat old-fashioned one, and resembled that view of the eighteenth-century constitution much criticized by reformers and even by Bentham himself. Nevertheless, if Bentham saw constitutionalism in terms of a system of patronage, it was not a narrow system that he envisaged. His objects were a widespread accountability and the identification of constitutive power by the legislator with the public interest.

3. Interests and Constitutional Democracy

Bentham did not believe that any interaction between constitutive and operative power advanced the public interest. The enlightened legislator should see the object of a constitution as identifying the interests of operative power with the universal interest via a constitutional democracy. To achieve this identification, constitutive power was recognized by Bentham as potentially the embodiment of the universal interest. The equation of the universal interest

[25] See ibid. 103.

with the varying interests of the individuals who comprise the community in a constitutional democracy was not taken by Bentham as one which needed elaborate justification. He often approached this subject in a negative way, arguing that the interests of the members of the community would be more likely to embody the universal interest than those of a monarch, aristocracy, or other ruling élite. He also argued that each individual's interest in his own security, subsistence, and abundance, and a general regard for relative equality, an interest existing without the additional power of rulers to effect the satisfaction of his desires in a sinister way, rendered the community, as an aggregate of individuals, the most appropriate repository of the universal interest. Even though individuals sought their own interests apart from those reckoned to comprise the universal interest, the effect of their actions on society as a whole was fairly limited when compared with that of the sinister interest of rulers.

A system of representative government was a necessary though not a sufficient condition for the identification of the interests of rulers and ruled. We are concerned here not only with the ruled acquiring the means of controlling the rulers but also with the way in which the representative system itself enhanced the development of the universal interest among the ruled. A single representative for a number of constituents could not obviously satisfy all the desires of all his constituents. The tasks involved in carrying out all of the varying desires of constituents would be too great for the one person to attempt to perform. He also could not satisfy desires which were held only by a few but not by a substantial number. Furthermore, he would not succeed in remaining in his position if he did not attempt to advance the interests of the greater number of his constituents which they shared in common. Whatever their individual desires might be, as individuals they shared in common the desires for security, subsistence, abundance, and relative equality. The representative would thus tend to advance these particular objects of desire and not others. In addition, the number of those who held constitutive power (in whom the universal interest was located) should be as great as possible, and hence Bentham advocated near universal suffrage based on an easily acquired literacy. Not only would this sort of representative system ensure that nearly all individual interests were taken into consideration in attempting to determine the universal interest, but the very participation of numerous members of the community in politics would enhance their moral and intellectual character.[26]

In spite of Bentham's argument, the critic of his position might still argue that the whole people were not suitable to serve as the repository of constitutive power and hence to represent the universal interest. Firstly, they lacked the intellectual ability to articulate and discern what was in the universal interest; and secondly, there was a tendency for the majority (whose opinions embodied the universal interest) to oppress the minority. As for the first criticism, Bentham would characteristically reply that the real obstacle among the people to their grasping what was in their own interest *and* in the interest of society was the operation of 'sinister-begotten prejudice', which was itself the offspring of sinister interest. Where the sinister interest of rulers no longer flourished, as in a representative democracy with extensive securities to prevent the abuse of power, the influence of prejudice would diminish. Furthermore, Bentham placed great emphasis on the dependence of intellectual aptitude on moral aptitude. Mere intellect was not sufficient to identify one's interest with the universal interest; moral aptitude—a regard for the greatest happiness—was also necessary. Even though numerous individuals had some difficulty in determining intellectually which of their interests coincided with the universal interest, they would, on balance, have a greater tendency to act correctly, as they had a higher degree of moral aptitude than any set of rulers. In addition, the knowledge required to judge one's rulers correctly was not

---

[26] In *First Principles Preparatory to Constitutional Code (CW)*, 141, Bentham writes: 'The advantage which the bulk of the population may be expected to reap in the article of moral character and conduct from such diffusion of political knowledge and the habit of attention to political subjects is neither less important nor less manifest not to say demonstrated by experience than in the article of intellectual vigour. In England, since the time when, by the question concerning parliamentary reform, minds least elevated in the conjoint scales of power and opulence have to so great an extent been led to apply themselves to the subject of legislation, the improvement that has had place in respect of moral conduct has been matter of observation and proportionable satisfaction to all those whose age has placed the means of observation in their power. Such in a word has been the effect in every country which has had the good fortune of witnessing the existence of this same cause. Witness Ireland during its golden age, France, Spain, Portugal, Naples, Piedmont.' In the above passage Bentham reveals a much greater awareness of the moral effects of participation than has usually been ascribed to him. See e.g. Carole Pateman, *Participation and Democratic Theory* (Cambridge, 1970), 19–20. See also G. J. Postema in *Philosophical Review*, 95 (1986), 487.

particularly great and might be obtained by a reading of newspapers or books (such as those written by Bentham himself).[27] Bentham also suggested that those unable to achieve even this modest competence through basic literacy might still seek advice: 'Aptitude through advice is within the reach of the least instructed: no one but has time for taking the opinion of whom general estimation points out as the best qualified for giving such advice of all who are within his reach.'[28] On numerous occasions Bentham pointed to the various states in the United States as possessing good government though based on differing groups of holders of constitutive power with widely based franchises.[29] That most of the states were considered well governed was evidence that whatever variations in aptitude existed from state to state, there was sufficient basic aptitude to choose and reject satisfactorily the various members of the different state governments.

The second criticism, that the majority of the people would use their power to oppress the minority, was considered by Bentham as being based on a logical confusion between a difference of opinion and a difference of interest. Holders of constitutive power would often disagree, he argued, but this disagreement was not such that the minority could not accept the will of the majority. The disagreement would not be over interests but rather over the means to realize those interests. Bentham referred to this sort of disagreement as a clash of opinion. But as all held constitutive power, their interests, say in security, would be the same. A clash of interests arose only between those whose interests were fundamentally opposed to the holders of constitutive power, that is to say, the possessors of operative power.[30] Bentham admitted that even in a constitutional democracy there would be those either in power or waiting in the wings for the downfall of the regime whose interests would be opposed to the universal interest, and he located at times this opposition in the unproductive classes of society. One might presume that they were unproductive because they possessed the power to ensure that others produced for their benefit.[31] The power to ensure that others produced while one did not was closely linked to the possession of political power.

---

[27] *First Principles Preparatory to Constitutional Code* (*CW*), 144–5.
[28] Ibid. 144.   [29] See ibid. 145–6.   [30] See ibid. 39.
[31] See ibid. 68–70.

4. The Extent of the Power of Government

Having established the plausibility of identifying the interests of the holders of constitutive power with the universal interest, the next step in Bentham's argument was for the legislator to maximize the *dependence* of operative on constitutive power. Government consisted of the distribution of political power, and the operative power of government was manifest in a distribution of offices. Each office had two characteristics: its functions and its rank in the scale of subordination. The power attached to a particular office was related to these characteristics. It has been shown elsewhere how Bentham defined the various functions of offices and arranged them carefully in distinct chains of command.[32] It has also been shown how he utilized 'securities for appropriate aptitude' to prevent or limit the abuse of power by those holding office.[33] What concerns us here is the way he saw securities working between constitutive and operative power and, in addition, one very important development in his theory which took place over the period during which he worked most intensively in constitutional theory.

Bentham listed six main securities (as well as a number of additional more specialized ones) for ensuring the dependence of operative on constitutive power.[34] The first was the obvious one of minimizing power in the hands of those who held operative power. Power, wrote Bentham, 'is of the essence of the situation: it is the instrument and the only instrument which he who is placed in that situation has to work with'.[35] Its diminution might be achieved in a number of ways: (1) by the 'fractionalization' of power by means of its division among a number of office-holders; (2) by the use of subordination to restrict power by placing it in the hands of higher or lower authorities; (3) by reducing the field of power by diminishing, for example, the geographical area, the number of people, the number of subordinate offices, or other areas of activity under the control of officials; (4) by reducing the sanctions possessed by officials to ensure compliance with orders. Indirect

---

[32] See F. Rosen, *Jeremy Bentham and Representative Democracy* (Oxford, 1983), 76–92.   [33] See ibid. 55–75.   [34] See UC cxiii. 34–6.
[35] *First Principles Preparatory to Constitutional Code* (CW), 30.

modes of reducing power might be established by the use of publicity and the influence of public opinion and also by ensuring that an office-holder's power, if exceeded or expanded, would be subject to legal punishment.[36] The second security was that of minimizing the amount of money at the disposal of government functionaries, and the third, the minimization of the remuneration paid to government officials. The fourth security was the exclusion of factitious dignity as a source of power which nearly always was used not only as power but also as a way of marrying 'prejudice' to sinister interest. The fifth security was the maximization of legal responsibility for the actions of officials through the courts, and the sixth, the maximization of moral responsibility through the influence of public opinion. Bentham established a number of other securities which were developed in detail and worked up into an elaborate system later in the *Constitutional Code* itself.[37] These included competitive examinations, arrangements to ensure attendance, and full publicity for all political activities. In addition, he recognized that there were other so-called securities widely employed by constitutional governments which he regarded as false securities. At one point[38] he listed three of these: (1) the exclusion of certain classes of society from the suffrage; (2) the use of two or more legislative chambers; and (3) the use of religion to secure moral aptitude or, in the use of oaths, to enhance legal responsibility.

On the whole, Bentham's doctrine of securities was designed to achieve accountable government through minimal government. There were other important means to enhance the dependence of operative on constitutive power (influence of public opinion and the representative system were two of these), but there is no doubt that the minimization of power, money, and factitious dignity in the hands of officials was the most important. There is, however, a measure of contradiction in Bentham's position. On the one hand, he argued that, in the relationship between constitutive and operative power, constitutive was dependent on operative power and, to enhance the former, one must enhance the latter. On the other hand, he argued that to secure appropriate aptitude on the

---

[36] UC cxiii. 38.
[37] See J. Bentham, *Constitutional Code*, i. ed. F. Rosen and J. H. Burns (Oxford, 1983), ch. 6, § 31; ch. 8, § 12; ch. 9, § 25 (*CW*), pp. 117–33, 168–70, 419–37.
[38] UC cxiii. 36.

part of officials (and hence their dependence on the constitutive power of the state) operative power must be minimized.

Bentham himself gradually became aware of this difficulty in his theory and especially of ambiguities in the notion of minimizing power. As he well knew from his experience in attempting to establish the panopticon prison, one source of government inefficiency and incompetence was the lack of power by officials to take necessary action in the public interest.[39] Constitutive power would not be served merely by minimizing power in a general way. Weak government has never benefited constitutional democracy. At some point between 1822 and 1827, when the first volume of the *Constitutional Code* was printed, Bentham changed his mind about the minimization of power. In a note dated 21 February 1827, Bentham wrote: 'Power maximized so as securities against abuse be so too', and this note was written on the earlier 1822 manuscript concerned with the minimization of power.[40] In the *Constitutional Code* itself, Bentham wrote: 'In no existing Code is the scope given to the power of ruling functionaries so ample as in the present proposed Code.'[41]

It is important to understand what this shift with regard to power in Bentham's theory entails. In part, it represents a needed clarification in his thought so that restrictions designed to limit the abuse of power are not confused with restrictions on the exercise of power. Bentham continued to take the view that all rule is evil, though admittedly the evil may be necessary. 'All government', he wrote characteristically, 'is a choice of evils. To govern is to do evil that good may come.'[42] It is a fairly simple step from this position to the one that whatever government governs least is best. But such a step would not take into account the way in which operative and constitutive power are linked, with the latter dependent upon the successful operation of the former. If government is too weak to serve the people, because power has been minimized, constitutive power might also be diminished. The people might not be able to ensure that desirable acts of government which ought to be enacted could be carried into effect. Once Bentham appreciated that the simple minimization of power was no security for good govern-

---

[39] See esp. Janet Semple, 'Jeremy Bentham's Panopticon Prison' (Ph.D. thesis, London University, 1990).   [40] UC cxiii. 39.

[41] *Constitutional Code*, vol. i, ch. 6, § 31, art. 13 (*CW*), p. 120.

[42] UC cxiii. 138.

ment, he was then able to concentrate on both the careful definition of power and the establishment of securities to prevent its abuse.

It may be tempting to see in this shift in Bentham's position a movement towards authoritarian government, if not something worse. Yet Bentham could defend his move as part of his account of constitutional liberty in which operative power most fully depended on constitutive power. Indeed, it would be an essential characteristic of the theory that operative power should not be limited for its own sake. Without sufficient operative power individuals could not be secure from foreign invasion, from other individuals in the state, and from the abuse of government power by other government bodies. Nevertheless, it might be argued that Bentham's position is very close to that of Hobbes in that the power of the state is maximized to establish the minimal conditions of civil peace and individual security. At a superficial level there is some resemblance, but Bentham, it must be recalled, placed his emphasis on the enhancement of constitutive power by the indirect means of the theory of dependence rather than on the enhancement of sovereign coercive power. Furthermore, the objectives sought by Bentham in the exercise of operative power were more extensive than that of ensuring civil peace. He also did not ignore the objective of limiting government, but he did not equate it with minimizing power. Bentham was closer in spirit to thinkers such as Montesquieu and Delolme who found an important source of liberty in the British constitution in the great executive power of the monarch. Because there were few *direct* limitations on his power, it was thought that the usurpation of executive power was improbable. Nevertheless, there were important indirect limitations, especially in the fact that funds for the executive were controlled by the House of Commons. In the same manner, Bentham proposed the maximization of operative power but with limitations on power imposed indirectly by the use of securities. In this way the dependence of effective operative power on constitutive power could be best achieved.

Within the framework of the interaction of constitutive and operative power, Bentham believed that the power of the people should be limited to that of appointing and removing government officials and scrutinizing their activities. He also recognized that there were times under bad governments when it was not just a matter of changing the personnel; the very 'texture' of the constitution ensured that only sinister interest prevailed. In these circumstances, Bentham observed, the government was like a country infected with plague.[43] He saw the only solution to a corrupt and oppressive constitution in the people rising up to change the form of government: 'In this case every man thus tormented must either lie down as motionless as he can under his torment, or rise up—and in conjunction with as many as he can get to join with him, rise up, and endeavour to rid the country of the nuisance.'[44]

[43] *First Principles Preparatory to Constitutional Code (CW)*, 128.
[44] Ibid.

5

Theory and Practice I: Bentham and the Greek Constitution of 1822

1. Bentham's 'Observations'

'To find the provisional Grecian Constitution in so high a degree conformable to the principle of the greatest happiness of the greatest number has been matter of considerable and no less agre[e]able surprize to me', wrote Jeremy Bentham on 9 February 1823, the day he began to draft his commentary on the first Greek constitution.[1] This virtually unknown work was commissioned during a period when support for the Greek cause in England, which had been growing since 1821, finally coalesced with the establishment of the London Greek Committee, the arrival in London of Andreas Louriottis to initiate negotiations for the first Greek loan, and the departure of Louriottis and Edward Blaquiere for Greece to begin the involvement of the London Greek Committee (and Lord Byron) in Greek affairs.[2] As Bowring and Blaquiere were in close contact with Bentham, and Bentham had been active in assisting the Greeks in various ways since the autumn

[1] *Securities against Misrule and Other Constitutional Writings for Tripoli and Greece*, ed. T. P. Schofield (Oxford, 1990), (*CW*), 183.

[2] These events have been recorded in the fairly extensive literature on philhellenism. See e.g. D. Dakin, *British and American Philhellenes during the War of Greek Independence 1821–1833* (Thessaloniki, 1955); C. M. Woodhouse, *The Philhellenes* (London, 1969); W. St Clair, *That Greece Might Still Be Free: The Philhellenes in the War of Independence* (London, 1972). On the events in Greece, see D. Dakin, *The Greek Struggle for Independence 1821–1833* (London, 1973). Little has been written on the specific contribution of Bentham and the Benthamites. See A. Dimaras, 'The Other British Philhellenes', in Richard Clogg (ed.), *The Struggle for Greek Independence* (London, 1973), 200–23; F. Rosen, 'Bentham's Letters and Manuscripts in Greece', *Bentham Newsletter*, 5 (1981), 55–8; P. Kitromilides, 'Jeremy Bentham and Adamantios Korais', and F. Rosen, 'A Note on Bentham and Korais', *Bentham Newsletter*, 9 (1985), 34–48, 49–50.

of 1821, his name appeared among the first members and
supporters of the London Greek Committee.[3] He was also well
known by this time as a jurist of international standing.[4] Thus, it
was natural for him to be asked to comment on the first efforts of
the Greeks at drafting a constitution.

Throughout February, Bentham devoted considerable attention
to his writings for Greece. The manuscripts which bear headings
connecting them with Greece were roughly of three sorts: detailed
studies of the various articles of the Greek constitution; some
general principles of constitutional law such as a justification for
placing sovereignty in the people; and more specific institutional
proposals like those which later appeared in the *Constitutional
Code*.[5] At the end of February, Bentham somewhat hastily put this
material together to form his 'Observations' so that Louriottis and
Blaquiere could take it with them when they departed for Greece
on 4 March.[6] At the time of their departure, he instructed Blaquiere
as to how he was to proceed in Greece. He requested that the cost
of translation and publication should not be paid by the Greek
government mostly because he wanted to ensure that the Greek
government did not have to take responsibility for the anti-
monarchical sentiments expressed in it. He also wanted the
'Observations' published with Greek and English versions in
parallel columns.[7] Blaquiere and Louriottis duly delivered the
'Observations' on 16 May to the Greek legislature where it was
received with great enthusiasm.[8] Bentham received two letters

[3] For lists of members of the London Greek Committee, see Appendices I and II.
See also Kitromilides, 'Jeremy Bentham and Adamantios Korais', 36 ff.

[4] See J. R. Dinwiddy, 'Early Nineteenth-Century Reactions to Benthamism',
Transactions of the Royal Historical Society, 5th Series, 34 (1984), 47–69; 'Bentham and
the Early Nineteenth Century', *Bentham Newsletter*, 8 (1984), 15–33.

[5] See *Securities against Misrule* (*CW*), pp. xxvi–xliii, 181–285.

[6] See UC xii. 103, Bentham to Blaquiere, 2 Mar. 1823; see also UC xii. 100,
Louriottis to Bentham, 14 Feb. 1823.

[7] UC xii. 103, Bentham to Blaquiere, 2 Mar. 1823.

[8] UC xii. 123, Blaquiere to Bowring, 16 May 1823: 'To day has been rendered
peculiarly interesting by what occurred in the Chamber of Representatives, when I
presented the Philosopher's works and observations, and made a speech . . .
Resolutions were immediately passed for translating the works and an appropriate
letter will also be written. I have found a man who is likely to devote the remainder
of his life to the study and propagation of Mr. B's principles. This man is a priest!!!
very amiable and enlightened. I am taking the necessary steps to set him to work.
But there is not a single type in G[reece] much less a press!!!' On 11 June, Blaquiere
wrote to Bowring (UC xii. 126) in a similar vein: 'Pray inform the Philosopher that
a most flattering letter has been voted to him by the Legislative Assembly, and that

thanking him for the 'Observations': the first from Alexander Mavrokordatos as Secretary to the provisional government, and the second from Ioannis Orlandos and Ioannis Skandilides who were President and Secretary of the Legislative Senate respectively.[9]

Contrary to Bentham's original plan, the Greek legislature announced that it would arrange for the translation into Greek 'with as much dispatch as may be . . . for the common use and benefit of the nation'.[10] In spite of these sentiments, it was obvious that neither the personnel nor the equipment existed in Greece to make and print such a translation, and the 'Observations' was never published. Nor was the work included in the collection of Bentham's writings edited by John Bowring in 1838–43. The only known copy, believed to be virtually complete, has been found in the vast Bentham archive at University College London and it, together with related manuscripts, has been published for the first time as part of the new edition of the *Collected Works*.[11]

In this chapter three major themes of the 'Observations' will be considered: (1) Bentham's thesis that the acceptance of popular sovereignty should lead to a transformation of the theory and

the observations are in a course of translation—In other respects he has a right to be amply satisfied with the devotion universally felt here.' In his book on the Greek revolution, Blaquiere later wrote: 'Mr. Bentham has given up all the energies of his powerful mind to the subject: and though Greece may not be enabled to profit by his sublime and benevolent labours so soon as the friends of humanity could wish, she already appreciates their value, with a degree of gratitude and zeal that does her public men and citizens the very highest honour' (*The Greek Revolution* (London, 1824), 310 n.).

[9] The 'conjecture' made by K. Triantaphyllopoulos ('Ypomnima tou Bentham peri tou prōtou ellēnikou politeumatos kai anekdotoi apantēseis tou Bouleutikou', *Praktika tēs Akadēmias Athēnon*, 37 (1962), 80–7) and repeated most recently by Pan. J. Zepos ('Jeremy Bentham and the Greek Independence', *Proceedings of the British Academy*, 62 (1976), 296–7) that the letter of thanks for Bentham's 'Observations' was delayed because the Greek government did not want to make a forthright stand on Bentham's hostility to monarchy is clearly false. Bentham received two letters of thanks for the 'Observations' which he subsequently published. See Bowring, iv. 580–1 (letters 1 and 2). The so-called delayed letter to which Triantaphyllopoulos refers was in fact a reply to a letter from Bentham which was in turn a reply to a letter from Alexander Mavrokordatos to Bentham introducing the two Greek Deputies, Orlandos and Louriottis, to Bentham (Bowring, iv. 581–3, letters 3 and 4). Triantaphyllopoulos and Zepos (and others) have also been confused by the fact that the Greek government responded twice to presentations by Bentham: on the presentation of the 'Observations' in 1823 and the presentation of the early draft of the *Constitutional Code* by Leicester Stanhope in April 1824. For the response of the Greek government to the latter, see Bowring, iv. 583 (letter 5).

[10] Bowring, iv. 581.   [11] See *Securities against Misrule* (*CW*), 216–56.

practice of constitutional government; (2) his use of the greatest
happiness principle to resolve problems arising from the exclusion
of the Turkish community from citizenship; and (3) his novel and
important contribution to constitutional theory in the doctrine of
'latent negatives'. Then the relationship between the 'Observations'
and Bentham's better-known work on constitutional government,
the *Constitutional Code*, will be explored. Finally, consideration will
be given to the allegation that the constitution of Epidaurus was a
mere 'façade' created by the Greeks to impress Europeans as to the
capacity of the Greeks to operate a Western, centralized government. This allegation raises not only the question of the point of
Bentham's commentary (if it was on a constitution not meant to be
operable) but also the general issue of the relationship of constitutional theory to practice.

2. Popular Sovereignty and the Division of Power

Unlike most earlier and even later writers on constitutional law,
Bentham believed that once the doctrine of popular sovereignty
was accepted as the basis of a constitutional system, the whole of
constitutional theory would have to be radically altered. This
meant, in his view, the rejection of the established doctrine of the
division of power. In his earlier writings, as we have seen, though
critical of Blackstone, he remained somewhat sympathetic to
Montesquieu and Delolme.[12] But so long as the British constitution
was held up for emulation and the American constitution praised in
so far as it embodied this principle (though in a different form), he
felt that no progress generally in constitutional theory and practice
was possible. For under the widespread influence of writers like
Montesquieu and Delolme liberal politicians throughout the world
looked to Britain or the United States for models of their
constitutions. By the time he was writing for the Greeks, he had
also become a sharp critic of Montesquieu and Delolme, and in his
'Observations' he explicitly dismissed their accounts of the British
constitution as 'the romance' and warned the Greeks not to take
their writings seriously.[13]

[12] See Ch. 3 above.
[13] *Securities against Misrule* (*CW*), 240.

In the 'Observations' Bentham discussed the theme of the division of power in the context of the Greek constitutional provision for sharing legislative power between the Legislative Senate and the Executive Council.[14] However, he soon developed his theme more generally, and took as his starting-point the principle of 'strict and absolute dependence' on the people of the state.[15] This principle affected the division of legislative power only indirectly, and its aim was to arrange the institutions of government in such a way that the will of the elector would be least thwarted and that government would be most accountable to it. For Bentham, this was best achieved, not through a direct democracy or a small republic, but through a representative democracy with a single legislative chamber elected by virtual universal suffrage in annual elections using the secret ballot. The executive and judicial branches of government were then devised to be as dependent upon the will of the legislature as the legislature was dependent upon the will of the electorate.

Bentham admitted that in certain circumstances the principle of the division of power could have beneficial consequences. Where legislative power in a state was independent of the people, its division could lead to moderate government, because the various bodies in the state possessing legislative power would compete for the favour of the people to advance their own interests. They would also be inclined to compromise among themselves to advance their interests further.[16] The result of this process would tend to favour the people generally, and produce a form of 'weak' government (as in England) which was preferable for the people than more absolutist regimes (as on the Continent).[17] Bentham could see the advantages of this 'weak' form of government sufficiently that he argued against the institution of the principle of absolute dependency in Britain, as this would produce, unless the laws generally were radically reformed, 'the consummation of

[14] See arts. 9 and 10 of the Greek provisional constitution of Epidaurus (1822). The version used here, the same as that used by Bentham, was printed in C. D. Raffenel, *Histoire des événemens de la Grèce* (Paris, 1822), 429–41. See *Securities against Misrule* (*CW*), 209–15, for the full text. The more widely circulated Greek/English version (*The Provisional Constitution of Greece* (London, 1823)) had not yet been published when Bentham wrote the 'Observations'. See also *Securities against Misrule* (*CW*), 219 ff. [15] *Securities against Misrule* (*CW*), 266.
[16] Ibid. 231–2. [17] Ibid. 232–3.

despotism and misrule; it would give to the laws . . . a strength altogether irresistible'.[18]

In spite of this caveat, Bentham argued that once the doctrine of popular sovereignty was accepted, there was no justification for the retention of the principle of the division of power. This was not an easy argument to establish, as it meant showing that what had hitherto been widely regarded as a 'good' principle was no longer so. The argument which he used was, nevertheless, a plausible one. Consider the United States, he began, where, in spite of the employment of a form of divided power, most officials were directly or indirectly removable by the people and hence accountable to them. To improve this government, he continued, suppose a king was appointed with a veto on all legislation and the power to appoint and dismiss all members of the executive branch of government. He argued that no benefit could arise from such an appointment nor from the appointment of a hereditary house of lords which would be necessary to support the monarchy. For Bentham, the main consequence of instituting divided power in a situation such as this (besides the fact that the people in general would have their votes devalued) was that government expenditure (now no longer controllable by the people) would increase dramatically, as it had in England under George III, and the burden of this expenditure would fall on the people.[19]

Bentham's argument rested on a deeper foundation, which he did not explore in the 'Observations' but which can be found in the manuscripts which were written at this time. This was simply that the exercise of popular sovereignty coincided more or less with the greatest happiness of the greatest number. He argued on the basis of interests that the people generally were more inclined (or found it in their interests) to support the greatest happiness of the greatest number. No other class of persons, he believed, would have that interest. But why should each individual see the greatest happiness of the greatest number as in his interest? In a characteristic passage, he wrote:

The way in which, by expression and effect given to the several individual wills, contribution is made to the universal happiness is this. If the result depended upon himself each individual would give expression and effect to such will as in his judgment would in the highest degree be conducive to

<hr/>

[18] *Securities against Misrule* (*CW*), 230.   [19] Ibid. 234.

his own greatest happiness, whatsoever became of the happiness of others, and consequently on most if not all occasions at the expence of the happiness of all others. . . .

But, in so far as the effect of it is by others seen or thought to be detrimental to their own happiness, the will of each individual finds an opponent and bar in the will of every other and in the will of all together a bar absolutely insuperable. On the other hand in so far as the effect of each one's will is by every other individual seen or thought to be conducive to his own greatest happiness the will of each one finds a support and coadjutor in the will of every other: in a word each separate interest finds a bar and that an insuperable one in every other separate and sinister interest: but each man's share in the universal interest finds an ally and coadjutor in every other man's share in the universal interest.[20]

Bentham did not argue that the universal interest was the sum of the interests of the individuals who made up the society. The universal interest was more or less fixed and definite and could be defined initially by such values as security, subsistence, abundance, and equality, all of which could be justified as being conducive to the greatest happiness. Individual interests were more variable, and often set individuals in opposition to each other in society, but they could be of a sort to join with the universal interest. For Bentham, the key point was that the individual's interest would be advanced and his happiness enhanced when his interests coincided with the general interest. And when they did not, he would be thwarted by the other members of the community (his allies and coadjutors). He also argued that through a representative system this process of alignment and advancement of interests would be strengthened and enhanced.[21]

Bentham did not argue that the will of the people *always* coincided with the greatest happiness principle. But he did argue that due to the various checks on self-interested actions, opposed to the general interest, that were built into the system, the tendency for the will of the people to coincide with the greatest happiness principle was strong. The division of power, however, disrupted this tendency and placed in power interests which could not easily be made to act in conformity with the greatest happiness principle. Indeed, the division of power was the main opponent to the

---

[20] Ibid. 265–6.
[21] See F. Rosen, *Jeremy Bentham and Representative Democracy* (Oxford, 1983), 41–54.

otherwise efficacious doctrine of popular sovereignty. In saying in the 'Observations' that the employment of the division of power deprived the people of their votes and their share of supreme constitutive power, Bentham also meant that the people (though perhaps gaining a dose of moderate government) were none the less being deprived of their happiness, that is to say, of the opportunity for their interests to be advanced in line with the greatest happiness.

3. The Greatest Happiness Principle and the Oppressed

Bentham's remark (cited above) that the conformity of the Greek constitution of 1822 to the greatest happiness principle was an agreeable surprise to him was based not on any explicit statement of the principle in the constitution, but on the implications of several key provisions.[22] These provisions contained numerous progressive 'enlightenment' principles, such as equality before the law, a wide suffrage, careers open to merit, and progressive taxation based on law, which Bentham generally favoured and considered justifiable by the greatest happiness principle. Although he was troubled generally by some constitutional provisions (e.g. division of power, judicial organization, etc.) it was in the exclusions from suffrage and political power that he saw the main threats to government based on the greatest happiness principle. This applied to the exclusion of women from politics, men under the age of 30 from becoming members of the Legislative Senate, and most importantly the exclusion of all non-Greeks from suffrage and office.[23] As for women, there does not seem to be any specific reference to female suffrage in the constitution, but Bentham was under no illusion that the Greeks had adopted this progressive idea. As elsewhere in his writings, though he favoured female suffrage and saw no difficulty with its institution if it was

---

[22] 'Art. 2. Tous les indigènes de la Grèce, professant la religion chrétienne, sont Grecs, et jouissent de tous les droits politiques. Art. 3. Les Grecs sont égaux devant la loi, sans distinction de rang ni de dignité. Art. 6. Tous les Grecs peuvent être appelés à tous emplois. Le mérite seul détermine la préférence. Art. 8. Les contributions aux charges de l'état son réparties dans la proportion de la fortune de chacun. Aucun impôt ne peut être exigé qu'en vertu d'un loi.'

[23] See arts. 1, 2, 6, 13. See also *Securities against Misrule* (*CW*), 259 ff.

combined with the use of the secret ballot, he thought it pointless to push a suggestion here that would not be at that time taken seriously.[24]

Bentham also anticipated his later critique of James Mill's exclusion from suffrage of everyone under the age of 40 in criticizing the provision to exclude those under 30 from legislative office.[25] But his main concern was with the limitation of political rights to Greeks only, which meant the exclusion of the Muslim and Jewish populations from suffrage and office. In the actual 'Observations' sent to Greece, Bentham dealt with this difficult problem in a most circumspect fashion. He did not mention the subject until the final pages of his text and then restricted himself to making suggestions as to how to minimize the opposition between the Greeks and those excluded groups.[26] In the manuscripts, however, he addressed himself to the situation more directly, as in the following passage:

The constitutive power—i.e., the power of choosing those by whom all operative power in all its degrees commencing with the supreme shall be exercised. The exclusion put on this occasion upon so large a part perhaps the largest part of the existing population is at present it should seem an unavoidable arrangement but it is a highly deplorable one. It entails upon the country the existing division, reversing only the position of the condivident races. It places the Turks under the Greeks [as] the Helots were in under the Spartans, in the situation that the Protestants in France were in under the Catholics, in Ireland the Catholics under the Protestants, in the Anglo-American United States the Blacks under the Whites. In no country can any such schism have place but in point of morality and felicity both races are, in howsoever different shapes, sufferers by it: the oppressors as well as the oppressed.

To lessen the opposition of interests—to bring them to coincidence as speedily as is consistent with security should therefore be an object of constant care and endeavour.[27]

This passage has been quoted at length because it contains several ideas of considerable interest. On the one hand, Bentham conceded that the Turkish population was or would be an oppressed class forming a substantial minority, perhaps even a majority in the

[24] *Securities against Misrule* (*CW*), 260. See also Lea Campos Boralevi, *Bentham and the Oppressed* (Berlin, 1984), 5–36.
[25] *Securities against Misrule* (*CW*), 260–2. See Rosen, *Jeremy Bentham and Representative Democracy*, 169, 227, and UC xxxiv. 302–3.
[26] *Securities against Misrule* (*CW*), 254–6.   [27] UC xxi. 192.

society. He considered the arrangement 'highly deplorable' and pointed out that the Greeks would suffer from this arrangement as much as the Turks. On the other hand, Bentham was willing to see the exclusion as an 'unavoidable arrangement', and was also, in conceptual terms, willing to accept the definition of the new state in terms of its being wholly Greek—that is to say, he was concerned with 'the greatest happiness of the greatest number of the political community in question'. The happiness of the excluded Turks became under this formulation 'a secondary object'.[28]

Bentham might have argued that the exclusion of the Turks from political suffrage and office was itself so gross a violation of the greatest happiness principle that the constitution could hardly be said to embody this principle. That he did not argue this was not due (as perhaps was the case for female suffrage) to a fear that the rest of his advice would not be accepted if he advanced this position. Bentham's acceptance of the situation was not prudential but conceptual. The object of any political society was firstly to provide for the security (the key ingredient in happiness) of its members. The war of independence was fought to rid the Greeks of Turkish rule and to secure for the Greeks their own state. Bentham could see that the security of this new state might initially have depended on the exclusion of the Turks. If they were not excluded, they might soon be in a position to oppress the Greeks again. While Bentham could accept this argument, he could also argue that the future security of the Greek state lay with the accommodation of the Turks. In the text of the 'Observations' Bentham attempted to move dialectically from the dictates of 'self-regarding prudence', that is the security of the Greeks, to a position of benevolence— called 'effective benevolence'—which was compatible with it.[29] If the main principle of 'self-regarding prudence' was to avoid the possibility of hostility by the Turkish community, the principle dictated by 'effective benevolence' was 'to treat them with as much kindness as the indispensable regard for your own safety will permit'.[30]

With regard to voting and representation, Bentham argued that

[28] UC xxi. 264.

[29] See *Securities against Misrule* (CW), 254. See also *Deontology, Together with A Table of the Springs of Action and Article on Utilitarianism*, ed. A. Goldworth (Oxford, 1983) (CW), 249–81, where this distinction is employed.

[30] *Securities against Misrule* (CW), 254.

the Turks could be given the vote without posing a threat to the Greeks. He took the view that so long as the Greeks were in the clear majority in the legislature, they could afford to grant the non-Greeks suffrage. If at any point the non-Greeks tended to out-number the Greeks in too many election districts, the voting age for non-Greeks might be increased beyond that for the Greeks.[31] In spite of this severe limitation on citizenship, Bentham believed that the introduction of non-Greeks to citizenship would eventually make them good citizens and would diminish the threat to the security of the Greeks. 'They would be raised to a situation high in dignity, as well as security', wrote Bentham, 'in comparison of the highest which any of them can occupy even in a Mahometan country at present' and 'to no Christian' (i.e. Greek), he continued, 'could in that case any Mahometan be, as such, an object of contempt'.[32] It might have been argued that in raising the aspirations of members of an oppressed class by granting them citizenship and then frustrating those aspirations by denying them *effective* citizenship the result might be to threaten the ruling class more than if the oppressed class were left in a downtrodden state. Bentham might well have accepted this argument, but he would then have replied that once integrated into the constitutional system, the non-Greeks would find a number of advantages in remaining in this system, however unjust and frustrating, rather than risking civil war. There would have been a number of issues on which some Greeks and some non-Greeks might agree and together form a majority in the electorate to see put into effect by a wholly Greek legislature. And the willingness of the non-Greeks to engage in constitutional politics rather than attempt rebellion or revolution would so enhance the security of the Greeks that further concessions might be forthcoming.

A second example which Bentham employed in the 'Observa-tions' of how 'effective benevolence' might be compatible with 'self-regarding prudence' concerned the possession of weapons by the two groups. Bentham assumed that in due course Greek males would be trained in the European style of warfare (organized in companies and battalions) and in the use of the musket and bayonet. Non-Greeks would presumably not be allowed to participate in this training nor to possess firearms the length of

[31] Ibid. 254–5.   [32] Ibid. 255.

muskets.[33] Nevertheless, Bentham argued that non-Greeks should
be allowed to carry swords and pistols so that they would be able to
defend themselves from attack. This could be achieved, he
believed, without arming them in a way which would threaten the
security of the Greeks. That is to say, they would have no training
in the use of the musket, and, in addition, would not be allowed to
carry concealable weapons such as daggers and very small pistols.[34]

Although Bentham confined his arguments in the 'Observations'
to the ways the non-Greek population could be treated with
benevolence without threatening the security of the Greeks, he was
at the time thinking of some consequences of this benevolence
which would extend beyond the Greek constitution. In the letter to
Blaquiere which accompanied the delivery of the 'Observations' to
him to be taken to Greece, he suggested privately:

supposing them [Muslims] treated with the gentleness there recommended
[i.e. in the 'Observations'] they might ere long be made willing
instruments for the liberation of the subjects of the Barbary Powers from
the existing Despotisms. The people are everywhere prepared for it, as I
have been satisfied by circumstances that have come to my knowledge, but
of which no intimation could be given in the paper intended for
publication, lest by that means the fulfilment of the prophecy should be
prevented by the divulgation of it. Natural and supposed irreconcilable
enemies would thus be converted into grateful and steady allies.[35]

Bentham had in the previous year worked with Hassuna D'Ghies,
the young ambassador from Tripoli, in devising ways to transform
and even to overthrow the established 'Mohamedan despotism' and
replace it with a more liberal regime, and it is to the knowledge
gained in this adventure that he probably referred in the letter.[36]
This additional dimension to the constitutional problem revealed
Bentham's wider concern with bringing happiness and good
government to the whole of the Ottoman Empire and beyond. The
Greek struggle for independence was the first step but not in the
sense of providing an example of a successful revolution. The key
to the spread of liberal government to the rest of the Middle East

---

[33] *Securities against Misrule* (*CW*), 255.

[34] Ibid.   [35] UC xii. 103, Bentham to Blaquiere, 2 Mar. 1823.

[36] *Securities against Misrule* (*CW*), pp. xv–xxxvi, 1–280; see also L. J. Hume,
'Preparations for Civil War in Tripoli in the 1820s: Ali Karamanli, Hassuna D'Ghies
and Jeremy Bentham', *Journal of African History*, 21 (1980), 311–22; and *Constitutional
Code*, i. ed. F. Rosen and J. H. Burns (Oxford, 1983) (*CW*), pp. xv–xvi.

lay with the way in which the Muslims resident in Greece were treated and the extent to which they were well treated depended, for Bentham, on the extent to which they could be admitted to citizenship and civic responsibility. It was for this prize that Bentham thought other Muslim peoples would be enticed to overthrow their despotic governments.

It is true that Bentham did not invoke a doctrine of universal natural rights or insist that the greatest happiness principle required the equal treatment of all persons in the state in suffrage and political rights. He would most probably have found such doctrines either pointless (given the nature of the revolutionary struggle) or dangerous. But he never suggested that where non-Greeks were deprived of political rights, they should in any way serve the interests of the Greeks or be exploited by them. His main aims were to minimize oppression and insecurity for both Greeks and non-Greeks, and he thought that this could best be done through a constitutional system which increasingly integrated the non-Greek community in a way which did not threaten the Greek community. It was clear, however, that unless the Greeks accepted these changes, they, as well as the non-Greeks, would be threatened, as they would have to maintain their superior position increasingly through force.

4. Latent Negatives

One discussion in the 'Observations' deserves special notice. In his examination of the division of power Bentham extended his analysis from the open vetoes on legislation (and by implication on the will of the people) possessed in this case by the Executive Council to an analysis of what he called 'latent negatives', that is to say, potential vetoes possessed by various officials by virtue of deficiencies in the way the constitution was itself drafted.[37] The possessor of the veto was, in effect, given a share of legislative power. He might be, as we shall see, a high official, a body of officials, or even a humble clerk.

Bentham contended that a number of articles in the Greek

---

[37] *Securities against Misrule (CW)*, 236–40.

constitution revealed the presence of a 'latent negative'. For
example, in article 24, the President of the Legislative Senate was
given the power to fix the days on which the session of the
assembly was to commence and to terminate. He thus had the
power to determine that the Senate would never meet, or, if
meeting, would cease to do so. Even though this President of the
Senate was elected to his position by the Senate itself, he
nevertheless would hold office for the duration of the session, and
there was no provision for his removal. This official also had the
power (in article 25) of calling an extraordinary session and thus
was free to keep the Senate in existence so long as it suited him or to
terminate it at will.

The President of the Legislative Senate was given other
opportunities to exercise a latent veto. By article 30, all legislative
acts were to be signed by the President and countersigned by the
Principal Secretary. If the President refused to sign, the act could
not become law. Similarly, in article 31, he was empowered to
transmit resolutions from the Senate to the Executive Council, but
Bentham noted that if he did not approve of a resolution, he could
refuse to send it on. Finally, in article 36, where each member of the
Senate was given the right to propose legislation, the President was
empowered to send it to a committee for examination. As Bentham
noted, he could simply omit to do so. Bentham also pointed to
similar latent negatives possessed by the Principal Secretary of the
Legislative Senate. In article 31, he was given the power to
countersign resolutions of the Senate, and in article 46 he was to
receive resolutions from the President for transmission to the
Executive Council. In both of these cases refusal or inaction might
lead to the end of these resolutions.

Bentham then turned to the 'latent negatives' possessed by
members of the Executive Council and the eight subordinate
ministers. For example, even where the Executive Council had
concurred in legislation and a particular law had been passed, it
might later turn out that a majority in the Council did not agree
with the law. This group of three could by article 54, which
empowered the Council to have laws executed by ministers,
simply omit to send the law to the minister, and the law would
become inoperative. Furthermore, if the minister who was to
execute the law did not approve of it, he could ensure that it was
not implemented. Finally, both the President of the Executive

Council and the Principal Secretary possessed a 'latent negative' by virtue of article 57 where they were empowered to sign, counter-sign, and seal all acts and decrees. Bentham especially wondered who was to keep the Seal of the state. The constitution did not specify who this might be, but he too might very well possess a 'latent negative'.

In the *Constitutional Code* Bentham took considerable pains to avoid the possibility that various officials might exercise vetoes on legislative power. Conspicuously absent from the *Code* were the officials whom he identified as possessing 'latent negatives' in the Greek constitution (e.g. President and Principal Secretary of the Legislative Senate). Bentham devised means by which legislative, executive, and judicial business would not languish. All officials could be removed by petition and vote. The use of 'deputes' ensured that government business did not come to a halt due to absence from office. The principle of 'single-seatedness' enhanced accountability in office so that those potentially exercising vetoes or otherwise thwarting the popular will could readily be identified and removed from office. But even in a narrow, technical sense, Bentham ensured that one official could not quietly prevent another from carrying out his duties.

To take one example, Bentham provided in the *Code* that the appointment of a civil servant was to be made by the appropriate minister and confirmed by the Prime Minister. A perfect oppor-tunity for quietly preventing an appointment of which he did not approve would appear to rest with the Prime Minister by his simply not confirming the appointment. This might be an opportunity perhaps for persuading the minister to appoint someone favoured by himself and perhaps hostile to legislation of which he disapproved. To avoid this 'latent negative' on the execution of legislation, Bentham provided that once the 'location instrument' making the appointment arrived at the Prime Minister's office, he must either appoint someone else or suspend the appointment made by the minister. If he did nothing, after a fixed period of time the appointment was automatically confirmed.[38] Bentham was not opposed to the Prime Minister being involved in making the appointment or, indeed, making the appointment himself. After all, the Prime Minister was free to dismiss the

---

[38] *Constitutional Code*, vol. i, ch. 9, § 17, art. 31 (*CW*), pp. 343–4.

minister if he so wished. Nevertheless, what he wanted to avoid
(and he did so successfully) was giving the opportunity to the
Prime Minister of thwarting or undermining the legislative/
executive process simply by inaction. In the *Code* he was forced to
act publicly and, by doing so, he was also forced to take
responsibility for his actions and thereby be accountable to those
who appointed him. Other bodies and offices throughout the *Code*
were carefully defined so that the exercise of 'latent negatives'
would be impossible. It might appear that Bentham was dealing
here with a fairly minor, technical matter, but once it is recalled
that this discussion arose from the earlier consideration of the
division of power and was closely related to Bentham's general
theory of democratic accountability, it may be seen as an important
theme in his theory of democratic government.

5. The 'Observations' and the Constitutional Code

When Bentham wrote the 'Observations' in February–March 1823,
he was actually engaged in drafting the *Constitutional Code*, begun
the previous year on the invitation of the Portuguese Cortes and
continued in 1823, partly encouraged by events in Greece.[39] A
number of proposals and suggestions made in the 'Observations'
were either taken from this early *Code* or subsequently appeared in
it. Portions of the considerable material on judicial organization
and procedure which appeared in the 'Observations' might well
have been a brief summary taken directly from an early version of
the *Code*, as a considerable portion of it was written in general
terms and made no direct reference to Greece.[40] Just as in the *Code*,
Bentham saw the judiciary as best headed by a single official, the
Justice Minister. The Greek constitution, however, though
possessing a Minister of Justice subordinate to the Executive
Council (article 20), vested judicial power in a body of eleven
officials who were chosen by 'the Government' and who then
chose from among themselves a President (article 86). One of the
deficiencies of the constitution was that it failed to spell out either
the duties of this body or the means by which its members were

[39] *Constitutional Code*, vol. i (*CW*), pp. xi–xxxi.
[40] *Securities against Misrule* (*CW*), 243–52.

chosen by the Senate and Executive Council together. Presumably, it was some sort of supreme tribunal, but no precise duties were given to it. Bentham characteristically criticized the provision for this body and proposed not only its abolition (with considerable savings in money and the avoidance of potential corruption) but also the elevation of the Justice Minister from relative obscurity, as a subordinate member of the executive, to head the judicial authority of the state.

In other suggestions for the organization of the judiciary Bentham followed closely ideas developed in the *Code*. He proposed that the state was organized into single-seated districts (i.e. one judge in each), with the judges appointed by the Justice Minister. Nearly all cases were to be heard in this one type of court. He also proposed here, as in the *Code*, that power be given to the electorate (a provision vigorously criticized later by John Stuart Mill) to dismiss (though not to appoint) judges.[41] He used here the system of substitutes who were unpaid (unless paid by the judges) deputies acting in place of the sitting judge in order to avoid delay in hearing cases.[42] Other provisions, such as two classes of jurors, the exclusion of lawyers from positions as judges, uninterrupted sittings of the judiciary, and judicial hearings open to all who wished to attend, also reappeared in the *Code*.[43]

Bentham's suggestions for the two other branches of government, though close to the *Code*, displayed at least one significant variation largely due to the fact that he modelled the proposals for the executive more closely on the American system than he did in the final version of the *Code*. The Greek Executive Council, to which he devoted considerable attention in the 'Observations', seemed to violate most of his principles of constitutional organization. It was composed of five members who were chosen from outside the legislature and who served for one year. The precise method of selection was not determined but was left to further legislation. The Executive Council was a powerful body which

[41] Ibid. 245–6. See J. S. Mill, *Considerations on Representative Government*, in the *Collected Works of John Stuart Mill*, ed. J. M. Robson, xix: *Essays on Politics and Society* (Toronto, 1977), 526, 528.
[42] *Securities against Misrule* (*CW*), 247, 251. At this point Bentham did not use the term 'depute' which he later adopted from the law of Scotland. See *Constitutional Code*, vol. i, ch. 5, § 2, art. 3 n. (*CW*), p. 31 n.
[43] *Securities against Misrule* (*CW*), 247–8, 251–2. See Rosen, *Jeremy Bentham and Representative Democracy*, 149–63.

performed a wide range of executive functions and, in addition, possessed a share of legislative power equal to that of the Legislative Senate.[44] Among its executive powers was included that of the appointment of all government employees. In legislative matters, it could veto any act passed by the Legislative Senate and make its own proposals for legislation.

In contrast to this arrangement, Bentham favoured a single legislature with the executive clearly subordinate to it. He saw in the Executive Council a body which could easily overwhelm and subordinate the rest of the government, and especially the Legislative Senate. Besides restricting its legislative powers and turning it into a true executive, subordinate to the legislature and giving execution and effect to legislation, Bentham proposed a basic simplification of the personnel and duties. In addition to the five members of the Executive Council, the constitution provided (article 20) for the appointment of eight ministers to deal with such matters as foreign affairs, war, justice, finance, and so on. Bentham recommended the abolition of these eight subordinate ministries and the elevation of one of the five members of the Executive Council to a position similar to that of the President of the United States with sole control of the entire executive branch of government. The remaining four members of the Executive Council would be subordinate to him and head four ministries similar to those of state, war, navy, and finance in the United States. 'If the business of the Greek nation', he remarked, 'is but carried on with a degree of aptitude and success not very much below that with which it is carried on in that confederated Commonwealth, the Grecian will be a happy people.'[45] At any rate, eight positions would have been abolished and the structure of the executive simplified. Bentham did not favour, however, the mere imitation of American practice, as he did not approve of the system of indirectly electing the President and the President's veto on legislation. He proposed instead that the Greek constitution was followed with the annual election of the executive (now limited by Bentham to a single person) by the legislature, so long as the executive no longer was able to veto legislation.

One interesting difference between Bentham's proposals here

[44] See constitution of Epidaurus, arts. 18–22, 52–84.
[45] *Securities against Misrule* (*CW*), 222.

and the *Constitutional Code* was that he had not yet developed the more elaborate scheme of thirteen ministers (plus the Justice Minister) which he later developed for that work and was content here to recommend the four which he believed constituted the American system.[46] In contrast, however, he recommended the continuation of the Greek proposal for annual elections of the executive by the legislature, while later in the *Code* he adopted the four-year term employed in the United States for the election of his Prime Minister.[47]

Bentham also considered appointments to various offices within the executive which in the Greek constitution was left wholly to the Executive Council itself. He proposed that the patronage of each government official should be limited so that the President under the newly proposed arrangement would appoint (and be responsible for) only the four ministers directly under him. They, in turn, would appoint the main officials in their respective ministries. Thus, the power of appointment would be diffused throughout the executive, without any one person or body of persons possessing too great a power of patronage. Furthermore, Bentham proposed clear chains of command and lines of responsibility within each ministry.

Bentham did not devote too much attention to monarchy in the 'Observations' partly because the Greek constitution was republican in form and partly because he did not want to stir up opposition to his other proposals among the numerous Westernized Greeks who, however partial towards republican government in principle, saw the acceptance of a European monarch on a Greek throne as a way of securing independence from Ottoman rule. Although he included a discussion of monarchy towards the end of the 'Observations' he seemed to disguise the discussion somewhat by placing it under the heading: 'Unapt arrangements inserted in the Spanish Constitution, and not in the Grecian'.[48] Nevertheless, the reader finds under this innocuous heading a typical late-Bentham discussion of the inaptitude and corruption surrounding the institution of monarchy in which his dislike of the institution is made abundantly clear.

[46] See *Constitutional Code*, vol. i, ch. 9, § 2, art. 1, § 26, art. 53 and n. (*CW*), pp. 171–2, 456–7 and n.

[47] Ibid. p. xxiv; ch. 8, § 5, art. 1, p. 156.

[48] *Securities against Misrule* (*CW*), 252.

6. Constitutional Theory and Practice

From the vantage-point of contemporary politics and political
theory, it takes a considerable imaginative leap to grasp the
importance given to constitutions in the 1820s. Nowadays not only
are constitutions written largely by civil servants but also, among
theorists, they have been devalued in importance when compared
with economic forces and such political factors as nationalism and
tribalism. Thus, there is a temptation to dismiss any constitution as
a façade behind which the real forces of politics and economics
operate. From this perspective Bentham's efforts to draft and
distribute constitutions throughout the world may seem ridiculous,
and the fact that leaders of new states seeking to establish
constitutional government beat a path to Queen's Square Place,
absurd.

There was a revival of interest in constitutional theory and
practice in the 1820s, as many new states were created out of the
break-up of former colonial empires. New constitutions were
adopted, revised, or implemented throughout Central and South
America, Greece, and in Spain and Portugal. Although this new
interest in constitutions was heavily indebted to the last great
period in the development of constitutional practice—the 1780s and
1790s when the American and French constitutions were written—
Bentham, for one, felt that further steps might be taken which not
only incorporated these new ideas and criticized those which were
not appropriate but also took full recognition of the most
important development since this period. If in the 1780s the seed of
constitutional democracy was planted, by the 1820s constitutional
democracy might be seen as a fully grown alternative to a variety of
European constitutions. Bentham was one of the few constitutional
theorists to have seen the significance of this development. In his
critique of the division of power he advanced, not the principle of
vox populi, vox dei, but the doctrine that a constitutional democracy,
based on popular sovereignty, could provide settled, moderate
government, without practices like the division of power which,
for whatever laudable reason they evolved, seemed now only to
thwart the will of the people. It was this doctrine which Bentham
later developed in full in his *Constitutional Code*.

During the 1820s Europe was full of revolutionary leaders

attempting to raise loans, armies, and public enthusiasm for their various causes or attempting to survive in defeat and disgrace on limited resources while planning for the future. Many of these leaders passed through or lived for a period in London, and, despite his reticence about seeing people, a number came to know Bentham. What did these adventurers hope to obtain from Bentham and why did they regard the establishment of a constitution as a crucial part of their various revolutionary activities? One answer to these questions is fairly obvious. The adoption of a constitution was a signal to the world of the willingness of these leaders to establish a government able to function within the European political tradition. This signal, however tentative, was essential, if European states were to be persuaded to support loans to the new governments and to recognize their diplomats. Nevertheless, a constitution also served other purposes. It established the nature of the regime (e.g. whether republican or monarchical), and the values it intended to uphold. In establishing various offices and institutions it represented the first step towards settled government.

It has been held that the constitution of Epidaurus of 1822 was not really a constitution at all and was no more than a façade designed to lead European powers to believe that Greece could be ruled by a centralized constitutional government.[49] William St Clair has put the matter most strongly: in Greece, the constitution 'never existed . . . except on paper': and in Europe it encouraged the false belief 'that the Greek Revolution was being conducted on progressive liberal principles'.[50] It is true that at the time the Greek constitution was written conditions in Greece were anarchic and actual government, in so far as it existed, was based on the localized rule of the *kapetanei* and forms of local or regional government which survived the break-up of Ottoman rule. Nevertheless, considerable efforts had been made to take the first steps towards national constitutional government. An assembly in Greece had adopted the constitution, and it was even revised by another assembly at Astros in 1823.[51] Although this body was more of an assembly of interested parties than a constitutional government,

---

[49] See Dakin, *The Greek Struggle for Independence 1821–1833*, 88.

[50] St Clair, *That Greece Might Still Be Free*, 94.

[51] For a brief account of these revisions, see Dakin, *The Greek Struggle for Independence 1821–1833*, 103–6.

there is little doubt that the constitution, if not operable, represented the ideals and aspirations of the Westernized Greeks who drafted it. Furthermore, they could see that it was in their interest to have established the constitution, even if the realization of their goal might have to await independence from Ottoman rule and victory by the Westernized Greeks over other Greeks who opposed a unified national government. To dismiss the Greek constitution of 1822 as merely a piece of worthless paper would require evidence that those who wrote it did not in fact want constitutional government, and there is no evidence to support this view.[52] Indeed, there is considerable evidence that the Westernized Greeks not only thought constitutional government to be good for

---

[52] Consider the following passage from Thomas Gordon's *History of the Greek Revolution*, 2 vols. (Edinburgh, 1832), i. 325: 'Such is a slight sketch of the constitution, excellent in theory, but totally unfit for the people to whom it was addressed; hardly did it see the light, when some of its best provisions were openly trampled upon, and others forgotten; indeed the organic law of Epidaurus soon became a dead letter, used only in the following years as a watchword for faction. It may appear surprizing, that its authors should have given institutions so thoroughly democratical to a nation, which, after groaning for centuries under despotism, was fast verging towards the worst kind of oligarchy, and that such a charter should have been accepted by the aristocrats, who made up a large portion of the assembly. No one in fact thought this mode of government practicable in Greece: but the ambition of so many individuals, (each afraid of seeing a rival invested with solid and permanent power), rendered it necessary to generalize, and ostensibly to refer every thing at short intervals to the mass of the people. Each man looked upon the constitution as a stepping stone to the highest offices, and its framers were not the least aspiring. Having no natural hold on the country from long residence or family connexions, their business was to oppose legal barriers to the great captains and primates; thinking themselves sure of success in a career where victory depended upon political finesse.' Gordon was an early philhellene, a member of the London Greek Committee, and a first-hand observer of many events during the early period of the Greek revolution. His strong condemnation of the Westernized Greeks and his general view of the constitution seem to be based on two assumptions which Bentham would not accept: firstly, that the Greek people generally were 'unfit' for constitutional democracy: and secondly, that the Westernized Greeks were somehow wrong to use constitutional government to advance their own interests. As for the first of these, Bentham believed that it was always in the interest of the people to have representative democracy and that it was the ruling classes rather than the ruled who threatened constitutional democracy. See Rosen, *Jeremy Bentham and Representative Democracy*, 185 ff. With regard to the second assumption, Bentham would not subscribe to a view which separated duty from interest. If the Westernized Greeks could establish constitutional democracy and subsequently gained from such an establishment (though without undermining the constitution) in Bentham's view, valuable motives would be established for supporting the constitution. See R. Harrison, *Bentham* (London, 1983), 130. Bentham could obviously see far more grounds for optimism than Gordon.

Greece but also that it would advance their own interests in the state.

If we can clear Bentham of the possible criticism that he wrote a commentary on a constitution that never existed, it might still be argued that he saw in the Greek constitution and in Greek society a greater potential for good government than was realistically present. It was not that he found good government present in Greece, but rather he found in Greece a 'clean slate', an absence of obstacles to good government. Here was a society not corrupted by the traditional political institutions of Europe and which might more easily adopt the institutions he proposed than a country like Great Britain. In the opening paragraph of an essay headed 'JB to Greek Legislators' on which the 'Observations' was partly based, Bentham called attention in the strongest terms to the unique position of Greece:

You enter upon your career under the most auspicious circumstances. Nothing to match them is to be found in history. Nothing to match them is to be found in present times. Obstacles which in other nations set up a bar to good government, and that bar an insuperable one, have no place in your case. You are not cursed with Kings. You are not cursed with Nobles. Your minds are not under the tyranny [of] Priests. Your minds are not under the tyranny of Lawyers.[53]

To this Bentham added shortly afterwards that Greece was fortunate in not possessing colonies: 'In this respect you have the advantage over Spain, Portugal, England, France and the Netherlands: in particular over Spain and Portugal.'[54]

There is some evidence that Bentham was aware of difficulties in establishing good government in new states, or at least was aware that conditions in new states were different from those in established ones.[55] At one point in his writings for Greece, he contrasted Greece with the new states of Latin America and pointed out that in Greece no settled habits of rule and obedience yet existed.[56] But he came very close to asserting that Greece was in some sort of privileged position and exempt from the ills of other

---

[53] *Securities against Misrule (CW)*, 193.   [54] Ibid. 195.

[55] Ibid. 185–6, where Bentham discussed the way in which uncertainties and dangers in new states led to a dependence of the individual on the whole and a tendency for the individual to make heroic sacrifices for the good of the whole. See also *Constitutional Code*, vol. i, ch. 6. § 25 arts. 42–3 (*CW*), pp. 83–4, where he explored the problem of a lack of experience and ability among leaders of new states.

[56] UC xxi. 211.

European states. One reason for Bentham's belief may have been the fact that he had little experience of a state like Greece which was genuinely new. Bentham realized that the United States (which in other respects served as a model for Greece) was not wholly appropriate as it was already fully established prior to independence.[57] The new states of Latin America also enjoyed settled European government prior to independence. Whatever Bentham thought of Ottoman rule, he did not think that the Greeks at the time were experiencing settled government and believed that they would not until constitutional government was fully secured.

If Bentham believed that Greece was in an advantageous position with regard to the establishment of constitutional democracy, as compared with European states, by virtue of the clean slate he found there, he did not go so far as to attribute virtues to the Greeks *because* they had no settled government. His assumptions that all political leaders were self-aggrandizing and potentially corrupt would prevent him from imputing to the Greeks virtues based on political innocence. Nevertheless, he was surely mistaken if he thought that it would be easier to establish constitutional democracy in Greece than in Europe, and, indeed, he would eventually come to see this for himself as he became further involved in Greek affairs.[58]

In spite of the subtlety of the theory and the novelty of some of the ideas, the Greeks for whom the 'Observations' was written were hardly prepared to engage in constitutional politics as opposed to the politics of the chiefs, that is to say, of money, weapons, families, and force. That Bentham took their first halting steps towards constitutional politics seriously was a source of considerable gratification to the Westernized Greeks, and this gratification was amply displayed in the official letters which passed between the new government and Queen's Square Place.[59] What Bentham proposed, however, was not simply a constitution suitable for Greece, but, in a sense, something more difficult for a new state to adopt. He proposed a constitutional democracy which would have made even greater demands on the Greeks to abandon traditional practices than the constitution they had themselves

---

[57] *Constitutional Code*, vol. i, ch. 6, § 25, arts. 42–3 (*CW*), pp. 83–4.

[58] See Bentham to Bolivar, 13 Aug. 1825, in *The Iberian Correspondence of Jeremy Bentham*, ed. P. Schwartz, 2 vols. (London and Madrid, 1979), ii. 907.

[59] See Bowring, iv. 580–92.

adopted. Bentham was one of a very few philosophers, politicians, and 'liberators' of the day who realized that a successful constitutional democracy could not depend on concentrated, independent executive power, and, indeed, he saw in this feature of many states (including Greece) a potential source of despotism. Strong leadership, especially military leadership, was a precondition for national independence, and it would be natural to translate this need, which was essential for political survival itself, into constitutional politics as a reliance on strong, independent executive power which would equal if not dominate the legislature. Bentham opposed this move however suitable it superficially appeared even to those involved in establishing the new state. In the 'Observations', as we have seen, he argued against the division of power in general terms and the institution of the Executive Council in particular.[60]

His general approach to constitutional democracy led him to emphasize the importance of elevating legislative power as the most important factor in government. Unless the legislature was supreme, the main task of government, to secure and advance the interests of the governed, could not be achieved. A strong, independent executive serving the interests of the people was as unlikely a prospect for Bentham as an enlightened monarch serving the interests of the people. Both were, almost by definition, in the grip of sinister interests by virtue of their lack of accountability to the people they supposedly served.[61]

[60] In the civil strife which developed in Greece in 1823 and 1824, the various factions claimed control of the Legislative Senate and Executive Council which were then established for a period in separate locations. Although the constitution cannot be blamed for the civil war, its design was such as to enable each of the contending forces to capture control of one of the major institutions and to proclaim itself the legitimate government. What was in many respects a struggle between different regions, groups, and personalities thus became a constitutional struggle as well. Although it is arguable that the political struggle became a constitutional struggle because of the special relationship between the Westernized Greeks and the constitution, it is also arguable that the design of the constitution itself encouraged the subsequent division.

[61] The novelty of Bentham's ideas, and the importance he gave to the Greek constitution, may be seen in the following remark by Lord Guilford, made approximately eighteen months after Bentham had written his 'Observations': 'When I wrote you my last letter ten days ago, proposing what I thought, and still think, would be the best Constitution for Greece, I forgot that you already had a Constitution, which, of course, must be observed in the convocation of your General Assembly. A stronger Executive Government will, however, be necessary, and one not subject to popular elections.' Archeio Spiridon Tricoupi, ELIA, Athens, Guilford to Tricoupi, 12/24 Oct. 1824.

It might be argued that constitutional practice since Bentham's day has tended to disprove this thesis. The most effective and enduring constitutional democracies have been those where executive power has been most developed, and in all constitutional democracies legislatures have played a much diminished role in the governmental process. Indeed, this development has led most commentators to see the emphasis in early democratic theory on legislatures actually making laws to be executed by a passive executive as evidence of the irrelevance of much of that early theory. Bentham's theory could accommodate a diminished active role by the legislature in the governmental process. It would oppose, however, independent executive power as destructive of democracy.

6

Theory and Practice II: Bentham and the First Greek Loan

Scholars have either ignored Bentham's involvement in the negotiations for the first Greek loan (as perhaps irrelevant) or have misconstrued it, so that this chapter represents the first attempt to state more clearly the nature of that role.[1] Such an attempt can only be successful by appreciating that Bentham's attempts to link theory with practice were probably doomed to failure from the start. His suggestions were rejected, not because they were impractical (for in many respects they were highly practical), but because they were based on critical principles whose only practical role was to undermine the ideological positions and personal opinions of those who were parties to the dispute. Bentham could lay bare the assumptions which led to the dispute in the first place, but he could not end the conflict by virtue of the suggestions themselves. For a philosopher entering the dim world of practice, his vision was, as we shall see, remarkably clear.

[1] William St Clair (*That Greece Might Still Be Free* (London, 1972), 210) mentions Bentham's involvement but is mistaken as to its object and outcome. G. F. Bartle has provided a fuller account of these events but no account of what precisely Bentham did. See 'Bowring and the Greek Loans of 1824 and 1825', *Balkan Studies*, 3 (1962), 62 ff. See also D. Dakin, *British and American Philhellenes during the War of Greek Independence, 1821–1833* (Thessaloniki, 1955), 77; A. Lignadē, *To Proton Daneion tēs Anexartēsias* [The First Loan of Independence] (Athens, 1970), 134–5, 168, 171, 179; and Pan J. Zepos, 'Jeremy Bentham and the Greek Independence', *Proceedings of the British Academy*, 62 (1976), 293. Most interpretations of Bentham's relationship with the Greek Deputies have depended on the correspondence between them published in E. Dalleggio, *Les Philhellènes et la Guerre de l'Indépendance* (Athens, 1949), 157–75. This collection was taken from copybooks in the General State Archives, Athens, and presents a misleading and incomplete account of their relationship. A fully edited version, taken from the original letters, will appear in the appropriate volumes of *Correspondence* in the *Collected Works of Jeremy Bentham* (forthcoming).

1. The Crisis of the First Greek Loan

The Greek Deputies Ioannis Orlandos and Andreas Louriottis, who arrived in London in January 1824 to negotiate the first loan on behalf of the Greek government, had good reason to regard Bentham as a friend. Louriottis had approached him in February 1823, at the time of his first visit to London, and from their meeting (and with the encouragement of Edward Blaquiere, John Bowring, and Leicester Stanhope), Bentham had already sent numerous books and manuscripts to Greece, including the early draft of his constitutional code.[2] As he had responded so positively to Louriottis's invitation in 1823 to draft the 'Observations' and to the Greek cause generally since Pikkolos's arrival in London in 1821, it was natural that, when in difficulty, they might turn to him for assistance.[3]

Although Bentham was not initially involved in the negotiations regarding the loan, he was in contact with the principal figures during this period.[4] Yet, when he wrote a long letter to Stanhope, dated 19 and 21 February, when the negotiations were being concluded, he did not mention the loan and referred to Orlandos and Louriottis only in connection with his own constitutional code.

[2] See above, Ch. 5. See also *Constitutional Code*, i, ed. F. Rosen and J. H. Burns (Oxford, 1983 (*CW*), pp. xvi ff. for the history of this work in relation to Greece. See also Bowring, iv. 580–92.

[3] For Bentham's early involvement in Greek affairs, see P. Kitromilides, 'Jeremy Bentham and Adamantios Korais', *Bentham Newsletter*, 9 (1985), 34 ff. and F. Rosen, 'A Note on Bentham and Korais', *Bentham Newsletter*, 9 (1985), 49.

[4] Soon after their arrival in January 1824 Orlandos and Louriottis made contact with Bentham. In an exchange of letters on 31 January, a dinner invitation for 6 February was eventually negotiated, and they returned for breakfast on 16 February. See UC xii. 180–1 and Diary of John Colls 1821–25, BL Add. MS 33563, fo. 130. See also UC xii. 186 where on 9 February a dinner invitation from Bentham was refused, though the breakfast meeting on the 16th may have replaced it. There is no evidence to suggest that the Greek loan was discussed at these meetings. There would have been other topics Bentham would have wanted to discuss such as the fate of his manuscripts, the prospect of his drafting a set of codes, and his offer to educate two Greek youths at his expense in England, but some discussion of the loan probably took place. Some evidence exists to suggest that Bentham had discussed the loan with Bowring prior to the arrival of Orlandos and Louriottis in London, as his Commonplace Book records among 'Dicenda to Bowring', dated 21 Jan., 'Suspicious Greek Loan' (see UC clxxiii. 105). It is not clear what Bentham had in mind, though he advised Bowring on matters in which they shared a common interest, e.g. the *Westminster Review* which Bentham financed and Bowring edited, and which was about to appear at this time.

This seems to indicate that he had paid little attention to the course of the negotiations.[5] Bowring, who, as Secretary of the London Greek Committee, took most of the responsibility for arranging the loan, seems to have been pleased with the outcome and with the fact that the loan had been oversubscribed three times. Even though the Greek Deputies were more concerned with obtaining the loan as soon as possible than with its terms, they were not in so desperate a position that they could not have raised the money by other means.[6] There were other offers (especially through French sources) and the apparent ease with which the second loan of £2,000,000 was raised the following year in London, without much reference to the London Greek Committee, provides evidence that there was plenty of money available for loans of this type.

But Bowring did not find negotiating with the Greek Deputies an easy task. He complained of their 'narrow-mindedness' and that they 'nearly wrecked the loan itself by miserable trifling about shadows'. 'They carried on their discussions with our capitalists', he continued in a letter to Byron, 'as if they were trading for old clothes.'[7] For a new country of no international standing, without even a settled government and with its very existence as an independent state still in the balance, it may seem remarkable that any loan could have been raised. But such loans had become commonplace in London for various European countries and for the new states of Latin America. London seemed awash with money for speculative investments of this kind which paid a high return and seemed fairly safe in so far as the wealth and territory of whole states seemed to back the loans. Although the loan was for £800,000 at 5 per cent interest, £100 of stock could be purchased for £59 payable in six monthly instalments from early March. Thus, only £472,000 could be raised, but the return for lenders was considerably enhanced by the discounted price they paid for the loan stock. In addition, the retention of two years' interest of 5 per cent of the nominal value of the loan and the establishment of a

---

[5] General State Archives, Athens, Stanhope papers, K. 121, fo. 39. Copy in UC xii. 190–200.

[6] See Dakin, *British and American Philhellenes*, 76.

[7] LGC papers, vol. xi, fo. S, 13 Feb. 1824. The Deputies also found the negotiations difficult. 'Quelle différence', they complained to Mavrokordatos, 'entre l'esprit du Patriotisme et celui qui préside aux Spéculations commerciales.' Benaki Museum, Mavrokordatos papers, Orlandos, Zaimēs, and Louriottis to Mavrokordatos, 3 Aug. 1824.

sinking fund of 1 per cent of the total seemed to give some additional security to lenders. Bowring himself hoped to make a considerable profit from the loan and invested £25,000 of his own money. Joseph Hume, one of the contractors, invested £10,000 and fairly large sums were invested by others.[8] If C. B. Sheridan was 'not sanguine' about the loan on 9 February, he quickly changed his mind when he saw the terms and urgently applied for £5,000 of stock.[9] The return on his investment would nearly amount to a very attractive 10 per cent per year, and such a return was guaranteed for at least two years.

Nevertheless, there were clouds on or just over the horizon. The speculative bubble, symbolized by the ample funds available for the Greek loans, would burst the following year with widespread panic and loss. Even in February 1824 there was considerable anxiety expressed in the newspapers about the soundness of various loans.[10] For Bowring, still young and fairly inexperienced as a city financier, the Greek loan represented his first major enterprise and he gambled a good deal of his wealth and reputation on it. His activities in liberal Spain had made him an associate of Bentham from 1820; his wrongful arrest in France as a spy in the spring of 1822 had brought him to public notice, and he obtained a good deal of support from leading reformers in London; his literary career was now being established; the first number of the *Westminster Review* which he edited appeared at this time; and with his assuming the post of Honorary Secretary of the London Greek Committee, he was about to become a public figure of some importance, at least to the readers of the *Morning Chronicle*, *Examiner*, and similar newspapers.[11] If he was anxious about the Greek loan, it was over reports from Greece that there was civil strife amongst various factions that was threatening to break out into civil war. As he sternly wrote to Alexander Mavrokordatos, then leader of the Greek government:

[8] See *Cobbett's Weekly Register*, 60 (4 Nov. 1826), 369–70.
[9] LGC papers, vol. v, fos. A³, Y³, C. B. Sheridan to Bowring, 9, 19 Feb. 1824.
[10] See e.g. *Morning Chronicle* (3 Feb. 1824).
[11] For Bowring's activities in Spain, and his introduction to Bentham, see below, Ch. 7. See also G. F. Bartle, 'The Political Career of Sir John Bowring (1792–1872) between 1820 and 1849' (MA thesis, London University, 1959); and *The Autobiographical Recollections of Sir John Bowring*, ed. L. B. Bowring (London, 1877). For his arrest in France, see J. Bowring, *Details of the Arrest, Imprisonment and Liberation, of an Englishman, by the Bourbon Government of France* (London, 1823).

On the pecuniary transactions of the government of Greece, any thing like disunion must have the most fatal consequences—The Greek Committee hope that a loan may be effected in this country on not disadvantageous terms; but it is of the highest importance that it should possess that moral guarantee which results from internal concord and good understanding.[12]

Bowring was bound to feel uneasy in his search for that elusive 'moral guarantee' for the success of the loan which he felt should emerge in Greece. His letter to Mavrokordatos was prompted by information from Lord Byron which had arrived in London in late November and early December. 'Lord Byron', wrote John Cam Hobhouse to Bowring, 'does not give an encouraging account of the government whose dissentions he declares to be more formidable to the cause of Greek independence than the Turkish enemy.'[13] Such remarks, supposedly by Byron himself, that 'all the stories of the Greek victories by sea and land are exaggerated or untrue' or 'as for the fleet it has never been to Sea at all until very lately—and as far as can be ascertained has done little or nothing' would only confirm Bowring's worst fears.[14] Furthermore, early reports from Leicester Stanhope confirmed those from Byron, which Hobhouse thought should not be made public.[15] Stanhope also asserted: 'I hope you will still succeed in obtaining a *small* Loan—say a hundred thousand Pounds. I think it is not feasible or even desirable under existing circumstances that Greece should obtain a larger sum.'[16]

For Bowring to receive intelligence and advice of this nature, just prior to and during the loan negotiations, must have been unsettling, even if none of these gloomy reports was actually published in the newspapers. For the *Morning Chronicle* 'the

[12] LGC papers, vol. v, fo. U^1, 27 Dec. 1823.

[13] Ibid. vol. iv, fo. G^3, 30 Nov. 1823.

[14] Ibid. vol. iv, fo. J^3, Charles Barry to Hobhouse, 1 Dec. 1823, quoting a letter from Byron, dated 28 Oct. 1823. The letter from Byron to Barry appears in *Byron's Letters and Journals*, ed. L. Marchand, 12 vols. (London, 1973–82), xi: '*For Freedom's battle*', 54.

[15] 'Since I received your last letter I have had sundry dispatches from Lord Byron which I think ought to be communicated to the Greek Committee—whether the Committee will think it their duty to act upon them as to make them public is another matter—I should rather recommend silence as the account from Greece is of the most discouraging nature'. Ibid. vol. iv, fo. L^4, Hobhouse to Bowring, 23 Dec. 1823. See also ibid. fo. V^4, Blaquiere to Bowring, 26 Dec. 1823: 'I shall make the most *prudent* use imaginable.'

[16] Ibid. vol. vi. fo. D, Stanhope to Bowring, 2 Dec. 1823. This letter was omitted from Stanhope's *Greece, in 1823 and 1824* (London, 1825).

independence of Greece, is hourly gaining strength'.[17] Bad news
tended to be discounted, as, for example, a report of Mavrokordatos
having been 'torn in pieces by the Hydriots' was explained as
'circulated by Russian agents', because Mavrokordatos was supposedly opposed to Russian influence in Greece.[18] According to the
Morning Chronicle, he had gone to Hydra 'to superintend the sailing
of the fleet, and has since returned to his duties of Secretary-
General to the Government'.[19] In fact neither the rumour nor the
correction was accurate. The truth of the matter was that he had
fled to Hydra in the spring of 1823 when the *kapetanei*, especially
Petrobey and Kollokotronis, had taken effective control of the
government, and his flight was clear evidence of the civil strife then
existing among the Greeks.[20] Nevertheless, in England among the
reformers there was a powerful optimism expressed in the
strongest support for the Greek cause. On the eve of the arrival of
the Greek Deputies in London to negotiate the loan, the *Morning
Chronicle* wrote in its 'City' column:

With the exception of Spain, every description of Continental public
securities continues to improve; for the industry and peace of the world
appear at present to rest on a firm foundation; and nothing but the
ambition and pride of Continental Kings can disturb a state of things so
beneficial to the human species. Greece alone requires the assistance of the
English nation. . . . Public Deputies from the Greek Government are
expected to arrive by the first Malta packet, and then, either by loan or by
some other device, will that assistance be given to the modern Greeks,
who . . . have strong claims on mankind for the extraordinary persever-
ance with which they have resisted the oppressive and degrading
Government of the Asiatic barbarians, who now pollute Europe with their
detestable principles. With liberal laws in the Peninsula and in Greece, the
commerce of Europe may be increased to an unbounded extent, and the
prosperity of mankind in a proportionate degree promoted.[21]

---

[17] *Morning Chronicle* (17 Dec. 1823).   [18] Ibid. (19 Nov. 1823).
[19] Ibid.
[20] See D. Dakin, *The Greek Struggle for Independence 1821–1833* (London, 1973),
104–6; St Clair, *That Greece Might Still Be Free*, 165–6.
[21] *Morning Chronicle* (12 Jan. 1824). This publicly expressed sentiment was
confirmed privately, as when Bowring wrote to Byron (4 Feb. 1824): 'There has
lately been a great interest excited in England among all parties for the Greek
cause—the clergy—the tories have come forward—and in conversation I had some
days since with Mr. Canning, he expressed the best feelings possible towards the
Greeks. The loan, I have no doubt, will be the most popular yet introduced on the
British market' (Murray archive, Box A21).

If the cause of Greece was to be seen in the context of resisting the tyrannies of the Holy Alliance, the loan for Greece should be seen as part of the vision of a growing prosperity throughout a world organized on liberal principles, and financed by capital and loans from London. By 1822 foreign states, some of which were not yet independent, had already borrowed approximately £10,150,000 in London.[22] Most of the loans were to European states: Denmark borrowed £3,000,000, Portugal £1,500,000, and Russia £3,500,000. But others were not: in 1824 Brazil borrowed £3,686,200 and in the next year £2,000,000. During this period Argentina borrowed £1,000,000 and Mexico £6,400,000.[23] These loans were not entirely successful. Speculation in Colombian and Chilean bonds had reduced some families to misery and a great deal of money had been lost.[24] Nevertheless, the mood was so positive and the speculation so feverish that a Mexican loan for £3,200,000 was floated just weeks before the Greek loan.[25] It was organized on similar lines, with £58 payable in five monthly instalments for £100 in stock at 5 per cent interest over a thirty-year period.[26]

In spite of rumours that the Mexican bonds were not authorized by the government and questions about the security for the loan, the *Morning Chronicle* thought the terms were good and reported brisk business.[27] While it urged 'the utmost caution' on the part of the contractors in light of the losses incurred by other South American loans, especially the Colombian loan, this reserve seems to have dissolved with news of the impending recognition of the new South American states, as putting an end to the uncertainty of their continued existence.[28]

With the arrival of the Greek Deputies in London, the *public* view of the prospects of the loan could not have been brighter. Whatever Stanhope may have written to Bowring about conditions in Greece, he was reported in the *Morning Chronicle* on 31 January as having arrived in the Morea believing confidently in 'the final

---

[22] J. Francis, *Chronicles and Characters of the Stock Exchange* (London, 1855), 266.
[23] Ibid. 280.   [24] See *Morning Chronicle* (15 Jan. 1824).
[25] See ibid. (27 Jan. 1824).
[26] No further loans could be raised for 12 months, and if more were raised after that period, a quarter of the new loan would be used to pay off the old. A sinking fund was established to redeem the loan amounting to £64,000 in the first and £32,000 in each succeeding year.
[27] See *Morning Chronicle* (27, 30 Jan., 3 Feb. 1824).
[28] Ibid. (3, 7, 11–12 Feb. 1824).

emancipation of the whole of Greece from the yoke of the Ottomans'.[29] 'He confirms', the report continued, 'all the victories obtained by the Christians both by sea and land, and also states that the greatest harmony prevailed amongst all the Chieftains.'[30]

Although the Greek loan was bedevilled by attempts by others to float loans at this time, the agreement was signed on 19 February and announced publicly the next day. The atmosphere surrounding the heavily oversubscribed loan may be seen in this report in the *Morning Chronicle* of 26 February:

On the Foreign Stock Exchange, the Greek Loan continues to command the chief attention of speculators, and also of those who want good interest for their money, with fair security for its payment. They have risen since yesterday 1½ per cent . . . [T]he Independence of Greece will, in every human probability, be completely established, and the richest parts of Europe and Asia will be sufficient guarantee to the Holders of Grecian Bonds, which will then undoubtedly be the best in Europe.

The buoyancy in the value of the loan survived the payment of the first instalment on 3 March, but by 20 March a different report began to appear in the *Morning Chronicle*: 'The friends of Greece regret that confidence is apparently declining in the solidity of the Greek Loan.' Two days later, the 'City' report noted: 'In Greek scrip scarcely a transaction is done, and its price is at present stationary. The long want of news from the Morea has in no small degree hurt the interest which was early taken in this Loan. The news of the capture of the Castle of Patras [by the Greeks] is hourly expected.'[31]

On 24 March, the *Morning Chronicle* presented a different sort of analysis and the first criticism of those responsible for the loan:

The Greek scrip is depressed far beneath its value, and this circumstance is not to be wondered at, for there is not one Foreign Loan now in the English market, which has been so completely abandoned to the test of public opinion, as that of the Christian descendants of the great civilizers of mankind. The effect of this neglect, no doubt, operates injuriously against this much injured nation; but whether the Loan be successful or not, the circumstance may retard, but cannot prevent their final triumph. There is not a public debt in the English market, which may not be, and occasionally is not, depressed by circumstances, but, with the exception of

[29] See *Morning Chronicle* (31 Jan. 1824).   [30] Ibid.
[31] Ibid. (22 Mar. 1824).

the Greek Loan, there is not a foreign Loan which is not powerfully supported by its Patrons, who conceive it to be a part of their duty, as it were, to nurse it, until it comes to maturity. The Greek Loan, however, like a stranger, is abandoned to the friendship of strangers, and strong indeed must its claim be on the public, since it has continued, under such circumstances, even to exhibit the emblem of respectability. It is the surprise of every friend of the final emancipation of Greece, that steps are not taken to strengthen the good opinion which only a few weeks ago British capitalists entertained of its resources.

This remarkable passage seems to shift the blame for the rapid decline in the value of the Greek loan from the absence of good news from Greece to the failure of the British backers to keep up the value of the loan. The reason for their failure is not revealed, but when favourable reports from Greece were printed on 31 March and on 3 April (though not many of them true), the Greek loan scrip remained seriously depressed. What could have happened during the first vital weeks of the loan's existence to threaten its chances of success?

2. Bentham as Reluctant Mediator

Bentham's involvement in what had become a bitter dispute between Orlandos and Louriottis on the one hand, and Bowring and the loan contractors on the other, began on 6 March when the two Deputies paid him a visit.[32] The loan agreement had already been signed and announced, the subscriptions taken, and the first instalment paid. With the *Florida* about to sail for Greece with £30,000 in gold and sovereigns and £10,000 in Spanish dollars at the end of March, it would be difficult to conceive of a worse time for such a dispute to develop. If Bowring and the contractors were fearful of civil strife in Greece, how much more anxious must they have been of such strife on their very doorstep in London. To their credit, none of the disagreements was aired in public at this time (though some emerged at the time of the Greek loan scandal in October 1826), but sufficient apprehension must have been aroused to depress the value of the loan, as we have seen, shortly after it was launched.

[32] Colls's Diary, BL Add. MS 33563, fo. 130.

Orlandos and Louriottis sought Bentham's assistance for two related difficulties. The first was the more general problem that the arrangements for the control over the loan and its distribution were organized so as to be, in the view of Orlandos, 'contre les intérêts de ma patrie'.[33] Bowring's search for security for the lenders had led him and the contractors to arrange for the loan to be placed in the hands of British Commissioners in Greece, such as Lord Byron or Leicester Stanhope, at whose discretion the money would be distributed. To a certain extent, the Deputies approved of this plan, as the Commissioners could keep the funds out of the hands of such leaders as Kollokotronis in the event that they happened to control the government. As there was no assurance as to who would control the Greek government when the funds arrived, the Commissioners could be seen to have an important role to play. But the Greek Deputies now believed that nothing less than the 'honour' of the Greek government, the nation, and themselves was at stake. The French, Russians, and Austrians, they believed, would say that they had sold Greece to the English, and the loan would compromise the interests of Greece towards the Holy Alliance and towards anyone else.[34] To a certain extent their fears were not without foundation. The security for the loan was supposedly the 'public lands' of Greece which could be sold at the end of the war to raise funds to repay the loan. Bowring had already suggested sending a surveyor to Greece to determine the extent and quality of these lands and opening an office in London to sell them. 'We could, I am sure, find capitalists to buy and colonists to cultivate them', he confided to Byron in Greece, adding, as if to forestall the view that Greece was being sold to the British, that 'it is important that every suggestion should come from the [Greek] Government'.[35]

The second difficulty was more specific, and it reveals the motive behind the Deputies turning especially to Bentham and addressing him in such flattering terms as 'Notre Père et protecteur de la Grèce' or 'Notre Ami et Père de notre patrie' after addressing him

---

[33] UC xii. 201, Orlandos to Bentham, 9 Mar. 1824. See earlier correspondence to which Orlandos refers in Louriottis papers, Centre for Neo-Hellenic Research, National Research Foundation, Athens, Σt¹, fos. 51–2.

[34] UC xii. 214, Orlandos and Louriottis to Bentham, 13 Mar. 1824. See also versions in Dalleggio, *Les Philhellènes*, 158–9, and LGC papers, vol. vi, fo. E²; vol. x, fo. E.   [35] LGC papers, vol. xi, fo. S, 13 Feb. 1824.

simply as 'Monsieur' in their earlier letters. According to the Deputies, twenty-four days before signing the loan agreement, they prepared a minute which they wished to insert into the contract (with which they were otherwise satisfied). They alleged that Bowring, anxious to avoid any further delay in signing the contract, gave the Deputies a solemn assurance that there would be no difficulty in having the minute signed by Joseph Hume and Edward Ellice, the two main Commissioners of the loan in London. Orlandos and Louriottis believed that Hume and Ellice were willing to sign the minute, but that Bowring was not, and they wanted Bentham to assist them in their dealings with Bowring. They also noted that they had reached agreement with Hume and Ellice that the Commissioners in charge of the funds in Greece were to be Byron, Gordon, and Lazarus Koundouriottis instead of Byron and Stanhope, as originally planned. Stanhope was about to be recalled to England and Gordon seemed likely to replace him, but the important point here was the suggestion that a Greek, Koundouriottis, was made one of the Commissioners in charge of the loan.[36]

Bentham's response to the invitation to act as mediator between the Deputies and Bowring betrayed some alarm and surprise, but he soon agreed to look into the matter and the Deputies were satisfied that he had undertaken the 'commission'.[37] Bentham, however, was much less happy to take on such a task than he indicated to the Deputies. The very next day he referred in a letter to Stanhope to the 'most unwelcome and useless commission' which 'has absorbed near two days of my time'. 'To gain me', he continued, 'I am called Protecteur de la Grèce, and so on flattered up to the skies.'[38] Bentham had been pleased with his relationship with the Deputies and especially with Orlandos ('Orlando and I are upon the best of terms', he wrote on 10 March, just prior to the approach of the Deputies).[39] He hoped that they could be useful to him in his plans to draft various codes for Greece, and with some relief noted to Stanhope: 'They are hot and suspicious, and full of

[36] UC xii. 212, Orlandos and Louriottis to Bentham, n.d., but possibly 10 Mar. 1824. See another version in Dalleggio, *Les Philhellènes*, 157–8.
[37] See UC xii. 202, Orlandos and Louriottis to Bentham, 11 Mar. 1824.
[38] LGC papers, vol. x. fo. C, Bentham to Stanhope, 10, 12, 13, 14 Mar. 1824.
[39] Ibid.

complaints quite ungrounded I believe ag[ainst] their best friend
B[owrin]g but as yet they seem kindly disposed as well as full of the
most extraordinary respect as towards me.'[40]

Besides his desire to assist Bowring and the Greek cause
generally, he thus had an additional reason for not denying the
request of the Deputies. Nevertheless, his suspicions of the
Deputies were confirmed first by Bowring and then by Blaquiere.
According to Bowring, the minute they had submitted three weeks
earlier was considerably different from the one they had just sent to
Bentham.[41] The earlier minute was not accepted by Bowring
because it obliged the Greek government to use the funds for
specific purposes, such as attacks on certain towns, and Bowring
thought that such restrictions would limit and discredit the Greek
government. It also expressly prohibited the money from going
into the hands of the Finance Minister, a provision which Bowring
thought would reveal the numerous rifts among the Greeks and
alarm the lenders. In addition, Bowring said that Hume and Ellice
would not give the Deputies 'uncontrolled power over the Loan,
nor be parties to *secret* agreements on behalf of any party, or class of
men whatever'.[42] Blaquiere confirmed Bowring's view, contrary
to that of the Deputies (i.e. that Hume and Ellice agreed with them
and that only Bowring was in opposition), by noting that 'Mr.
Hume is also dissatisfied with the deputies'.[43] However much
Bentham laboured in the next weeks to assist the Deputies, he
always remained close to Bowring. 'All the eulogisms (you will
see),' he wrote to Bowring, 'are for Hume and Ellice who deserve
not . . . a tenth part of what you do.'[44] To Stanhope, Bentham
noted: 'It appears but too plainly there is a sad want of wisdom and
temper even in Orlando, of whom I had and still have a much
higher conception than of the others. Poor soul! considering the
state of the public mind in their country, how could it have been
otherwise.'[45]

[40] UC xii. 219–20, Bentham to Stanhope, 14 Mar. 1824. This letter may be a
continuation of the letter to Stanhope referred to in n. 38. See also xii. 191 for a
draft.

[41] UC xii. 213, Bowring to Bentham, 12 Mar. 1824.

[42] Ibid.

[43] UC xii. 215, Blaquiere to Bentham, 12 Mar. 1824.

[44] LGC papers, vol. vi, fo. F², Bentham to Bowring, 14 Mar. 1824.

[45] LGC papers, vol. x, fo. C, Bentham to Stanhope, 10, 12, 13, 14 Mar. 1824.

3. Bentham's Proposal

Much of Bentham's lengthy correspondence with Orlandos and
Louriottis at this time was directed towards persuading them to see
their position more clearly. At the outset he took the view that
there was an identity of interest between the lenders in London and
good government in Greece, as the repayment of the loans would
depend on responsible government being established in an independent Greece. As the interest of the Commissioners, who
represented the lenders, would be to further this aim, Bentham
believed that their discretion in the payment of the loan was crucial
to its success. In this respect, Lord Byron, though appreciating the
difficulty of the task of the Commissioners, took the same view as
Bentham.[46] Bentham also believed that the interests of the
Westernized Greeks would be best secured by the proposed
arrangement, as the Commissioners would naturally favour men
like Mavrokordatos rather than Kollokotronis.[47]

In spite of Bentham's analysis of the problem in terms of
'interests', Orlandos and Louriottis were not persuaded to accept
the established arrangements. They clung to the view of the
importance of the 'honour' of the nation. As for the loan, 'les
finances sont à une nation, à un Gouvernement', 'ce que le sang est
à un homme, à un corps humain'.[48] With the help of various
advisers they set forth several new proposals which would achieve
what they desired. Firstly, they wanted to change the wording of
their agreement from 'à l'usage du Gouvernement Grec' to 'à
l'ordre du Gouvernement Grec' so that the funds held by the
Commissioners in Greece would have to be paid over to the Greek
government when requested. Secondly, if they conceded that the
Commissioners might take charge of the loan on Zante (the Ionian
Island under British administration) they also insisted that
Koundouriottis should be nominated as one of the Commissioners.
The proposed changes would effectively take the power to dispose
of the loan out of the hands of the British, and, as Koundouriottis

[46] See 'For Freedom's battle', *Byron's Letters and Journals*, xi. 73, Byron to Bowring,
10 Oct. 1823, 141–2, Byron to Samuel Barff, 26 Mar. 1824.
[47] LGC papers, vol. x, fo. D, Bentham to Orlandos and Louriottis, 12 Mar. 1824.
See also UC xii. 206–11.
[48] LGC papers, vol. x, fo. F, Orlandos and Louriottis to Bentham, 16 Mar. 1824.
See also UC xii. 242 and Dalleggio, *Les Philhellènes*, 163–5.

was on the side of the Westernized Greeks (indeed, he was the brother-in-law of Orlandos), he would tend to ensure that the funds remained in safe hands. Bentham was not entirely pleased with the proposal, and revealed this displeasure by suggesting that while 'ordre' in the context may imply a positive idea of honour, 'usage' carried no dishonour for the Deputies and for Greece.[49] He also feared that if Kollokotronis dominated the government, the Westernized Greeks might still see the funds from the loan pass directly into his hands. In addition, Bentham had also been told by J. Hamilton Browne, the philhellene and former official of the Ionian government, of the relationship between Koundouriottis and Orlandos and that Koundouriottis would be unacceptable to many Greeks, as he had a special interest as a Hydriot in favouring the Greek islands.[50] Nevertheless, Bentham seemed willing to accept their proposal so long as the Commissioners knew secretly that they could exercise discretion in passing the funds over to the Greek government in order to avoid giving the funds to the wrong people.

Bentham's main difficulty with this proposal seems to have been with the Commissioners themselves. Stanhope, on whom Bentham depended most, was about to be recalled to London by Canning.[51] Gordon, who had said that he would go to Greece, had backed out once before and might again decline at the last minute. As for Byron, whose days were numbered, it seems that he was not entirely to be trusted. Bentham noted that James Mill 'has launched forth in declaration of his being a prodigy of inconsistency and caprice . . . that he could not be depended upon for two moments together'.[52] Bentham argued prophetically that the main security

---

[49] UC xii. 233, Bentham to Orlandos and Louriottis, 15 Mar. 1824.

[50] See UC xii. 223–32, James Hamilton Browne to Stanhope, 14 Mar. 1824.

[51] Dakin, *British and American Philhellenes*, 74; St Clair, *That Greece Might Still Be Free*, 193.

[52] LGC papers, vol. x, fo. G, Bentham to Bowring, 20 Mar. 1824. Bentham, however, did not agree with Mill, though he admitted to not knowing much about Byron: 'but I have never found to my recollection a man to advance any position so determinately without considerable specific grounds: and by his connections he is in a way to have political fruits in abundance' (ibid.). Stanhope, however, seems to have shared Mill's opinion, and wrote to Bowring on 11 February from Missolonghi: 'Do not trust Ld. B[yron] with yr. money. He is too generous with his own and he will be almost as much so with yours.' See LGC papers, vol. vi, fo. Z. This passage was omitted from the published version of Stanhope's letters. See *Greece, in 1823 and 1824*, 111–13.

for the loan would depend on the continuity of the Commissioners in Greece and there was no provision in the loan agreement for Commissioners to appoint their own successors. The possibility existed, he believed, that there would be no English Commissioners to supervise the distribution and use of the loan.[53]

In the numerous letters which passed between Bentham, Bowring, the Deputies, and a host of others attempting to sort out these problems, the idea of four Commissioners to supervise the loan, with two British and two Greek, was raised. Orlandos and Louriottis had suggested this possibility, as had Hamilton Browne,[54] so that the idea was not new to Bentham. But Bentham used the idea to set forth a novel plan for Orlandos and Louriottis to end the dispute which so threatened the success of the loan. He suggested that there should be two British and two Greek Commissioners; one of the Greek Commissioners would be Koundouriottis and the other would be from the opposing party, but Orlandos and Louriottis would have the power to choose this latter Commissioner.[55] When it is appreciated that the 'opposing party' was that of the arch-enemy Kollokotronis, who had been used by Bentham throughout these negotiations to justify not placing the loan 'at the order' of the Greek government lest he came to power and misappropriated the funds, the novelty of the proposal is striking. On further inspection, its utility also becomes evident. In the first place, by accepting the principle of the four Commissioners, Bentham took the emphasis off the problem of the equal relationship between the lenders (or the London Greek Committee) and the Greek government. In concentrating on the Commissioners it was also implied that they would retain the power to decide whether or not to release the money and to whom it should be released. With equality among the Commissioners, the honour of the Greek government was preserved without the government gaining the power to order the release of the money. Secondly, the two rival Greek Commissioners would serve as a

[53] LGC papers, vol. x, fo. G, Bentham to Bowring, 20 Mar. 1824. See Bentham's writings on this theme in *Constitutional Code*, vol. i, ch. 8, § 4, ch. 9, § 6 (*CW*), pp. 154–6, 215–17.
[54] See UC xii. 242 and another version in LGC papers, vol. x, fo. F, Orlandos and Louriottis to Bentham, 16 Mar. 1824. See also Dalleggio, *Les Philhellènes*, 163–5. For Hamilton Browne, see above, n. 50.
[55] Louriottis papers, Σt¹, fo. 59, Bentham to Orlandos and Louriottis, 17 Mar. 1824. See also UC xii. 245, and LGC papers, vol. x, fo. Jb.

check on each other, and they would not easily be able to combine against the two British Commissioners who would more probably be united. But as Bentham offered to Orlandos and Louriottis the patronage of choosing the person from the opposing party, they could more easily accept this person as one of the Commissioners.

Orlandos and Louriottis were obviously struck by the boldness of Bentham's proposal, and it seems that the arrangement not only would have satisfied them but also would have redeemed the honour of Greece.[56] They did not even raise the issue of the relationship of the Commissioners to the Greek government. Their only reservation was an unwillingness to choose Kollokotronis himself who they thought would destroy the harmony of the Commissioners. They nominated instead Anagnostis Pappajannopoulos, a close friend and adviser to Kollokotronis.

It now appeared that Bentham had at last laid the foundations for resolving the dispute between Bowring and the Greek Deputies. But to his obvious disappointment, he was unable to persuade Bowring to accept his proposal.[57] Bowring's initial response does not appear to have survived, but it is possible to reconstruct his position from a letter in reply from Bentham. Bowring's main objection, according to Bentham, was that the two rival Greek Commissioners 'would unite in a scheme of depredation for mutual benefit'.[58] Bentham denied that this was likely to occur and argued that the existence of even one British Commissioner would have been sufficient to denounce publicly any such plan. Furthermore, if the Greeks were able to combine on a sufficiently stable basis to plunder the loan, Bentham argued prophetically that no group of Commissioners could ultimately prevent them.

Bowring's rejection of Bentham's plan was not based on its impracticality. In his search for the 'moral guarantee' that the loan would be repaid, the funds not squandered, and, perhaps most importantly, that individual Greeks would not profit from it, Bowring would not find Bentham's emphasis on interests and incentives especially appealing to his moral sensibilities. Bentham did point to what the Greeks needed: an Audit Board and a legislature composed of good representatives. If an incorruptible

[56] UC xii. 243, Orlandos and Louriottis to Bentham, 17 Mar. 1824. See also Dalleggio, *Les Philhellènes*, 165–6.
[57] See LGC papers, vol. x, fo. G, Bentham to Bowring, 20 Mar. 1824. See also UC xii. 246–8, which may have been part of the same letter.   [58] Ibid.

Audit Board could be established, he suggested to Bowring, '*they should be the Commissioners at once*'.[59] But in the absence of these institutions and people, Bentham did not turn away from the Greeks to champion potentially unreliable British Commissioners. In a revealing passage, he wrote:

Orlando has made great sacrifices, Mavrocordato has made great sacrifices. These you are quite satisfied of. Yet their obtaining for their sacrifices any the smallest compensation, you seem to consider a public calamity, and determined if possible to prevent it. For my part, as above, I see not how it would be possible for you to prevent it: nor if you could, do I see why it should be desirable. Every thing indeed depends upon the quantum: and if they could obtain more than a due compensation, so they naturally enough, though not certainly, would. But even supposing them to obtain too much, this with all its bad effects would have one good effect: namely the encouraging them and others to make upon occasion the like sacrifices in future.[60]

If Bentham was willing to see private interest serve as an incentive to further the public good, Bowring's more moralistic outlook tended to resist a solution in this direction. For Bowring, the enhancement of private interest at the expense of the public interest was precisely the evil to be avoided at all costs, and he steadfastly resisted all moves by Orlandos and Louriottis and the Westernized Greeks to use the loan to advance their own positions. Bentham did not see such a development as the main problem and, indeed, he saw it as providing the incentives needed to establish a stable and successful government in Greece.

If Bentham attempted to persuade Orlandos and Louriottis to think in terms of 'interests' rather than vague rhetorical notions such as 'honour', he also attempted to persuade Bowring to abandon his moralistic stance and regard private interests in a positive manner. If he persuaded one side, he did not succeed with the other, and what is perhaps most paradoxical is the fact that Bowring's eventual loss of money and reputation, as revealed during the Greek loan scandal in 1826, was based on his own confusion of public and private interest. Bentham never condemned or even criticized Bowring for his apparent misdeeds, largely because he appreciated the fact that Bowring had done more than anyone else (except perhaps Blaquiere) to advance the Greek cause

[59] Ibid.   [60] Ibid.

in England. That Bowring sought to profit from his involvement was to be expected. If Bowring were to be criticized, it would be (in Bentham's eyes) for a moral rigidity which prevented a fairly simple accommodation of the aspirations of the Greeks. This failure led to the paralysis of activity surrounding the loan about which the *Morning Chronicle* complained.

4. The Fate of the First Greek Loan

Bentham and the Greek Deputies continued to correspond into the autumn of 1824 and occasionally after that time, but Bentham's close involvement in the various problems surrounding the Greek loan soon passed. He acknowledged 'no small magnanimity on their part in their entering so readily into a proposal of so novel a complection',[61] but in the end, he recommended that the Deputies had to accept the existing arrangements or look elsewhere for their money.[62] Bowring was persuaded to show some flexibility in the arrangements and in the end he accepted Koundouriottis as the third Commissioner along with Byron and Stanhope, with Stanhope to be replaced by Thomas Gordon. Apart from the brief moment when Bentham seemed allied with the Deputies against Bowring, he remained loyal to his friend. He even joined in the fruitless suggestion that Bowring might be appointed consul for the Greek government in England.[63] His sympathy for the Deputies soon evaporated, and in August 1825 he described his relationship with them in the bitterest terms:

Such a compound of ignorance, groundless suspicion, insincerity, faith-lessness, incivility, negligence, quarrelsomeness, weakness of judgment,

---

[61] See LGC papers, vol. x, fo. G, Bentham to Bowring, 20 Mar. 1824.

[62] UC xii. 252–62, Bentham to Orlandos and Louriottis, 22–3 Mar. 1824. See also LGC papers, vol. x, fo. I.

[63] Ibid. Bartle, 'Bowring and the Greek Loans of 1824 and 1825', 63, citing a letter from Orlandos and Louriottis to Archbishop Ignatius on 26 April 1824, suggests that the proposal was made after the dispute between Orlandos and Louriottis and Bowring, but Bentham's letter reveals that it might have been made in the midst of the dispute as a way of reconciling Bowring and the Deputies. Furthermore, the suggestion may have originally come from Joseph Hume (or possibly from Bowring himself), but not from Bentham (as Bartle suggests), although Bentham vigorously supported the proposal.

pride, vain-gloriousness, frivolity, and in the whole together incapacity for political business, I could not have conceived unless I had witnessed it. To me, from first to the last, their expressions were full of the same affection and respect. But, all hopes of bringing them into any good course having compleatly failed, I at last pleaded by occupations as an excuse for ceasing to correspond with them, and declining to receive a colleague of theirs, Zaime, upon his arrival here. I have but too much reason for the apprehension that they are but a fair specimen of their Countrymen at home. A guerilla warfare seems to be all they are fit for.[64]

As for the control of the first Greek loan, events soon overtook the flimsy arrangements made by Bowring and the London Greek Committee. When the first instalment reached Greece, Byron was dead and Stanhope was preparing to return with Byron's body to England. Gordon, who was to replace Stanhope, eventually refused to go to Greece at this time, as did Hobhouse who had agreed at one point to replace Byron. In effect there were no approved British Commissioners to supervise the payment of the loan until Hamilton Browne and H. Lytton Bulwer arrived just before the third instalment of the loan reached Greece. The earlier instalments were held at Zante by the bankers Barff and Logotheti who refused to release the funds supposedly because there were not enough Commissioners to supervise the distribution. As the Greek government was desperate for money, Blaquiere, who arrived with the first instalment, managed to raise a modest sum on the security of the funds in the bank. At last, Barff, on his own initiative, paid the money directly to the Greek government, and when Hamilton Browne and Lytton Bulwer arrived, they were in a poor bargaining position. They were hardly known in Greece and did not possess the stature of Byron and Stanhope. With £80,000 of the loan already paid to the Greeks, concessions from them for the additional £50,000 would be hard to obtain. The third instalment of £50,000 slipped through their hands as they fell seriously ill, and they received little more than a receipt for the loan. Abandoning negotiations, they returned to England.[65]

It is impossible to say if Bentham's plan would have fared better, but his emphasis on ensuring the continuity of Commissioners in

---

[64] Bentham to Simon Bolivar, 13 Aug. 1825, in *The Iberian Correspondence of Jeremy Bentham*, ed. P. Schwartz, 2 vols. (London and Madrid, 1979) ii. 907.
[65] See St Clair, *That Greece Might Still Be Free*, 215–16; Dakin, *British and American Philhellenes*, 84 ff.

Greece pointed to a serious fault in Bowring's strategy. Further-more, Bentham's awareness of the need to reconcile the Greeks by securing their interests as well as those of the lenders and, in addition, the need to persuade the Deputies of the identity of interest between lenders, contractors, Deputies, Commissioners, and the Westernized Greeks, such as Mavrokordatos and Koundouriottis, might have enabled some recovery to take place in the standing of the loan in London.

Nevertheless, neither the Deputies nor Bowring could fully respond to the ideas presented, largely because they approached the problem in ways that did not admit of solution. The nationalism of the Greek Deputies tended to obscure their perceptions of interest which should have made them less suspicious of the contractors of the loan and the London Greek Committee in London. Bowring's moralistic position led him to deny the importance of incentives for the Greeks and to miss a fairly simple accommodation of the aspirations of the Greek Deputies. However clear was Bentham's vision, he could not persuade those who were unable to see clearly what was at issue.

PART II

IDEOLOGY

And those who claim to be the originators and leaders of these revolutions do not originate or lead anything; their sole merit is identical with that of the adventurers who have discovered most of the unknown lands, namely the courage to go straight ahead while the wind blows.

(Alexis de Tocqueville, *Recollections*)

In 1823, London was peopled with exiles of every kind and every country; constitutionalists who would have but one chamber, constitutionalists who wished for two; constitutionalists after the French model, after the Spanish, the American; generals, dismissed presidents of republics, presidents of parliaments dissolved at the point of the bayonet, presidents of cortes dispersed by the bomb-shell; the widow of the Negro chief king Christophe, with the two princesses, her daughters, of the true royal blood, 'black and all black;' the dethroned Emperor of Mexico; and whole swarms of journalists, poets, and men of letters. London was the Elysium (a satirist would say, the Botany Bay) of illustrious men and would-be heroes.

(Count G. Pecchio, *Semi-serious Observations of an Italian Exile*)

7

Blaquiere's Liberalism and Mediterranean Nationalism

Edward Blaquiere, impetuous and often impecunious Irishman of Huguenot descent, English naval officer during the Napoleonic wars, and early apostle of liberalism, had numerous intellectual heroes, but two were especially memorable: Niccolò Machiavelli and Jeremy Bentham.[1] He admired the *Discourses on Livy* and regretted that so few read this work instead of the *Prince*.[2] For the regeneration of Italy in the early nineteenth century, Blaquiere believed that the task would be difficult but could be eased somewhat not only by the study of Machiavelli's *Discourses* but also by a 'proper application of Mr. Bentham's principle of utility', both of which 'would shew the people of Italy that sound morals are the indispensable companions of good government'.[3]

The conjunction of Machiavelli and Bentham will strike some readers as odd, especially as Bentham himself wrote 'Anti-Machiavel' letters early in his career. Blaquiere's enthusiasm for Machiavelli may only have been temporary, and he is eager to point to others, besides Machiavelli and Bentham, such as Bacon, Grotius, Beccaria, Filangieri, and Montesquieu, who have contributed to the advancement of 'moral and political science'.[4] Nevertheless, the joining of Machiavelli and Bentham reveals a good deal about Blaquiere, especially that conjunction of ruthlessness and political idealism which characterized his approach to politics.

Blaquiere's books are not now read, and he is known, if at all, mostly from studies of philhellenism and Byron and, to a lesser

---

[1] See Signor F. Pananti, *Narrative of a Residence in Algiers*, ed. E. Blaquiere (London, 1818), 458 n.–60 n. (editor's note).

[2] Blaquiere also admired the *Prince* and believed that the work had never 'formed a single tyrant'. He was prepared to argue that 'the works of no writer furnish a more unexceptionable body of maxims, in favour of religion, morality, and good government, than those of Niccolò Machiavelli' (ibid. 460 n.).

[3] Ibid. 457.

[4] Ibid. 459 n.

extent, as a follower of Bentham. To William St Clair, his ideas are 'unexceptionable' and his books are 'an unattractive mixture of instant history, conventional sentiment, and tired rhetoric'.[5] John Bowring, whose friendship with Blaquiere cooled after the latter had returned to London in 1824, deliberately understated his importance both to Greece and to Bentham in his biography of Bentham so that Blaquiere's importance at this time has not been appreciated.[6] Bowring omitted to point out that it was through Blaquiere that he was able to meet Bentham for the first time in 1820, and he seems to have forgotten the warm public thanks he gave to Blaquiere, upon being released from prison in France in 1822, for his active support.[7]

Due to the judgements of various modern writers and Bowring's intentional minimization of Blaquiere's importance, his writings and political ideas have been virtually ignored. In the 1820s, however, no foreigner was more highly regarded in Greece. When Bulwer wrote that 'Mr. Blaquiere though even these people smile at his enthusiastic accounts of their country, is by far the most popular foreigner who has visited it',[8] Alerino Palma, the Italian philhellene whose *Greece Vindicated* prompted the investigations into the Greek loan, criticized Bulwer for suggesting that the Greeks were smiling about Blaquiere's writings, when, in fact, only those in England who had adopted the opposing doctrine of Stanhope were smiling. Palma praised Blaquiere as follows:

I can pay Mr. Blaquiere a well-merited tribute by thus publicly saying, that of all the persons sent to Greece by the Committee, not one has been able

[5] W. St Clair, *That Greece Might Still Be Free* (London, 1972), 141; see also D. Dakin, *British and American Philhellenes during the War of Greek Independence, 1821–1833* (Thessaloniki, 1955), 43, where Blaquiere is called 'that radical, international busybody'. Among writers on Byron and philhellenism, only Harold Nicolson (*Byron: The Last Journey, April 1823–April 1824*, (new edn., London, 1948), 67, 277) portrays Blaquiere in a sympathetic manner.

[6] See Bowring, x. 474–5, 514–15. See also C. Gobbi, 'Edward Blaquière: Agente del liberalismo', *Cuadernos Hispano-americanos*, 350 (1979), 306–25.

[7] See J. Bowring, *Details of the Arrest, Imprisonment and Liberation, of an Englishman, by the Bourbon Government of France* (London, 1823): 'My excellent friend Blaquiere (whose name I cannot introduce without the expression of the warmest gratitude and admiration, for the courage, ardor, and devotion, with which he has pleaded my cause, and watched over and consoled my sufferings,), was with me at that moment, and accompanied me to the Town-house' (8). Note that the failure to acknowledge the importance of Blaquiere was repeated in the posthumously published *The Autobiographical Recollections of Sir John Bowring*, ed. L. B. Bowring (London, 1877).

[8] H. Lytton Bulwer, *An Autumn in Greece* (London, 1826), 104.

like himself to conciliate the affections of the nation. He is looked upon as a Greek, and, according to the constitution modified at Astros, he can at any time be admitted to the advantages, which are enjoyed by the Greeks themselves.[9]

In the opinion of these contemporary commentators, Blaquiere's effectiveness and popularity in Greece far surpassed even those of Byron. But such was not the case in England. Hobhouse minimized his importance as early as July 1823 in writing to Byron: 'Never fear about Blaquiere, he is not our agent. We pay some of his expenses and he writes us letters but he is not in your line and cannot be in your way.'[10] And by the time Blaquiere returned to England in 1824, following his attempted delivery of the first instalment of the Greek loan, his views were wholly out of favour.[11]

1. Blaquiere, Bowring, and Bentham

To understand the varying reactions to Blaquiere in Greece and in England, it is perhaps best to begin with an account of his relationship with Bentham, for it is from this relationship that the London Greek Committee was eventually established and, without it, it would never have flourished. Bentham had known the naval officer (never higher in rank than a lieutenant) at least since 1813, when the first reference to Blaquiere occurs in Bentham's correspondence.[12] Blaquiere had earlier read Bentham's *Traités de législation* (1802) and had even purchased in 1806 a copy for the garrison library in Gibraltar.[13] His first letter to Bentham coincided with the publication of Blaquiere's first book, *Letters from the Mediterranean*, containing numerous references to the *Traités* and

[9] Count Alerino Palma, *Greece Vindicated* (London, 1826), 269.

[10] *Byron's Bulldog: The Letters of John Cam Hobhouse to Lord Byron*, ed. P. W. Graham (Columbus, Oh., 1984), 335 (Hobhouse to Byron, 8 July 1823). See also BL Add. MS 36460, fo. 123, Hume to Hobhouse, 16 Sept. 1823.

[11] For the dispute with Stanhope and Blaquiere's return to England, see Ch. 9 below.

[12] See *Correspondence*, viii (1809–16), ed. S. R. Conway (Oxford, 1988) (*CW*), 330–2, Blaquiere to Bentham, 7 July 1813.

[13] See E. Blaquiere, *An Historical Review of the Spanish Revolution* (London, 1822), 547.

high praise for Bentham himself.[14] Although Blaquiere quoted from a number of prominent authors of the Enlightenment, such as Voltaire and Rousseau, he clearly had a special place for Bentham. Bentham regarded this obvious attempt at flattery as one of Blaquiere's 'eccentricities', though he allowed Blaquiere to visit him where 'in the course of a year or two he partook several times of such potatoes and water as the hermitage affords'.[15] After this brief contact, Blaquiere ceased to correspond or visit, and Bentham ascribed this not to any ill-feeling but, as he wrote to his brother, to 'the finding himself perhaps not able to satisfy to his own satisfaction this or that question which he apprehended might be put to him'.[16]

After he left the navy, Blaquiere had no obvious source of income and lived in Paris, 'a place of abode which state of his finances renders a rather more convenient one than London'.[17] Blaquiere seemed short of funds and certain of his expenses were paid by Bentham for his services in Spain and Greece and by the London Greek Committee.[18] He often wrote to Bowring during his fund-raising tour around Britain for additional money for his expenses, and it was Bentham who paid for his first journey to Greece in 1823.[19] Although his father was an officer in the British army and the family was supposedly connected to that of Lord John de Blaquiere, there is evidence that some members of the family lived in considerable poverty in Ireland.[20]

Blaquiere must have earned some money from his books and journalism, but it is not clear exactly what he did between 1814 and 1819 when he again came into contact with Bentham. Bentham described him in 1820 as 'in all points perfectly honourable and spotless-benevolent disinterested generous yet not prodigal, [but]

---

[14] See *Letters from the Mediterranean*, 2 vols. (London, 1813), i. 218 n.–219 nn., 284 n., 303 n.–304 n., 382–3 and n.; ii. 294 n.

[15] UC x. 25–9, Bentham to Baron De Lessert, 28 Nov. 1820.

[16] BL Add. MS 33545, fos. 443–6, Bentham to Samuel Bentham, Sept. 1820.

[17] UC x. 25–9, Bentham to De Lessert, 28 Nov. 1820.

[18] See Hobhouse to Byron (n. 10 above); LGC papers, vol. xi, fo. O[5], Blaquiere's accounts (1824); BL Add. MS 33545, fos. 436–8, Bentham to Samuel Bentham, 11 Aug. 1820; UC xii. 119, Blaquiere to Bentham, 8 Aug. 1823.

[19] See e.g. LGC papers, vol. vii, fo. X, Blaquiere to Bowring, 22 Jan. 1824; fo. Y, Blaquiere to Bowring, n.d.; UC xii. 119, Blaquiere to Bentham, 8 Aug. 1823.

[20] See Gobbi, 'Edward Blaquière: Agente del liberalismo'; UC x. 25–9, Bentham to De Lessert, 28 Nov. 1820; LGC papers, vol. vii, fo. X, Blaquiere to Bowring, 22 Jan. 1824.

there is a good deal of the Irish enthusiasm, and a little more than enough of Irish impetuosity and eccentricity in his turn of mind'.[21]

By the time Bentham wrote these words in 1820, Blaquiere had again entered his life. He wrote from Southampton that he was about to set out for Spain to witness 'a great people struggling for their liberties'.[22] He also intended (though he did not make this clear to Bentham) to collect materials for a book and, using his various letters of introduction and copies of Bentham's books, to see if the new government might make use of Bentham's ideas.[23]

Blaquiere felt that the impending meeting of the Cortes would propose modifications of the constitution of 1812, and he suggested that Bentham present 'the ameliorations which appear necessary to render it complete'. If they reached him in Madrid, he assured Bentham that these proposals 'shall find their way to the fountain head'.[24] A further letter from Bordeaux informed Bentham that Blaquiere was planning to arrange for the translation of the *Traités* into Spanish, and Bentham was stimulated by these letters to develop his writings on colonies intended to persuade the Cortes 'to emancipate all Spanish America'.[25] When Blaquiere reached Madrid in June 1820, he quickly arranged with his main contact, José Joaquín de Mora, the editor of the liberal daily newspaper *El Constitucional*, for a translation of the *Traités* and eventually other Dumont versions of Bentham's works into Spanish. He also encouraged Bentham to send him other writings which he would attempt to publish.[26] By early August, Bentham was in possession of a translated extract from *El Español Constitucional*, published monthly in London, which revealed that the Cortes, in formulating new civil and criminal codes, 'will invite the celebrated English jurisconsult, Mr. *Jeremy Bentham*, if he should be inclined to go to Spain to contribute, by his own vast acquirements, to the great

---

[21] UC x. 25–9, Bentham to De Lessert, 28 Nov. 1820.
[22] *Correspondence*, ix (1817–20), ed. S. Conway (Oxford, 1989) (*CW*), 430, Blaquiere to Bentham, 4 May 1820.
[23] Ibid.
[24] Ibid. 430–1.
[25] Ibid. 458–9, Bentham to Blaquiere, 5 June 1820.
[26] Ibid. 493–7, Blaquiere to Bentham, 26 June 1820. Note that this plan was temporarily suspended as another translator, Ramón Salás, was brought to his attention. See BL Add. MS 33545, fo. 431, Blaquiere to Samuel Bentham, 6 July 1820. See also P. Schwartz, 'Bentham's Influence in Spain, Portugal, and Latin America', *Bentham Newsletter*, 1 (1978), 34–5.

work of our legislation'.[27] The 'invitation' was obviously inspired by Blaquiere, and if Bentham was unwilling to go to Spain, he was very willing to codify. All he required was 'encouragement', by which he meant 'from a competent quarter, a competent assurance that, as soon as brought to light, it would receive the requisite attention, and take its chance of being put to use'.[28]

If in June Blaquiere had set off for Spain, by September he had apparently created a stage on to which Bentham was being applauded supposedly to act his greatest part. From Bentham's perspective events in Spain seemed especially favourable not only to liberal views in general but also to his more theoretical efforts at codification. Blaquiere's letters were full of news and made it seem as if in the struggles then going on in Spain the future of liberal civilization was at stake. He also did not fail to link Spain with other European struggles, especially that going on in Naples. 'Public attention, at Madrid', he wrote at one point, 'is said to be divided between the proceedings of the Cortes and the patriots of Italy. Having felt the blessings of freedom here, their sympathy has become more acute than that which is experienced amongst those nations of Europe that are as yet in a state of comparative slavery.'[29]

With Blaquiere in Spain, a friend of his named John Bowring, 'a young mercantile man', used his connection with Blaquiere to try to establish contact with Bentham and, though he presented a pamphlet of his own and various letters he had received from Blaquiere, Bentham would not spare the time to see him.[30]

---

[27] UC xxii. 85. Bentham was obviously pleased to receive this invitation, but he decided to decline, as he felt unable to travel to Spain. He proposed instead that the Spanish Ministers of Justice and Finance nominate two young Spaniards to take up residence at 19 York Street and share Bentham's garden, where he would 'convert them into legislative draughtsmen, and as I produced they might translate' (BL Add. MS 33545, fos. 436–8, Bentham to Samuel Bentham, 11 Aug. 1820).

[28] BL Add. MS 33551, fos. 1–20, Bentham to Mora, 19 Sept. 1820.

[29] Blaquiere to Bentham, 15 Aug. 1820, printed in the *Traveller* on 28 August 1820. Blaquiere was perhaps more candid when he admitted in 1828 that Louriottis, for example, was poorly treated when he first came to Spain in 1823 to obtain assistance for the Greek cause. 'His reception among the Spanish Liberals was not very creditable.' E. Blaquiere, *Letters from Greece; with Remarks on the Treaty of Intervention* (London, 1828), p. xx n.

[30] UC xiii. 7, Bentham to E. Bell, 5 Sept. 1820; BL Add. MS 33545, fos. 443–6, Bentham to S. Bentham, 5 Sept. 1820. The pamphlet Bowring gave to Bentham was *Observations on the State of Religion and Literature in Spain, made during a Journey through the Peninsula in 1819* (London, 1819). The copy in the British Library (CT

Nevertheless, Bentham soon appreciated the fact (as Bowring doubtlessly informed him) that Bowring had numerous contacts of his own in Spain and especially in the Cortes.[31] Within a month of his refusing to see Bowring, Bentham could write to him: 'Now that you have taken me under your protection, there are some hopes for me.'[32] With Blaquiere in Spain and Bowring in London, the pattern which was to mature in the context of Greece was now established. From Bentham's point of view, Blaquiere was 'disinterestedness and generosity itself'.[33] And soon Bowring was 'one of the most extraordinary, if not the most extraordinary man, I ever saw in my life'.[34]

Bentham awaited only what would be the most elusive invitation— that the Spanish Cortes would invite him to draft a code or set of codes.[35] 'You never knew Bentham in better health, or more animated than he is now,' wrote James Mill in June 1821, but he also added prophetically: 'If out of all this we should get him engaged in the making of a code, it would be well; but in the mean time a great deal of precious time is wasted.'[36] Perhaps from his antipathy towards Bowring, who so quickly became a valuable ally of Bentham, Mill was able to see through all the activity generated by Blaquiere and Bowring and appreciate that far from advancing Bentham's ideas as a theorist and philosopher, they were merely using Bentham to enhance the liberal political doctrines in which they so fervently believed. Blaquiere and Bowring had created a stage for the advancement of ideology, on which Bentham was to play a special role as the most celebrated jurist of his day. Bentham himself saw the stage as an opportunity (through the construction of various codes) to link theory with practice. He soon learned that this was not to be the case first in Spain, then in Portugal, and finally in Greece.

127 (1)) is inscribed to Bentham with Bowring's name and address, as though he hoped to use it to start a correspondence. See also UC cvi. 252, Colls's Diary entry for 4 August 1820 recording Bowring's first visit.

[31] BL Add. MS 33545, fos. 443–6, Bentham to Samuel Bentham, 5 Sept. 1820.
[32] Bowring, x. 516. Bentham to Bowring, Sept. 1820.
[33] BL Add. MS 33551, fos. 22–33, Bentham to Mora, 22 Sept. 1820.
[34] UC x. 57–64, Bentham to Blaquiere, 9–19 Dec. 1820.
[35] See *Constitutional Code*, i, ed. F. Rosen and J. H. Burns (Oxford, 1983) (*CW*), pp. xi ff.
[36] Dumont MSS, Geneva, 76/21–2, Mill to Dumont, 8 June 1821, *Iberian Correspondence of Jeremy Bentham*, ed. P. Schwartz, 2 vols. (London, 1979), i. 539.

Bentham was already widely read in Spain by lawyers and men of letters who had known Dumont's *Traités* since its publication in 1802. Blaquiere and Bowring found there a ready audience for the play they were to enact. The play, however, was not one based on Bentham's theory, nor was it even Benthamism, but a variation of nineteenth-century liberalism. In a revealing letter to Dumont, written in November 1820, just after he had left Spain to return to Paris to work on his book, Blaquiere sketched out a proposal 'to promote a closer union and clearer understanding between the liberal thinkers throughout Europe'.[37] Dumont was supposedly to represent the Genevan republic; Blaquiere reported confidently that he would gain the support of Bentham 'not to mention . . . all those distinguished characters who form his circle'. In Paris, he claimed to have already the support of Benjamin Constant and his friends and felt confident that he could enlist leading men in Spain, Naples, and Portugal. As for Germany 'and the other northern parts of Europe', he added with less confidence that he would be forthcoming with suggestions when he had received Dumont's initial response to his proposal. The proposal was as follows:

to establish a *bureau de correspondance* at Paris—and that the communications sent here from different points, should be published once or twice in each month. We should thus be enabled to concentrate the *public opinion* of Europe in the french Capital, and I need scarcely point out to your penetrating mind, what a powerful influence such a work must exercise, as also its effect in successfully opposing the encroachment of tyranny and arbitrary power.[38]

The omission of Germany and 'the other northern parts of Europe' from the proposal shows what emphasis Blaquiere placed on the development of liberal ideas in the currently volatile Mediterranean basin, to which he had brought the thought of Bentham. But what he had brought was Bentham, the liberal, who was willing to devote his time to work for freedom in these countries. Where Mill was apprehensive that Bentham might have been wasting valuable time, Blaquiere wrote with pride that Bentham had 'occupied himself incessantly with the interests of Spain during the last six months'.[39]

---

[37] Dumont MSS, 74/83–8, Blaquiere to Dumont, Nov. 1820, *Iberian Correspondence*, i. 358.   [38] Ibid. i. 359.   [39] Ibid.

2. Blaquiere's Doctrine

Blaquiere's proposal reflects his conception of the practical use of ideas. Liberal thinkers from all over Europe were to cultivate public opinion to oppose tyranny and advance liberal ideas. The proposal may seem harmless enough, and the Bentham who is portrayed was the Bentham already seen by Europeans—the Enlightenment figure whose ideas on punishment, law, and so on were appropriate to nations professing 'liberal opinions'. Was not Blaquiere merely supplying the link with practice as a devoted disciple should?

To answer this question in the affirmative would be to ignore the existence of Blaquiere's own political doctrine which consisted of two somewhat incompatible ideas. On the one hand, he strongly supported the nationalist aspirations of countries like Spain, Portugal, Italy, and Greece, based on, as he once put it, 'the imprescriptible right of a whole people to legislate for itself'.[40] On the other hand, he looked to an international community of liberals to lead the struggle for national self-determination, and to an alliance between liberalism and constitutionalism which would legitimize and make possible the concrete realization of this 'imprescriptible right'. The right of national self-determination, however, became the most important right in his liberal credo.

Blaquiere's position developed slowly in his writings. In 1813, he exhibited mostly an attraction to the Mediterranean countries and an interest in their 'regeneration', but he did not explicitly identify this regeneration with nationalism. The perspective he adopted was, for the most part, that of a British naval officer. For example, he followed an anti-French line and pointed out the strategic value of the Mediterranean area to Britain, especially in relation to the eastern empire.[41] In his later writings, his attitude towards France and, for that matter, Britain and the United States became more critical. For example, he criticized the United States for not helping to liberate South America, and Britain, having 'liberated Europe from the iron yoke of Bonaparte', for not proclaiming the independence of South America.[42] As for France, despite his

---

[40] Count G. Pecchio, *Anecdotes of the Spanish and Portuguese Revolutions*, ed. E. Blaquiere (London, 1823), p. viii.

[41] E. Blaquiere, *Letters from the Mediterranean*, i, p. vi.

[42] Pananti, *Narrative of a Residence in Algiers*, 14 n., 400 n.–401 n.

appreciation of the role of the French Revolution in influencing movements for the 'regeneration' of the Mediterranean, he was highly critical of the regime which was to attack Spain in 1823, and he was never sympathetic to Napoleon ('one of the greatest enemies public liberty has had in Europe') whose navy he had opposed for many years.[43]

In place of the Holy Alliance, Blaquiere looked to liberal opinion and liberal parties in numerous countries to support nationalist movements. Spain became the first such country to move towards national 'regeneration', and Bentham became the symbol of liberal idealism on an international stage.[44] 'If the Legislator of Queen-square-place be not a Cosmopolite', he asked rhetorically at one point in his book on Spain, 'where is one to be found?'[45]

Although Blaquiere went to Spain ostensibly to collect materials for his own book, he was not a passive observer. Even his efforts on behalf of Bentham were directed at bringing together liberal ideas and nationalist aspirations. He also viewed Spain as part of a movement which had spread to Portugal, Italy, and Greece and would soon spread even further. Nevertheless, the doctrine he espoused was not entirely coherent. As he looked to the nation and its 'regeneration', he seemed to lose sight of the individuals whose liberty he ultimately sought to protect. He was impatient of human diversity and complexity. For example, when writing of religion in Spain, he argued for no limits to religious toleration 'except those which may be opposed to it by morality and reason', and he looked forward to 'the day on which Protestant and Catholic shall meet in the same temple, to adore one common Father, [as] . . . the greatest triumph ever obtained by humanity'.[46] On the other hand, he was critical of the Jews, allowed to return to Spain under the new constitution, for not being sufficiently tolerant of others despite their seeking toleration for themselves.[47] Blaquiere's liberalism did not seem to accommodate so easily the rights of different groups of people in the state as it did the more abstract rights of the nation itself.

[43] Pananti, *Narrative of a Residence in Algiers*, p. xiii.
[44] For references to Bentham in Blaquiere's *An Historical Review of the Spanish Revolution*, see 528, 547, 553–4, 565–7, 582–5.
[45] Ibid. 585 n.
[46] Ibid. p. xi.
[47] Ibid. 547. See St Clair, *That Greece Might Still Be Free*, 208.

3. The Legitimation of Murder

Blaquiere's doctrine developed most fully in the context of Greece, and it is here that the contrast between Bentham's theory and Blaquiere's doctrine becomes most evident. If Bentham's theory might be used in a detached manner to assess the value of various constitutional arrangements and to reveal difficulties, perhaps even fallacies, which are implicit in certain arguments, Blaquiere's writings were more closely related to practice and were used to legitimate various arrangements. Blaquiere wrote as a rhetorician; his aim was to persuade the British to support the Greek cause and he did so in large part by arguing that the cause was a legitimate one.

Blaquiere's *The Greek Revolution* and his earlier *Report on the Present State of the Greek Confederation* were as much part of the events they were intended to depict as they were accounts of them.[48] Both works were closely connected with the establishment of the London Greek Committee itself. The journey to Greece in March 1823 by Blaquiere and Louriottis, carrying Bentham's 'Observations' for the Greek government and stopping at Genoa to enlist the support of Lord Byron, represented the first steps taken by the newly formed Committee, and led to the arrangement of the expedition to be sent to Greece in the autumn of 1823 and later, in 1824, to the first Greek loan. When Blaquiere returned to England he presented his *Report* (with additions) formally to the Committee on 13 and 20 September 1823. On 20 September he also announced in a prospectus that he was preparing his book, *The Greek Revolution*, for the press.[49] At this time Leicester Stanhope replaced him in Greece as the agent of the Committee, while he devoted his time to raising funds for the expedition and working on the book. Blaquiere's writings were thus closely related to the early development of the London Greek Committee. Though it would be wrong to see his views as reflecting or representing those of the Committee as a whole, in so far as many would dissent from aspects of them, it is no exaggeration to claim that these writings

[48] *Report on the Present State of the Greek Confederation* (London, 1823); *The Greek Revolution* (London, 1824).

[49] See L. Droulia, *Philhellénisme: Ouvrages inspirés par la guerre de l'indépendance grecque 1821–1833* (Athens, 1974), 61.

were not only as important to the Greek cause in Britain as any other activities of the London Greek Committee but were also intimately associated with these activities and served as a force for their realization.

Blaquiere's *Report* was widely circulated and attempted to achieve three related ends: firstly, to suggest that Greece had a legitimate constitutional government, as established at Epidaurus in January 1822 and revised at Astros in the autumn of 1822; secondly, to minimize the criticisms of the Greeks for committing atrocities against the Turks; and thirdly, to establish that the British had a duty (or at least that it was in their interest) to support the Greek cause. The arguments advanced in support of these contentions were developed more fully in his longer and more interesting work, *The Greek Revolution*, which was published in 1824.

A major theme of this book was that Turkish rule over Greece was illegitimate, a necessary argument in light of the fact that the Holy Alliance had declared that the Ottoman Empire was and had been the legitimate government in Greece. Blaquiere distinguished between the revolutionary struggles in Italy and Spain on the one hand as civil struggles, and the war in Greece on the other as one against illegitimate rule. The Greeks, in his view, had suffered enormous deprivation and degradation without security of life, liberty, religion, and property. They had, he argued, two sorts of claims on Europe. In the first place the Greeks were the direct descendants of the ancient Greeks whose art and literature formed the basis of European civilization. Secondly, the Greeks were Christians, burdened and oppressed under infidel rule. Furthermore, modern Greece was strongly influenced by the ideas and events of the French Revolution of 1789. The Revolution brought Greece more into contact with Western Europe. Commercial contacts were greatly increased. During the Revolutionary wars there was a rapid expansion of the Greek navy which became a major trading force in the Mediterranean and which brought considerable prosperity to the Islands. But perhaps most important was the spread of education which developed considerably at this time. 'It did not . . . require much discernment to foresee', he observed, 'that this intellectual revolution would, at no very distant day, be followed up by one of another kind.'[50] Events in Europe

[50] *The Greek Revolution*, 18–19.

were not only influential in bringing about the Greek Revolution, they rendered it inevitable.[51] The special position in which Greece found itself at the Congress of Vienna, with Russia (and especially with John Capodistrias, of Greek origin, playing a special role) taking an interest in an independent Greece but with all of their hopes completely dashed, led to an inevitable revolution. The rise of the secret society, the Eteria, could be linked with the failure of Greece to secure the prospect or hope of independence at this time.

Many of the sentiments Blaquiere set forth (especially about the legacy of ancient Greece and the plight of the poor Christians under Ottoman rule) were commonplaces in the pamphlet literature and newspapers of the time. But Blaquiere had a more serious task to accomplish, namely to justify the struggle for Greek independence almost as if it were a modern struggle against 'colonialism' and in the process provide a persuasive argument which amounted to nothing less than the legitimization of murder.

The expression 'the legitimation of murder' may seem too emotive for what might be regarded as the inevitable excesses of such a struggle, where few prisoners were taken and massacres on both sides had occurred. Blaquiere condemned the massacre perpetrated by the Turks at Chios (Scio) in the strongest terms, but his attitude towards the Greeks' massacre of Turks at Tripolizza in October 1821 was different. Before examining Blaquiere's argument, let us consider this account of the Tripolizza massacre taken from the journal of the philhellene W. H. Humphreys:

As soon as the Greeks had entered the town in force, they [the Turks] sued for quarter, but in vain; the barbarians [the Greeks] went from house to house sparing neither age nor sex, and the work of slaughter continued the whole night. . . . The fires, shots, screams of agony and terror, and shouts of these monsters formed a night of dreadful horror. . . . Never was a town so completely pillaged: not the most trivial article was to be found in the houses, the boards were ripped up in the search for plunder, the windows and doors were broken up, and not even a single lock left to them.

As they were thus busied in pillaging, it was not till the third day after the assault that these wretches, as if not satisfied with the number of victims they had already devoted to most cruel deaths, determined on destroying those [women and children] that remained in the huts of the old camp. They stripped and drove them away intending to shoot them near a

[51] See ibid. 24.

deep pit at some distance from Tripolitsa; but the thirst for blood was too great to enable them to wait so long, and they covered the road to the spot destined for their butchery with bodies of women clasping their infants to their bosoms and children clinging to their mother. . . .

The hour of retribution for the Turks had come and nowhere could fitter executioners have been found. However deserved, however well merited might have been their fate, yet it could not make the perpetrators of it less detestable nor hardly less guilty. 'We have done no more to them than they used to do to us,' was always their excuse. . . .

They disabled their prisoners by cutting off their arms and legs and then lighted fires under them while yet alive to burn them slowly to death, and they severed the heads of the most lovely female forms and replaced them with the heads of dogs for their sport.

Such are the modern Greeks, debased, degraded to the lowest pit of barbarism. [That] they are unworthy of·emancipation, is a natural idea which their national and individual depravity gives rise to.[52]

In another passage, Humphreys agreed with Lord Byron that, to remove the causes of this depravity, the Greeks needed their liberty rather than continued slavery, but none the less, as we have seen in the material quoted above, he condemned unreservedly the Greek massacre and the character it reflected.

Although Blaquiere did not deny that atrocities took place, he would not condemn the Greeks for committing them. He also tried to set the record straight by correcting some false reports of the massacre which had appeared in Raffenel's *Histoire des événemens de la Grèce*.[53] It was not true, he asserted, that several hundred Greeks died while fighting among themselves for the spoils.[54] Nor was it true that the Albanians who were promised safe conduct as they left Tripolizza were killed.[55] They left under an arrangement, with their arms, for Epirus. Blaquiere was most probably correct, but close attention to such details as these does not minimize the horror of what occurred, and one cannot help feeling that Blaquiere was more concerned with minimizing the massacre than with close attention to historical fact.[56] For the most part, Blaquiere repeated the arguments he used in the *Report*, but developed them in considerable detail. He appreciated that Tripolizza was a double

[52] *W. H. Humprheys' First 'Journal of the Greek War of Independence'*, ed. Sture Linnér (Stockholm, 1967), 62–5.   [53] Paris, 1822.
[54] Ibid. 372–3. See Blaquiere, *The Greek Revolution*, 146–7.
[55] Raffenel, *Histoire*, 371; Blaquiere, *The Greek Revolution*, 147.
[56] See Blaquiere, *The Greek Revolution*, 146–7.

disaster for the Greeks. It alienated European supporters by showing a side of the Greeks which left little to distinguish them from the Turks, and by acknowledging that the Greek government was ineffectual in that it could not control the chiefs and soldiers who supposedly fought in its name. Furthermore, as none of the considerable booty which was found at Tripolizza was obtained by the government itself, the government failed to acquire any financial stability or security from this notable victory. The booty went to the irregular chiefs and their followers.

Nevertheless, he refused to condemn the Greeks for the massacre, and put forward two arguments which he used both in the *Report* and in *The Greek Revolution*. The first was that this sort of massacre was neither rare nor confined to uncivilized countries, and the second was that the previous actions of the Turks accounted for, if not justified, the actions of the Greeks. As for the first argument, he took the view in the *Report* that the excesses committed at Tripolizza, when all the circumstances were known, 'will appear mild, when compared to those committed by the best disciplined and most civilized troops in Europe in many instances during the last fifty years'.[57] In *The Greek Revolution*, he wrote:

Those who so harshly judge the conduct of the Greeks at Trippoliza, and other points, would do well to recollect the battle of Agincourt, Siege of Magdeburgh, ravages in the Palatinate under Turenne, the treatment of the Scotch after the battle of Culloden, various events of the North American war, the massacre of both parties in Ireland, the assaults of Jamael, Prague, and Belgrade; not to mention the many other instances of cruelty, which stain the page of history.[58]

Blaquiere was not suggesting that massacres like Tripolizza occurred often among civilized states, but that there were times when the social compact broke down and such results had followed. Thus, Greece might be no different from other civilized societies when it had a settled government within an independent state. Nevertheless, his argument was not Hobbesian, in that Hobbes might well have settled for the restoration of Turkish rule. Blaquiere was more ambitious: he sought national independence and self-government and was willing to justify murder and massacre to achieve it.

As for the view that the Greeks were as barbarous as the Turks,

[57] Blaquiere, *Report*, 11.   [58] Blaquiere, *The Greek Revolution*, 154 n.

Blaquiere thought on the one hand that the excesses of the Greek soldiers had been 'most wantonly exaggerated' and on the other hand, given the experience of oppression by the Turks, such excesses might be excused.[59] With regard to Tripolizza, he wrote, 'that animosity which generally inflames the victorious assailant, was aggravated by the accumulated oppressions of centuries, and by recent atrocities on the part of the infidels, of so dreadful a caste, that they seemed to cry aloud for retribution and vengeance'.[60] 'If it could be shewn,' he continued, 'that the infidels had preserved the life of a single armed Greek who fell into their hands, from the breaking out of the contest till the storming of Tripolizza, then, indeed, might there be something like a plausible pretext for a great deal of what has been said.'[61] Even the disease which broke out in Tripolizza from the dead bodies following the massacre and which forced the Greeks to abandon the town was 'caught probably from the Turks'.[62]

4. Constitutionalism and the Greek People

The task of legitimizing murder was not confined to justifying massacre or making scapegoats of the Turks. Blaquiere also needed to present the Greeks in the most positive light—as Europeans capable of settled constitutional government, able and willing to repay their debts, and closely identified with the ideals of the European Enlightenment. He dwelled at length not only on the provisional constitution of Epidaurus but especially on the convention at Astros which met to revise the constitution. Whatever the realities of Greek politics (and Blaquiere was not blind to them), he presented a picture of constitutional progress in Greece which would have impressed the Greeks themselves. 'The assemblage of a congress at Epidaurus', he wrote, 'has been justly regarded as a new era in the Greek Revolution.'[63] He emphasized 'the anxiety of all classes to witness the formation of a government' and the qualifications of the sixty or so representatives, many of whom 'had for the most part received a liberal education in the west of

[59] Blaquiere, *Report*, 11; *The Greek Revolution*, 146.
[60] Blaquiere, *The Greek Revolution*, 146. [61] Ibid. 148.
[62] Ibid. 168. [63] Ibid. 177.

Europe'.[64] Blaquiere depicted the subsequent meeting at Astros in the following terms: 'Whether we regard the importance of the measures decided there, or the dignity and moderation with which the deliberations were carried on, the meeting at Astros may be justly considered as one of the most impressive and interesting events of the struggle.'[65]

The deliberations at Astros, where consideration was given to new constitutional provisions, the development of civil and penal codes, the introduction of public education, and the establishment of agencies for collecting taxes, were 'more calculated to illustrate the real spirit of the cause for which Greece is contending'.[66] Blaquiere was well aware that his account of Greek constitutional development was incomplete, that one had to consider the realities as well as the aspirations. 'The attempt to regenerate a people who have been long weighed down by tyranny, and exposed to the influence of a corrupt and demoralizing government,' he wrote, 'is a task of infinite difficulty, and must ever encounter obstacles almost insurmountable.'[67] With regard to the adoption in Greece of Bentham's constitutional theory, he appreciated the fact that 'Greece may not be enabled to profit by his [Bentham's] sublime and benevolent labours so soon as the friends of humanity could wish'.[68]

Nevertheless, what mattered to Blaquiere was the aspiration and not the reality, for it was the aspiration of the Greeks to develop an independent European constitutional government which provided the legitimizing force in his political doctrine. The aspiration was so strong and elevated that the means to achieve the end, however brutal, could be explained away. If, for Bentham, the constitution of Epidaurus was an ideal which he might explore critically and in the process provide support for the aspirations of the Westernized Greeks while urging them to adopt an even better constitution, for Blaquiere, the ideal itself became reality in the sense that it could be used to legitimate massacre and plunder. In the deadly realm of ideology, the distinction between virtues and vices become blurred. The same people were at once 'weighed down by tyranny, and exposed to the influence of a corrupt and demoralizing government'[69] and possessed of 'as much, if not more virtue

[64] Ibid. 177–8.   [65] *Report*, 6.   [66] Ibid. 9.
[67] *The Greek Revolution*, 117.   [68] Ibid. 310 n.   [69] Ibid. 117.

among the Greek peasantry than any other in Europe'.[70] At times, his assertions approached the realm of fantasy as when he compared the Greeks with the newly independent Latin Americans:

However invidious it may be thought to institute a comparison between the Greeks and those nations of the southern hemisphere, who have shaken off a yoke scarcely less galling than that of the infidels, the immense superiority of the former in almost every quality and attribute required by those who would enter the arduous career of national independence, must strike the most superficial observer.[71]

Or when referring to the potential prosperity of the Greeks, he could write: '[It] is surely no exaggeration to say, that, with a population at once so ingenious and industrious, a climate unequalled, and a soil the most productive that could be named, their prospect of wealth and prosperity is almost boundless.'[72] For Blaquiere, the true basis of the Greek government lay with the people, and the people had the capacity to resist those Greeks who did not subscribe to the aspirations which Blaquiere had identified as legitimate. In attempting to rebut the assertion that Greek politics was full of dissent and faction, he wrote:

It is a most remarkable fact, that in all the disputes which have arisen between the leaders in Greece, the people have invariably maintained the strictest neutrality, never taking any share or mixing themselves up with either party. It would, in truth, be impossible to witness the celebrated, but not always infallible, maxim of *vox populi vox dei* more exactly realised than in the undeviating line of conduct observed by a people who had been so long erased from the list of nations.[73]

Blaquiere was trying to argue that the ordinary people had the means and the will to resist men such as Kollokotronis and the other chiefs who led irregular forces and who opposed efforts to establish a national government. It was true that the ordinary Greek was oppressed as much by these Greeks as he was by the Turks, and would have no reason to be particularly well disposed towards them. But it was also true that the success of these chiefs against the Turks made them far more popular than the Westernized Greeks such as Mavrokordatos whom Blaquiere supported but who were unable to mount successful military campaigns against the Turks.

---

[70] *The Greek Revolution*, 296.   [71] Ibid. 303–4.   [72] Ibid. 302.
[73] Ibid. 311 n.

'The people', for Blaquiere, became an abstraction, yet not one without the capacity to strike at their leaders. For example, he suggested at one point that the captains and the primates of the Morea who acted without principle and purely to advance their own interests were 'held in just abhorrence by the people, but so closely watched, that the time is not far distant when they will be called upon to render a terrible account for their misdeeds and perfidy'.[74] So powerful and watchful a court of final judgement could only be an abstraction—representing the Greek nation as Blaquiere thought it should be. Blaquiere fully understood the power and appeal of nationalism, even if he failed to appreciate its dangers.

[74] Ibid. 312–13.

8
Stanhope's Liberalism

'It is necessary to state', wrote Leicester Stanhope in 1857 (he was then the earl of Harrington) 'that I have been a liberal in politics all my life.'[1] What he meant by this declaration is by no means clear. Throughout his life, and especially in his youth, Stanhope, though a professional soldier, had been engaged in political controversy, mostly on the side of reform.[2] *The Military Commentator* (1813), his first pamphlet, contained a thorough critique of several aspects of military law and an especially strong attack on the practice of flogging.[3] The publication of the pamphlet, even anonymously, displayed a good deal of courage, as his printer and publisher, John Drakard, had suffered a £200 fine and a sentence of eighteen months for seditious libel after publishing an attack on flogging two years earlier.[4]

Stanhope achieved public notice from his campaign in India in favour of liberty of the press, which culminated in the suppression of the *Calcutta Journal* and the expulsion of John Silk Buckingham, the editor, from India for reprinting Stanhope's pamphlet on the press in India.[5] He was also a frequent speaker in the Court of

---

[1] L. Stanhope, *The Earl of Harrington on the Maine-Law; on the Law of Libel, as Opposed to the Declaration of Truth and the Defence of Character; and Other Subjects* (Derby and London, 1858), 22.

[2] As a soldier Stanhope saw action in South America and in India. He was a strong supporter of the administration of the marquis of Hastings in India where he was made deputy quarter master-general in 1817 and created CB in 1818 for services during the Mahratta War in 1817–18. He was retired on half-pay with the rank of lieutenant-colonel in June 1823 though promoted to full colonel in 1837. See *DNB*.

[3] *The Military Commentator; or, Thoughts upon the Construction of the Military Code of England, Contrasted with that of the Codes of Other Nations: Together with Remarks upon the Administration of that Code, Particularly with Regard to Military Flogging* (London, 1813).

[4] See J. R. Dinwiddy, 'The Early Nineteenth-Century Campaign against Flogging in the Army', *English Historical Review*, 97 (1982), 312–13.

[5] See J. S. Buckingham, 'Greece in 1823 and 1824', *Oriental Herald and Colonial Review*, 3 (1824), 335; see also 5 (1825), 438. See L. Stanhope, *Sketch of the History and Influence of the Press in British India* (London, 1823). See also G. Bearce, *British*

Proprietors against many of the policies of the Directors of the East India Company.[6] His energies were then transferred to Greece, and he became the agent of the London Greek Committee in Greece from September 1823 until he was recalled by Canning in 1824 for, in his own words, 'being too republican'.[7] His involvement with Greece continued in England, and he became a major figure in the controversies surrounding the Greek loans and the Greek loan scandal in 1826.[8] He also claimed to have been banished from Ireland for advocating Catholic emancipation, but his most enduring campaign in his later years was for temperance, and he became an untiring advocate of the introduction of a Maine-Law (prohibiting the sale of alcoholic beverages) into Britain.[9]

Stanhope's reputation today is based almost wholly on his involvement in the struggle for Greek independence, though he is usually mentioned as an important advocate of liberty of the press in histories of British rule in India. Nevertheless, with regard to Greece, he is known almost entirely as a fervent disciple of Bentham whose ideas he applied with a 'single-minded concentra-

Attitudes towards India, 1784–1858 (Oxford, 1961), 97 ff.; P. Griffiths, *The British Impact on India* (London, 1952), 269 ff.; and W. H. Wickwar, *The Struggle for the Freedom of the Press 1819–1832* (London, 1928), 275–9. Not all accounts have been sympathetic. See K. Ingham, *Reformers in India, 1793–1833* (Cambridge, 1956), 108.

[6] See C. H. Philips, *The East India Company, 1784–1834* (London, 1949), 2–5, where he depicts the quarterly meetings of the General Court of Proprietors as a popular senate. 'Aspirants to fame in the Commons often used the General Court as a training ground, notable among these being George Tierney, Charles and Robert Grant, Douglas Kinnaird and Joseph Hume' (3). Stanhope also spoke frequently in debates. For example, on 21 March 1821 he spoke on 'Prize Property' and on 4 April 1821 he contributed to the debate on Canning and liberty of the press in India. On 29–30 May 1822 Stanhope also discussed press freedom at the debate at East India House. He was not popular with the Directors: 'for the Directors hate Buckingham, Kinnaird and me most cordially', BL Add. MS 36464, fo. 46, Stanhope to Hobhouse, n.d. (1827?). Stanhope also urged various newspapers and journals to criticize British policy in India. See e.g. his letter against slavery in India, addressed to the duke of Gloucester as Patron and President of the African Institution, dated 20 June 1822 and reprinted in the *Calcutta Journal* (6 Jan. 1823), 77–9.

[7] L. Stanhope, *The Earl of Harrington on the Maine–Law*, 25 n. Stanhope had planned to return to England in the summer of 1824 on his own initiative as he was unwell and sought to avoid the hot weather. See *Greece, in 1823 and 1824* (new edn., London, 1825), 189–190 (Stanhope to Bowring, 18 Apr. 1824): 'and as I am, from ill health, unable to remain in Greece during the hot weather. . . . As soon as I have made the necessary arrangements with respect to the loan I shall start for England. My ambition would lead me to remain in Greece, but my health and affairs render my return indispensable.' See also 170 (Stanhope to Bowring, 9 Apr. 1824).

[8] See below, Ch. 13.   [9] See *The Earl of Harrington on the Maine–Law*.

tion . . . to the regeneration of Greece'.[10] The Benthamite
Stanhope and the romantic poet Lord Byron have been presented
by modern historians as forming two opposing poles of doctrine
and attitude in Greece.[11] The well-known anecdote of Stanhope
proposing that Byron read Bentham's work *A Table of the Springs of
Action*, and Byron's blunt reply—'What does the old fool know of
springs of action; My——has more spring in it'—has supposedly
epitomized their differences.[12] The contrast between the soldier
Stanhope, called the 'Typographical Colonel', rushing around
Greece establishing newspapers, Lancasterian schools, and utilitarian
societies, and the poet Byron trying to lead a band of unruly Suliots
into battle with traditional Greek costume and a helmet larger than
that of Kollokotronis himself, has become an abiding theme of
modern writers.[13]

Both Blaquiere and Stanhope became associated with Bentham
and both saw themselves as 'liberals' during this period when
liberalism was first emerging as a political ideology. We have seen
how Blaquiere 'used' Bentham to advance and strengthen liberal
ideas in Spain but his own ideas were far removed both from
Bentham's theory and from that moderate constitutionalism which

[10] W. St Clair, *That Greece Might Still Be Free* (London, 1972), 159. St Clair adds
that this devotion to Bentham 'was one of the strangest manifestations of
philhellenism' (159). See also L. Marchand, *Byron: A Biography*, 3 vols. (London,
1957), iii. 1136; Marchand, *Byron: A Portrait* (London, 1971), 423–4; Doris Langley
Moore, *The Late Lord Byron: Posthumous Dramas* (London, 1961), 75, 523; Moore,
Lord Byron: Accounts Rendered (London, 1974), 407, 421, 424; and C. M. Woodhouse, *The Philhellenes* (London, 1969), 105.

[11] See e.g. C. Brinton, *The Political Ideas of the English Romanticists* (Ann Arbor,
Mich., 1966; 1st pub. 1926). 155–6; R. E. Zegger, *John Cam Hobhouse: A Political
Life 1819–1852* (Columbia, Mo., 1973), 124; L. Crompton, *Byron and Greek Love*,
(London, 1985), 318.

[12] See Marchand, *Byron: A Biography*, iii. 1136, where the source of the anecdote
is given as Hobhouse. In Stanhope's own version, Byron returns after the incident to
borrow this very work of Bentham. See *Greece, in 1823 and 1824*, 543. While there is
little doubt that Stanhope and Byron discussed Bentham, it is worth noting that
Byron hardly mentions Bentham in his correspondence from this period. Nor does
William Parry include the anecdote in *The Last Days of Lord Byron* (London, 1825). It
is possible that Hobhouse who saw Stanhope frequently at this time heard the
anecdote related by Stanhope and suitably embellished it.

[13] See e.g. Marchand, *Byron: A Biography*, iii. 1136; *Byron: A Portrait*, 424;
Moore, *The Late Lord Byron*, 61. Not all recent writers have seen Bentham and
Byron in opposing terms. See e.g. M. Foot, *The Politics of Paradise: A Vindication of
Byron* (London, 1988), 102 n. Foot may have been influenced by Crompton's *Byron
and Greek Love*.

characterized his approach to politics. Similarly, Stanhope's reputation as a friend and follower of Bentham should not be accepted without critical scrutiny.[14] In his earlier pamphlets on flogging and liberty of the press, despite ample quotations from Plato, Montesquieu, Hume, Beccaria, Rousseau, Godwin, and Milton which appear as headings to chapters and in other contexts, Bentham was not mentioned.[15] Bentham's *On the Liberty of the Press and Public Discussion* (1821) would surely have been as relevant as any other text to Stanhope's campaign for press freedom in India, and, indeed, he used it later in Greece.[16] Stanhope had probably never read Bentham before they met for the first time in May 1823.[17] Bentham was so surprised by the sudden appearance of this so-called disciple that he referred to him in a letter as 'my ever dear and invaluable though so late found friend'.[18] Nevertheless, Stanhope did present himself, for whatever reasons, in his letters from Greece to Bowring and the London Greek Committee (which form the basis of *Greece, in 1823 and 1824*) as a follower of Bentham, and thus earned for himself this well-known reputation. But Stanhope's doctrine, like Blaquiere's, was far removed from Bentham's theory and, to complicate matters further, stood in direct conflict with that of Blaquiere who, like Stanhope, referred to himself as both a 'liberal' and a follower of Bentham. The object of this chapter is to explore Stanhope's doctrine, its 'liberal' character, and his relationship to Bentham.

1. Greece: European or Asian

During the struggle for Greek independence, one of the major issues of debate was whether or not Greece should be considered a

[14] See e.g. W. Thomas, *The Philosophic Radicals* (Oxford, 1979), 164.

[15] See Stanhope, *The Military Commentator; Sketch of the History and Influence of the Press in British India.*

[16] Bowring, ii. 275–97. Stanhope might have seen the review of Bentham's pamphlet in the *Calcutta Journal* on 16 Apr. 1822. He eventually used an excerpt from this work in the prospectus for *Hellenika chronika*, one of the newspapers he established at Missolonghi.

[17] Diary of John Colls, BL Add. MS 33563, fo. 122, entries for 1, 19 May 1823.

[18] Stanhope papers, General State Archives, Athens, K. 121, fo. 74, Bentham to Stanhope, 26 Oct. 1823.

European nation. By custom and tradition, and even in appearance, there was little to distinguish the Greeks from the Turks under whom and with whom they had lived for centuries. In methods of warfare and in political organization, they continued to follow Turkish ways even after they had begun to fight for their independence, and one major task of the Greeks themselves and the European philhellenes (like Blaquiere) was to persuade other Europeans that, in supporting the Greek cause, they were rescuing a European nation, Christian rather than Muslim, whose ancient civilization was the very spring from which European civilization flowed. From this perspective the class of Westernized Greeks produced by the Greek diaspora who were educated and had lived in Europe became key figures for the future of Greece, as they would ultimately take control of the government of their country. Most supporters of Greek independence took the view that the Greeks were essentially European, and were prepared to deal with a figure like Alexander Mavrokordatos who, whatever his actual power in Greece, symbolized the Westernized Greeks and formed the key link in the chain between Europe and a European Greece.

Stanhope did not share the view of most philhellenes. After two months in Missolonghi, he declared in a letter to Bowring: 'In all this connected with Greece consult those Anglo-Indians who understand the character of Asiatic nations. It is for this reason that I find myself quite at home in Greece.'[19] If Blaquiere saw the Greek struggle for independence as an extension of the liberal struggles in Spain, Portugal, and Naples, Stanhope viewed Greece in terms of developments in Asia: 'I consider the effects which have been brought about by the press and by education in Hindoostan, and the efforts making in favour of freedom by the Greeks, to form an epoch in the history of Asia.'[20]

In ascribing an 'Asian' character to the Greeks, Stanhope did not intend to idealize them. 'You must never forget,' he wrote to Bowring at one point, 'that you are not administering to men but to children.'[21] At another point he wrote: 'The people of Greece know nothing of liberty. How should they, after centuries of

[19] *Greece, in 1823 and 1824*, 80 (Stanhope to Bowring, 14 Jan. 1824).

[20] Ibid. 544. See also 246: '*My opinion is, that the struggle, however protracted, must succeed, and must lead to an improvement in the condition, not only of Greece but of Asia*' (italics in original).

[21] Ibid. 112–13 (Stanhope to Bowring, 11 Feb. 1824).

Turkish domination? They require to be taught the elements—the ABC of good government.'[22] His method of teaching the Greeks was described as follows:

It is my practice, when the natives visit me, to draw their attention to those points which are most essential to their welfare, and to put the matter in a point of view that will interest them, and set their minds in labour. For example, if I wish to recommend military discipline to them, I speak of the combined operations and close order observed by their ancestors . . . speaking of education, I lament that their Turkish masters should have deprived their children of the means of acquiring that knowledge which their great forefathers so eminently possessed.[23]

In spite of the patronizing tone adopted by Stanhope, he wanted the Greeks to develop and succeed in their struggle. He did not agree with the view which Capodistrias ascribed to Lord Londonderry and to the British government of rendering 'Greece as insignificant and harmless as possible, and to make her people like the spiritless natives of Hindoostan'.[24] However much he lamented the actual state of the Greeks, Stanhope favoured the establishment of an independent constitutional republic run entirely by the Greeks themselves. He saw his role in Greece (as in India) as one of preparing the 'natives' for independence and self-government. Such preparation would require careful attention and a firm hand.

2. Authoritarian Liberalism

Using a distinction employed by Elie Kedourie, it is possible to distinguish between 'Continental' and 'Whig' theories of nationality, with Blaquiere subscribing to the former and Stanhope to the latter.[25] Where Blaquiere was prepared to accept brutality and even murder for the sake of national independence (and was widely admired by the Greeks for his position), Stanhope looked to self-governing republics on Swiss or American models, not because he was a republican (as opposed to a monarchist) but because he

---

[22] Ibid. 67 (Stanhope to Bowring, 3 Jan. 1824).
[23] Ibid. 47–8 (Stanhope to Bowring, 18 Dec. 1823).
[24] Ibid. 12 (Stanhope to Bowring, 13 Oct. 1823).
[25] See E. Kedourie, *Nationalism* (rev. edn., New York, 1961), 132–3.

thought that such a form of government would enable all Greeks
(and others) to live together peacefully. He was proud of the mixed
monarchy of the British constitution but thought it inappropriate
to Greece, where a monarchy would have to be so strong to rule
the Greeks that it would soon become a tyranny.[26]

Instead of risking a foreign monarchy and possible tyranny to
gain independence, Stanhope urged them to support 'the constitution, the laws, the security of person and property, and the liberties
of the Greeks'.[27] His position was clearly 'Whiggish', and perhaps
'liberal', though neither term can be employed in this context with
much accuracy. Nationalism in his view played a subordinate role
to good constitutional government, and such a position brought
him into conflict with those Greeks and philhellenes who saw their
struggle as a desperate one for national independence. Most Greeks
would have dismissed as absurd Stanhope's preoccupation with
newspapers, education, utilitarian societies, and legal codes at a
time when their very survival was at stake. But in his view, mere
survival under any conditions was not worth the struggle, for
without constitutional liberty, the Greeks would be little better off
than under the Turks.

Stanhope's position was not without paradox. If, on the one
hand, he supported the Greeks in their struggle for liberty, his
treatment of them as being similar to the Indians was at best
patronizing and at worst authoritarian. Stanhope's attitude towards
many Greeks seems infused with that 'authoritarian counter-
current' in liberal thought whose source was in British rule in India
and which, as Eric Stokes has observed, had led 'serious men from
Chatham onwards' to wonder 'whether the possession of a
despotically-ruled empire might not prove fatal to the cause of
liberty in England'.[28] By the beginning of the nineteenth century, a
'superiority complex' had already developed, Indian institutions
were regarded as hopelessly corrupt, and reform, if at all possible,
would have to proceed on European lines.[29] Stanhope seems to
have absorbed the 'superiority complex' which intermingled with

---

[26] See *Greece, in 1823 and 1824*, 141 (Stanhope to Odysseus, 15 Mar. 1824); 123
(Stanhope to Bowring, 21 Feb. 1824).

[27] Ibid. 139 (Stanhope to Odysseus, 15 Mar. 1824).

[28] E. Stokes, *The English Utilitarians and India* (Oxford, 1959), p. xi.

[29] P. Spear, *The Nabobs: A Study of the Social Life of the English in Eighteenth-
Century India* (London, 1932), 136.

his liberal creed. The 'superiority complex' made him not only patronizing and condescending but it also obscured his vision so that the reality of Greece was at times hidden from his view behind the categories and concepts he brought from India.

3. Stanhope and Mavrokordatos

Consider, for example, his attitude towards Mavrokordatos, whom at several points he treated as an upstart native rather than as one of the main leaders of a new European state and much admired by Blaquiere, Byron, Bentham, and other supporters of Greek independence. In urging Mavrokordatos to improve the fortifications at Missolonghi, Stanhope observed:

I told Mavrocordato months back that he should call upon every individual to devote a fortnight's labour to this object, and should himself be the first to take off his coat and show a good example. He smiled—said yes—did nothing, complained piteously, and, as usual, ended in courteous begging.[30]

Stanhope's relationship with Mavrokordatos reveals a good deal about this combination of authoritarianism and liberalism in his thought. Before arriving in Missolonghi, he seemed willing to accept the general estimate of Mavrokordatos. He reported the opinion of Capodistrias to Bowring, after their meeting in Geneva, that Mavrokordatos was 'a man of great probity and finesse—qualities that are rarely found together, but very essential in his situation'.[31] From Cephalonia a month later, he reported that 'the whole nation seem to look up to him as their friend'.[32] After meeting at Missolonghi, Stanhope outlined his numerous plans for newspapers, hospitals, a postal service, and so on, and again reported favourably to Bowring:

Mavrocordato is a favourite with the islands, the people of Western Greece, and the legislative body. He is now president of that body, and is sent round here to settle affairs in this quarter. I find him good natured, clever, accommodating, and disposed to do good. He has rather an

---

[30] *Greece, in 1823 and 1824*, 415 (Stanhope to Bowring, 29 May 1824).
[31] Ibid. 15 (Stanhope to Bowring, 18 Oct. 1823).
[32] Ibid. 35 (Stanhope to Bowring, 26 Nov. 1823).

ingenious than a profound mind. He seems, at all times, disposed to concede, and to advance every good measure; and I consider it a grand advantage for Greece that he is now in power at Missolonghi.[33]

In spite of Stanhope's favourable opinion, one might wonder if saying that Mavrokordatos possessed 'rather an ingenious than a profound mind' was meant as a compliment. Perhaps Stanhope felt that Mavrokordatos could not (as a Greek) grasp the profundity of Stanhope's vision of Greece as an independent constitutional republic, based on a free press, widespread publicity in government, and a universal system of education. This suspicion of Mavrokordatos grew quickly as Stanhope struggled with him over the next fortnight to establish what he considered to be the first 'free press' in Greece.[34] 'Prince M. is a good man,' he wrote. 'Do not imagine, however, that he is a friend of liberty in a large sense.'[35] Three weeks later, Stanhope declared to Byron (who was defending Mavrokordatos) that 'I knew him to be an enemy to the press, although he dared not openly to avow it.'[36] In a subsequent letter sent to Bowring a week later Stanhope not only repeated his criticisms of Mavrokordatos but he 'disqualified' him from membership of European society:

Mavrocordato is a clever, shrewd, insinuating, and amiable man. He wins men, at first, by his yes's and his smiles. He is accessible and open to good counsel; but he pursues a temporizing policy, and there is nothing great or profound in his mind. He has the ambition, but not the daring or the self-confidence required to play a first part in the state. His game, therefore, is to secure the second character either under the commonwealth or under a king. The constitution is said to be his child, but he seems to have no parental predilections in its favour. And what, after all, can you expect from a Turk or Greek of Constantinople?[37]

Although Stanhope would later intensify his attack on Mavrokordatos and criticize even his use of the title of 'Prince', the foundations of a profound antipathy, one incidentally not shared by Bentham, Byron, or Blaquiere, were laid.

[33] Ibid. 41–2 (Stanhope to Bowring, 16 Dec. 1823).
[34] Ibid. 56 (Stanhope to Bowring, 23 Dec. 1823): 'I feel proud that in Greece, as in Hindoostan, I have contributed to the first establishment of a free press. There was a press, indeed, at Calamata, but it was under the control of Ipsilanti, and the one at Corinth was merely used for registering decrees and proclamations.'
[35] Ibid. 63 (Stanhope to Bowring, 2 Jan. 1824).
[36] Ibid. 93 (Stanhope to Bowring, 24 Jan. 1824).
[37] Ibid. 100 (Stanhope to Bowring, 31 Jan. 1824).

The amiable and diplomatic Mavrokordatos must have found Stanhope a difficult man with whom he was forced to work. By comparison, the eccentric and unpredictable Byron was a steady and co-operative ally. To the European philhellenes, Mavrokordatos was a friend: Shelley had dedicated *Hellas* to him; Bentham saw an identity of interests between the holders of the Greek loan scrip and Mavrokordatos in Greece in that both sought to establish a stable, prosperous, independent European state. Mavrokordatos had wooed and won over Byron to his camp; he had induced him to come to Missolonghi, thereby ensuring that his links with Europe were strong. With Byron as Commissioner of the loan and agent for the London Greek Committee, this mosquito-infested town, built on a swamp, and no other part of Greece could become the centre of power no matter into how many factions the government was divided. The money raised by the loan would be channelled through Missolonghi and would thereby strengthen the hand of the Westernized Greeks.

Stanhope placed all these assumptions in doubt. He arrived in Greece with no strong commitment to the Westernized Greeks. He wanted to involve the 'natives' in his activities and saw Mavrokordatos as almost a foreigner with little in common with the Greek population. He also wanted to overcome the division of the Greeks into factions and unite the country behind the constitution. As Mavrokordatos represented one faction among many, he could not be regarded by Stanhope simply as an ally. In addition, Mavrokordatos had supported the republican constitution, and Stanhope regarded his willingness to accept a European monarchy imposed on Greece as a condition for achieving independence as a special form of treason. Furthermore, for Stanhope, the test for supporting the constitution was support for the establishment of a free press, and Mavrokordatos's fearfulness about the establishment of the newspapers at Missolonghi made him an enemy in Stanhope's eyes to liberty and to the constitution.

For Mavrokordatos, however, the harm that might be done by the newspapers was very different from that imagined by Stanhope. Mavrokordatos realized that the newspapers would have little impact in Greece where they would not be widely circulated or read. Their impact would be abroad and such strong support for liberty of the press would not be welcomed by the Holy Alliance which Mavrokordatos wanted to enlist, if possible, in support of an independent Greece or at least not make more hostile to such a conception. Like Orlandos and Louriottis, he also did not want to appear too strongly allied with the British, nor would he wish to be known as having sanctioned so radical a political doctrine as that advocated by Stanhope. The Holy Alliance (as Stanhope found out personally when he attempted in 1825 to visit Milan, then under Austrian rule[38]) might not recognize the authoritarian tone behind the politics of reform or, if they did, might discount it as being a way of extending British authority in Greece.

4. Stanhope, Odysseus, and Greek Unity

Mavrokordatos was directly threatened by Stanhope when the latter began in January 1824 to court Odysseus, the military chief who controlled much of eastern Greece. As Stanhope was not satisfied with an alliance with one faction and sought to raise his own sights above the squabbling parties in Greece which had already engaged in civil war, he found in Odysseus (then in control of Athens) a means by which he might attempt to bring unity to Greece before the proceeds of the loan arrived and were distributed. He wanted to find in Odysseus a man, like himself, seeking to rise above faction and unite the country under a system of constitutional liberty, a military man dedicated to reform and the establishment of a free press and schools. Odysseus obliged and reflected with approval what Stanhope wanted him to be. Stanhope's vanity, as well as his doctrine, led him to form this much-criticized relationship. William St Clair has wryly observed that 'Odysseus was certainly the most unusual Benthamite ever to burn a village or slit a throat. Had it been possible', he continued, 'to change an oriental brigand into an enlightened champion of constitutional liberty by addressing him flattering letters, then Stanhope would have succeeded.'[39] Even though Stanhope made a number of proposals to Odysseus which invoked the name of Bentham, Stanhope, as will be shown, was not mainly interested in establishing Bentham in Greece, but himself and his own doctrine.

[38] See 'Tyrannical Conduct of the Austrian Authorities towards the Honourable Leicester Stanhope', *Oriental Herald and Colonial Review*, 5 (1825), 437–41.
[39] St Clair, *That Greece Might Still Be Free*, 191.

Odysseus saw in Stanhope a great opportunity to divert the proceeds of the loan, as well as the supplies and arsenal at Missolonghi, into his hands. In flattering Stanhope by posing as an idealized Greek version of the Englishman, he was still advancing his own interests. Each man saw in the other an image of himself as well as the opportunity to obtain what he wanted. Both seemed flattered by the roles they were supposed to play.

Stanhope left Missolonghi at the end of February 1824 and journeyed to Athens to work with Odysseus to unite the various interests of eastern and western Greece by first convening a congress at Salona. In a letter to Byron, written shortly after his arrival, Stanhope depicted Odysseus in the most flattering terms:

I have been constantly with Odysseus. He has a very strong mind, a good heart, and is brave as his word; he is a doing man; he governs with a strong arm, and is the only man in Greece that can preserve order. He puts, however, complete confidence in the people. He is for a strong government, for constitutional rights, and for vigorous efforts against the enemy. He professes himself of no faction, neither of Ipsilanti's nor of Colocotroni's, nor of Mavrocordato's; neither of the Primates, nor of the *Capitani*, nor of the foreign king faction. He speaks of them all in the most undisguised manner. He likes good foreigners, is friendly to a small body of foreign troops, and courts instruction. He has established two schools here, and has allowed me to set the press at work.[40]

To Bowring Stanhope wrote in similar terms:

The Chief Odysseus has been a mountain robber, has never bowed in bondage to the Turks, has served under Ali Pacha, has been chosen Governor of Eastern Greece, has refused to give up Athens to a weak government, and has lately sympathised with the people, and taken the liberal course in politics. He is a brave soldier, has great power, and promotes public liberty. Just such a man Greece requires.[41]

His expectations of the congress at Salona were equally high:

The congress at Salona will go great good. Eastern and Western Greece, and the islands, will unite to put the constitution in force, to get the revenues placed in the public coffers, and to promote military co-operation. Many of the chiefs of the Morea, together with the legislative body, and the great mass of the people, will approve these measures, and

---

[40] *Greece, in 1823 and 1824*, 125–6 (Stanhope to Byron, 6 Mar. 1824).
[41] Ibid. 134 (Stanhope to Bowring, 11 Mar. 1824).

their combined interests will form such a preponderating power, that all the little factions will be forced to follow the strong current.[42]

Stanhope seemed much happier in Athens than in Missolonghi and even busier. He quickly established a third newspaper, the *Free Press of Athens*, with an appropriate motto, taken from Bentham, 'Publicity is the Soul of Justice'.[43] A church was being transformed into a Lancasterian school (with further funds requested from the London Greek Committee and the Society of Friends), and Stanhope even planned to form 'a utilitarian society, for the purpose of establishing and fostering all useful measures'.[44]

He laid plans for the congress at Salona and began to journey there. He sent Humphreys to Missolonghi to ensure that Byron and Mavrokordatos would attend, and he addressed other leaders of the various factions to the same end. He hoped to establish a unified government to receive the first instalment of the Greek loan and return to England before the onset of the hot summer weather. He knew that the country was rife with faction—'the foreign king, the Ipsilanti, the Mavrocordato, the Petrobey . . . the Colocotroni faction', though he also believed that Odysseus did not belong to any of them.[45]

From Salona, Stanhope saw three parties: 'Mavrocordato, the oligarchs of the islands, and some of those of the Peloponnesus, and the legislative body' who stood for 'order and a mild despotism, either under a foreign king or otherwise'; 'Colocotroni, and some of the captains, and some of the oligarchs of the Morea' who stood for 'power and plunder', but whose fortunes at that moment seemed in decline; 'Ipsilanti, Odysseus, Negris and the mass who are now beginning to embrace republican notions, finding that they cannot otherwise maintain their power'.[46] While Stanhope was not so naïve as to believe that Odysseus had become a republican from mere choice or conviction, he none the less backed this party and recommended the inclusion of Odysseus in the five-man Executive Council, Ypsilanti as President of the legislature, General Kolliopoulos as Minister of War, and Negris as Minister of State. 'The object of the measure', he wrote to Bowring, 'is to break the force of contending factions, and to confound the traitors who are for a

[42] Ibid. 134–5 (Stanhope to Bowring, 11 Mar. 1824).
[43] Ibid. 135.   [44] Ibid. 136.
[45] Ibid. 139 (Stanhope to Odysseus, 15 Mar. 1824).
[46] Ibid. 198 (Stanhope to Bentham, 4 May 1824).

foreign king.'[47] What is important about this remark is that Stanhope's measures at this point seemed less directed at reconciling all factions and more at undermining the position of Mavrokordatos. Stanhope had believed that Mavrokordatos was opposed to the congress at Salona, and he was probably correct, even though Mavrokordatos had been prepared to attend it with Lord Byron before the latter died. Stanhope's courtship of Odysseus directly threatened Mavrokordatos's position as the link between the European philhellenes and Greece. Without the maintenance of that position, he could not gain control over the loan and use the money to direct the various military chiefs, including Odysseus. Stanhope placed all these plans in jeopardy, not because Odysseus was an obvious choice to lead the country, but because Stanhope's political doctrine led him to denigrate Mavrokordatos and to see Odysseus in the special way he did.

5. Stanhope's Ideological Use of Bentham

Stanhope's political ideas belong to the realm of ideology. Even though they lacked any philosophical foundation, they possessed a certain coherence and were especially useful as a way of guiding practical judgement and action. While many Europeans would find themselves confused, if not utterly bewildered, by events in Greece, both Blaquiere and Stanhope seemed to know exactly what to do, and neither displayed the hesitation and perplexity which characterized Byron at Cephalonia and later at Missolonghi, and Bentham in his involvement in the dispute over the Greek loan.

Blaquiere's ideology has been depicted in terms of a Mediterranean nationalism which contained elements of early liberalism.[48] Stanhope's ideology might also be given a geographical appellation, that of Asian, but he was prepared to apply it anywhere that 'native' peoples sought liberty and independence. Stanhope's ideology also contained elements of early liberalism—a secular republican state, responsible to the people, based on liberty of the press, publicity, and universal education. Unlike Bentham, however, Stanhope did not simply hold out a coherently formulated

---

[47] Ibid. 202 (Stanhope to Bowring, 7 May 1824).
[48] This is not to suggest that Blaquiere's nationalism and liberalism were ultimately compatible. See Kedourie, *Nationalism*, 109.

ideal, designed to appeal to people who held liberal opinions and
who sought liberal institutions. Stanhope's achievement was more
directed at practice, and, in courting the warlord Odysseus, who
was to die in a year, probably killed by his fellow Greeks, he
revealed most fully the authoritarian side of his liberal creed.
Odysseus could rise above the squabbling factions either because he
could promise all things to all men or because he could eventually
crush the other factions. Doubtless, Odysseus himself had no
ambition to lead the Greek nation, and only sought to profit
sufficiently from his involvement with Stanhope to enrich himself
and secure his position in eastern Greece. Yet, Stanhope wanted to
see in him a greater figure, and had he remained in Greece to
distribute the money from the loan, he might have enabled
Odysseus and others like him to rise to more than military
prominence. One wonders what liberal institutions and practices
the world would have seen in a Greece ruled by these leaders.

As we have seen, Stanhope did not appear to have read much
Bentham and did not meet him until the spring of 1823, with
Bentham showing some surprise at this sudden appearance of a
dedicated disciple. Nevertheless, Stanhope's reputation as a disciple
of Bentham was largely created by himself. If Blaquiere's *The
Greek Revolution* referred to Bentham twice, largely to the effect
that his ideas, though relevant and appreciated, were not immediately applicable until the bloody struggle was successfully resolved,
Stanhope's *Greece, in 1823 and 1824* is notable for nearly three dozen
references to Bentham. At times, Stanhope simply praised
Bentham, as when he gave (in a letter to Bowring) this report of
Bentham's activities to the Zurich Committee: 'The venerable
Bentham, with a spirit of philanthropy as fervent, and a mind as
vast as ever, had employed his days and nights in contemplating
and writing on the constitution of Greece, and in framing for her a
body of rational laws, the most useful of human offerings.'[49] Or,
when he decided to use an excerpt from Bentham's pamphlet *On
the Liberty of the Press* for the prospectus for *Hellenika chronika*, he
referred to it as 'all comprehensive and conclusive'.[50] Bentham
would, of course, have seen the originals or copies of these letters.

More frequently, however, Stanhope would report at length on

---

[49] *Greece, in 1823 and 1824*, 7 (Stanhope to Bowring, 10 Oct. 1823).
[50] Ibid. 50 (Stanhope to Bowring, 20 Dec. 1823).

his attempts to advance Bentham's various projects, or, at least, his versions of them. For two of his proposed newspapers he took mottoes from Bentham: 'The greatest good of the greatest number' for the *Hellenika chronika* and 'Publicity is the Soul of Justice' for the newspaper at Athens.[51] He also included references to Bentham and brief articles on his work and its importance in various numbers of the *Hellenika chronika* and the *Greco telegrapho*.[52] In addition, he reported on various efforts to recruit the two Greek boys to be educated at Bentham's expense at Hazelwood School.[53] On 9–10 April he presented Bentham's early draft of the *Constitutional Code* to an assembly of Greeks who had met near Argos with the following words:

I presented Mr. Bentham's manuscript on government to them observing that they should prefer his aid to that of the Holy Alliance, for if they followed his maxims, they would be free and powerful; whereas, if they accepted the hollow friendship of despots, though adorned with ribbons and gold chains, they must relapse into long and hopeless servitude.[54]

According to Stanhope, therefore, according to his rhetoric at least, without Bentham the Greeks might relapse into a 'long and hopeless servitude' under the domination of the Holy Alliance. But Stanhope's actions on behalf of Bentham were less successful than his rhetoric. The manuscript of the *Constitutional Code*, which he brought with him to Greece in the autumn of 1823, was not presented to the Greek government until April 1824. Although there were numerous circumstances which may have prevented him from going to the seat of government (such as an uncertainty as to whether or not such a government existed and the absence of a

[51] See ibid. 41 (Stanhope to Bowring, 16 Dec. 1823). The original (LGC Papers, vol. vi, fo. F) reads: 'The greatest good of the greatest many', as though Stanhope was unsure of Bentham's phrase. See also *Greece, in 1823 and 1824*, 78 (Stanhope to Bowring, 14 Jan. 1824); 135 (Stanhope to Bowring, 11 Mar. 1824); 167 (Stanhope to Bowring, 9 Apr. 1824).

[52] See e.g. *Greece, in 1823 and 1824*, 90 (Stanhope to Bowring, 21 Jan. 1824); see also n. 50 above and F. Rosen, 'Bentham's Letters and Manuscripts in Greece', *Bentham Newsletter*, 5 (1981), 55–8.

[53] See e.g. *Greece, in 1823 and 1824*, 52 (Stanhope to Bowring, 20 Dec. 1823); 207–9 (Stanhope to Bowring, 14 May 1824); and 288–9 (Bentham to Stanhope, 23 Sept. 1823).

[54] Ibid. 173 (Stanhope to Bowring, 9 Apr. 1824). See also 196–8 (Stanhope to Bentham, 4 May 1824).

completed text from Bentham), Stanhope never gave the manuscript any priority and never expressed any opinion about the delay in its presentation. He probably used the occasion to present the manuscript as part of his attempt to unify the various factions at Salona. When Stanhope wrote to Bentham after its presentation that 'were your code ready, it would, I think, be immediately adopted in Greece', he would have known merely from the fact that the *Code* was written in English that few Greeks would have been able to read it, and there were no plans by the government to adopt any of Bentham's codes.[55] As for Bentham's plan to educate the two Greek youths at Hazelwood School in Birmingham, Stanhope enthusiastically made it his own. From Missolonghi in December 1823, he reported to Bowring:

I have heard of two extraordinary boys here. One is ten years of age, and possesses a great talent for making extempore poetry; the other is a little Jew, of seven years old, whom the Turks converted, *par force*, on account of his calculating powers. I have sent to Jannina for them, and, should they answer the description, I shall send them home to Mr. Bentham, to be educated at Hill's School, (Hazelwood).[56]

This report seems to have come to nothing and a month later Stanhope revealed plans to Bowring to announce Bentham's proposal in an insertion in the *Hellenika chronika*:

He [Stanhope] should consult the wisest men on this subject. He should endeavour to obtain the offspring of parents who have been prominent in rescuing Greece from the Satanical rule of the Turks, and have been firm in promoting her liberties; also, children of ingenuous disposition, of healthy frames, of superior natural talents, and who are likely hereafter to have an influence in the state.[57]

Again, nothing seems to have developed from this initiative, and in May 1824 Stanhope wrote to Konstantinos Botzaris and Kollokotronis, himself, offering, on Bentham's behalf, to educate two of their sons.[58] Stanhope issued his invitation from Zante, as he

---

[55] Ibid. 197 (Stanhope to Bentham, 4 May 1824); 48 (Stanhope to Bowring, 18 Dec. 1823). See also *Constitutional Code*, i. ed. F. Rosen and J. H. Burns (Oxford, 1983) (*CW*), p. xxx, for Bentham's connection with Theodore Negris, which was established by Stanhope and came to nothing.

[56] *Greece, in 1823 and 1824*, 52 (Stanhope to Bowring, 20 Dec. 1823).

[57] Ibid. 87 (Stanhope to Bowring, 18 Jan. 1824).

[58] Ibid. 207-9 (Stanhope to Bowring, 14 May 1824).

prepared for his own departure, and the invitations seem almost an afterthought. In the event, Stanhope failed to organize the education of the Greek youths, although he had ample time to do so. As we shall see, Blaquiere successfully brought nine Greek youths (including two for Bentham) to England several months later.[59] Indeed, this venture was one of the more successful of the London Greek Committee, but Stanhope, for all of his apparent enthusiasm, did not carry out Bentham's wishes, and one wonders to what extent the emphasis on sons of famous men or on youths of great ability was Stanhope's rather than Bentham's. Blaquiere avoided conditions such as these and simply chose youths who were representative of the country as a whole.

Stanhope used Bentham's name most when he was engaged in controversy, though the controversy may not have been initially about Bentham himself. For example, when Mavrokordatos and others at Missolonghi resisted the move by Stanhope to put the extract from Bentham's pamphlet on press freedom in the prospectus of the *Hellenika chronika*, Stanhope not only raised the general problem of censorship, but, more importantly, the additional problem of suppressing 'the thoughts of the finest genius of the most enlightened age—the thoughts of the immortal Bentham'.[60]

In several arguments with Byron, Stanhope either used Bentham or, it seems, Bentham was the occasion of their argument. 'His Lordship', wrote Stanhope, 'then began, according to custom, to attack Mr. Bentham.'[61] But the dispute was actually about freedom of the press and the argument about Bentham was incidental. Either Byron criticized Bentham because he knew Stanhope would rise to the bait or Stanhope used Bentham to gain a kind of moral ascendancy over Byron. 'I said [to Byron]', wrote Stanhope characteristically, 'that it was highly illiberal to make personal

---

[59] See below, Ch. 9. See also A. Dimaras, 'The Other British Philhellenes', in Richard Clogg (ed.), *The Struggle for Greek Independence* (London, 1973), 209 ff.; 'Foreign, and Particularly English, Influences on Educational Policies in Greece during the War of Independence and Their Development under Capodistrias, 1821–1831' (Ph.D. thesis, London University, 1973); and G. F. Bartle, 'The Greek Boys at Borough Road during the War of Independence', *Journal of Educational Administration and History*, 20 (1988), 1–11.

[60] *Greece, in 1823 and 1824*, 55 (Stanhope to Bowring, 23 Dec. 1823).

[61] Ibid. 97 (Stanhope to Bowring, 28 Jan. 1824). This passage does not appear in the original letter from Stanhope to Bowring. See LGC papers, vol. vii, fo. C[3].

attacks on Mr. Bentham before a friend who held him in high estimation.'[62]

Douglas Dakin has speculated that had Byron lived and Stanhope and Byron stayed on to supervise the loan, Stanhope might have gone far to achieve national unity.[63] He has also suggested that Canning's decision to arrange for the recall of Stanhope was based not on deference to the Turks or to the Holy Alliance, but on his belief that Stanhope's opposition to Mavrokordatos was such as to threaten British policy which favoured Mavrokordatos as an alternative leader in Greece to Capodistrias who was regarded as pro-Russian.[64] Although, in the eyes of the British government, Stanhope's potential success may have required his recall (as he was at the time a soldier on half-pay), Stanhope actually achieved very little in Greece, and his reputation as an ardent disciple of Bentham does not stand up to scrutiny. What was important for Stanhope was not that he was a disciple of Bentham but his own ideology. His ideology led him to seek unity in Greece, but not through the supposedly pro-British Mavrokordatos. He spurned this upstart 'native' by bringing together all of the 'natives' under his own authority or, like the Rousseauian 'Lawgiver', that of the laws and the constitution of the country.

Stanhope's ideology was to have profound consequences (as will be seen in Chapter 9) on the arrangements for the payment of the Greek loan and on the dispute with Blaquiere. It was an ideology (like Blaquiere's) which accommodated Bentham's ideas *at its own level* without absorbing the philosophical foundations of Bentham's thought. Both Stanhope and Blaquiere used Bentham in two ways: firstly, in a very practical way to open doors and to bolster up their own positions; and secondly, to give their particular brands of liberalism an authenticity and respectability which they otherwise lacked. Without Bentham, Blaquiere's liberalism became a brutal form of nationalism; and Stanhope's liberalism might become an authoritarian doctrine far removed from the liberal principles, such as liberty of the press, on which it was supposedly based.

Even in later years, Stanhope never ceased to invoke Bentham's name, especially when he referred to law reform and, in particular,

---

[62] Ibid. This passage also does not appear in the original letter from Stanhope to Bowring.

[63] *British and American Philhellenes during the War of Greek Independence, 1821–1833* (Thessaloniki, 1955), 74.   [64] Ibid.

to the reform of the Courts of Chancery at whose hands he, like many others, had suffered.[65] But he continued to adapt Bentham to his own uses. In 1852, by then the earl of Harrington, Stanhope wrote: '[I]n the words of my late friend, Jeremy Bentham, [the existing constitution] produced "the greatest happiness to the greatest number for the longest period of time," of any system of government recorded in the annals of history.'[66] The occasion of the speech was Stanhope's attack on proposals to introduce the secret ballot on the grounds that it would undermine the 'ancient constitution'. It is not entirely surprising that Stanhope used Bentham's name to oppose a reform that Bentham had in fact strongly supported during his lifetime.

[65] See *The Earl of Harrington on the Maine-Law*, 12, 28, 38.
[66] Ibid. 37.

9
Conflict and Confusion in Early Liberalism

1. Blaquiere Returns to Greece

The arrival of the first instalment of the Greek loan in Zante at the end of April 1824 brought the doctrines of Blaquiere and Stanhope into sharp conflict, a conflict which revealed most fully the differences between their two types of liberalism. Before Blaquiere had arrived in Greece, Stanhope had in a sense already thrown down the ideological gauntlet, though, given the lapse of time for letters to pass between Greece and England (from six weeks to eight months), he would most probably not have been aware of the development of Stanhope's position. In addition, though many of Stanhope's letters to Bowring (which were printed in *Greece, in 1823 and 1824*) were circulated among the leading figures and read at meetings of the London Greek Committee, it is not clear how much of the correspondence was actually seen by Blaquiere who was travelling around Britain and absorbed in the completion of his own book, *The Greek Revolution*.[1]

---

[1] Much of Stanhope's correspondence was edited and printed in the form in which it was written. At some points, probably due to the large number of letters which were edited in a brief period, there is some confusion; at other points editorial decisions were taken to eliminate mistaken, misleading, or repetitious material which would not make sense when the letters were published in sequence. Nevertheless, some revealing passages were either added or suppressed. The letter of 2 Dec. 1823 (see Ch. 6 above) in which Stanhope suggested that Bowring should raise only 'a small loan' of not more than £100,000—'I think it is not feasible or even desirable under existing circumstances that Greece should obtain a larger sum'—was not included in *Greece, in 1823 and 1824* (new edn., London, 1825) (see LGC papers, vol. vi, fo. D). Nor was this comment on Lord Byron, incorporated in the letter of 11 Feb. 1824: 'Do not trust Ld. B[yron] with yr. money. He is too generous with his own and he will be almost as much so with yours' (LGC papers, vol. vi, fo. Z). A copy of a letter to Parry, incorporated into a letter to Bowring, dated 16 May 1824 (see *Greece, in 1823 and 1824*, 211–13), was omitted from the published volume. In it,

Blaquiere must have arrived at Zante full of hope and with a feeling of considerable accomplishment. Behind him were the troublesome negotiations over the loan and the difficulties of raising funds for the expedition led by Parry which had preceded him to Greece. Although letters received from Byron and Stanhope had revealed the nature of the civil strife in Greece, the proceeds of the loan were seen by Blaquiere as the means of finally uniting the Greeks behind a 'national' party led by Mavrokordatos.[2] In the first days after his arrival the full horror of the situation soon became known. Firstly, Byron was dead. Not only was the news of his death a considerable personal shock, but as Byron had remained loyal to Mavrokordatos, he would also have supported Blaquiere's position of channelling the funds for the war through the prince. Secondly, Stanhope was gone, and was probably at Salona with Odysseus. 'Stanhope has managed matters in such a way', he wrote to Bowring, 'as to have left Mr. Barff in total ignorance of his movements.'[3] In a short time Blaquiere would be worried more about Stanhope's ideas than his absence. Thirdly, Blaquiere could see that the absence of Thomas Gordon (who was still deliberating in Scotland as to whether or not he would go to Greece and, if so, when he would go) exposed the foolish policies of not providing replacements for Commissioners in the event of death or non-arrival, and, on a personal note, of not making him a Commissioner. 'It has been a sad blunder', he wrote to Bowring, 'not to

Stanhope is highly critical of Parry's achievements in Greece: 'Your answers to my queries are not clear to my mind; however I hope they may prove satisfactory to your employers' (LGC papers, vol. viii, fo. B[3]). Perhaps most puzzling is the omission in the original letter of the incident regarding Bentham, Byron, and liberalism which appears on 96–8 of *Greece, in 1823 and 1824*. See LGC papers, vol. vii, fo. C[3]. The material may have been added from another source or, perhaps, Stanhope wanted to use Bentham here to boost his own liberal credentials. Other letters were simply not included in *Greece, in 1823 and 1824*: see LGC papers, vol. v, fo. X, Stanhope to Bowring, 30 Nov. 1823; fo. Z, Stanhope to Bowring, 2 Dec. 1823; fo. D[1], Stanhope to Bowring, 6 Dec. 1823; fo. E[1], Stanhope to Bowring, 8 Dec. 1823; fo. H[1], Stanhope to Bowring, 10 Dec. 1823; vol. vii, fo. I[3], Stanhope to Bowring, 1 Feb. 1824; and fo. P[5], Stanhope to Bowring, 27 Mar. 1824. Although it is tempting to speculate about the reasons for the various omissions, no common thread is clearly evident except perhaps for the fact that a number of the letters took up to eight months to arrive in London and may have arrived after Stanhope himself returned and began work on the volume.

[2] LGC papers, vol. viii, fo. V, Mavrokordatos to Blaquiere, 16/20 Apr. 1824.
[3] Ibid. fo. Y, Blaquiere to Bowring, 29 Apr. 1824.

invest me with Gordons powers, as we intended at first.'[4] Blaquiere soon became aware that Stanhope, as the only authorized British Commissioner, would become the key figure in obtaining the release of the funds from the bankers Barff and Logotheti, where they had been placed according to the agreement reached in London between the Greek Deputies and the London Greek Committee. Finally, Blaquiere arrived to find Parry sick and mad in the lazaretto in Zante.[5] Within a month, he would have to face the depressing fact that Parry's expedition 'has been of *no earthly use* in that the whole of the money has been thrown into the sea'.[6]

After a month, during which time he rushed frantically around Zante trying to sort out the problems he had found, he seemed to have lost his customary buoyancy. 'I would sooner have lost my right hand', he wrote, 'than come out to cut such a figure in the eyes of this ill-fated people.'[7] Stanhope returned to Zante on 12 May and soon the opposition between them intensified:

Blaquiere has been with me this morning. He is dreadfully alarmed. He has had a moving letter from Mavrocordato. The Turkish fleet is out. The fortresses in Negropont are relieved. The Egyptians and Ottomans are coming on, and the loan is all in Barff's counting-house. My opinion is known to you. The Turkish fleet, when collected, is always master at sea. Their fortresses will, therefore, be relieved, their troops will effect their landings and succeed in their first efforts, but with the winter comes the ebb: then is the time for the Greeks to commence their blockades and sieges, and to march. Judge from experience which is right B[laquiere] or I.[8]

With the departure of Stanhope for Britain on the *Florida* with Byron's body on 25 May 1824, and the arrival of the second instalment of the loan, also locked away with Barff and Logotheti, Blaquiere became even more bitter. Two months had now passed without any of the money being passed to the Greeks. The second instalment contained only a letter from Bowring to Stanhope who

---

[4] Ibid. Regarding Gordon's return to Greece, see also vol. ix, fo. T, Gordon to Bowring, 13 June 1824; fo. C^2, Gordon to Bowring, 20 June 1824; vol. x, fo. Q^3, Gordon to Hume, 26 Sept. 1824.

[5] Ibid. vol. viii, fo. Y, Blaquiere to Bowring, 29 Apr. 1824.

[6] Ibid. fo. B^2, Blaquiere to Bowring, 8 May 1824.

[7] Ibid. fo. U^2, Blaquiere to Bowring, 15 May 1824.

[8] *Greece, in 1823 and 1824*, 224–5 (Stanhope to Bowring, 22 May 1824).

had by this time departed for England, and no further instructions regarding the loan. Blaquiere wrote in anger to his friend Bowring:

Pray do not be surprised if I am hurt and irritated beyond expression at this treatment, but great as my annoyance at these proofs of personal slight and inattention may be, it is completely absorbed . . . [by] the irreparable injury done to Greece and the Greek cause by this concatenation of mismanagement and folly which has kept the money locked up . . . nearly two months, without there being yet the most distant prospect of its release . . . you keep us in a state of profoundest ignorance of every thing, an ignorance which renders our situation absolutely intolerable.[9]

As for Stanhope, Blaquiere now freely admitted that 'had he remained in this country there could have neither been cordiality nor co-operation between us'.[10] In writing to Bentham, Blaquiere noted at this time: 'By what he has said, and which I have written, you will have easily perceived that we are completely at issue.'[11] Blaquiere was at this time thoroughly disgusted not only with Stanhope but also with Bowring and the London Greek Committee:

We are fairly distracted by the shocking conduct of the committee. Nor can I describe to you their [the Greek Deputies'] unmingled rage at the idea of being treated so shamefully. Should B[owring] show you the letters I have written to those concerned, you will be able to judge of my own feelings and treatment throughout this transaction, a treatment that has filled me with disgust, and almost induces me to return to England at once to tell the *friends of liberty*, that they have as little sense of justice and liberality as those whom they would decry! Trusting to God that this conduct of the G. Committee, may not cause the total destruction of Greece . . .[12]

Blaquiere's predicament can be explained partly by the unfortunate sequence of events including the death of Byron, departure of Stanhope, and non-arrival of Gordon, or, for that matter, of Koundouriottis from Hydra; partly by the mismanagement of the arrangements for the disposal of the loan by the London Greek Committee; and partly by the personalities of Blaquiere and Stanhope. With Blaquiere never fully trusted by some members of the London Greek Committee, and Stanhope, vain, arrogant, and

[9] LGC papers, vol. ix, fo. U, Blaquiere to Bowring, 14 June 1824.
[10] Ibid., Blaquiere to Hume.   [11] Ibid. fo. U, Blaquiere to Bentham.
[12] Ibid.

always drawn to the heart of controversy, it is tempting to
understand the nature of their dispute, however agonizing and
momentous, as a purely personal one. The irritating conflicts
between Stanhope and Byron (as will be seen in Chapter 10) were
often personal, with Byron expressing his growing annoyance with
Stanhope's manner and Stanhope disapproving of Byron's behaviour. Yet the complete opposition between Blaquiere and
Stanhope was not the result of a clash of personalities, especially as
there was so little direct contact between them. As we shall see, the
conflict was an ideological one.

2. Blaquiere versus Stanhope: The Context of Conflict

Their differences can only be fully understood in terms of a clash of
ideologies emerging out of early liberalism. The extent to which
this was understood by those surrounding Blaquiere and Stanhope
is not entirely clear. Palma, whose *Greece Vindicated* contained a
sharp critique of Stanhope, understood perfectly well that there
was a conflict between them which had a profound effect on the
outlook and behaviour of leading figures in the London Greek
Committee:

His [Stanhope's] behaving in a contrary manner, and the conduct of
Messrs. Trelawney, Fenton, Humphreys, etc. indisposed the [Greek]
Government towards the London Committee; gave weight to the reports
that Greece was sold to the English, and was to be treated like East India;
made the deputies less attentive to the counsels of the Committee, which
were founded, not on the reports of Blaquiere, but on those of Stanhope,
by which the members not only divested themselves of their enthusiasm,
but also adopted a coolness almost hostile, and even went so far as to
deliberate whether the money should or should not be sent to Greece.[13]

Palma believed that 'the harm he [Stanhope] did was not done
intentionally, but with an idea of promoting the benefit of the
Greeks and of the English'.[14] In other words, Stanhope was neither
a rogue nor a fool; he was motivated by principles and 'ideas'. And
Blaquiere, in Palma's view, had made the clearest analysis and

[13] A. Palma, *Greece Vindicated* (London, 1826), 244.
[14] Ibid. 245.

prescriptions for Greece, especially in his *Narrative of a Second Visit to Greece*, the reply to Stanhope, which Palma discussed at length.[15]

Not many other figures involved with the Greek loan saw the differences between Stanhope and Blaquiere as clearly as Palma. Some tended to see the conflict more in terms of reactions to personalities than to ideas generally. 'I am sorry to see Mr. B's warm feelings and ultra zeal carrying him so very far beyond the scale of moderation which we might expect and require in our agent', wrote Joseph Hume after having examined Blaquiere's letters from Greece at this time.[16] 'Blaquiere has written me an insane letter from Zante,' wrote Hobhouse, 'he is a zealous imbecile.'[17] But Hobhouse would also respond on a personal level to Stanhope, as when Stanhope urged him to replace Byron in Greece:

Stanhope called—and used every argument to second what Hume urged last night—he told me that he knew of no man who could do what I could do in Greece—no man in England. He said I might gain absolute control over the councils—and actually form the government.

I stated my fears and objections—and told him unfeignedly that I thought myself unequal to action in such a crisis—and also that it seemed to me absurd to attempt to found or save a state in the *holidays*, for I must come back by February next.[18]

Hobhouse reacted to Stanhope's belief that he might gain 'absolute control' over the state not in terms of any pattern of authoritarian ideas expressed by Stanhope but in terms of Stanhope's personality. His reaction was to puncture Stanhope's vanity rather than to argue about the truth of his ideas.

Others at the time would see part of what was at issue between Blaquiere and Stanhope without recognizing that there was a dispute. When Gordon discussed the first Greek loan, he noted that the English 'were too much inclined to erect themselves into a Board of Control, and meddle in matters beyond their competence'.[19] In spite of this allusion to the position of Stanhope (or perhaps to Hume or Bowring), Gordon went on to praise both Stanhope and Blaquiere for their respective roles in Greece without

---

[15] See ibid., esp. 266–9.
[16] LGC papers, vol. ix, fo. W², Hume to Bowring, 30 June 1824.
[17] Ibid. fo. Y¹, Hobhouse to Bowring, 17 June 1824.
[18] BL Add. MS 56549, fo. 20, Hobhouse Diaries, 8 July 1824.
[19] T. Gordon, *History of the Greek Revolution*, 2 vols. (Edinburgh, 1832), ii. 274.

mentioning any dispute between them, or, so it seems, between Byron and Stanhope.[20] If there was a conflict of political ideas, for Gordon, it was between liberal and conservative principles with all of the philhellenes considered 'liberal' and the conservatives linked with support for the Holy Alliance and opposition generally to Greek independence.[21] The latter, from a number of different perspectives, tended to criticize all aspects of the Greek struggle for independence. Philip James Green, former British consul for the Morea, criticized the Greeks for the atrocities at Tripolizza, Stanhope for violating the terms of his appointment in the army by serving in Greece, Blaquiere for giving absurd and extravagant accounts of events in Greece and of the resources of the Greeks available to repay the loan, Byron and Stanhope for squabbling, and the organizers of the Greek loans for floating loans which would never be repaid.[22] As we shall see, the Tory press would seize upon any opportunity to discredit the activities of the London Greek Committee and the reformers associated with it so that from the perspective of total opposition the dispute between Stanhope and Blaquiere might seem of little consequence.

For those who travelled to Greece at this time and published their memoirs, their views often depended on where they were and with whom they were associated. Waddington, who was a fairly detached observer, did not see any dispute between Blaquiere and Stanhope. For example, he agreed with Stanhope (as opposed to Byron) that the newspapers published at Missolonghi would do no harm, though he put it with less enthusiasm: '[I]f they can be productive of no great utility, [the newspapers] will at least do very little injury.'[23] He also favoured self-government for the Greeks (though he was not sure that they could achieve it) rather than the imposition of a foreign king.[24] But his overall view was critical of all the activities of foreigners in Greece:

In spite of all that has been said and written to the contrary, I am of opinion that the personal service of foreigners in Greece is still, as it ever has been, entirely useless. Those who present themselves with arms and rules of

[20] T. Gordon, *History of the Greek Revolution*, 2 vols. (Edinburgh, 1832) ii. 78–83.

[21] Ibid. ii. 279–80.

[22] P. J. Green, *Sketches of the War in Greece* (London, 1827), 69 ff., 146 n.–147 n., 162, 170, 173 n.–174 n. See also Blaquiere's 'Reply to Green' in *Letters from Greece*, (London, 1828) 139–98.

[23] G. Waddington, *A Visit to Greece in 1823 and 1824* (2nd ed., London, 1825), 173.   [24] Ibid. 167–8.

discipline are despised and maltreated; their tactics are ridiculed, and themselves condemned to starvation. Those who import theories and principles ready cut and dried in the West, soon perceive, or ought to perceive, that their counsels are inapplicable to the state of the country, and impracticable. Those who would introduce schools, and laboratories, and hospitals, are considered to be innocent enthusiasts, who have sadly mistaken the *moment* for their exertions. The few who have brought money are allowed to spend it, indeed, but not without great jealousy and suspiciousness from the very persons who are devouring it as a spoil or a right.[25]

Those who were with Byron at Missolonghi tended to criticize Stanhope and especially Parry. Julius Millingen, who served as a physician to Byron and later joined the Turks, emphasized the lack of co-operation between Byron and Stanhope and rejected Stanhope's belief that Greece should have a republican form of government.[26] But his strongest criticism was of Parry and of the failure of the London Greek Committee to appreciate the fact that Parry was an ignorant and drunken man whose presence in Missolonghi led to the failure of the expedition.[27] Nevertheless, the ideological link between Byron and Blaquiere, in that both supported Mavrokordatos, did not pass unnoticed. 'Had Mr. Blaquiere found Lord Byron in life and health,' wrote P. Gamba, 'what innumerable benefits would immediately have accrued to Greece!'[28] W. H. Humphreys, protégé of Gordon whom he met in Greece in 1821, returned with Parry to Missolonghi in 1824 and soon became a staunch supporter of Stanhope, especially in his efforts to unify the country. In his memoir, Humphreys followed Stanhope in attacking Mavrokordatos and in praising Odysseus, and he virtually blamed Mavrokordatos for the death of Byron.[29] Handing the money over to the Greeks, as was eventually done by Bulwer and Browne, without the precautions advocated by Stanhope 'caused all but their utter ruin'.[30] Like Stanhope, he

---

[25] Ibid. 174–5.

[26] J. Millingen, *Memoirs of the Affairs of Greece* (London, 1831), 92. See W. St Clair, *That Greece Might Still Be Free* (London, 1972), 183.

[27] Ibid. 94 ff., 177.

[28] P. Gamba, *A Narrative of Lord Byron's Last Journey to Greece* (London, 1825), 280–1.

[29] W. H. Humphreys, 'Journal of a Visit to Greece', in *A Picture of Greece in 1825: As Exhibited in the Personal Narratives of James Emerson, Esq., Count Pecchio, and W. H. Humphreys, Esq.*, 2 vols. (London, 1826), ii. 203 n.–204 n., 207–18, 278–9.

[30] Ibid. ii. 261 n.

favoured a republican form of government rather than a European monarch, and also, like Stanhope, he found Parry 'to be a blustering worthless character'.[31] Most importantly the account of the retention of the loan by Barff and Logotheti agreed substantially with that of Stanhope as opposed to the account given by Palma.[32] Nevertheless, Humphreys did not refer to the dispute between Stanhope and Blaquiere, perhaps because he had little actual contact with Blaquiere, or possibly because he preferred to concentrate on Mavrokordatos. Surely, Blaquiere would have been included in this remark: 'Every Englishman who arrived in Greece was greatly prepossessed in favour of Mavrocordato, and we all at first thought him a princely fellow as well as a Prince: but he is neither the one nor the other.'[33]

On the whole, those writers whose roots lay in the nationalist movements of the Mediterranean (e.g. Pecchio, Gamba, Palma) sympathized with the views held by Blaquiere, while many, if not most, of the British philhellenes adopted some of the views of Stanhope.[34] Other British travellers, of course, condemned the views of both. But few saw the ideological conflict between Stanhope and Blaquiere as of crucial importance to the so-called Benthamite involvement in Greece and, indeed, to the development of liberalism generally.

In fairness to the contemporaries of Stanhope and Blaquiere, it is true to say that there were a great many other issues which concerned the British besides the administration of the first Greek loan. Even for the reformers, like Hobhouse, Sir Francis Burdett, Edward Ellice, Sir James Mackintosh, Bowring, and others, who were strong supporters of the London Greek Committee, Greece was only one among several causes which occupied their time. During 1823 when the Committee was founded, there was great concern with the fate of Spain following the invasion by France, and the Spanish Committee raised more money at this time than

[31] W. H. Humphreys, 'Journal of a Visit to Greece', ii. 206.

[32] See ibid. ii. 220 ff.

[33] Ibid. ii. 203 n.–204 n. Like Humphreys, J. Emerson is also sympathetic to Stanhope and Odysseus and hostile to Mavrokordatos. See 'Journal of a Residence among the Greeks in 1825', in *A Picture of Greece in 1825*, i. 110–11, 158, 340, 349; see also the assessment by Frank Abney Hastings, Finlay papers, British School of Archaeology at Athens, H. 3 [S. 8.2 (a)], fo. 3b–d, n.d., c.1824.

[34] See Palma, *Greece Vindicated*; Gamba, *A Narrative of Lord Byron's Last Journey to Greece*; and Pecchio, 'A Visit to Greece in the Spring of 1825', in *A Picture of Greece in 1825*, ii.3–195.

the Greek Committee.[35] After 1824, Catholic Emancipation began to occupy the attention of reformers. When Hobhouse finally decided not to go to Greece as a replacement for Byron, he became absorbed more with this issue.[36]

The interest in Spain and Greece of these reformers might be seen as itself part of the development of liberalism in Britain, a development which was also controversial. 'The divergence of popular radicalism from liberalism,' John Belchem has argued, 'was the most important "ideological" development in the 1820s, overshadowing the emergence of Ricardian socialism.'[37] Belchem's study of Henry Hunt ('Orator' Hunt) has usefully shown the strength of the new liberal current in spite of Hunt's strictures on the inconsistency and hypocrisy of its leading figures.[38] Hunt appeared at the public meeting for Greece which was held on 15 May 1823 to launch the subscription for the funds which would later finance the expedition of Byron, Stanhope, and Parry to Greece. Among the speakers were Lord Milton, John Smith, Mackintosh, Lord John Russell, Lord William Bentinck, Hobhouse, John Sidney Taylor, Lord Archibald Hamilton, Charles Brinsley Sheridan, and William Smith.[39] Hunt's intervention was intentionally mischievous, as he chided those attending the meeting for giving relatively small sums to the Greek cause and for having delayed for two years to call a public meeting. More importantly, he called attention to the contrast between such eloquent speeches about liberty in Greece and a reluctance to respond to conditions of oppression in Britain. William Cobbett took a similar line in criticizing those supporting the relief of the Spanish following their meeting in June 1823:

They want no *real* change. All they want in the present case is to make a noise about liberty and freedom, and independence, and glorious revolution, but they will suck you down a hundred thousand pounds of the

---

[35] By the end of September 1823, the Greek Committee had raised nearly £7,000 while the Spanish Committee had raised more than £19,000. See *Morning Chronicle* (27, 29 Sept. 1823).

[36] See BL Add. MS 56549. Between September 1824 and August 1825, with the exception of his involvement in Byron's affairs, Hobhouse became preoccupied by Catholic Emancipation and, to a lesser extent, with the founding of London University.

[37] J. Belchem, *'Orator' Hunt: Henry Hunt and English Working-Class Radicalism* (Oxford, 1985), 9. [38] Ibid., see 166 ff.

[39] See *Morning Chronicle* (16 May 1823).

public money, at the very *same moment*, and make nothing of it. Nay it seems to clear their throats; for the more they swallow the louder they bawl.[40]

The suspicions of Hunt and especially of Cobbett were to be proved correct in the collapse of the Greek loan in 1825 and revelations of the loan scandal in 1826 (to which Cobbett devoted enormous space in the *Weekly Register* under the heading of 'Greek Pie'). For both, the involvement of the reformers in Greece and Spain was simply a way of prattling on about liberty without doing anything about it and profiting from their involvement in the various subscriptions and loan. From the perspective of Hunt and Cobbett the very development of liberalism, with its internationalist perspective and interest in trade and finance, was a greater issue than the various currents at work within this new and developing doctrine.

If popular radicalism diverged from and became a critical voice of liberalism, so might the development of working-class radicalism be seen in a similar manner. For Noel Thompson, 'the years 1824–7 were to see not only the articulation of the theoretical foundations of a distinctively anti-capitalist and socialist political economy but also discussion of its scope, method, content and aims'.[41] The establishment of the London Mechanics' Institution virtually paralleled that of the London Greek Committee, and the same figures tended to support both of them. The controversies which surrounded the foundation of the London Mechanics' Institution have been regarded as of greater ideological significance in the development of political thought than has that between Blaquiere and Stanhope in the London Greek Committee.[42]

As for the public at large, the problems of Greece were seen in numerous contexts. For the government, and especially for Canning (who was then Foreign Secretary), the problem of Greece was largely a problem of intricate diplomacy—of how to minimize Russian influence in Greece and promote British interests while at the same time remaining relatively neutral in the eyes of the Holy

---

[40] *Cobbett's Weekly Register*, 46 (21 June 1823), 731.

[41] N. W. Thompson, *The People's Science: The Popular Political Economy of Exploitation and Crisis 1816–34* (Cambridge, 1984), 11.

[42] See E. P. Thompson, *The Making of the English Working Class* (Harmondsworth, 1968), 817–18. See also Ch. 10 below.

Alliance and the Ottoman Empire. The solution to the problem allowed the London Greek Committee to exist without much government interference except for the recall of Stanhope, but the Committee's role was seen in the context of international diplomacy rather than in terms of the development of liberalism. Investors treated the Greek loan as perhaps the most exotic, though not the most risky, of the numerous foreign loans floated in London during this period. Indeed, interest in Greece as an investment was far greater than interest in Greece as a charitable cause.

In politics, the older division between Tories and Whigs tended to obscure the new liberal currents, and the opposition of the Tories and the Church of England clergy to support for the Greeks, reflecting the position of the government, was decisive in delaying the development of much support for Greece even as late as 1823. Although membership of the London Greek Committee showed considerable unity between radical reformers and more traditional Whigs, it was difficult to entice English Tories to support the cause at all. Support came especially from Scotland, Ireland, the English Whigs, the new industrial towns of Liverpool and Manchester, the nonconformist churches (especially the Society of Friends), and the City of London. In this division between those who would support the Greek cause and those who would not, the further division among liberal supporters would not appear significant.

3. Blaquiere versus Stanhope: The Nature of the Dispute

If the dispute between Blaquiere and Stanhope was not prominently before the public, and, if appearing at all, it was partially submerged among numerous other issues, why should it seem of significance for the development of liberal thought in the early nineteenth century? The answer to this question is a complex one. At the simplest level, it is clear that the dispute between Blaquiere and Stanhope was of crucial importance to the activities of the London Greek Committee and to English philhellenism. That this has not been recognized is largely due to the fact that few scholars have studied the papers of the London Greek Committee. Where they have been examined, scholars have recognized the importance of the dispute.[43] What was publicly known was very different from what went on behind the scenes, and the nature and bitterness of the dispute can only be seen in the unpublished correspondence contained in that archive.

Even so, the significance of the dispute cannot be appreciated from the papers themselves. What has also obscured the nature of the conflict has been the fact that both Blaquiere and Stanhope have been considered disciples of Bentham. Not only would an .ideological dispute between them make no sense but their very involvement in Greece would tend to be conceived within the general framework of the 'Benthamite' involvement in Greece. But when we have examined Bentham's theory of constitutional liberty, the main features of the very different ideological positions of Blaquiere and Stanhope emerge more clearly. Neither Blaquiere's nationalism nor Stanhope's authoritarianism is present in Bentham's theory, if only because his theory has recognizable limits with regard to practice while the ideological positions of Blaquiere and Stanhope differ from Bentham's theory precisely because they are fundamentally oriented towards practice. This is not to deny that Bentham wanted his various legal reforms and codes put into practice, but to say that he hoped they would be accepted, not because they were 'liberal' but because they had passed the test of utility and provided for the greatest happiness of the greatest number. He knew that liberals rather than conservatives would be inclined to accept his theories, and he welcomed their interest in them. But to acknowledge this connection with practice does not commit one to a liberal ideology. Many liberals, as we have seen, considered Bentham as a liberal like themselves. Especially in Spain Bentham attempted to meet Blaquiere's requests for material on liberal themes (for instance, on the liberty of the press) which Bentham approved on theoretical grounds.

But Bentham's theory should not be confused with liberalism as a political ideology. In the first place, as theory, it was more

---

[43] Compare e.g. the account of the dispute in Dakin, *British and American Philhellenes during the War of Greek Independence, 1821–1833* (Thessaloniki, 1955), 73 ff. with A. D. Lignadē, *To Prōton Daneion tēs Anexartēsias* (Athens, 1970), 197–323. Dakin, who did not dwell on the dispute, did not use the London Greek Committee papers for his study. Lignadē, who made extensive use of the papers, was well aware of the dispute.

broadly conceived than the narrower political doctrine to which it became related in the 1820s. Bentham's utilitarianism drew on a considerable philosophic tradition with its roots in Locke and Hume; and his theory of constitutional liberty grew out of his critique of the achievements of Montesquieu.[44] Although there is a tendency to identify liberalism as a political doctrine with this larger philosophic tradition (E. Halévy's work suffers from this confusion), clearly the larger tradition could relate to a number of political doctrines, indeed, to conservatism as much as to liberalism.[45] In the second place, Bentham was considered, even in the 1820s, as a major figure of the Enlightenment and in this sense he belonged politically more to the eighteenth century where religious scepticism, economic freedom, and constitutional and individual liberty in the mould of Voltaire, Montesquieu, Delolme, Helvetius, and others were more part of a literary tradition and meant something different from the doctrines associated with liberalism in the early part of the nineteenth century. In making these points (and particularly the latter) there is no intention here to attempt to question (as others have done) the enormous influence which Bentham undoubtedly had on the reform movements of the Victorian era.[46] Many men of differing political persuasions read and utilized Bentham's ideas (as indeed they were meant to be utilized) and many (though by no means all) might be called 'liberal' in politics. The crucial point here is not Bentham's influence but his place in liberal ideology. What should now be clear from this study of the ideas of Blaquiere and Stanhope is that Bentham had little to say about nationalism in the nineteenth century or about political development in Asia, though he was perfectly willing for his ideas to be used, if possible, in those contexts as well as in many others.

In the dispute between Blaquiere and Stanhope several problems crucial to the development of liberalism as an ideology emerged in

[44] Most books on Bentham's utilitarianism or on his legal and moral philosophy reflect this wider philosophical dimension of his writing and have little to say about Bentham's contribution to liberal doctrine. See e.g. D. Baumgardt, *Bentham and the Ethics of Today* (Princeton, NJ, 1952); H. L. A. Hart, *Essays on Bentham* (Oxford, 1982), and G. J. Postema, *Bentham and the Common Law Tradition* (Oxford, 1986).

[45] See Ch. 1 n. 8 above.

[46] For the most recent contribution to this important debate, see S. R. Conway, 'Bentham and the Nineteenth Century Revolution in Government', in R. Bellamy (ed.), *Victorian Liberalism* (London, 1990), 71–90.

a striking manner. The most important was the problem of the extension of liberalism to the context of a non-European state where nationalist aspirations had to be weighed against liberal values. Blaquiere's position was clear, and in his support for national independence at virtually any price, with money and other assistance channelled to those who could grasp the idea of *national* independence, he seemed at times in advance of the Greeks themselves.

Stanhope's position was more problematic. In his opinion, the struggle for independence was not fuelled simply by nationalism, for Greece was essentially a non-European state. The process which has been called in the twentieth century, 'nation-building', in Stanhope's view, should go hand in hand with the war of liberation, if the Greeks were not to replace the despotism of the Turks with another despotism of their own making. Paradoxically, in so far as the Greeks themselves were considered to be unable to manage their own affairs (and, indeed, unable to manage the money that they themselves had borrowed) as they had not yet formed a European state, the need for some other party to manage their affairs raised another spectre, that of authoritarianism, this time mixed with paternalism in giving the people what they ought to want. In attempting to establish a free press, schools, utilitarian societies, a postal service, and hospitals in Greece, Stanhope was not following a Benthamite programme or even fulfilling Bentham's ambitions. He was dealing with a problem that Bentham had never conceived—how to transform an essentially non-European state into a European republic.

When Bentham wrote 'Securities against Misrule' for the use of Hassuna D'Ghies in Tripoli his object was to show a non-European ruler what liberal values he might introduce into his state without threatening his position as ruler.[47] He was presenting D'Ghies with a useful theory but was not showing him how to transform the state into which he would be introducing the theory into another kind of state. He also did not deal with the problem of the construction of a European state in a non-European setting. Stanhope's project raised problems never faced by Bentham, problems more suited to ideology than to theory, of the means by

[47] *Securities against Misrule and Other Constitutional Writings for Tripoli and Greece*, ed. T. P. Schofield (Oxford, 1990) (*CW*), 23–141.

which such a transformation might be effected. If Bentham's idea of introducing free speech, a free press, and publicity into an absolute Muslim state without endangering the power and authority of the ruler seems problematic, precisely because he holds up the theoretical ideal without developing the ideological framework to guide action, Stanhope's own project was equally problematic in so far as he believed that his experience in India, as a soldier in a colonial army (however complex British rule in India was at this time), somehow provided him with a unique insight into how to proceed in Greece. But that unique insight was simply that the Greeks were not European and were to be treated like children. He also took from his struggle with British authority the belief that the improvement of the Greeks was only possible where liberal institutions were introduced, the people were gradually accustomed to their use, and the leaders were disposed to accept and promote them. Nevertheless, such a paternalist attitude could work mainly in a 'colonial' setting and then only in one where rulers were disposed to tolerate the introduction of liberal values. Such conditions could hardly be expected to have developed in Greece (though some commentators thought that with Stanhope, Greece was destined to assume the same colonial status as British India), and, as a result, Stanhope's position seemed to some observers to be confused and out of place. The apparently absurd picture of the 'Typographical Colonel' rushing around Greece establishing newspapers, schools, and societies reflected more the untenability of Stanhope's position than any special 'Benthamite' influence.

4. Blaquiere and Stanhope in London

Despite Stanhope's apparent eccentricity there is no doubt that in London his ideas were received with much greater sympathy than Balquiere's, especially by Bentham who distinctly failed to rally behind the position of Blaquiere. Even though Blaquiere recovered his spirits sufficiently to recruit the Greek youths for education in Britain (as Stanhope failed to do), and returned in the *Amphitrite*, flying the Greek flag and carrying produce from Greece to be sold as additional security for the Greek loan, with the result that the value of the Greek loan improved for the first time since its launch, his prodigious efforts went without much appreciation. Blaquière's fears that Canning and the government might refuse to allow the ship to come to London were unfounded, but he was disappointed at the refusal of the Committee, and especially his friend, Bowring, to respond to his arrival. Due to the death of one of the boys during the journey, the *Amphitrite* was held in quarantine in Standgate Creek, but Blaquière did not hear from Bowring.[48] When he had at last heard from Joseph Hume, he learned of the 'sad state of things between the Committee and Deputies' and noted sardonically that 'we blame the dissensions of Greece, and we lead the way'.[49] By this time his only fear was: 'that some disagreeable retort may escape me in seeing persons who have acted so shamefully to me . . . I cannot however look back on that treatment without feeling all the indignation of a man who is conscious of having done his duty in every respect.'[50]

Nevertheless, within a week four of the Greek youths were presented by Bowring at a dinner given by the Lord Mayor at the Mansion House. Dressed in national costume, they entertained the large crowd with appropriate songs and dances, 'according to the style of their country'.[51] In the meantime, Blaquière presented to the Committee cannon balls made of marble from the Parthenon (to symbolize the absence of iron or lead in Greece) and a Turkish flag captured by Marcos Botzaris just before he died.[52] In November 1824 Blaquière presented his accounts and expenses to the Greek Committee, with a frank statement of the desperate plight of the Greeks, especially the 15,000 refugees from Candia and Ipsara—'starving with hunger and without cloathes to cover them or beds to lay on!'[53] As for his relationship with Stanhope, he added sarcastically in his report:

Should the Committee express any surprise that there are no *items* in my account for the support of the Press or establishment of Lancasterian Schools, be good enough to say that Col. Stanhope left nothing for me to

---

[48] See LGC papers, vol. xi, fo. U², Blaquiere to Bowring, 13 Oct. 1824; see also fo. Q², Blaquiere to Bowring, 10 Oct. 1824.

[49] Ibid. vol. xi, fo. Z², Blaquiere to Bowring, 15 Oct. 1824.

[50] Ibid.

[51] *Oriental Herald and Colonial Review*, 3 (1824), 447.

[52] Ibid.

[53] LGC papers, vol. xi, fo. O⁵, Blaquiere to Bowring (for Committee), 19 Nov. 1824.

do in that important field. If circumstances over which the Philanthropic Colonel had no control have prevented his excellent views from being carried into effect, he is not the less entitled to praise.[54]

He submitted a bill for £150 to cover his expenses, noting that virtually the whole of the past eighteen months had been devoted to the Greek cause.[55] He must not have been entirely pleased when he received only £126 for his troubles.[56]

Despite Blaquiere's considerable efforts to advance Bentham's projects in Spain and Greece there seems to have been little contact between them once he returned to Britain. Stanhope became more closely involved with Bentham and assisted him in the completion of his chapter on the 'Defensive Force' in the *Constitutional Code* as well as furthered some of his aims through various friends.[57] Stanhope's volume was rushed into print and was in circulation by October 1824.[58] This rapidity was intended to defend Stanhope against such charges as being responsible for delaying the payment of the loan or being at odds with Lord Byron. To Bowring he wrote in July: 'I know not what you mean by saying that I was the cause of the Loan being recalled. This may be a convenient tone for certain persons to assume but will it stand the test of discussion.'[59] If such a view that Stanhope was responsible for the non-payment of the loan was in circulation, Stanhope only partially rebutted it. He took the view that Barff and Logotheti held back the loan on the grounds that they were not authorized to release it without the presence of other Commissioners besides Stanhope. But he also suggested (as we have seen) that he did not share Blaquiere's belief that the payment of the funds was a matter of great urgency. As he wrote a year later in 1825: 'On my return to England, I implored the commissioners of the Greek loan to assume a rigid control over the money, or no benefit would accrue from it—Greece would be

[54] Ibid.   [55] Ibid.
[56] Ibid. fo. G⁶, Blaquiere to Bowring, 18 Dec. 1824.
[57] See *Constitutional Code*, i, ed. F. Rosen and J. H. Burns (Oxford, 1983) (*CW*), p. xxviii. For example, J. S. Buckingham, who was introduced to Bentham by Stanhope, published a number of articles on Bentham in the *Oriental Herald and Colonial Review*. See S. T. King, 'James Silk Buckingham 1786–1855: Social and Political Reformer' (MA thesis, London University, 1933).
[58] See LGC papers, vol. xi, fo. E⁴, Richard Ryan to Bowring, 27 Oct. 1824. It is worth noting that Ryan, who edited the book, thanked Bowring for his revisions and suggestions.
[59] Ibid. vol. ix, fo. M⁴, Stanhope to Bowring, 22 July 1824.

ruined, and the *dividends would* NEVER, NEVER *be paid.*'[60] Surely, the
consequence of his letters from Greece and his advice on returning
to England would have been to incline Bowring, Hume, Ellice, and
others to delay making hasty arrangements to pass over the money
to the Greeks and to increase friction between themselves and the
Greek Deputies, Orlandos and Louriottis, in London. Blaquiere
had little doubt that it was Stanhope who was responsible for the
failure to make definite arrangements to pay the loan to the Greeks
prior to his departure for England. His *Narrative of a Second Visit to
Greece*, written largely as a reply to Stanhope's *Greece, in 1823 and
1824*, contained the following comment on Stanhope's recently
published challenge to Bowring to judge between the views of
Blaquiere and Stanhope:

Would to God that experience had proved that the apprehensions of the
Government, my own fears, as well as those of Prince Mavrocordato and
so many others, were not destined to be realised! In less than ten days after
the above was penned [Stanhope's letter to Bowring], Ipsara was
destroyed, and more than four thousand men, women, and children, were
put to the sword![61]

Stanhope replied to this criticism in the second edition of his book,
which reprinted Blaquiere's comments:

I never would have given up the British loan till I had seen the foundations
of order laid, and a reasonable ground for hoping that the dividends would
be faithfully discharged. 'Tis false, however, to say that I withheld the
British loan and that the consequence was the fall and massacre at Ipsara.
On the contrary, long before the loan arrived, I took precautionary
measures with the Greek Government to prepare for its security,
reception, and employment; and at my suggestion, commissioners were
sent for that purpose to Zante. I called, too, upon Count Logotheti and
Mr. Barff, to render up the loan, provided certain wholesome measures
should be adopted; but they refused on the plea of my not being
empowered (in consequence of the death of Lord Byron and the absence of
Colonel Gordon) to draw the money; and again, because the government
of the Ionian Isles had forbidden the money to be sent to Greece. Within
ten days after this refusal, but long before the money could have operated
any thing in their favour, the brave Ipsariots were overpowered.[62]

[60] 'Letter of the Hon. Leicester Stanhope to the Editor of Blackwood's
Magazine', *Oriental Herald and Colonial Review*, 7 (1825), 114.
[61] *Narrative of a Second Visit to Greece* (London, 1825), 63 n.–64 n. See also *Greece,
in 1823 and 1824*, 407 n.–408 n.
[62] *Greece, in 1823 and 1824*, 433–4 (Stanhope to Count Metaxas, 12 May 1825).

On two counts Stanhope's defence was defective. Firstly, Blaquiere's criticism was not simply that the massacre of Ipsara could have been prevented if Stanhope had secured the release of the money, but that Stanhope was wrong in stating that there was no imminent danger to the Greeks. There was danger and the massacre at Ipsara was evidence of it. Secondly, Stanhope seems to have denied that he had influence with Logotheti and Barff with respect to the loan funds lodged with them. Nevertheless, he claimed a good deal of credit for urging all parties *not* to pay over the money until numerous conditions had been met. Furthermore, Palma produced in *Greece Vindicated* evidence from correspondence between Stanhope and the bankers Barff and Logotheti (omitted from Stanhope's volume) to show that it was Stanhope and not the bankers who argued that the loan should not be released.[63] In addition, Palma suggested that Stanhope upon his return to London tried to annul the loan and would have succeeded but for opposition from Ellice and Burdett.[64]

Nevertheless, Blaquiere's brand of nationalism found little enthusiasm in London, in spite of his own prodigious efforts on behalf of the Greeks. Even though Stanhope could not, in the end, control the payment of the loan, his views led to increasing mistrust between the Greek Deputies and the London Greek Committee. Blaquiere continued to sympathize with the Greek Deputies and eventually made his last journey to Greece on their behalf to defend their behaviour in London. In *Letters from Greece*, his last book, Blaquiere neither mentioned Bentham nor praised his writings. Though written after the Greek loan scandal of 1826 in which Louriottis's name was not untarnished, he none the less found he 'more sinned against than sinning'.[65] As for the loans, he made this comment:

In recommending that an attempt should be made to negotiate the *First Loan*, I considered, as I still do, that the resources of Greece, if properly managed, were fully equal to the payment of interest and principal . . . With respect to the *Second Loan*, while I admitted the necessity of negotiating it, I did so in the belief that the proceeds would have been very

[63] See esp. 237–42.
[64] Ibid. 237. Both of these views were shared by the Greek Deputies. They also felt that the London Greek Committee disapproved of Blaquiere. See Benaki Museum, Mavrokordatos papers, Orlandos, Zaimēs, and Louriottis to Mavrokordatos, 3 Aug. 1824. [65] London, 1828: 168 n.

differently appropriated. If I had for an instant imagined, that instead of being applied to the liquidation of the first Loan, and otherwise employed to supply the real wants and necessities of the cause, rather than becoming the prey of ruthless and unprincipled speculators; that instead of hastening the independence of Greece, and thus enabling her to commence the work of repayment, it was destined to be divided among a knot of greedy individuals, or squandered in the furtherance of projects as useless as they were preposterous, I should most certainly as the friend of Greece, and of those whose property was thus destined to be wantonly sacrificed, have felt it my duty to protest in the face of England and of Europe, against that fatal transaction.[66]

Blaquiere no longer saw in London fellow liberals working for a common cause, but rather 'ruthless and unprincipled speculators' and a 'knot of greedy individuals'. He remained true to his beliefs and continued to support the Greek cause and, more generally, the cause of nationalism in the Mediterranean basin. He died in 1832 supporting Mendizabal's expedition to establish a constitutional monarchy in Portugal.[67]

[66] Ibid. 166–7. He also believed that no third loan could be raised until financial affairs in London were placed in other hands, as those who held power had abused it. See Benaki Museum, Archive 9, fo. 9, Blaquiere to Speliadē (Secretary of the Legislative Assembly), 2 May 1827.

[67] See Bowring, x. 475, and C. Gobbi, 'Edward Blaquière: Agente del liberalismo', *Cuadernos hispano-americanos*, 350 (1979), 306–25.

10

'The Last Days of Lord Byron'

1. The Attack on Bentham and Stanhope

The myth of Stanhope, the Benthamite soldier, and Byron, the romantic poet, forming two opposing poles of doctrine and attitude in Greece was based in part on Stanhope's *Greece, in 1823 and 1824*. But the work which developed the thesis of Stanhope v. Byron was actually written as a reply to Stanhope. Of the numerous books, articles, and poems published after the death of Byron, William Parry's *The Last Days of Lord Byron*, published in 1825, was the only one to concentrate almost wholly on the supposed opposition between Stanhope and Byron. It also linked Stanhope and Bentham by incorporating a notorious chapter which lampooned Bentham's life-style.

In the 1820s Bentham's reputation was at its peak, and he was perhaps the most highly regarded English philosopher and jurist of his day. When Hazlitt wrote in *The Spirit of the Age* (1825) that Bentham's 'name is little known in England, better in Europe, best of all in the plains of Chile and the mines of Mexico', he was only partially correct.[1] Bentham was well-known throughout Europe and Latin America, largely due to the widespread dissemination of Dumont's French versions of his writings, especially the *Traités de législation*.[2] But he was *also* well-known, though not necessarily approved of, in England, where, besides his reputation as a jurist and legal reformer, he had a growing reputation as an advocate of radical reform which included the advocacy of representative democracy based on universal suffrage.[3]

---

[1] W. Hazlitt, *The Spirit of the Age; or, Contemporary Portraits*, ed. E. D. Mackerness (London, 1969), 19.

[2] *Traités de législation, civile et pénale*, ed. É. Dumont, 3 vols. (Paris, 1802). On Dumont, see C. Blamires, 'Étienne Dumont: Genevan Apostle of Utility', *Utilitas*, 2 (1990), 55–70.

[3] See e.g. *Plan of Parliamentary Reform, in the Form of a Catechism* (London, 1817) (Bowring, iii. 433–557); *Bentham's Radical Reform Bill, with Extracts from the Reasons*

To the Tory press, Bentham's position was an anathema and few opportunities were lost to pour scorn on his ideas or on his disciples. When Parry's book was published, it was eagerly received, not so much for its account of Byron (who was himself regarded with some ambivalence), but for the chapter on Bentham. *The Times* devoted a whole column to its review, which consisted largely of the lengthy extract from Parry's book describing what Byron supposedly called 'Jerry Bentham's Cruise'—his custom of jogging through the streets of London for exercise, his alleged encounter with a prostitute called the 'City-barge' (on account of her bulk) in Fleet Street, his supposed habit of taking his meals at odd hours, his vanity in admiring his own works in a bookseller's window, and other practices which apparently were told often to the amusement of Byron in Missolonghi.[4] In an introductory paragraph Parry was introduced in *The Times* as 'Major Parry, a gentleman who was with Lord Byron during the season of his Lordship's operations in Greece'. Bentham was depicted as:

a person whom some retired tradesman [i.e. Francis Place] and self-dubbed philosophers [possibly James Mill] put on a level with Bacon or Locke— with Solon or Lycurgus; but who, we suspect . . . will rank with the theorists and fanatics of the puritanic age—with the fifth monarchy-men— with the John Lilburns and Praise-God Barebones of the Commonwealth.

The introduction concluded:

We may merely add, that Jeremy Bentham is too elaborately odd for a great man: a great man may be occasionally odd by accident, or from the circumstances of education; but he never doggedly sets about doing every thing differently from other men, in order to be thought a genius because he is eccentric.

In August 1825, J. G. Lockhart (the biographer of Scott) reviewed the book in *Blackwood's Edinburgh Magazine*, another strong Tory periodical.[5] By this time, Lockhart at least had figured out, as *The Times* had not, that Parry was neither a major nor a gentleman. This discovery, however, made him no less attractive, and he was

---

(London, 1819) (Bowring, iii. 558–97). See also J. R. Dinwiddy, 'Bentham's Transition to Political Radicalism, 1809–10', *Journal of the History of Ideas*, 36 (1975), 683–700.

[4] *The Times* (19 May 1825).

[5] 'Parry's Last Days of Lord Byron', 18 (1825), 137–55. The ascription of the article to J. G. Lockhart may be found in Walter E. Houghton (ed.), *Wellesley Index to Victorian Periodicals 1824–1900*, 4 vols. (Toronto, 1966–87), i. 17.

depicted as 'a Firemaster, in our navy, and had, through a long life, served in such a way as to secure a high character for bravery, honesty, and intelligence and skill in his profession'.[6] For Lockhart, Parry was 'a plain man', 'a doing man', and 'plainly . . . incapable of inventing these things'.[7] Like *The Times*, *Blackwood's* proceeded to print the lengthy extract about Bentham, comparing it not unfavourably with Hazlitt's essay in *The Spirit of the Age*.

Blackwood's was obviously inspired by *The Times*, as were other journals, especially in North America, and it seems that Bentham was hurt by the damage to his reputation.[8] Nevertheless, Bentham did not actually play much of a role in the book which was directed primarily at discrediting Stanhope. If *The Times* conveniently forgot about Stanhope, Lockhart in *Blackwood's* did not, calling him 'a crack-brained enthusiast of the regular Bentham breed'.[9]

2. The Character of William Parry

William Parry, a somewhat obscure figure, was given responsibility for organizing the brigade of artillery and arsenal in the expedition arranged by the London Greek Committee and dispatched to Greece in November 1823. He was employed by the London Greek Committee on the recommendation of Thomas Gordon who was using him to organize his own expedition (see Chapter 11) until he withdrew as leader and passed Parry on to the Committee. Even in his relationship with Gordon, Parry displayed obvious signs of psychological instability. He tended to idealize Gordon as a great leader not only to be given faithful and devoted service but also to be defended against all sorts of imagined slights and attacks.[10] When the London Greek Committee hesitated to commit itself to the expedition which Parry was organizing (largely due to Gordon's indecision about leading it), Parry would characteristically attack the Committee in letters to Gordon

[6] Ibid. 138.   [7] Ibid. 138–9.
[8] See Bowring, xi. 66–7; J. R. Dinwiddy, 'Early Nineteenth-Century Reactions to Benthamism', *Transactions of the Royal Historical Society*, 5th Series, 34 (1984), 49.
[9] 'Parry's Last Days of Lord Byron', 139.
[10] See Gordon papers, Aberdeen University, 1160/21/9/27, Parry to Gordon, 21 May 1823; 1160/21/9/30, Parry to Gordon, 25 May 1823.

('*Questions Absurd, Resolutions Ridiculous*'), when the reason for the hesitation lay primarily with Gordon himself.[11] To Gordon, he pretended to be the practical and useful servant, always flattering his master, if only by seeing everyone else as inferior and confused. Even where the Committee was slavishly following Gordon's proposals for sending the brigade of artillery and arsenal to Greece, Parry's impatience with their concern to consider alternative plans, however briefly, was transformed in his letters into contempt for the Committee which bordered on accusations of treason. Gordon, however, seemed either blind or indifferent to Parry's deficiencies. When W. H. Humphreys met Parry for the first time, he was afraid that he was 'non compos', even though his 'braggadacio chimeras' were 'highly diverting'. 'He is as ardent in eulogizing you', he wrote to Gordon, 'as he is in vituperating every body I have yet heard him speak of.'[12] Gordon simply replied that Parry 'is really a worthy, and friendly man, and capable of giving you much practical instruction, that cannot be found in books.'[13] But not everyone shared this view and, with the withdrawal of Gordon from the expedition, the Committee was anxious that Gordon provide a financial guarantee for Parry's work in Greece.[14] The Committee eventually accepted Gordon's personal recommendation and a further subscription to 'the cause' of £250.[15] In recommending Parry, he wrote:

Now from my knowledge of the man I can have no hesitation in saying— that I am persuaded he is not only ready but most eager to go—and that it would be impossible for the Committee to find a man in his situation so capable of rendering essential service. His real merit is considerably obscured by his excessive desire of hearing himself talk. But his character appears to me highly reputable, and his principles strictly honorable.[16]

Bowring was only slightly less enthusiastic, when he wrote that Parry 'is certainly the only man whom we could find so well

---

[11] Ibid. 1160/21/9/34, Parry to Gordon, 1 June 1823.

[12] Ibid. 1160/21/9/70, Humphreys to Gordon, 14 Oct. 1823.

[13] Ibid. 1160/21/9/72, Gordon to Humphreys, 20 Oct. 1823. Parry could impress others. Blaquiere, who seems to have met him in connection with Gordon, wrote at the time: 'Parry and a few old Sergeants would be an immense acquisition' (ibid. 1160/21/9/12, Blaquiere to Gordon, 27 Mar. 1823).

[14] See ibid. 1160/21/9/51, Bowring to Gordon, 26 Aug. 1823.

[15] See LGC papers, vol. iii, fo. H[1], Gordon to Bowring, 27 Aug. 1823; and Gordon papers, 1160/21/9/63, Bowring to Gordon, 1 Sept. 1823.

[16] LGC papers, vol. iii, fo. H[1], Gordon to Bowring, 27 Aug. 1823.

adapted to the undertaking he is about to be engaged in'.[17] Joseph Hume, however, seemed somewhat less satisfied with Parry's appointment and asked Gordon as late as November 1823 to send Parry 'a series of instructions for his guidance' including injunctions to follow Stanhope's orders and 'to control his own temper and feelings if any thing unpleasant should occur.'[18] 'I have great fears,' he continued, 'from Mr. Parry's warm and lusty disposition and, after the confidence we have placed in him, it will be much to be regretted if he should disappoint our just expectations.'[19] Nevertheless, the problem with Parry would not turn out to be his 'warm and lusty disposition', as Hume feared, except as it led to drunkenness, but the tendency seen by Humphreys (who at that time had no reason to be hostile to him) for Parry's paranoid mind to eulogize one man and attack everyone else. While he was working for Gordon, he could do little harm, although it is curious that Gordon, who took him to Scotland in the spring of 1823, was so blind to his faults. Parry's flattery and obsequiousness seems to have acted as sedatives on those on whom he bestowed such dubious attentions. If he did Gordon little harm, Gordon's recommendation would prove fatal, and in the employ of the London Greek Committee, Lord Byron, and Leicester Stanhope, there would be ample scope for the operation of Parry's destructive personality. By the time Blaquiere arrived in Zante with the first instalment of the Greek loan, and the death of Byron had driven the mad Parry to the lazaretto there, he would report:

[T]here is no doubt whatever of his [Parry] being one of the greatest rascals unhung, and as great an imposter; for it now appears that he is totally ignorant of nearly all those points which induced the Committee to send him out. So detested has he made himself at Missolonghi, that all the

[17] Gordon papers, 1160/21/9/63, Bowring to Gordon, 1 Sept. 1823. Bowring was, none the less, very positive in recommending Parry to Byron. On 22 July 1823, Bowring wrote: 'Parry the man who will accompany and head the rest is a strong-minded, practical operator, whose services cannot but be highly valuable to the Greeks.' On 18 August he noted: 'After long consultations among the Military Gentlemen who belong to it [the Committee], a plan of Col Gordon has been adopted to send to Greece under the control of a very intelligent fire-master who was Genl Congreve's right hand man—and understands the manufacture of every species of destructive arms and missiles . . .' See Murray archive, Box A21. For Gordon's role in the expedition, see below, Ch. 12.

[18] Ibid. 1160/21/9/78, Hume to Gordon, 4 Nov. 1823.

[19] Ibid.

English who are there, say they will quit it immediately should Mr. Parry come back.[20]

Blaquiere had every reason to be sympathetic with Parry for both were opposed to Stanhope's policies in Greece, but Blaquiere's opposition was ideological and Parry's personal. Faced with the débâcle of the expedition organized by Parry, he could see with regret that a great mistake had been made: 'Upon the whole, it is deeply to be regretted we had not made more careful inquiries as to his character. As a sot and a drunkard Mr. P is unrivalled; and will you believe it all the people at Missolonghi agree.'[21]

3. The Myth of Parry and Byron

Parry's expedition left England in November 1823 and for various reasons did not reach Greece until early February 1824. He was expected to serve under Byron and Stanhope, to establish an arsenal in Greece, and to instruct the Greeks in artillery. In this task he was accompanied by nine English craftsmen.[22] The time he actually spent with Byron amounted to only a few weeks from 5 February to Byron's death on 19 April. Parry, Byron, and Stanhope were together in Missolonghi for only sixteen days.

The bare facts of what occurred during this brief period are not in dispute, but their significance is not easy to determine. If Parry in fact accomplished little or nothing, neither, for that matter, did Byron or Stanhope, or most of the philhellenes who went to

[20] LGC papers, vol. ix, fo. R, Blaquiere to Bowring, 7 June 1824. This letter also provides further evidence than has been known as to Parry's madness at Zante after Byron's death. Cf. Doris Langley Moore, *The Late Lord Byron: Posthumous Dramas* (London, 1961), 186 n.

[21] LGC papers, vol. ix, fo. R, Blaquiere to Bowring, 7 June 1824. W. H. Humphreys wrote in similar terms: 'Parry unfortunately proved to be a blustering worthless character, who had found no great difficulty in imposing on the Committee in London, and had come out with strong recommendations to Lord Byron, who entrusted all his operations to him; which effectually put a stop to the chance of his being able to commence any enterprize whatever, and the badly conducted expedition of the Committee was rendered a useless expenditure.' See 'Journal of a Visit to Greece', in *A Picture of Greece in 1825*, 2 vols. (London, 1826), ii. 206.

[22] See D. Dakin, *British and American Philhellenes during the War of Greek Independence, 1821–1833* (Thessaloniki, 1955), 59–60.

Greece. So much of what was accomplished belongs to the realm of symbol and gesture. If the money for the entire expedition was wasted, it can none the less be argued that the very existence of the expedition encouraged subscriptions to the first Greek loan. For whatever actually happened in Greece, the newspaper reports of the expedition in London were most encouraging. The British expedition was of enormous symbolic value and no symbol was more powerful than that of Byron. And for Stanhope to invoke Bentham, the liberty of the press, and constitutional liberty was perhaps more important than the fact that he actually did little. Even the two newspapers he established at Missolonghi were largely of symbolic value. What actually occurred in Greece was less important than the symbols generated by the very presence of these major actors on the historical stage.

The appreciation of the importance of these symbols and symbolic actions does not mean that the reality of what actually took place in Missolonghi is being neglected. The 'reality' was failure, and the reasons for this failure will occupy us in due course.[23] Here, however, in the realm of ideology, the significance of the expedition has to be seen more in terms of the generation of a series of myths which have absorbed the attention of writers to the present day. We have already referred to a number of myths, especially the one that Stanhope was in fact a disciple of Bentham. In exposing this myth, we have been able to see more clearly the terms of the ideological conflict between Stanhope and Blaquiere. To see this conflict in the clearest light, it is necessary to expose other myths surrounding Parry, Byron, and the tragic expedition to Missolonghi. One myth is that of the down-to-earth practical William Parry, who provided assistance and comfort to Byron during his last days. Another myth is the account of the relationship between Byron and Stanhope depicted in *The Last Days of Lord Byron*.

As for the practical and helpful Parry, one can judge the power of this myth from the manner in which those writing 150 years after the events still subscribe to it. 'Reading the numerous accounts of these exciting days,' writes William St Clair, 'one sometimes gets the impression that Parry was the only normal man among dozens of neurotics.'[24] 'The firemaster's sound practicalities', notes Leslie

[23] See below, Ch. 12.
[24] *That Greece Might Still Be Free* (London, 1972), 177.

Marchand, 'seemed a relief after his [Byron's] experiences with the indecisive Mavrokordatos and the "typographical Colonel".'[25] According to Doris Langley Moore, 'it was a comfort to him [Byron] to have an intelligent down-to-earth factotum at his command, fatherly and protective (he was twenty years Byron's senior) yet deferential too, a good companion over glasses of brandy and water'.[26]

Although the writers who have made these remarks are careful to point to Parry's failure as firemaster and leader of the expedition, and perhaps his inclination to drunkenness, the failure is not ascribed to a serious defect in Parry's personality and character. Not all modern writers, however, accept this positive view of Parry. Woodhouse points out that Byron 'alone' found Parry good company.[27] Nicolson emphasizes that Parry quarrelled with virtually everyone with whom he came into contact.[28] Yet even Nicolson, despite his awareness of his deficiencies, is drawn to Parry: 'For Parry was no fool. Uneducated but shrewd, besotted but vigorous, pretentious and yet devoted, plausible and yet in his own way sincere, crude and yet intensely emotional, Parry emerges as a very definite, and not wholly unsympathetic personality.'[29] Nicolson points out at length and with eloquence the mutual attraction of Byron and Parry with Parry depicted as providing relief from Byron's difficulties and frustrations in Missolonghi and acting as a lightning conductor for Byron's emotional outbursts which, in absorbing the force of the storm, protected Byron.[30] Nevertheless, having examined Parry's previous relationship with Gordon, one can see in his attachment to Byron merely the repetition of a psychological pattern of passionate attachment and devoted service to one man coupled with a paranoid distrust and dislike of everyone else. Rather than provide relief and comfort for Byron, it is more likely that Parry isolated Byron, encouraged his heavy drinking and that antisocial and self-destructive side of his personality that Byron himself was partly attempting to overcome by coming to Greece in the first place.

Byron was more susceptible to Parry's influence than Gordon,

[25] L. Marchand, *Byron: A Biography*, 3 vols. (London, 1957), iii. 1175. The passage is repeated in *Byron: A Portrait* (London, 1971), 439, where the point is made more strongly.   [26] Moore, *The Late Lord Byron*, 171.

[27] C. M. Woodhouse, *The Philhellenes* (London, 1969), 111.

[28] H. Nicolson, *Byron* (new edn., London, 1948), 210–11.

[29] Ibid. 211.   [30] Ibid. 211–12.

who, for the most part, dealt with Parry only from a distance and was able to minimize the effects of his fawning, loquacious, single-minded devotion to him. Byron was vulnerable: a poet, entirely out of his depth in military matters, finding the acceptance of responsibility burdensome and boring, he was also totally frustrated in his ambition for military success in Greece. He lacked ideological commitment in a setting that required it, if any progress (of whatever value) was to be made. Blaquiere and Stanhope (however limited their success and however restricted their perceptions of the world) were able to act largely because they worked from within frameworks carefully defined by ideas oriented to practice. The poet, perhaps, like the philosopher, is not especially oriented towards ideologically programmed action. Bentham in Greece, as in Spain, would have only symbolic value and the same may be said for Byron in Greece. From the point of view of Stanhope, Byron 'had no opinions at all at least no fixed opinions and he frequently said so himself'.[31] From the perspective of one who saw clearly the road he was to take, Byron must have been a disappointment. Perhaps this is why Stanhope sought ludicrously to introduce him to the 'opinions' of Bentham. In place of fixed opinions Byron had 'very strong' feelings and he confessed to Stanhope that he quarrelled with everybody.[32] What a relief then to discover in Parry someone with whom he need not feel inferior for lack of opinions, with whom he would not quarrel (as Parry would only serve and amuse him), and into whose apparently practical and busy hands he could delegate the various day-to-day responsibilities that had evolved from his presence (with funds) in Greece. He need not even quarrel with others, as Parry would do it for him. Byron did not need Parry to supply information about military matters, and there is no evidence that he did so. The relationship between them was not constructive at all. 'P[arry] was officious, pompous, and jealous of any having access to, or influence with Lord B.', wrote James Kennedy who provided this picture of Byron's household in Missolonghi:

The household appeared in confusion: all the servants had uniforms, each according to his fancy, and some of them were of the most grotesque kind: they seemed to have exchanged duties; the cook, for example, became

---

[31] BL Add. MS 56549, fo. 162, Hobhouse's Diary, n.d.

[32] Ibid. Hobhouse also wrote: 'He quarrelled with Stanhope—but made it up as often and said give me your honest right hand.'

groom, and the groom became something else, and *vice versâ*; each appeared to be doing something else than that which lay within his province.[33]

Whatever his influence on Byron, it would hardly seem to have been positive and most probably Parry's role was one of increasing the chaos and confusion. According to Stanhope, Byron 'did little—but shoot pistols—and ride—and drink punch with *Parry* . . . whom he laughed at'.[34] Millingen described their relationship more vividly:

> It was soon perceived that the brandy-bottle was Parry's Castalian spring, and that, unless he drank deep, his stories became dull. Lord Byron, in consequence, took constant care to keep him in good spirits; but unfortunately, partly from inclination, and partly to keep him company, he drank himself to the same excess.[35]

Were their relationship only defined in terms of mutual drunkenness, it might not have been so destructive. The excessive drinking was merely a symptom of the underlying dependence, and even this might not have been destructive if Byron did not depend on Parry nearly as much as Parry depended on Byron. While Gordon merely employed Parry, Byron developed a deep need for him, even though it became readily apparent that by giving Parry the power and responsibility implicit in the absurd appointment to 'Major' in the artillery brigade, such an appointment meant the virtual destruction of the brigade. The more Byron needed Parry, the more Parry served Byron alone, and his admiration for and attraction to Byron was accompanied by a bullying hostility towards anyone else. The pattern that Parry established with Gordon would be carried on even more venomously in Greece.

4. The Myth of Opposition between Byron and Stanhope

If the relationship between Byron and Parry has formed so powerful a myth, even more powerful is that which depicts the

---

[33] J. Kennedy, *Conversations on Religion with Lord Byron and Others* (London, 1830), 307.   [34] BL Add. MS 56549, fo. 163, Hobhouse's Diary, n.d.
[35] J. Millingen, *Memoirs of the Affairs of Greece* (London, 1831), 117.

polar opposition between Stanhope and Byron, so much favoured by historians and which has served to obscure the real ideological differences between Blaquiere and Stanhope. The depiction of Stanhope as the 'Typographical Colonel' and Byron's supposed reaction to Stanhope's offering Bentham's *Table of the Springs of Action* to him are commonplaces of nearly every account of Byron's last days in Missolonghi, and reflect this myth.

One of Parry's well-known qualities which endeared him to Byron in Missolonghi was his ability to act as a mimic. If he supposedly entertained Byron often with his accounts of 'Jerry Bentham's Cruise', he later put his ability to mime and caricature to impressive use in his book. When Stanhope included a number of anecdotes in *Greece, in 1823 and 1824* to portray his positive relationship with Byron, Parry took these very anecdotes and transformed them in his own book into evidence for the thesis of fundamental opposition between the two men. According to Parry,

I have already more than once alluded to their disputes; and if Colonel Stanhope was right, we must condemn Lord Byron. The Greek Committee have thanked the former, and have thus tacitly censured the latter. In bringing the two before the reader, I wish him to decide betwixt them. I had to choose my party on the spot; and I do not pretend to be impartial, for I never sided with Colonel Stanhope.[36]

Parry also brought Bentham into this picture of Byron and Stanhope. One reason for their opposition was 'the fact of Colonel Stanhope having laboured to cast a considerable degree of censure on Lord Byron, chiefly, as it appears to me [Parry] because he was not an admirer of Mr. Bentham'.[37] Parry also invited the reader, in effect, to choose who was correct, a Byron who would 'rather ridicule Mr. Bentham's oddities than discuss his principles', or a Stanhope who allegedly censured Byron for being a 'Turk' for not appreciating Bentham's liberal principles.[38]

What Parry omitted to say is that he was supposed to have been working for both Byron and Stanhope, and there was no need for him to choose one party or the other. But he would not have been drawn to the temperate Stanhope who also might have been a better judge than Byron of the skills he claimed to possess.

[36] Parry, *The Last Days of Lord Byron*, 227–8.   [37] Ibid. 225.
[38] Ibid. 226.

Psychologically, Parry wanted to be attached to one person and Byron was the ideal candidate. His emphasis on a division between Byron and Stanhope was additionally a way of justifying his own actions in Greece. He developed his theme to the fullest extent. If Stanhope wanted to establish schools throughout Greece as part of the struggle for independence, Byron was portrayed as proclaiming: 'Give Greece arms and independence and then learning.'[39] Byron was also depicted as so repelled by Stanhope's preoccupation with printing presses instead of warfare that he 'felt much relieved by at last finding a practical man [i.e. Parry] near him, in whom he could confide'.[40] Parry repeated these disagreements between Byron and Stanhope at several points in the book. In one example, he wrote:

In the course of the day, I also observed, that Lord Byron, in addition to his other difficulties, did not agree very cordially with Colonel Stanhope. The Colonel was anxious to establish schools, erect printing-presses, and secure liberty, by promulgating theories concerning it. Lord Byron seemed willing to leave the form of the government to be settled by circumstances hereafter. He wanted the Greeks first to conquer their national independence, and then enter into a compact for the security of individual rights. Colonel Stanhope, I understood, had been very active in establishing a newspaper at Missolonghi, and Lord Byron said, had his will been uncontrolled, it should not have been done.[41]

Mavrokordatos was another source of dispute:

Lord Byron, who had no love for theories of government in the then condition of Greece, attached himself to the party of Mavrocordato and practical civil order; Colonel Stanhope, the champion of liberal opinions, the great man for a press and newspaper, united himself at Athens with Odysseus and the other military chieftains, and seemed to wish that all the supplies sent out from England might be placed under their control. Henceforth all that Byron had done was to be undone; and what he was doing was to be opposed.[42] . . .

His [Stanhope's] hostility to Mavrocordato had been so marked, that there gradually arose an opinion, among both Greeks and English, strengthened by the Colonel's own conduct, that he was endeavouring to break up the establishment at Missolonghi, and remove all the stores belonging to the committee to Athens. This report, like the others, was conveyed to Lord Byron, and he not having parted with Colonel Stanhope on very good terms, it added much to the disagreeableness of his feelings.

[39] Parry, *The Last Days of Lord Byron*, 16.   [40] Ibid. 25.
[41] Ibid. 32–3. See also 82–4.   [42] Ibid. 84–5. See also 37.

He had before attributed both neglect and deceit to the [London] Greek Committee or some of its agents; and this report of the proceedings of their special and chosen messenger [Stanhope], made him, in the irritation of the moment, regard them as acting even treacherously towards him.[43]

Even Byron's death was used by Parry to develop this extreme polarization of Byron and Stanhope, with Stanhope hoping that Byron would be buried in the Parthenon at Athens but Byron having supposedly expressed a desire to be buried in England.[44] Parry also presented Byron's supposed opinions of many leading figures, including Stanhope, putting these remarks in quotation marks as though they were a summary of actual remarks made by Byron himself. Thus, Byron allegedly said this about Stanhope:

Here too is the chief agent of the Committee, Colonel Stanhope, organising the whole country. He leaves nothing untouched, from the general government, to the schools for children. He has a plan for organising the military force, for establishing posts, for regulating the administration of justice, for making Mr. Bentham the apostle of the Greeks, and for whipping little boys in the newest and most approved mode. He is for doing all this, without a reference to any body or any thing; complains bitterly of a want of practical statesmen in Greece, and would be glad I believe, to import a large supply of Mr. Bentham's books, and scholars. Mavrocordato he openly beards, as if the Prince knew nothing of Greece, and was quite incapable of forming a correct opinion of its interests. At the same time, he has no funds to carry all his projects into execution. He is a mere schemer and talker, more of a saint than a soldier; and with a great deal of pretended plainness, a mere politician, and no patriot.[45]

This is a mere excerpt from Byron's supposed remarks about Stanhope which range considerably further—from Stanhope's desire personally to govern Greece to Byron's own plans supposedly to include Bentham and Stanhope as 'heroes' in the next cantos of *Don Juan*.[46] Parry especially used Bentham to bring out the antipathy between Byron and Stanhope. If Stanhope had used Bentham to bolster up his own ideas and proposals, Parry satirized Bentham in an attempt to show that Byron rightly mocked Bentham in his various encounters with Stanhope.[47] Nevertheless, satire was neither Parry's only weapon nor even the one he most often used. The tone of the whole book was remarkably bitter and

---

[43] Ibid. 105–6.   [44] See ibid. 143–4.   [45] Ibid. 189.

[46] See ibid. 189–92.   [47] See ibid. 235–41.

never more so than when depicting the relationship between Byron and Stanhope, as in this concluding passage:

In the pursuit of his own schemes, he [Stanhope] broke up the brigade Lord Byron had been at so much pains in forming; he in a manner reversed and destroyed all Byron had done, and not only cast, as far as lay in his power, odium on the memory of his noble friend, but did a great injury to the Greek cause.[48]

5. Myth and Evidence

However Parry attempted to create the myth of opposition between Byron and Stanhope, the surviving evidence suggests a different interpretation of their relationship. Stanhope clearly appreciated Byron's importance and reputation in Greece. While awaiting Byron's arrival in Missolonghi, he wrote to Bowring: 'Lord Byron's presence here is anxiously solicited by the government and people' (16 December 1823); 'all are looking forward to Lord Byron's arrival as they would to the coming of a Messiah' (31 December); 'Lord Byron has this moment arrived. He was received with military honours and popular applause' (5 January 1824).[49] All of Stanhope's general remarks about Byron in his correspondence reflect this respect for his importance and, in addition, his letters display the good-humoured bantering that had developed between them. For example, when Stanhope objected to contributing £100 to the support of the demoralized philhellenes who were supposed to be trained to serve in the artillery corps, Byron, he said, 'insisted upon having my £100, and threatened, if I refused it, to libel me in my own Chronicle'. Knowing that Byron disapproved of his newly created paper and would hardly have been an enthusiastic contributor, Stanhope replied: 'Upon this I took fire, and declared that, if he would do so with all the strength of his powerful and sarcastic mind, I would pledge myself to subscribe double the sum. Am I not a swaggerer.'[50]

Byron also engaged in this sort of banter, and on the issue of the press at a later date he wrote:

---

[48] Parry, *The Last Days of Lord Byron*, 308–9.

[49] Stanhope, *Greece, in 1823 and 1824* (new edn., London, 1825), 42, 60, 71.

[50] Ibid. 82 (Stanhope to Bowring, 7 Jan. 1824).

[F]rom the very first I foretold to Col. Stanhope and to P[rince] Mavrocordato that a Greek Newspaper (or indeed any other) in *the present state* of Greece—might—and probably *would* lead to much mischief and misconstruction—unless under *some* restrictions—nor have I ever had anything to do with either—as a Writer—or otherwise, except as a pecuniary Contributor to their support on the outset which I could not refuse to the earnest request of the Projectors. Col. S[tanhope] and myself had considerable differences of opinion on this subject—and (what will appear laughable enough—) to such a degree that he charged me with *despotic* principles—and I *him* with Ultra-radicalism.[51]

Earlier, when still in Cephalonia, Byron wrote to Bowring giving this estimate of his new colleague:

I am happy to say that Colonel Leicester Stanhope and myself are acting in perfect harmony together—he is likely to be of great service both to the cause and to the Committee, and is publicly as well as personally a very valuable acquisition to our party on every account. He came up (as they all do who have not been in the country before) with some high-flown notions of the sixth form at Harrow and Eton, &c; but Col. Napier and I set him to rights on those points, which is absolutely necessary to prevent disgust, or perhaps return; but now we can set our shoulders *soberly* to the *wheel*, without quarrelling with the mud which may clog it occasionally.[52]

The Harrovian Byron and the Etonian Stanhope, while disagreeing on some points, were in basic agreement on many more. Both insisted that they would speak the truth about conditions in Greece and, unlike Blaquiere, fully brought to light the dissent and factions existing at the time.[53] Both joined together in subscribing funds for an artillery brigade in Missolonghi.[54] Stanhope supported the plan for Byron to take on the payment of the Suliots and to organize the expedition to Lepanto with Parry's artillery.[55] He also sympathized with Byron's difficulties in dealing with the Suliots and thought their conduct might have provoked Byron's first illness in February

---

[51] *Byron's Letters and Journals*, ed. L. Marchand, xi: *'For Freedom's battle'* (London, 1981), 138–9 (Byron to Samuel Barff, 19 Mar. 1824).

[52] Ibid. 83 (Byron to Bowring, 26 Dec. 1823).

[53] See ibid. 64 (Byron to Stanhope, 25 Nov. 823); *Greece, in 1823 and 1824*, 31–2 (Stanhope to Bowring, 26 Nov. 1823); *'For Freedom's battle'*, 64–5 (Byron to Bowring, 29 Nov. 1823), 66–70 (Byron to Greek government, 30 Nov. 1823), 71 (Byron to Mavrokordatos, 2 Dec. 1823), 72 (Byron to Bowring, 7 Dec. 1823).

[54] *Greece, in 1823 and 1824*, 39 (Stanhope to Bowring, 13 Dec. 1823).

[55] Ibid. 43 (Stanhope to Bowring, 16 Dec. 1823).

1824.[56] Furthermore, both Byron and Stanhope accepted a system
of Commissioners to supervise the payment of the loan.[57] And
both held out, as a major object of their policies in Greece, the
reconciliation of the various parties.[58] As a result, Byron appeared
more in favour of Stanhope's efforts to reconcile the various parties
at Salona than was suggested by Parry. There is no reason to doubt
his sincerity (whatever reservations Mavrokordatos might have
had) when he wrote to Stanhope that 'P[rince] Mavrocordato and
myself will go to Salona to meet Ulysses—and you may be very
sure that P.M. will accept any proposition for the advantage of
Greece.'[59] Similarly, Byron reported to Barff: 'In a few days—
P[rince] Mavrocordato and myself—with a considerable escort
intend to proceed to Salona at the request of Ulysses and the Chiefs
of Eastern Greece—to concert if possible a plan of Union between
Western and Eastern Greece—and to take measures offensive and
defensive for the ensuing Campaign.'[60] The delays in undertaking
this journey occasioned by bad weather and flooding were genuine.
By the time the weather had eased, however, Byron's fatal illness
had begun.[61] Although Stanhope was suspicious of the delay which
ultimately prevented Mavrokordatos and Byron from reaching
Salona, he never doubted that Byron supported his policy, and
tended to blame Mavrokordatos.[62]

When Byron died, Stanhope was in Salona awaiting his arrival.
In a letter to Bowring, written when the news of Byron's death had
just arrived, Stanhope wrote:

The soul of Byron has taken its last flight. England has lost her brightest
genius—Greece her noble friend. To console them for the loss, he has left
behind the emanations of his splendid mind. If Byron had faults, he had
redeeming virtues too—he sacrificed his comfort, fortune, health and life
to the cause of an oppressed nation. Honoured be his memory! Had I the

[56] Ibid. 116 (Stanhope to Bowring, 18 Feb. 1824); see also 124 (Stanhope to
Byron, 6 Mar. 1824).
[57] 'For Freedom's battle', 73 (Byron to Bowring, 10 Dec. 1823); 142 (Byron to
Barff, 26 Mar. 1824); *Greece, in 1823 and 1824*, 183 (Stanhope to Byron, 19 Apr.
1824).
[58] 'For Freedom's battle', 80 (Byron to Kinnaird, 23 Dec. 1823); 132 (Byron to
Kennedy, 10 Mar. 1824).
[59] Ibid. 137 (Byron to Stanhope, 19 Mar. 1824).
[60] Ibid. 140–1 (Byron to Barff, 22 Mar. 1824).
[61] Ibid. 146 (Byron to Bowring, 30 Mar. 1824).
[62] *Greece, in 1823 and 1824*, 181 (Stanhope to Bowring, 14 Apr. 1824).

disposal of his ashes, I should place them in the Temple of Theseus or in the Parthenon in Athens.[63]

These words seem written with sincerity, and there is no reason to connect them, as Parry did, with a move by Stanhope to use the body of Byron to gain more power and prestige for Odysseus by having him buried in Athens rather than in Missolonghi or in England. Stanhope seems in these remarks merely to have wanted to honour Byron if he was to be buried in Greece by having him buried in an appropriate setting.

This discussion of the numerous points of agreement between Stanhope and Byron will, one hopes, establish a background against which the relatively few points of disagreement can be measured. There were obvious differences in temperament and personality. Stanhope seems to have found Byron a difficult man with whom to work. For Stanhope, Byron's explosive personality, his keen wit and playfulness, his erratic temperament, seemed to clash with Stanhope's more earnest, determined, and wilful disposition. Stanhope, however, was more absorbed with Byron's personality than was Byron with Stanhope's, for it was Stanhope who recorded various conflicts with Byron, which Parry then used for his own purposes. Byron's letters and journal are remarkably free of criticism of Stanhope or even of reports of conflict.

One continuing source of disagreement between the two men was over the various newspapers which Stanhope was attempting to establish in Greece. Within a day of Byron's arrival at Missolonghi, Stanhope reported to Bowring: 'His Lordship . . . thinks the press will not succeed. I think it will.'[64] Nevertheless, Byron contributed £40 in aid of Stanhope's project.[65] But there was little doubt that the two differed, and, at first, it seemed that Stanhope feared that Byron's opposition would jeopardize what he considered a most vital project.[66]

He summarized his conversation with Byron as follows:

He [Byron] said that he was an ardent friend of publicity and the press; but he feared that it was not applicable to this society in its present combustible state. I answered that I thought it applicable to all countries, and essential here, in order to put an end to the state of anarchy which at present

---

[63] Ibid. 191–2 (Stanhope to Bowring, 30 Apr. 1824).
[64] Ibid. 73 (Stanhope to Bowring, 6 Jan. 1824).   [65] Ibid.
[66] Ibid. 92–3 (Stanhope to Bowring, 24 Jan. 1824).

prevailed. Lord B. feared libels and licentiousness. I said that the object of a free press was to check public licentiousness, and to expose libellers to odium. Lord B. had mentioned his conversation with Mavrocordato to show that the Prince was not hostile to the press. I declared that I knew him to be an enemy to the press, although he dared not openly to avow it. His Lordship then said that he had not made up his mind about the liberty of the press in Greece, but that he thought the experiment worth trying.[67]

Byron's views did not change and Stanhope reprinted a note from Byron written in March 1824, where he stated that 'the Greek newspaper had done great mischief both in the Morea and in the islands, as I represented both to Prince Mavrocordato and to Colonel Stanhope that it would do in the *present* circumstances, unless *great caution* was observed'.[68]

There is no doubt that there was a strong difference of opinion about the way Stanhope set about establishing freedom of the press in Greece. Byron made no effort to conceal his disapproval and Stanhope took every opportunity to attempt to persuade his colleague of the 'error' of his ways. However, there is no evidence that their disagreement either undermined their respective positions or even placed in question their continued co-operation as the representatives of the London Greek Committee. Byron was primarily concerned not with the newspaper, but with organizing the ill-fated expedition against Lepanto and dealing with the troublesome Suliots. Although the establishment of the various presses was a major preoccupation of Stanhope, he was not significantly blocked by Byron to retard his progress. Indeed, one senses that he found in Byron's opposition additional reasons for the zealous pursuit of his ends.

Another point of disagreement between them on which Parry dwelled was the incident involving the restitution of an Ionian boat which had been captured by the Greeks and brought to Missolonghi. Byron urged the return of the cargo and, when Mavrokordatos and the Greeks refused, he provided the funds to meet the demands of Captain Yorke in the English brig *Alacrity*, which had come to claim restitution. Stanhope apparently disagreed and he wrote at length to Bowring describing the incident and his subsequent

---

[67] *Greece, in 1823 and 1824*, 92–3 (Stanhope to Bowring, 24 Jan. 1824).

[68] Ibid. 126. The note (not printed by Marchand) was attached to a letter (6 Mar. 1824) from Stanhope to Byron by Byron and then sent to the London Greek Committee. A second note dealing with the Suliots appears at 124.

conversation with Byron where he argued that 'the affair was conducted in a bullying manner, and not according to the principles of equity and the law of nations'.[69] The conversation then became heated and Byron, according to Stanhope, began an attack on Bentham.[70] Apparently, once published in Stanhope's volume, this account was reprinted in various newspapers, and Parry saw it as the conduct of Byron being 'sharply censured' without Byron having the opportunity to reply.[71] Parry also used the passage to launch a number of criticisms of Stanhope, but the question at issue here is whether or not Stanhope intended his account to constitute a censure of Byron. The humorous tone of the exchanges suggests that Stanhope included the passage partly as an example of the passionate but good-natured conversations that took place between them.

It is worth noting that Byron also wrote with some passion about the incident to Bowring, but the object of his concern was not Stanhope but the Greeks whom he accused of indulging in ridiculous behaviour by taking up 'buccaneering'.[72] Although he complained in another part of this letter of being 'tired of hearing nothing but talk—and Constitutions—and Sunday Schools—and what not etc.—all excellent things in their time and place—and *here also* whenever they have means—money—leisure—and freedom to try the experiment', and was probably referring to Stanhope, his overt references to Stanhope continued to exhibit full confidence in

[69] Ibid. 96 (Stanhope to Bowring, 28 Jan. 1824).

[70] Ibid. 96–8: 'His Lordship started into a passion. He contended that law, justice, and equity, had nothing to do with politics. That may be; but I will never lend myself to injustice. His Lordship then began, according to his custom, to attack Mr. Bentham. I said, that it was highly illiberal to make personal attacks on Mr. Bentham before a friend who held him in high estimation. He said, that he only attacked his public principles, which were mere theories, but dangerous;—injurious to Spain, and calculated to do great mischief in Greece. I did not object to his Lordship's attacking Mr. B's principles; what I objected to were his personalities. His Lordship never reasoned on any of Mr. B's writings, but merely made sport of them. I would, therefore, ask him what it was that he objected to? Lord Byron mentioned his Panopticon as visionary. I said that experience in Pennsylvania, at Milbank, etc. had proved it otherwise. I said that Bentham had a truly British heart; but that Lord Byron, after professing liberal principles from his boyhood, had, when called upon to act, proved himself a Turk . . . When he wished me good night, I took up the light to conduct him to the passage, but he said, What! hold up a light to a Turk!' See above, Ch. 9 n. 1, regarding the absence of this passage from the original letter.

[71] See Parry, *The Last Days of Lord Byron*, 231.

[72] *'For Freedom's battle'*, 102 (Byron to Bowring, 28 Jan. 1824).

him.[73] Byron, therefore, gave no indication that he had been 'severely censured' by Stanhope, and Stanhope's account only suggests the passionate and lively exchanges that were, as we have seen, a feature of their relationship. As for the mockery of Bentham that Stanhope recorded and Parry utilized to such effect, it is worth noting that Bentham's name was not even mentioned in all of Byron's letters and in the journal written in Greece in 1823–4.[74] Clearly, Bentham was not a subject that preoccupied him. Parry may have been partially correct in suggesting that Stanhope was 'flattering himself indirectly into the good graces of a great man', but there is no evidence that Bentham's ideas were a real point of contention between Byron and Stanhope.[75] Indeed, there is some evidence that Byron was not entirely unsympathetic to Bentham's ideas.[76]

As for the portion of the letter to Bowring in which Stanhope said that the Committee should not trust Byron with its money but which was not published by Stanhope, it might be interpreted as supporting Parry's thesis.[77] But it only supports the view that Stanhope personally disapproved of Byron, and the fact that he suppressed the letter is evidence that he was careful to avoid giving any impression that he sought to censure him or that they pursued opposing policies in Greece. Stanhope's disapproval of Byron's life-style would provide Parry with no grounds for seeing Byron and Stanhope as locked in struggle in Greece or for choosing one 'side' as opposed to the other. In spite of obvious personal differences, Stanhope and Byron, for the brief period during which they served together, were capable of acting together on many issues to advance the Greek cause as agents of the London Greek Committee.

6. Parry's Antipathy to Stanhope

What were Parry's real motives for writing the book? He was too bitter a man to write an objective account of Byron's last days, and

---

[73] 'For Freedom's battle', 102–3 (Byron to Bowring, 28 Jan. 1824).

[74] Ibid., as Index.   [75] Parry, *The Last Days of Lord Byron*, 237.

[76] See *Greece, in 1823 and 1824*, 542–3. Byron's and Bentham's ideas developed from the same Whig tradition. See Malcolm Kelsall, *Byron's Politics* (Brighton, 1987).   [77] See above, Ch. 9 n. 1.

his bitterness revealed the true object of his work. He was mainly concerned to attack and discredit Stanhope, not for Stanhope's attitude towards Byron, but for his treatment of him. There were two issues of consequence: (1) the question of the mechanics under Parry leaving Missolonghi and returning to England; and (2) the control of the weapons and stores which Parry brought to Missolonghi.

On 18 February, shortly after Parry arrived in Missolonghi and the arsenal was established, and three days after Byron suffered the epileptic fit, an incident occurred which frightened a number of the craftsmen who had come to Greece. This was the death of Sass, a Swedish philhellene, who was shot after an argument with a Suliot while guarding the arsenal. During this time, the Suliots were increasingly restive and numerous incidents took place between them and the resident foreigners.[78] Feeling no longer safe in Missolonghi, six of the craftsmen wanted to return to the Ionian Islands and then to England. Stanhope apparently provided the funds for their return, and Parry was furious both with them and with Stanhope who agreed to their demands.[79]

When Stanhope reported the events to Bowring, he wrote:

In consequence of the foregoing and other events, the workmen in the laboratory have refused to stop here. I must plainly state to you, that while the Suliots remain, the persons of Europeans are not safe in Missolonghi. Parry, Hodges, and Gill, will, however, remain, and they, with the assistance of the natives, can perform all the work required of them by the committee.[80]

In his next letter to Bowring, Stanhope discussed the issue at greater length. The expedition of Parry and the artificers was a major commitment of the London Greek Committee, and the departure of the six craftsmen after only two weeks in Greece would be interpreted as a major disaster. Stanhope wrote:

The result has been, that six of the mechanics have resolved on returning home. I listened to their complaints and their claims; I told them, that the Suliots would depart forthwith, and that all would then be quiet. They, however, doubted my authority; said that they had come out to labour peaceably,—that they would, however, risk all against the Turks, but that

[78] See St Clair, *That Greece Might Still Be Free*, 179.
[79] See Parry, *The Last Days of Lord Byron*, 65–6.
[80] *Greece, in 1823 and 1824*, 119 (Stanhope to Bowring, 18 Feb. 1824).

they did not come to Greece to be assassinated, and to leave their families destitute. I repeated that the Suliots were about to depart, but said, that if they were resolved to return home, they had a right to receive pay up to the day of their departure, and £10 each, promised to them by the committee, to defray the expense of their home passage, after the expiration of their service. For all these acts, I alone am responsible. With respect to the result, I am of opinion that the loss of six able mechanics is much to be regretted; still, as other workmen may be found to labour in their stead, the laboratory may be carried on most effectually, under the guidance of Parry, Gill, and Hodges.[81]

It is clear that Stanhope did sanction the departure of the craftsmen, but not without attempting to persuade them to remain. They felt, however, that Stanhope (and in this they were correct) would not be able to remove the Suliots, the source of their difficulties, from Missolonghi. Byron, at this time, was still recovering from the application of leeches to his temples after the fit, and was hardly able to assume much responsibility.[82] Nevertheless, he took a kindly interest in their plight and wrote to the Ionian banker Samuel Barff:

Six Englishmen will be soon in quarantine at Zante—they are artificers—and have had enough of Greece in fourteen days—if you could recommend them to a passage home I would thank you,—they are good men enough—but do not quite understand the little discrepancies in these countries—and are not used to see shooting and slashing in a domestic quiet way or (as it forms here) a part of house-keeping.—If they should want anything during their Quarantine—you can advance them *not more* than a dollar a day (amongst them) for that period—to purchase them some little extras—as comforts—(as they are quite out of their element) I cannot afford them more at present.—The Committee pays their passage.[83]

Several weeks later, Byron added in a letter to James Kennedy this postscript about Stanhope: 'Perhaps they [the artificers] are less to blame than is imagined, since Colonel Stanhope is said to have told them, *"that he could not positively say their lives were safe."* I should like to know *where* our life *is* safe, either here or any where else?'[84] In this letter Byron seemed to accept that Stanhope bore some blame for the departure of the craftsmen. But note the way that he

[81] Ibid. 120–1 (Stanhope to Bowring, 21 Feb. 1824).
[82] See *'For Freedom's battle'*, 115–16 (Byron to Barff, 21 Feb. 1824).
[83] Ibid. 118–19 (Byron to Barff, 21 [22?] Feb. 1824).
[84] Ibid. 133 (Byron to Kennedy, 10 Mar. 1824).

reported Stanhope's view in the passive voice rather than indicating what Stanhope actually said. It is probable that Byron was reporting Parry's account which, as in other instances, was only half-true. Stanhope did say that while the Suliots were present Europeans were not safe in Missolonghi, but he also energetically tried to persuade the mechanics to remain. And Byron, himself, did not even refer to Stanhope in his letter to Barff. In other letters of Byron, Parry's views are occasionally reported, but Byron, with a strong commitment to accuracy, usually put some distance between what he knew to be true and what he was simply repeating. Another point of interest is that Stanhope took full responsibility for the action of the craftsmen. This assumption of sole authority would surely have troubled Parry, though, given Byron's illness, it would have been the correct action to take.

The second issue was the attempt by Stanhope to remove stores and ammunition from Missolonghi to Athens. For Parry, this seemed to mean the destruction of the brigade that he and Byron had built up. He presented a highly legalistic argument in support of his contention that Stanhope had no right to the stores that had been sent out under his authority, subject to the orders of Lord Byron and with the agreement of Mavrokordatos.[85] Furthermore, as Byron had paid for the preservation of the stores, Stanhope, according to Parry, had even less of a claim to them.[86] He also thought that as their presence in Greece was subject to the authority of Mavrokordatos, the lawful head of the Greek government, Stanhope had no right to reject that authority in favour of Odysseus.[87] Finally, Parry argued that with the death of Byron, 'the brigade, stores and all, were wholly under my orders . . . I was responsible for them both to the committee and to Prince Mavrocordato.'[88] 'In spite, however, of his having no right to dispose of any part of the stores, or of the brigade,' he continued, 'and in spite of the commandant [Parry] of both being within his reach, he broke it up by his own orders, and, as I have said, in defiance of my representations.'[89]

No one in the London Greek Committee would share Parry's account of Stanhope's authority in Greece. Stanhope had gone to Greece as an equal representative with Byron. From his numerous references to Parry prior to the latter's arrival, it is clear that both he

[85] Parry, *The Last Days of Lord Byron*, 302–3.   [86] Ibid. 303.
[87] Ibid. 304.   [88] Ibid. 305.   [89] Ibid. 306.

and Byron were planning to assume joint command when he arrived.[90] This is especially evident in the joint letter Stanhope and Byron addressed to Mavrokordatos just after Parry's arrival where Mavrokordatos was invited, not to assume a position of power or authority, but merely to suggest ways that the arsenal might be of use to him.[91] Furthermore, when Stanhope first arrived in Athens and wrote to Byron requesting that one of the remaining men accompany a supply of powder, lead, shot, and four guns to Athens, Byron simply replied that 'what can be spared will be sent'.[92] Nevertheless, it is clear from Byron's letter that Parry was not only reluctant to part with this material but was also being allowed considerable autonomy with Byron's illness and Stanhope's absence.[93]

Parry's illusions about his position and authority probably owe a good deal to his relationship with Byron, especially after Byron fell ill on 15 February. At this time he began to rely more on Parry and, for example, referred often to 'Stanhope's and Parry's Reports' (rather than Stanhope's and Byron's) as sources of information for the Committee in London.[94] Besides the considerable autonomy granted to Parry to run the arsenal Byron took the view that whatever was being done in Missolonghi was being accomplished by Parry alone.[95] Nevertheless, while Byron would report Parry's outrageous comments and complaints about the leading figures of

---

[90] See *Greece, in 1823 and 1824*, 10 (Stanhope to Bowring, 13 Oct. 1823); 23 (Stanhope to Bowring, 2 Nov. 1823); 40 (Stanhope to Bowring, 16 Dec. 1823); 46–7 (Stanhope to Bowring, 18 Dec. 1823); 50–1 (Stanhope to Bowring, 20 Dec. 1823); 70 (Stanhope to Bowring, 5 Jan. 1824); 83 (Stanhope to Bowring, 7 Jan. 1824); 89 (Stanhope to Bowring, 21 Jan. 1824); 101 (Stanhope to Bowring, 31 Jan. 1824); 103 (Stanhope to Bowring, 4 Feb. 1824); 109 (Stanhope to Bowring, 7 Feb. 1824).

[91] 'For Freedom's battle', 104–6 (Byron and Stanhope to Mavrokordatos, 5 Feb. 1824).

[92] *Greece, in 1823 and 1824*, 128 (Stanhope to Byron, 8 Mar. 1824); 'For Freedom's battle', 137–8 (Byron to Stanhope, 19 Mar. 1824).

[93] 'For Freedom's battle', 137–8: 'Parry is to answer for himself on his own articles—if I were to interfere with him—it would only stop the whole progress of his exertions—and he is really doing all that can be done without more aid from the Govt. which neither works nor pays.'

[94] Ibid. 117 (Byron to Kinnaird, 21 [22?] Feb. 1824); 125 (Byron to Moore, 4 Mar. 1824); 136 (Byron to Kinnaird, 13 Mar. 1824); 139 (Byron to Bowring, 19 Mar. 1824); 146 (Byron to Bowring, 30 Mar. 1824).

[95] Ibid. 145 (Byron to Kinnaird, 30 Mar. 1824): 'Capt. Parry is doing all that circumstances will permit in his department, and indeed in many others, for he does *all* that is done here.'

the London Greek Committee, he never actively supported him.[96] However much Byron may have enjoyed Parry's remarks about Stanhope, he saw his role at one point as one of making peace between them.[97] Nor did Byron see Parry as a disruptive force in Missolonghi. It seems as though Byron and Parry faced the abyss of failure by forming a psychological suicide pact. They drank together and amused each other with one to face death and the other madness.

Parry, however, was to have a last lunge at the one man his paranoid mind thought had been intent on destroying him. Stanhope, like Byron, was complimentary of Parry during the two weeks the three were together in Missolonghi.[98] If, according to Byron, Parry and Stanhope already had disagreements, they were not evident in Stanhope's correspondence which at this time mentioned only Parry's plans and industriousness. But Parry was unable to maintain his initial momentum (called in retrospect by Millingen 'much ado about nothing').[99] With the revolt of the Suliots, the departure of the craftsmen, Byron's illness, and Stanhope's journey to Athens, conditions changed dramatically, and neither Byron nor Parry seemed able to surmount the hurdles fortune had placed in their paths. Reports from Hodges and Gill, the two assistants who remained in Missolonghi, revealed to Stanhope that efforts to print the prospectus of the newly established *Greco telegrapho* had been 'again and again thwarted by Parry'.[100] In response to Stanhope's new initiative with Odysseus, Parry supposedly 'went about with his eyes and hands up, saying "Horrible, horrible!! a conspiracy is formed against the government, and an Englishman [Stanhope] is at the head of it." '[101]

Stanhope's last contact with Parry occurred when they met in May 1824 at Zante, where Stanhope ordered him to return to the arsenal at Missolonghi.[102] With Parry's refusal, he severed contact

[96] Ibid. 108 (Byron to Hancock, 5/7 Feb. 1824): 'Parry says Blaquiere is a humbug;—to which I say nothing.'

[97] See ibid. 109.

[98] See *Greece, in 1823 and 1824*, 112 (Stanhope to Bowring, 11 Feb. 1824); 113 (Stanhope to Bowring, 15 Feb. 1824).

[99] Millingen, *Memoirs of the Affairs of Greece*, 97.

[100] *Greece, in 1823 and 1824*, 174 (Stanhope to Bowring, 9–10 Apr. 1824).

[101] Ibid. 184 n. (Stanhope to Bowring, 18–19 Apr. 1824); see also 301–3 (Hodges and Gill to Stanhope, 4 Mar. 1824); 447 (Hodges to Stanhope, 5 Sept. 1824).

[102] Ibid. 224 (Stanhope to Bowring, 22–4 May 1824): 'I then desired him to proceed to Missolonghi. He refused, saying he had no means of carrying on the

and soon returned to England on the *Florida* with the body of Byron. By this time Parry had so attached himself to Byron and so worshipped his memory that, given the peculiarities of his personality, an equivalent amount of hatred was directed towards Stanhope. If Bentham was hurt by Parry's book, it must be appreciated that Stanhope bore the brunt of the attack. In the second edition of his book, Stanhope appended a brief note (undoubtedly referring to Parry) and a lithograph of an extract from a letter from Byron to himself in which Byron spoke highly of him. In the note, Stanhope wrote:

Among the numerous Calumnies which have been industriously circulated in this country relative to my conduct in Greece, is that of my having acted in factious opposition to Lord Byron. The degraded quarter from whence the mass of these charges proceed, and their total want of truth, absolutely precludes me from replying to them in any manner whatever; but I cannot forbear quoting the testimony which his Lordship himself bears in my favour.[103]

7. Parry versus Hunt

Stanhope's dignified condemnation of Parry's volume did not end the controversy that has surrounded it to the present day. Stanhope himself replied to Lockhart's review in *Blackwood's* in a letter published by his friend J. S. Buckingham in the *Oriental Herald and Colonial Review*.[104] The *Examiner*, the weekly newspaper edited by Leigh and John Hunt, responded to the attack on Bentham which was published in *The Times*.[105] So far as the *Examiner* was

public service, and should wait Colonel Gordon's arrival. He continued swaggering and blustering till I told him that I had nothing more to say to him since he had disobeyed my orders.'

[103] *Greece, in 1823 and 1824*, 551.

[104] 'Letter of the Hon. Leicester Stanhope to the Editor of Blackwood's Magazine', *Oriental Herald and Colonial Review*, 7 (1825), 113–16.

[105] *Examiner* (22 May 1825), 32. See above, n. 4. For some years both John and Leigh Hunt had been friendly with Bentham, and often reviewed or discussed his writings in the *Examiner*. See e.g. the review of the *Rationale of Reward* that appeared just after *The Times* article and reply (29 May 1825: 335–6). See also *Correspondence*, viii, ed. S. R. Conway (Oxford, 1988) (*CW*), 252: 'The editor of the *Examiner*—Hunt, has taken me under his protection, and trumpets me every now and then in his paper, along with Romilly' (Bentham to Mulford, 9 July 1812). See also 256–9,

concerned, Bentham's stature was far above that inhabited by the writers from The Times; and, as for Parry, he was described as 'lately a caulker, but now calling himself a Major . . . this exceedingly ignorant, boasting, bullying, and drunken individual'. A year later, on 2 April 1826, the Examiner published an open letter to Parry from Leicester Stanhope in which Parry's book was criticized and Stanhope defended. To this letter John Hunt, the editor of the newspaper, appended the following note: 'This man was a caulker in the dock-yards, and is—(not to repeat the worst of him)—a slanderer, a sot, a bully, and a poltroon. Who wrote the book to which he has prefixed his name, we cannot exactly say; but he himself cannot write ten words of English.'[106]

At this time, Parry was negotiating with a Captain Robert Ramsay to assist in a plan to form a naval force for Argentina and was to go with him to South America at a salary of £400 per year. When Ramsay read the letter and note in the Examiner in 1826, he broke off these negotiations, and Parry proceeded to sue John Hunt for libel, claiming £1,000 damages. Parry v. Hunt came to trial on 14 June 1827 in a new and spacious courtroom at the Guildhall.[107] A large and excited crowd assembled and were thoroughly absorbed by the trial which lasted nine hours.

Hunt's defence was that his depiction of Parry was factually correct. Parry had slandered Bentham and Stanhope. Ample evidence was forthcoming as to his almost constant state of

372–4 for early correspondence between Bentham and Leigh Hunt. Bentham also knew Henry Hunt, a son of John Hunt, who worked on the Examiner, and for whom at one point Bentham arranged accommodation in one of his houses to be shared with Walter Coulson, a former amanuensis who worked on the Morning Chronicle and became editor of the Traveller. See BL Add. MS 33551, fos. 1–21, Bentham to Mora, 19 Sep. 1820; BL Add. MS 33545, fos. 423–4, Bentham to Samuel Bentham, 4 July 1820. John Hunt would have perhaps another reason for defending Bentham, as his nephew Marriott Hunt, apparently a son of Leigh Hunt, joined Parry's expedition as a surgeon, but fell ill during the voyage to Malta and returned to England. See LGC papers, vol. iii, fo. N¹, Marriott Hunt to Greek Committee, 13 Sept. 1823; vol. v, fo. O¹, Parry to Bowring, 27 Dec. 1823; Greece, in 1823 and 1824, 342–3 (Bowring to Stanhope, 7 Feb. 1824); Stanhope papers, General State Archives, K.121, fo. 114.

[106] Examiner (2 Apr. 1826), 212–13. Stanhope's letter bore the date of 14 May 1825.

[107] The lawsuit brought by Parry was not discussed by scholars prior to William St Clair's article in 1970 which brought it to light. See 'Postscript to The Last Days of Lord Byron', Keats–Shelley Journal, 19 (1970), 4–7. The account here relies on the reports of the trial in The Times and the Examiner.

drunkenness. He drank, testified Robert Laycock, one of the mechanics who accompanied him to Missolonghi, 'by word of mouth', that is to say, straight from the brandy bottle, and according to Lega Zambelli, a servant of Byron, was on two occasions seen in a state of complete intoxication lying on the floor with a bottle by his side. The account of the trial in the *Examiner* did not fail to point out that Parry could be identified in court by the redness of his nose. As to his cowardice, his returning home supposedly to shave when he was supposed to be attacking a Turkish vessel which had run aground established that trait. That Parry boasted of abilities he did not possess, for example, of making Congreve rockets (indeed, he claimed to have made the improvements before Congreve), was brought out by Leicester Stanhope.

The most difficult part of the defence was concerned with Parry's capacity to write the book in the first place, for if he did not write it, the name of the real author had not yet been revealed. In the whole trial the testimony of witnesses was surrounded by frequent outbursts of laughter and no less so in this part where Parry's capacity to write the book was under scrutiny. Bowring, secretary of the London Greek Committee, thought Parry incapable of writing the book on his own and noted that the materials on which the book was based, which were shown to him, were not sufficient to make up the book as published. One publisher, a Mr Knight, testified that Parry was introduced to him as Captain Parry ('and I fully expected to have seen that Captain Parry who had been so frequently towards the North Pole'). After inspecting the materials which Parry had accumulated, he declined to publish them and said that they were not the same as had appeared in the book. Mr Lacey, of another publishing firm, Knight & Lacey, which published the book, admitted that Parry had received 'some assistance in the arrangement of the work' (*The Times*), and the person who gave this assistance will not be an unfamiliar name to readers in the twentieth century, although the revelation of the name of Thomas Hodgskin hardly caused a ripple at the trial.

Hodgskin's reputation nowadays rests upon his being an early writer on political economy who made a major contribution in the 1820s to raising working-class consciousness through a critique of capitalist political economy, as in his book *Labour Defended against the Claims of Capital*, published in 1825, the same year as Parry's

Last Days of Lord Byron.[108] Hodgskin was also involved with Joseph Clinton Robertson in the founding and editing of the *Mechanics' Magazine* and the two rightly claimed that they had been instrumental in founding the London Mechanics' Institution, the distant forerunner of Birkbeck College. That Parry should have linked up with Hodgskin is not wholly surprising, for he was especially conscious of belonging to the artisan class. Throughout the period prior to his departure for Greece, when he was organizing the equipment for the arsenal and the artillery stores, Parry, as has been noted, was a scathing critic of his employers, the London Greek Committee. He even suggested that he and his fellow artisans might do a better job:

> *Had I the means I would have called a meeting of the Operative Men of the City of London* to *whom I* am generally known and I have no hesitation in saying that an ample Subscription would at once have been raised and the Greeks Assisted Practically without the least Chicanery and the Cause would have been felt in that way to give the desired Stamina to the Useful Classes and the only means of pressing so Just a Cause.[109]

It is tempting to suggest that Parry's (and Hodgskin's) critique of Bentham and Stanhope was an early attack from the left on this so-called attempt to apply Benthamite utilitarian values in Greece. Nevertheless, the notions of 'left' and 'working class' were not yet developed in Britain or in Greece and such an interpretation will not stand up to examination. There was no proletariat in Greece and hence no 'working-class consciousness' and the artisans who went to Greece from Britain thought that their enemy was Parry or the Suliots rather than Stanhope or Bentham. Furthermore, we have seen that the real doctrinal struggle in Greece took place within the early development of liberalism and in the tensions involved in the attempt to accommodate nationalist aspirations within liberal ideology.

The involvement of Hodgskin in writing the book was probably based as much on personal as on ideological considerations. In fairness to Parry, however, it seems clear that the book contains his

[108] See E. P. Thompson, *The Making of the English Working Class* (Harmondsworth, 1968), 855–7, 912. On Hodgskin generally see E. Halévy, *Thomas Hodgskin*, trans. A. J. Taylor (London, 1956). Both Parry's and Hodgskin's books were published by Knight & Lacey.

[109] Gordon papers, 1160/21/10/18, Parry to Gordon, 2 June 1823.

ideas and reflects his personality and Hodgskin's involvement in it was, as St Clair suggests, of 'the ghost-writer's art at its best'.[110] Neither Hodgskin nor Parry would have known Bentham very well.[111] A former naval lieutenant, who had been placed on half-pay, Hodgskin published in 1813 *An Essay on Naval Discipline* criticizing the system of impressment.[112] At approximately this time he met Francis Place and through Place became involved with James Mill and Bentham. Nevertheless, there was little direct contact between him and Bentham, and it was James Mill who provided some guidance in the research undertaken during his journey to northern Europe which was published in 1820 as *Travels in the North of Germany*.[113] During this time, however, he displayed a considerable interest in Bentham's ideas, and, for example, asked Place for copies of all his works, took an interest in Place's version of *Not Paul but Jesus*, in Bentham's pamphlet on special juries, and, referring to an article he had written on penal law, Hodgskin commented to Place: 'Mr Bentham will see I have paid him the honour he merits. It is right for us little fry to reverence our great master in all that relates to Laws.'[114] After four years in Edinburgh, where he knew Robertson, he came to London in 1822 and found a position on the *Morning Chronicle* with the help of James Mill.[115] The following year, he and Robertson (together with Knight & Lacey, the publishers) launched the *Mechanics' Magazine*, an

[110] St Clair, 'Postscript to *The Last Days of Lord Byron*', 6. Parry's letters demonstrate that, despite difficulties with grammar, he could put ten words together.

[111] According to Bowring, in his biography of Bentham, Parry did visit Bentham once, but Parry's account even of the bare facts of the visit did not square with the recollection of Richard Doane, Bentham's amanuensis, who was a member of the party. See Bowring, xi. 66. Colls's Diary does not record any visit from Parry at this time, though part of Bentham's 'Constitutional Code' and other material were sent to him via Bowring to carry to Greece. See BL Add. MS 33563, fo. 127 (entries for 1, 4 Nov. 1823). Bentham may have seen Hodgskin at least once. See *Correspondence*, ix, ed. S. R. Conway (Oxford, 1989) (*CW*), 288 (Bentham to Place, 5 Nov. 1818). Nevertheless, most contact was second-hand through Francis Place.

[112] London, 1813. See Halévy, *Thomas Hodgskin*, 31.

[113] Edinburgh, 1820. For details of this involvement, see W. H. Burston, *James Mill on Philosophy and Education* (London, 1973), 89, 93–6. See also *Correspondence*, ix (*CW*), 147–51 (Bentham to Place, 14, 17–18 Jan. 1818).

[114] BL Add. MS 35153, fos. 126 (15 Feb. 1820), 129 (4 Apr. 1820), 198 (29 Apr. 1821).

[115] See T. Kelly, *George Birkbeck: Pioneer of Adult Education* (Liverpool, 1957), 77–8. See also 76–145 for an excellent account of the establishment of the London Mechanics' Institution.

attractive journal of popular applied science, recording new inventions with numerous plates and illustrations. Towards the end of that year Hodgskin and Robertson began to establish the London Mechanics' Institution, and it is interesting to note how the dates run in parallel with the establishment of the London Greek Committee.

The dispute which followed between Francis Place on the one hand who sought to involve wealthy patrons in the establishment of the Institution (as the only practical way to make it succeed) and Hodgskin and Robertson on the other hand who wanted to keep the London Mechanics' Institution solely in the hands of artisans and mechanics has been recorded on several occasions and has been regarded by E. P. Thompson as an important 'ideological conflict' in the development of working-class consciousness.[116] Even though Hodgskin apparently argued that 'Men had better be without education . . . than be educated by their rulers' and Robertson contended that 'If the money were placed on the table before them, they ought to reject it, as they would the greatest evil', the differences between them and Place were not as clear cut as Thompson and others have supposed.[117]

On a personal level Place felt a special friendship for Hodgskin whom he had known for many years and treated as a member of his family.[118] He thought that Robertson had misled Hodgskin and had made 'a fool if not a rogue' of him.[119] Not only did Place accuse Robertson of trying to dominate the London Mechanics' Institution and reduce it to a committee under his control but he also accused him of the embezzlement of subscriptions which had been collected via the *Mechanics' Magazine*.[120] The dispute was acrimonious but it was won by Place. The two Honorary Secretaries were replaced and wealthy patrons were used to launch the Mechanics' Institution. However, the dispute was not an ideological one, but more narrowly one over the means to establish what was thought desirable by all who were involved. Robertson tried to make it into a dispute over doctrine without great success. Hodgskin, however, kept in touch with Place and Dr Birkbeck,

---

[116] Thompson, *The Making of the English Working Class*, 817–18. For a recent work on Place, see Dudley Miles, *Francis Place: The Life of a Remarkable Radical 1771–1854* (Brighton, 1988).

[117] T. Kelly, *Radical Tailor: The Life and Work of Francis Place (1771–1854)* (London, 1972), 13.   [118] BL Add. MS 27823, fo. 240 (Place MSS).

[119] Ibid. fo. 257.   [120] Ibid. fos. 287–8.

and continued to play a role as a lecturer at the London Mechanics' Institution. Place's disagreement with Hodgskin over the latter's ideas was mainly over his adoption of the Godwinian belief in the possibility of a society without government.[121] It is true that Knight & Lacey, publishers of the *Mechanics' Magazine*, also published the book and that it was reviewed in the journal.[122] But here the extract which was printed was not the attack on Bentham or the critique of Stanhope, but some supposed remarks of Lord Byron to the effect that the management of Mechanics' Institutions should belong entirely to mechanics, the point at issue between Place and the editors of the journal. Furthermore, Hodgskin and Place continued to meet throughout this period. Place recommended Hodgskin on 13 April 1826 for the post of editor of the *Mechanics' Magazine* (admittedly reflecting his dislike of Robertson as much as his attachment to Hodgskin).[123] His diary records other meetings with Hodgskin in 1826, and though Place was bitter about what Hodgskin and Robertson had done at the founding of the London Mechanics' Institution, he thought them foolish and dishonest but not ideologically in opposition. It should also be remembered that Bentham and Place were allied in extending their radical views to the artisan classes, and Bentham himself expressed at this time a doctrine which looked forward to a period of increasing equality and security to which Hodgskin would not have objected.[124] In Bentham's writings on religion, parliamentary reform, and constitutional government, one may find a theory of false consciousness and *political* exploitation which would encourage rather than oppose enquiries into economic exploitation which were beginning to be developed at this time.[125]

The jury in *Parry* v. *Hunt* took only forty minutes to reach a decision, and the decision was a curious one. Parry was awarded £50 rather than the £1,000 he sought, largely on the grounds that

[121] See ibid. fo. 369 (Place to Birkbeck, 11 June 1825).

[122] See *Mechanics' Magazine*, 4 (6 May 1825), 67–8.

[123] BL Add. MS 35146, fo. 11 (13 Apr. 1826).

[124] See Kelly, *George Birkbeck*, 118 n., quoting E. Lowenthal, *The Ricardian Socialists* (New York, 1911), 83: 'But in his constructive theory and his hope for the future, he is more nearly allied with Bentham than with even the predecessors of Karl Marx.' See also J. R. Dinwiddy, *From Luddism to the First Reform Bill: Reform in England 1810–1832* (Oxford, 1986), 42.

[125] See e.g. 'Supreme Operative', in *First Principles Preparatory to Constitutional Code*, ed. T. P. Schofield (Oxford, 1989) (*CW*), 149–226.

the jury did not consider him *profoundly* ignorant as one of the
alleged libels had suggested. That he was a coward, a slanderer, a
drunk, a bully, and ignorant was fully accepted. The verdict of the
jury, however, has not been the verdict of scholars. If opposition
between the utilitarian and the poet has been shown to be mythical,
perhaps a new myth has already begun to replace it, that of the
working-class victim of bourgeois Benthamism. For Doris Langley
Moore, Parry's book is 'the best, most vigorous, most convincing
account by any eye witness of Byron's final struggles in Greece, his
personality in sickness and despair, and the personality of his
plausible adversary, Colonel the Hon. Leicester Stanhope.'[126]
Despite the fact that the Tory press warmed to Parry to a great
extent, Moore writes: 'It was Parry's misfortune not to be a
gentleman—very obviously not a gentleman. . . . The book was
scornfully handled by most reviewers and its author rejected
everywhere.'[127] She finds Parry's account of 'the absurdities of
Jeremy Bentham's theories applied to Greece' convincing, even
though Bentham's theories were never applied to Greece.[128] The
fact that Parry was awarded only £50 in damages at the end of the
trial is regarded as 'no easy feat for a former dockyard labourer to
achieve in the 1820s, contending with aristocratic witnesses like
Stanhope and learned witnesses like Bowring, and facing a jury of
twelve middle-class citizens'.[129] A reading of the summary of
Justice Best's summation to the jury in fact reveals a strong bias
towards Parry and a hostility towards liberty of the press which
was rejected by the jury itself.

One cannot help but feel that Parry has attracted some inverted
snobbery in the twentieth century, just as he did from the Tory
press in his own day. Moore dismisses the testimony of other
working-class men that Parry was a drunkard on the grounds that
'it would have been difficult for two men of lowly rank to refuse to
oblige a dictatorial gentleman who asked for their support'.[130]

[126] *The Late Lord Byron*, 169.
[127] Ibid. Besides *The Times* and *Blackwood's Edinburgh Magazine* (discussed above), the following notice appeared in the *Gentleman's Magazine*, 95 (June 1825), 518: 'The Author before us appears to be a man of strong natural sense, with an honest old soldier's heart, and all that John Bullism about him, which evinces a sturdy determination to speak his mind, in utter disregard of person or party.'
[128] *Lord Byron: Accounts Rendered* (London, 1974), 425.
[129] Ibid. 426–7.
[130] Ibid. 427.

Even Parry's insanity is waved aside as something 'held against him as though insanity were a fate reserved for the disreputable'.[131]

The myth of Parry as victim is as false as the myth of opposition between Stanhope and Byron. These myths have arisen because the structure of ideas—in the form of theory *or* as ideology—has not been taken seriously. Without regard for intellectual context, it is possible to repeat what various individuals say but difficult to reconstruct its meaning. It is in undertaking the latter that myths such as these are formed, and so attractive and appealing (especially in the twentieth century) is the opposition between philistine utilitarian and romantic poet, between the earnest Stanhope and the wayward Byron, or the working-class victim of bourgeois Benthamism, that their repetition without critical investigation is commonplace. Nevertheless, only by approaching such myths from the reality of the larger context of ideas can one see the significance of the relations between the main figures at Missolonghi.

[131] Ibid.

11

Tories, Whigs, and Philhellenism

The development of philhellenism in Britain was not only influenced by the conflicts within early liberalism which had so marked an effect on the fortunes of the London Greek Committee. Philhellenism was also influenced by the ideological division between Whigs and Tories which strongly influenced the pattern of support generally in Britain for the struggle for Greek independence. In this chapter Tory opposition to active support for Greece will be shown to have had a decisive effect in curbing the growth of philhellenism in the period from the uprising in March 1821 until the founding of the London Greek Committee two years later. In a curious way the nature of this opposition largely ensured that the issue would become a partisan one that was reflected in the composition of the London Greek Committee itself as consisting largely of Whigs and radical reformers. Nevertheless, contrary to numerous commentators who have seen the Committee as somehow ignoring if not betraying philhellenism in representing a narrow ideological position, it is argued here that the Committee was largely successful because it drew on broad philhellenic sympathy that existed throughout Britain.[1]

1. Early Attempts at Fund-Raising

The uprising against the Turks in early 1821 appealed nearly as much to those who opposed liberal reform and revolutionary

---

[1] See e.g. C. M. Woodhouse, *The Philhellenes* (London, 1969), 80–1: 'Such were the prime movers in establishing the London Greek Committee: Whigs and Radicals, lawyers and parliamentarians, poets and antiquarians, merchants and reformers, Scots and Irish and other vicarious nationalists; but few philhellenes.' See also W. St Clair, *That Greece Might Still Be Free* (London, 1972), 155; E. S. De Beer and Walter Seton, 'Byroniana: The Archives of the London Greek Committee', *Nineteenth Century*, 100 (1926), 398–9.

movements on the Continent as to those who had supported them. *The Times*, for example, showed early support for Greece, and besides dwelling on the obvious connection between Britain and Greece as 'Christian' nations and on the supposed links with classical and hence 'European' civilization, argued that there were also important commercial advantages for Britain in reducing the power of the economically stagnant Ottoman Empire.[2] The government policy of supporting Turkey (or at best of remaining neutral) so as to reduce the possible influence of Russia was vigorously opposed as being feeble in conception and likely to produce the opposite effect of enhancing Russian influence in Greece. In a striking passage, *The Times* also wrote on 29 September 1821:

England has been accused by strangers of greater coldness towards the Greeks on this occasion, than becomes a free and Christian people. So far as regards the *people* of this country, we may be allowed to say, that it is not part of the constitution of Englishmen to speak loudly or boastingly of what they feel on any subject, where they are conscious of being unable to vindicate their declarations by their deeds. They are restrained from acting on behalf of Greece by the condition to which their rulers have reduced them.

Besides displaying a genuine sympathy towards the Greek struggle, *The Times* mentioned two themes that appeared in newspapers of varying political persuasions: firstly, the failure of the British to respond as they should to the Greek need for assistance; and secondly, that the reasons for this failure lay almost entirely with the government rather than with the people in general. These themes were repeated in the *Morning Chronicle* when it noted that 'it is a reproach to this country that the fate of the unfortunate Greeks, now struggling to emancipate themselves from a most odious tyranny, excites so little interest among us'. The *Morning Chronicle* accounted for this by also blaming the government:

The whole body of the Tories are now trained to scent danger at a distance. It would give them pleasure, in other circumstances, to see the feeble remnant of the Greeks emancipated; but they will not countenance the

---

[2] See *The Times* (1 Aug. 1821). In this article the pamphlet by K. Polychroniades, *Remarks on the Present State of Turkey, Considered in Its Commercial and Political Relation with England* (London, 1821), is quoted at length on the commercial advantages to Britain that would follow Greek independence.

smallest violation of the rights of legitimacy, even in the person of the Grand Turk.[3]

That early support for Greece existed across a wide band of political opinion may also be seen from the fact that the classical scholar Dr J. Lempriere's appeal for support for Greece was initially addressed to the *Courier*, normally a paper reflecting ministerial views.[4] A committee was formed at that time including Lords Lansdowne, Aberdeen, Elgin, Belmore, Mount-Morris, and others. Lempriere was by no means the first person to support publicly the Greek cause nor did his support differ from that being expressed throughout the press. But he did make the first appeal for funds and that he did so in October 1821 is evidence of early British support for Greece. According to Lempriere, however, 'I am not aware that the Committee did any thing, as government unfortunately for the honor of England, listened more to the representatives of the oppressors than to the cries of the oppressed.'[5] That the *Courier* briefly supported the Greek cause was a source of astonishment to later philhellenes who faced continual opposition in its pages. Referring to Lempriere's appeal, E. H. Barker wrote of the editor of the newspaper: 'This passage shews the *real* sentiments of the rogue; but he changed his note in a very few days, when he found that they were unpalatable to our Government.'[6]

Determined political opposition from the government gradually filtered through society to prevent a considerable body of philhellenic support from being expressed in public meetings and subscriptions.[7] It is not true, as Virginia Penn has suggested, that 'Philhellenism grew slowly in England, but its progress was

---

[3] *Morning Chronicle* (4 Oct. 1821).

[4] Lempriere's appeal appeared in the *Courier* on 9 October 1821 and was widely reprinted elsewhere. See *Traveller* (11 Oct.); *Examiner* (14 Oct.); *Morning Chronicle* (11 Oct.).

[5] LGC papers, vol. i, fo. J², Lempriere to Barker, 26 Mar. 1823.

[6] Ibid. fo. W⁴, Barker to Bowring, 4 May 1823.

[7] By December 1821, the *Courier* abandoned its policy of support for the Greeks and, according to the *Morning Chronicle*, 'we see, from the language of *The Courier*, they are now seriously determined to do what they can to *exterminate* the Greeks' (27 Dec. 1821). The *Courier* also exploited as much as possible the accounts of the atrocities at Tripolizza which led to a polarization of views with the *Morning Chronicle* absurdly defending the Greeks by pointing to similar atrocities committed by the English after the Battle of Culloden and during the Irish rebellion. See *Morning Chronicle* (27 Dec. 1821). See also *Morning Chronicle* (28 Dec. 1821), where a letter, signed 'Philo-Veritas', concludes with the observation: 'I have only to hope, that the Grand Turk in his last will and testament . . . has left fifty of his fattest wives to the friendly care and guardianship of the Editors of *The Courier*, as a mark

steady'.[8] Strong expressions of philhellenism were evident in
England by the summer and autumn of 1821, but such expressions
were discouraged by government policy and attitude. By the end of
1821 it was clear that most loyal Tories, whatever their personal
feelings regarding the suffering Christians and the fate of Europe's
classical inheritance, were expected to support the government
policy of neutrality. Neutrality meant not raising funds and not
sending men and equipment to assist the Greeks in the war. Once
these expectations were fully appreciated, even charitable assistance
for the Greeks became highly politicized with only the programme
of relief inspired by William Allen and carried out by the Society of
Friends escaping government hostility.[9] Only when Canning
became Foreign Secretary on the death of Lord Castlereagh in 1822
was a more flexible policy towards Greece adopted, and this
development enabled the London Greek Committee to be formed
in early 1823.[10] Canning could see that private subscriptions could
go hand in hand with official neutrality, thereby allowing British
influence to develop in Greece without placing Britain in opposition to the Holy Alliance. But there was no steady growth of
philhellenism; it was strong by the summer of 1821, but was
repressed in response to the government, and was only permitted
to develop in 1823. This domestic politicization of the Greek
struggle is important in explaining two significant facts about
philhellenism in 1823. Firstly, when Bowring and Blaquiere
founded the London Greek Committee, they were able to draw on
a philhellenic spirit still in existence after two years. Even though
this spirit had not been allowed full expression, its strength had not

of respect and esteem for their well-meant advocacy of Mahometanism!' Government influence, however, was not confined to the newspapers. Others seemed to
take their cue from what was perceived to be government opinion. For example,
when the Revd George Browne, Trinity College, Cambridge, sent two subscriptions to the *Morning Chronicle* to assist the 'Distressed Greeks', one on his own behalf
and the other on behalf of the Masonic Lodge of which he was Master, he was forced
to withdraw the latter subscription because of protests from the Grand Master, the
duke of Sussex, and others, that he was wrong to introduce 'political topics into the
bosom of a Lodge of Masons' (*Morning Chronicle* (27 Dec. 1821)). Browne himself
thought that he was making only a charitable donation for the relief of suffering, but
he readily complied with the request.

[8] Virginia Penn, 'Philhellenism in England (1821–1827)', *Slavonic Review*, 14
(1935–6), 366.
[9] Ibid. 370–1. See also *Life of William Allen with Selections from his Correspondence*, 3
vols. (London, 1846), ii. 260 ff., 323 ff., 363.
[10] See St Clair, *That Greece Might Still Be Free*, 139–40, 142–3. See also *Byron's
Bulldog: The Letters of John Cam Hobhouse to Lord Byron*, ed. Peter W. Graham

diminished, and the London Greek Committee could never have succeeded without the support existing since 1821. Secondly, that the motivating force behind the London Greek Committee in 1823 was mainly men like Bowring, Blaquiere, Hume, Burdett, and Hobhouse reflected the fact that only a group of people strongly opposed to the government (unlike the philhellenes of 1812) could form a successful Committee to assist the Greeks. In other words, only a highly political body could succeed in this politicized atmosphere.

2. Formation of the London Greek Committee

At the beginning of March 1823, with Blaquiere and Louriottis setting off for Greece with Bentham's 'Observations' and with plans to visit Byron during the course of their journey, the indefatigable Bowring began a massive correspondence that would lead to the formation of the London Greek Committee. He started by writing to MPs, inviting them to join the Committee and to contribute to the cause.[11] They, in turn, wrote to other prominent figures, and the list grew quickly with the main object being to move as soon as possible towards a public meeting.

Not everyone who was approached agreed to join the Committee. Some, like Lord Lansdowne (who had been associated with Lempriere's efforts and saw no new developments to justify another attempt) and Dr Henry Holland, declined membership of the Committee but none the less made contributions to it once it was established.[12] Some simply declined without giving reasons.[13]

(Columbus, Oh., 1984), 326 (Hobhouse to Byron, 2 Mar. 1823): 'Canning has certainly for the present taken quite a different line from Castlereagh and is more supported by some of us than by some of his own party.' See H. V. Temperley, *The Foreign Policy of George Canning, 1822–1827* (London, 1925), 319–37; Wendy Hinde, *George Canning* (London, 1973), 384 ff.

[11] See LGC papers, vol. i, fo. K, Bowring to William Roscoe, 1 Mar. 1823, where he refers to a meeting on 28 February consisting mainly of MPs.

[12] Ibid. fo. T, Lord Lansdowne to Bowring, 11 Mar. 1823; fo. M^1, Dr H. Holland to Bowring, 17 Mar. 1823.

[13] See e.g. ibid. fo. A^1, Pascoe Grenfell to Bowring, 14 Mar. 1823; fo. D^1, William Manning to Bowring, 15 Mar. 1823; fo. F^1, Spencer to William Smith, 15 Mar. 1823; fo. P^1, James Barnett to Bowring, 18 Mar. 1823; fo. U^1, Dr Burney to Chairman of Greek Committee, 21 Mar. 1823; fo. V^1, N. Slade to Chairman of Greek Committee, 22 Mar. 1823; fo. V^2, William Rose to Chairman of Greek Committee, 31 Mar. 1823.

Others were especially forthright in declining membership. Among the reasons given included statements to the effect that Britain should maintain the 'strictest neutrality' between Greece and Turkey, that the Foreign Enlistment Act would preclude service by British soldiers in Greece, that the very enterprise of establishing an association to support a war in which the country was not engaged was illegal, and that raising funds to relieve economic distress in Britain was more urgently required than raising money to assist the Greeks.[14] Even more important, perhaps, was the strong feeling that 'loyal and intelligent men will not take any steps to further a cause which *they think* is in opposition to the sentiments of the acting powers and directly opposed to the policy to which they are bound to adhere'.[15] Nevertheless, the founding of the London Greek Committee was more usually warmly welcomed, especially by those early phil-hellenes like Robert Chatfield who 'began almost to despair of our own countrymen taking a part in her cause, even in the least offensive and unobjectionable way'.[16]

As Bowring's list of Committee members grew, he also extended his contacts to other cities and towns in Britain. From the outset, it was intended that the Committee should be national in scope and draw on similar committees elsewhere. He even attempted to make contact with the government to suggest that the Committee, and especially Blaquiere, might be useful to it.[17]

The most important person assisting Bowring in extending the Committee was another indefatigable writer of letters, E. H. Barker (1788–1839), who served as an informal assistant secretary to the Committee and was especially useful because of his contacts with more traditional philhellenes. Barker was a classicist, a former amanuensis to the noted scholar Samuel Parr, and was then living in Thetford in reduced circumstances.[18] Like Bentham, he had been in regular contact with Adamantios Korais and, by the time the Committee was formed, had already added to the considerable

[14] See ibid. fos. Q–R, James McQueen to John Maxwell, 5 Mar. 1823; fo. I², Charles Monck to Chairman of Greek Committee, 26 Mar. 1823; fo. H³, W. M. Leake to Joseph Hume, 4 Apr. 1823; fo. R⁴, Lord Stanhope to Chairman of Greek Committee, 2 May 1823.

[15] Ibid. fo. B⁵, *Gallant*, 1 (10 May 1823).

[16] Ibid. fo. N, Chatfield to Barker, 8 Mar. 1823.

[17] See ibid. fo. N², Bowring to J. Reeves (copy), 26 Mar. 1823.

[18] See *DNB* for a somewhat critical account of his life.

pamphlet literature that had appeared in 1822.[19] In this pamphlet he seemed to have had little hope of raising a sum of money for the Greeks, though he thought that a campaign was possible to repeal the Foreign Enlistment Act which would enable men to go to Greece to fight the 'holy war'.[20] With the founding of the Committee, however, he seemed to be spurred to action, and his correspondence and support were so energetic that it is possible to speak of two Greek Committees, one based in London and run by Bowring and the other in East Anglia with Barker as its secretary.

Barker was active, for example, in the formation of the Cambridge Committee which would play an important role in fund-raising.[21] His link with traditional philhellenism ensured that the London Greek Committee as a whole was as much imbued with a love of Greece, ancient and modern, and a sympathy for her sufferings as with an ideological commitment to liberalism. At the minimum the co-operation of Barker and Bowring brought together traditional Whigs and reform-minded liberals in a purposeful manner. At times this co-operation approached incredulity, as when Barker learned that some of the Greek youths brought by Blaquiere for education in England might be sent to Hazelwood School in Birmingham, an establishment much admired by reformers. Barker wrote vigorously to Bowring to say that he had never heard of Hazelwood School and thought that the Greek boys should have the best education available at such institutions as Charterhouse, Christ's Hospital, Winchester, and so on. He had no idea of the extent to which Bowring and others had spurned traditional forms of education and thought it was a matter of not having sufficient funds.[22] But on the whole, Barker produced a steady stream of useful information and suggestions for Bowring which enabled him to extend the range of the Committee

---

[19] See *A Letter Addressed to the Rev. T. S. Hughes* (Southampton, 1822). A second, expanded edition also appeared in 1822, and further editions in 1823.

[20] Ibid. 23.

[21] Thomas Gordon wrote in his *History of the Greek Revolution* (2 vols. (Edinburgh, 1832)), ii. 79 n.: 'It would be ungrateful not to notice the unwearied zeal and very meritorious exertions of the Rev. Mr. Barker of Thetford, who advocated with his pen the cause of Greece.'

[22] See LGC papers, vol. xi, fos. M[4], T[4], Barker to Bowring, 1 Nov., 4 Nov. 1824. On the education of the Greek youths, see G. F. Bartle, 'The Greek Boys at Borough Road during the War of Independence', *Journal of Educational Administration and History*, 20 (1988), 1–11.

considerably beyond the confines of the London-based reformers who constituted its core.

By 29 March 1823 the London Greek Committee was sufficiently formed that Bowring could issue an initial list of fifty names of a Committee 'of the most distinguished and respectable individuals in the country' which met 'from time to time at the Crown and Anchor Tavern'.[23] Bowring's strategy of enlisting the support of Whig MPs, especially those most disposed towards reform, was successful, as nearly half of the members on the list were MPs. The Greek community in London was represented by J. Mavrocordato, N. Ralli, and D. Schinas, the last of whom had been publicly active from 1821 but who would be eventually forced to resign due to financial irregularities in handling subscriptions.[24] There were, of course, familiar names of those active in the cause of reform such as Sir Francis Burdett, Lord Erskine, J. C. Hobhouse, Joseph Hume, Zachariah Macaulay, Thomas Moore, Sir James Mackintosh, and Lord John Russell. Bentham and David Ricardo were members, though James Mill and Francis Place were not. The final list of eighty-four names contained some notable additions such as Byron, Leicester Stanhope, Thomas Campbell, and Henry Brougham who joined after the Committee had been formed. The classicists Chatfield, Lempriere, Parr, and Barker also appeared on the second list.[25]

Besides forming the Committee, Bowring organized weekly meetings at the Crown and Anchor Tavern. Approximately eight to ten members usually attended, although only a few, like Hume and Hobhouse, attended regularly.[26] Thus, while some continuity of attendance can be observed in the minutes of the various

---

[23] See *Morning Chronicle* (29 Mar. 1823) (reprinted in Appendix I). Other lists circulated earlier. See the list of 25 members, drawn up on 8 March and enclosed in a letter from Bowring to Byron, 14 Mar. 1823 (Murray archive, Box A21).

[24] See LGC papers, vol. v, fo. T², Cockerell to Bowring, 2 Feb. 1824; vol. vi, fos. W¹, X¹, Y¹, Z¹, A², B², C² (Feb.–Mar. 1824) (correspondence between Cockerell, Schinas, and Bowring).

[25] See Appendix II. Not all members appear on the list. Frank Abney Hastings was elected to the Committee in November 1824, long after the full list had been published. See Finlay papers, British School of Archaeology at Athens, H. 3 (S. 8. 2 (a)), fo. 18.

[26] See *Byron's Bulldog*, 333 (Hobhouse to Byron, 11 June 1823): 'Between ourselves there is not so much sympathy for foreign patriots as could be wished—all the efforts, money, time, and talking, all come from the same set of people . . . about four or five good men and true.'

meetings, there was considerable variation in attendance and participation which tended to result in most decisions being taken by Bowring himself as Honorary Secretary. The difficulty of finding others, besides Bowring, willing to take on the major chores of the Committee may be illustrated by the attempts which were made to appoint a Treasurer. The minutes of the meeting of 15 March 1823 record that Zachariah Macaulay was invited to be Treasurer.[27] At the meeting of 22 March Hume, William Smith, Hobhouse, and Evans were deputed to persuade John Smith to act as Treasurer.[28] Presumably, Macaulay had not accepted. The process of persuasion seems to have lasted until 19 April when Smith agreed.[29] At the public meeting on 15 May, in response to criticism from Henry Hunt about the arrangements for the disposal of the funds, it was announced that there were three Treasurers: John Smith, Edward Ellice, and Sir J. D. Forbes.[30] On 24 May the minutes record the appointment of a Committee of Auditors consisting of Hume, Ricardo, William Smith, Douglas Kinnaird, and Thomas Campbell, though these auditors were not mentioned at the public meeting the week before.[31] Although obvious concern was shown by members of the Committee to check the expenditure of funds and there is no evidence of misappropriation at this stage, clearly the absence of a single Treasurer with time and energy to devote to the job led to an even greater delegation of *de facto* power to Bowring who ran the Committee in most respects.

The minutes of the Committee indicated a great deal of activity and this activity was soon reflected in the press. Even a 'literary' subcommittee was formed consisting of Hobhouse, Sheridan, Schinas, and Thomas Campbell.[32] In a brief time many of the articles about Greece (except those taken directly from foreign papers) originated with the Committee. In addition, a series of reports, announcements, and subscription lists were regularly published.

The large number of MPs on the Committee facilitated communication between the Committee and the government. At the meeting on 12 April, William Smith was asked to obtain from Canning the government's views on assisting refugees.[33] He

---

[27] LGC papers, vol. iii, fo. A.   [28] Ibid. fo. C.
[29] Ibid. fos. G–H.   [30] *Morning Chronicle* (16 May 1823).
[31] LGC papers, vol. iii, fo. L.   [32] Ibid. fo. I.   [33] Ibid. fo. F.

reported two weeks later that while the government could not promise to assist refugees, it would not impede their passage through British territory or require passports from them.[34] In May, just after the public meeting, Joseph Hume reported on a meeting with Canning about the misconduct of British consuls in Greece and the problems of Greek refugees then in Switzerland.[35] These communications reflect the usefulness of the MPs not only in legitimizing the Committee before the wider public, but also in providing useful links with the government.

The public meeting took place at the Crown and Anchor Tavern on 15 May, and the report of the meeting covered a full page of the *Morning Chronicle*.[36] According to the newspaper, 'The meeting was most numerous and respectable, and the sympathy and enthusiasm which were manifested on this occasion, gave the strongest assurance of success to the objects which they were assembled to promote.' With Lord Milton in the chair, a series of speeches followed. Besides Lord Milton, the audience heard John Smith, Sir James Mackintosh, Lord John Russell, Lord William Bentinck, John Cam Hobhouse, John Sidney Taylor, Lord Archibald Hamilton, Charles Brinsley Sheridan, William Smith, John Wilks, and several others. The speeches were fairly predictable, as the various speakers passionately reaffirmed their commitment to civil and religious liberty and to the cause of Greece. There were some allusions to the Tory opposition to support for Greece, as in this passage from a speech by Sir James Mackintosh:

If we speak of the interests of liberty, they call it revolutionary rant—if we speak of the interests of religion, they call it the cant of fanaticism—if we give utterance to the sentiments we are bound to cherish for the great teachers, instructors, and ornaments of mankind, they deride us for using the common-places of school-boys—if we venture to hail the prospect of the second civilization of Greece, and to look forward with delight to another Athens, rising with new arts and eloquence to rival, if possible, the glory of her predecessor—they reproach and laugh at us, as the dupes of a visionary philosophy—as misguided enthusiasts in the cause of impracticable civilization, and unattainable improvement.

---

[34] LGC papers, vol. iii, fo. I (Minutes, 25 Apr. 1823).
[35] Ibid. fo. M (Minutes, 31 May 1823).
[36] See *Morning Chronicle* (16 May 1823).

3. Subscriptions for the Greeks

Once the public meeting had taken place and funds began to come to the Committee, Bowring began to publish lists of subscribers.[37] These lists, unlike the list of Committee members, reveal a wider base of support for the Committee than has been generally assumed.[38] But fund-raising for Greece was not a simple matter, and a good example of the difficulties involved may be seen in the successful attempt to obtain a donation from the City of London Common Council.

When the announcement was made of a move to obtain a subscription for Spain in the Common Council, the Greek Committee decided to send a delegation as well.[39] The Greek petition seems to have been a last-minute affair, but a deputation including Lord Milton, Lord Erskine, J. Smith, W. Evans, J. Hume, J. C. Hobhouse, and Bowring attended the meeting on 10 June. The meeting voted £1,000 for Spain and referred the Greek petition to a committee.[40] On 14 June the *Morning Chronicle* recorded another meeting of the Common Council at which the committee reported having met representatives from the Greek Committee. It then recommended that £500 should be given to the Greek Committee. Within the Council, however, a move was made to increase the sum to £1,000, the same amount as had been given to the Committee for Spain. During the debate as to the legality of using money to buy 'war-like stores' to be used against nations with which Britain was friendly, the Lord Mayor said that he had taken up the matter with the officers of the Common Council. The Recorder and City Solicitor thought the decision to vote these sums was illegal, but the Common Serjeant believed it legal.[41] The Lord Mayor claimed (though he was challenged by members) that 'this was the only time that the Court had voted money to one Power against another, both of the Powers being in

[37] See *Morning Chronicle* (19 May, 26 May, 9 June, 23 June, 18 July, 5 Aug., 1 Sept., 29 Sept., 30 Oct. 1823, 26 Jan., 15 Mar. 1824).
[38] See Appendix III for a list of major contributions to the Greek Committee.
[39] See *Morning Chronicle* (6 June 1823); see also LGC papers, vol. iii, fo. N (Minutes, 7 June 1823).
[40] *Morning Chronicle* (11 June 1823).
[41] Ibid. (14 June); See also ibid. (9 July 1823).

amity with Great Britain'.[42] But the majority, fortunately for the
Committee, were not influenced by these legal opinions and saw
their support for the Greeks as an issue of support for freedom in
both Spain and Greece. It was finally decided also to give the Greek
Committee £1,000.

Although much of the fund-raising burden fell on Bowring, he
was fortunate to have E. H. Barker's assistance. The Committee
recognized the importance of Barker's role as early as 22 March
1823 when it passed a special resolution to co-operate with him.[43]
Barker knew that a good deal of philhellenism existed at
Cambridge University and he set out to nurture it.[44] 'Mr. Hughes,
Mr. Pryme, myself, and other individuals,' he wrote, 'are going to
form a Committee [at Cambridge] for the receipt of subscriptions,
which will be appropriated to the Greek Cause, and not to the relief
of the fugitive Sciots like the Quaker-Subscription.'[45] Barker
clearly intended that whatever subscriptions he helped to raise were
to be used to assist the Greeks to win the war, and he was willing to
leave 'charitable' fund-raising to the Society of Friends.[46] In T. S.
Hughes and George Pryme he had two useful, if diffident, allies.
An early supporter of the Greeks, Hughes wrote a strong pamphlet
after the massacre of the Sciots in 1822.[47] As a Tory, a fellow of
Emmanuel College, Cambridge, and a clergyman, he was an ideal
person for Barker to enlist in support of the Committee.[48] At first,
he was made a member, but because of his 'ticklish' position as
examining chaplain to the bishop of London, his name was
withdrawn on Barker's advice, so as to enable him to escape
censure and be useful in other ways.[49]

George Pryme was a prominent Whig, a fellow of Trinity
College, a member of Lincoln's Inn (though he only briefly

---

[42] *Morning Chronicle* (14 June 1823).

[43] LGC papers, vol. iii, fo. B (Minutes, 22 Mar. 1823).

[44] This optimistic view was not universally shared. As one correspondent put it,
'nothing has given me so mean an opinion of the English University men as their
indifference or rather hostility to the Greeks' (LGC papers, vol. i. fo. U²,
C. Maclaren (Scotsman's Office) to Barker, 30 Mar. 1823).

[45] Ibid. vol. i, fo. Z¹, Barker to [?], 21 Mar. 1823.

[46] Ibid. vol. i, fo. L³, Barker to Bowring [?], 13 Apr. 1823.

[47] *An Address to the People of England in the Cause of the Greeks, Occasioned by the
Late Inhuman Massacres in the Isle of Scio* (London, 1822).   [48] See *DNB*.

[49] LGC papers, vol. i, fo. O⁴, Barker to Bowring, 30 Apr. 1823. Note that
Hughes's name does not appear on the lists of members of the Committee. Cf. St
Clair, *That Greece Might Still Be Free*, 145.

practised law), and an early lecturer in political economy at Cambridge.[50] Though ideologically closer to Barker, he was well aware that his own politics might form an obstacle to the success of a Cambridge Committee. As he wrote to Barker in May 1823:

I have not been inattentive to your communications respecting the Greek cause, but I find a few willing tho lukewarm; and the rest careless at best; some of them perhaps hostile, tho not avowedly so. Hughes has been here but little. . . . He is better fitted for obtaining a meeting, not merely from his zeal, but because he is a Tory. If anything is moved by a Whig it is immediately supposed to be a party measure and my own politics are so decided that I should only do mischief by taking a very active part. Your heading of the Resolutions by the word '*Political*' has and will I fear operate against us. The County is too much occupied with agricultural distress and grievances at home and both there and in the Town. Public spirit is a young and tender plant. On the whole I fear nothing can be done; at best no meeting will I think be called.[51]

Pryme's pessimism about the formation of a Cambridge Committee moderated somewhat when he accepted membership of the Committee in June 1823 (though his name did not appear on the list), and he reported that a branch might be formed at Cambridge.[52] In November, Hughes drew up a brief address for a Cambridge Committee and sent it to the press.[53] Pryme reported setting up the Committee itself, but again said he would not be active in it.[54] Elliott attended the first meeting and supplied an account of it for Barker:

But difficulty occurs in regard to the want of efficient members. Pryme is decidedly too much known as a Whig, and ultra Whig, and Hughes who would be the most proper man is too much occupied. . . . Peacock, Whewell, and Sedgwick are all, I think, on the Committee, and will be most valuable members. It seemed to me the time I was with them that there was no one, who had thoroughly made himself master of the question, and it certainly is a fault of the London-Committee that they are so lax in sending down information to the Country-Committees. . . . But in truth the whole matter rests in London on Mr. Bowring, and it is astonishing that he has done so much as he does.[55]

---

[50] See *DNB*.
[51] LGC papers, vol. i, fo. X⁴, Pryme to Barker, 7 May 1823.
[52] Ibid. vol. iii, fo. N (Minutes, 7 June 1823).
[53] Ibid. vol. iv, fo. H², Hughes to Bowring, 20 Nov. 1823.
[54] Ibid. fo. P², Pryme to Bowring, 22 Nov. 1823.
[55] Ibid. fo. S², Barker to Bowring, 29 Nov. 1823, containing an extract of a letter from Elliott to Barker.

However much the London Committee had been deficient, clearly a Cambridge Committee was launched, and at least one of the English universities had responded. Even the duke of Gloucester, as Chancellor of the University, had made a contribution. A distinguished list of scholars joined the Committee.[56] Hughes was Secretary, and the Committee often met at Pryme's house.[57]

Barker's efforts extended beyond the Cambridge subscription. He had early links with American philhellenes and urged Bowring to develop them.[58] When he heard that the American writer Washington Irving was in London, he immediately suggested that Bowring 'lay an embargo on him till he has produced something on the Cause'.[59] He also favoured (as did others) the idea of a public dinner to raise funds and proposed a dinner with the defeated Spanish General Mina, then living in seclusion in Britain, as the main guest and with the proceeds to be split with the Spanish Committee. Barker especially thought that a dinner would appeal to the Tories who had been so reluctant to contribute:

This scheme of a dinner would certainly take John Bull's curiosity and suit his stomach too. The very Tories will fall into the trap, and the more readily if you give a public notice of all of the toasts, which will be proposed; let those toasts be free from every political allusion, which can offend the *delicate* ears of Toryism.[60]

In terms of more practical success in fund-raising, Barker was behind most subscriptions that took place in East Anglia. He was

[56] See *Morning Chronicle* (19 Dec. 1823) for the Cambridge Address (dated 20 Nov. 1823) and list of members of the Cambridge branch committee. The list included: Professor C. Hewett, MD, Downing College (Treasurer); Professor P. P. Dobree, MA, Trinity College; Professor A. Sedgwick, MA, Trinity College; Revd W. Okes, MA, Caius College; E. Rogers, MA, LM, Caius College; Revd G. A. Browne, MA, Trinity College; George Pryme, MA, Trinity College; Revd J. Scholefield, MA, Trinity College; Revd J. Romilly, MA, Trinity College; Revd H. V. Elliott, MA, Trinity College; Revd E. B. Elliott, MA, Trinity College; William Whewell, MA, Trinity College; Revd T. S. Hughes, MA, Emmanuel College (Secretary); S. Pope, MA. Emmanuel College; W. Hustler, MA, Jesus College; Revd J. Lodge, MA, Magdalene College. Inaccuracies in spelling in the original have been corrected.
[57] See *Autobiographic Recollections of George Pryme, Esq. M.A., edited by His Daughter* [A. Bayne] (Cambridge, 1870), 143. See also 144 for a brief account of a visit by Orlandos, Louriottis, and Hobhouse to Pryme's house in July 1824.
[58] See LGC papers, vol. iii, fo. A[1], William Thornton to Barker, 24 June 1823; fo. R[1], Barker to Bowring, 17 Sept. 1823; vol. iv, fo. K[5], Barker to Bowring, 8 Jan. 1824.   [59] Ibid. vol. iv, fo. K[5], Barker to Bowring, 8 Jan. 1824.
[60] Ibid.

associated with William Keer Brown and helped persuade the duke of Grafton to contribute £50 and thereby lay the foundations for a Suffolk Committee.[61] He was also in touch with developments in Manchester, Birmingham, and Liverpool, and was a strong supporter of Blaquiere's efforts at fund-raising.[62] He worked steadily and enthusiastically encouraging subscriptions far into 1824, even after the loan had been launched and subscriptions were no longer urgently needed.[63] Even though he himself had little money (he could only contribute 2 guineas to the subscription), he did not hesitate to approach rich and poor alike.[64] Barker also possessed good judgement about how to proceed with the subscription. For example, he criticized Blaquiere for placing so radical a person as Joseph Parkes in charge of the subscription in Birmingham, and was quick to see the value of John Gladstone in Liverpool.[65] Finally, his enthusiasm was important in encouraging Bowring to continue when the latter seemed dispirited, especially in early 1824. When he learned in June of that year that Bowring was resigning as Honorary Secretary, he wrote: 'If you alone attend, and have to address yourself to the *shade* of the Chairman, still I maintain that all will be well. . . . For in point of fact you have had to manage half the business *yourself.*'[66] He also believed that the Committee should remain in existence, even though the amount of money now being subscribed had substantially diminished. For Barker the Committee could still be 'a point of union—a

[61] Ibid. fo. T², W. K. Brown to Bowring, 25 Nov. 1823; fo. D⁴, Brown to Bowring, 14 Dec. 1823; fo. I⁴, Barker to Bowring, 19 Dec. 1823; fo. K⁵, Barker to Bowring, 8 Jan. 1824; vol. v, fo. A², Brown to Bowring, 18 Jan. 1824; fo. E², Barker to Bowring, 21 Jan. 1824; fos. G²–H², Brown to Bowring, 23 Jan. 1824; fo. Q², Barker to Bowring, 1 Feb. 1824; vol. viii, fo. S, Barker to Bowring, 27 Apr. 1824.

[62] See ibid. vol. iv, fo. S⁵, Barker to Bowring, 13 Jan. 1824; vol. v, fo. E², Barker to Bowring, 21 Jan. 1824; vol. vi, fo. O⁴, Barker to Bowring, 5 Apr. 1824; vol. ix, fo. U³, Barker to Bowring, 15 July 1824.

[63] See ibid. vol. viii, fo. T¹, Barker to Bowring, 7 May 1824.

[64] See Bodleian Library, MS Bodl. 1004, fo. 177, Thomas Quayle to Barker, 28 July 1823: 'I thank you for your kind notice from the Greek Committee. Poverty not my Will *dissents*. Whatever I should give to the Greek Objects would be, bonâ fide, so much taken from my Creditors, on whose forebearance I am living. . . . But without any Exaggeration, I am not only in debt, but nearly penniless.'

[65] See LGC papers, vol. ix, fo. U³, Barker to Bowring, 15 July 1824; vol. vi, fo. O⁴, Barker to Bowring, 5 Apr. 1824, where he writes regarding Gladstone: 'an M.P., a friend of Canning, member of Liverpool Committee, an excellent speaker . . .'

[66] Ibid. vol. ix, fo. N², Barker to Bowring, 25 June 1824.

theatre for action—a centre for information—a focus for sympathy—
a sun to diffuse light and heat throughout the country'.[67]

4. Blaquiere's Fund-Raising Journey

After Blaquiere had returned from his first visit to Greece and had
been replaced by Stanhope in the expedition of the autumn of 1823,
he agreed in November of that year to attempt to enlarge the
subscription by a tour of a number of provincial towns and cities
including Winchester, Southampton, Salisbury, Bath, Bristol,
Birmingham, Manchester, and Liverpool.[68] Blaquiere's determination to extend the subscription beyond the limited confines of the
London Committee and his general enthusiasm for the Greek cause
made him a good choice for this difficult task. Writing from
Winchester, he gave a clear account of his method of attack:

I stopped at Basingstoke, saw the Rector, a determined ultra, gave him the
pièces and think I left him greatly softened. Wrote strong letters to Mr.
Jervoise the Hampshire County Member, and to Sir Thomas Baring—
urging both to come to the aid of the committee. In reaching this place
[Winchester] last night, I immediately saw Mr. Hitchen the Editor of the
Hampshire Telegraph. Found him uncommonly well disposed—proposed
a long article for his next no. which you will receive, and begged he would
see the Banker, who has already entered into our views and will receive
subscriptions. I have just returned from Mr. Richards who keeps a large
school. He is going to do all he can for us and even asked me to dinner—If
my visit to this place be followed up by a letter or two from Mr. Sheridan
and any one else who happens to be acquainted with the Neighbourhood,
there is no doubt of an immediate subscription.—and should there be one
here, you need not despair of any other place—[69]

Hitchen, the editor of the *Hampshire Telegraph*, does seem to have
been well disposed towards the Committee. He had printed a full
account of Blaquiere's *Report* in September, and after Blaquiere's
visit, reprinted the 'Cambridge Address', which had been prepared

[67] Ibid. fo. A[1], Barker to Bowring, 8 June 1824.
[68] Ibid. vol. v, fo. M[3], Blaquiere to Bowring, 13 Feb. 1824.
[69] Ibid. vol. iv, fo. Y[2], Blaquiere to Bowring, 27 Nov. 1823.

by T. S. Hughes.[70] That Blaquiere chose to emphasize the
Cambridge Address was partly due to its recent publication (it was
dated 20 November); yet it also enabled him to emphasize that the
London Greek Committee was drawing on the larger philhellenic
tradition that had been submerged since 1821 rather than on the
narrower ideological liberalism behind the London Committee. He
used E. B. Elliott's *Appeal from the Greek Committee to the British
Public in General, and Especially to the Friends of Religion* to the same
effect. Elliott, a signatory of the Cambridge Address, a clergyman
of the evangelical school and member of the Clapham Sect, is an
excellent example of the type of person Blaquiere hoped to use to
attract new people to the Greek cause.[71] But Blaquiere did not
entirely neglect his other interests and apparently left some copies
of the prospectus of the new *Westminster Review* for Hitchen to
distribute.[72]

Some initial success in Winchester was followed by a brief visit
to Southampton where he arranged for forms to be printed on
which subscriptions might be received and wrote anxiously to
Bowring to obtain further copies of his own *Report* and Elliott's
Appeal. He also urged Bowring 'to get the religious leaders about
Town to write down to their friends in the Country—relative to
preaching and otherwise promoting the Subscription'.[73] Besides
enlisting the support of local politicians and approaching the editors
of provincial newspapers and bankers to accept subscriptions, he
hoped to enlist the support of Church of England clergy, using the
Cambridge Address and Elliott's *Appeal* to do so. As Blaquiere was
then living in Southampton, the *Southampton County Chronicle
and Isle of Wight Journal* carried a number of articles favourable to
the Greek cause, and several more appeared during this visit.[74] But
Blaquiere was soon off to Bath where he found his visit fairly
promising: 'Having just taken a coup d'œil of the Pump Room, it
strikes me, much good seed may be sown in this seat of gout and
gossip. My hopes are such here, that I have determined to prolong

[70] See *Hampshire Telegraph and Sussex Chronicle* (29 Sept., 22 Dec. 1823).
[71] See *DNB*. See also LGC papers, vol. iii, fo. E⁴, E. B. Elliott to Bowring, 23
Oct. 1823; vol. iv, fo. J¹, Elliott to Bowring, 31 Oct. 1823; fo. C², Elliott to
Bowring, 14 Nov. 1823; fo. F³, Elliott to Bowring, 28 Nov. 1823.
[72] Ibid. vol. iv, fo. O³, Hitchen to Blaquiere, 2 Dec. 1823.
[73] Ibid. fo. H³, Blaquiere to Bowring, 31 Nov. 1823.
[74] See issues for 1, 15 Nov., 6, 13 Dec. 1823.

my stay a day or two.'[75] He found support in both the *Bath and Cheltenham Gazette* and the *Bath Chronicle*. The former had already printed a long article on the worthiness of the Greek cause and had defended Blaquiere against an attack by *Blackwood's Edinburgh Magazine*.[76] It now published the Cambridge Address, as did the *Bath Chronicle* which noted that 'the cause has been warmly espoused at Winchester; and at Cambridge, a public subscription has been headed by a liberal donation from the Chancellor [the duke of Gloucester] of £100'.[77] Despite this considerable publicity and apparent good will, Blaquiere was well aware of the 'paramount importance for the Committee to dispel prejudice and *repel* the attempt to connect its generous efforts with a spirit of party'.[78] In his use of the Cambridge Address he clearly sought to achieve these ends. But despite the Cambridge Address and Elliott's *Appeal*, the Church of England clergy seemed reluctant to support even a 'holy' war. For example, when Blaquiere tried to obtain support at Salisbury, he wrote to Bowring:

I have sounded a number of clergy in this *ancient seat of religion* and find the[y] don't like the idea of Lord B[yron]'s being made too prominent in the Greek question—the Rev John Greenly of the Cathedral—He is to be your correspondent here, recommends our being careful not to offend the cloth by bringing his Lordship too much into the foreground—look to this will you.[79]

Blaquiere was more enthusiastic about his prospects in Bristol, the next stop on his journey. 'I think there is every probability of a branch committee here', he wrote to Bowring. 'I have had more calls and seen more enthusiasm than any where else.'[80] On the same day as he wrote these words, the *Bristol Gazette* in a long editorial welcomed Blaquiere to the city and, in publishing the Cambridge Address, urged a similar development for Bristol.[81] In this material, and in a letter written on the same day but published a week later, Blaquiere stressed not only that he was appealing to all

---

[75] LGC papers, vol. iv, fo. X³, Blaquiere to Bowring, 12 Dec. 1823.
[76] See *Bath and Cheltenham Gazette* (18 Nov. 1823).
[77] Ibid. (16 Dec. 1823); *The Bath Chronicle* (18 Dec. 1823).
[78] LGC papers, vol. iv, fo. X³, Blaquiere to Bowring, 12 Dec. 1823.
[79] LGC papers, vol. vii, fo. S, Blaquiere to Bowring, n.d.
[80] Ibid. vol. iv, fo. S⁴, Blaquiere to Bowring, 24 Dec. 1823.
[81] *Bristol Gazette* (25 Dec. 1823).

parties and sects but also and especially that this was a struggle waged by Christians for their own survival.[82] As he put it more directly in a letter to Bowring, 'we shall at all events get the *Christians* of England into a corner out of which I defy them to creep without putting their hands in their pockets'.[83] Blaquiere was intent on establishing a local association and referred to those already established in England and Scotland.[84] In addition, the *Bristol Gazette* offered to receive subscriptions at the newspaper office.

When Blaquiere left Bristol, Sir Charles Elton, the noted Whig from Clifton and a member of the London Committee, took over the task of organizing the subscription, though he was considerably less optimistic about its prospects than was Blaquiere. If on 9 January Elton wrote to Bowring that the formation of a branch committee had been announced in the *Bristol Journal*, a week later he wrote to say that operations had been suspended pending further information from London, some instructions regarding how they should proceed, and a clearer statement of how the money was to be used.[85] In his letter to the *Bath Gazette*, Blaquiere had distinguished between the aid being given for the assistance of refugees by the Society of Friends and the object of the London Greek Committee to assist the Greeks to win their armed struggle. But many potential subscribers were obviously uneasy about such an object which involved supporting a foreign war, especially one towards which the government was neutral, even if it was a war between Christians and 'infidels'. Nevertheless, Elton continued to collect private subscriptions, though he noted with some disappointment that the subscriptions fell 'very far below our expectations', because 'the more opulent members of the mercantile community' had not been generous, partly because they had set a low average subscription and failed to secure larger sums.[86] He pressed on with the collection of private subscriptions and even brought to Bowring's attention that some ladies of Bristol had formed a branch committee to raise money to ransom captured Greek women.[87] At a gala dinner for members of the Bristol

---

[82] Ibid. (1 Jan. 1824).
[83] LGC papers, vol. iv, fo. S⁴, Blaquiere to Bowring, 24 Dec. 1823.
[84] *Bristol Gazette* (1 Jan. 1824).
[85] LGC papers, vol. v, fos. X¹, Z¹, Elton to Bowring, 9, 16 Jan. 1824.
[86] Ibid. fo. N³, Elton to Bowring, 13 Feb. 1824.   [87] Ibid.

Institution in early March 1824, Elton, in one of the toasts, spoke eloquently in support of Greece.[88] By the end of April, he sent to Bowring approximately £100.[89] If Bristol did not live up to Blaquiere's initial expectations, his efforts were not entirely unsuccessful, and one wonders if more might have been achieved with more positive leadership.

After leaving Bristol, Blaquiere set out for Gloucester and Worcester which appear to have been the low points of his entire journey. 'I could not have thought this country possessed two places so degraded and narrow minded', he wrote to Bowring, after having abandoned fund-raising there to seek refuge in Birmingham.[90] In Gloucester, he was armed with letters of introduction to Sir William Guise, but Guise, acting 'in a most rascally manner', refused to see him. Blaquiere not only sent him a strong letter of protest but also wrote to six members of the Corporation 'exposing their Chief Magistrate in his true light, very broadly hinting that, if all the patriotism and public spirit of Gloucester was not shut up in Sir W. Guise, they would come forward in aid of Greece'.[91] As for Worcester, 'the very sight of the place congealed me'.[92]

Blaquiere found Birmingham, and then Manchester and Liverpool, more to his taste, and while he was able to achieve some success in Bath and especially in Bristol, the new industrial cities seemed more responsive to the Greek cause. But nevertheless, he did not stay long in Birmingham. He was in contact with Joseph Parkes, a member of the Committee, who reassured him by the end of January that he had planned a public meeting for Birmingham and 'it will turn out the most numerous and influential public meeting held in this town for many years past'.[93] The subscription at Birmingham moved forward slowly, with Parkes still planning the meeting in late October 1824.[94]

In Manchester, however, Blaquiere found an active committee already in existence. George Hadfield, the Manchester attorney, later MP for Sheffield, and an active figure in the Congregational

[88] See *Bristol Gazette* (4 Mar. 1824).
[89] LGC papers, vol. viii, fo. A¹, Elton to Bowring, 30 Apr. 1824.
[90] Ibid. vol. iv, fo. H⁵, Blaquiere to Bowring, 2 Jan. 1824.
[91] Ibid.   [92] Ibid.
[93] Ibid. vol. v, fo. D², Parkes to Blaquiere, 20 Jan. 1824.
[94] Ibid. vol. ix, fo. V⁴, Parkes to Bowring, 27 July 1824; see also vol. xi, fo. M⁴, Barker to Bowring, 1 Nov. 1824.

Church, took the lead in organizing a branch committee in October 1823.[95] Although he experienced some difficulty at the outset, he could report by the beginning of November that he was definitely organizing a subscription.[96] By the end of November, the *Manchester Guardian* announced in a positive vein the formation of a committee and the forthcoming launch of an appeal.[97] Like others who had attempted to obtain broad support for the appeal, Hadfield was anxious to include both the clergy, the town officers, and the Tories. As for the Church of England clergy, he wrote:

They are not hostile to it, but many of them express a doubt whether the measure will meet with the approbation of Government and appear as if they were afraid of compromising themselves—the Dissenting Clergy who have large Congregations do not make the same objections, and I hope will be induced to espouse the Cause with zeal.[98]

At the same time, he approached the leading officers of the town:

I waited personally upon the Boroughmen and Chief Officers of the Town. . . . They have however promised to give something as private individuals but not in the capacity of public officers . . . for in this Town, the leading men will do nothing of this nature, without there is first shewn an example, or a demonstration on the part of the Government—.[99]

The Tories generally proved most reluctant to support the appeal. In mid-December, Hadfield reported to Bowring that he had delayed the commencement of a general subscription 'from a wish to bring the Tories into the scheme; their leading men have been repeatedly applied to, and though they do not absolutely refuse, I can not hope that the disposition will become general amongst them to support the Cause as they ought'.[100] A week later the general appeal, signed by George Hadfield and several others, was published in the *Manchester Guardian*.[101] What was striking about the subscription was that most individual contributions on the

---

[95] See *DNB*.
[96] LGC papers, vol. iii, fo. G³, Hadfield to Bowring (?), 7 Oct. 1823; fo. S⁴, Hadfield to Bowring, 1 Nov. 1823.
[97] *Manchester Guardian* (29 Nov. 1823).
[98] LGC papers, vol. iii, fo. S⁴, Hadfield to Bowring, 1 Nov. 1823.
[99] Ibid. vol. iv, fo. E², Hadfield to Bowring, 18 Nov. 1823.
[100] Ibid. fo. Y³, Hadfield to Bowring, 12 Dec. 1823.
[101] *Manchester Guardian* (20 Dec. 1823). The appeal was signed by Hadfield, John Potter, James Oughton, Edward Baxter, E. J. Lloyd, G. W. Wood, Robert H. Greg, and Mark Philips. Hadfield gave £40 and the others gave 10 guineas each. The appeal was followed by a list of 35 supporters, most of whom gave 5 guineas or less.

various lists were no more than 5 guineas, and many were less than 2 guineas.[102]

Blaquiere was impressed by the generosity of those asked to contribute: 'From all I saw, nothing can be more admirable than the Spirit here—5 and 10 Guineas are put down with more facility than *one farthing* could be got from our noble and religious aristocracy.'[103] He was equally struck by the way committee members put aside their own concerns to collect 'from house to house'.[104] Many of the small contributions, listed in the *Guardian*, were most probably raised in this manner. On 8 January, Blaquiere addressed the branch committee and read a number of documents. He reported to Bowring that 'all seemed to be highly pleased and voted me thanks', and the *Guardian* devoted 1½ columns to the meeting.[105] By mid-February Robert Hyde Greg, a member of the committee, sent £500 to the London Committee with a promise of more to come, and by May 1824, he sent nearly £200 as a second instalment.[106]

Blaquiere's final stop on this fund-raising odyssey was in Liverpool where, prior to his arrival, no definite steps had been made to raise a subscription.[107] 'If a stir be made here and a committee formed,' he wrote to Bowring, 'it will certainly be owing to my visit.'[108] He quickly set to work and described his efforts as follows:

One of my first cares here, as in every other place, has of course been to secure the Press—on calling upon the Editor of the *Liverpool Courier* the great Tory paper this morning, he handed me over his last no. from which I have cut out the enclosed leading article—If you could get this inserted in the Sun or Chronicle, it would have the very best effect. I have seen a number of persons today, and have little doubt but that a committee will be formed, though I confess this is one of the last places on earth where I should expect to see any public spirit except in what [is] related to its local interests. The trading spirit on one side, and the corrupt influence on the other, has taken full possession of Liverpool.[109]

[102] See *Manchester Guardian* (20 Dec. 1823, 10 Jan., 12 Jan., and 7 Feb. 1824).
[103] LGC papers, vol. iv, fo. J⁵, Blaquiere to Bowring, 7 Jan. 1824.
[104] Ibid. fo. L⁵, Blaquiere to Bowring, 8 Jan. 1824.
[105] Ibid. See also *Manchester Guardian* (17 Jan. 1824).
[106] LGC papers, vol. v, fo. C³, Greg to Bowring, 11 Feb. 1824; vol. viii, fo. J³, Greg to Bowring, 18 May 1824.
[107] See ibid. vol. v, fo. M³, Blaquiere to Bowring, 13 Feb. 1824.
[108] Ibid. vol. iv, fo. Q⁵, Blaquiere to Bowring, 12 Jan. 1824.
[109] Ibid. fo. T⁵, Blaquiere to Bowring, 13 Jan. 1824.

Not only did Blaquiere make good progress with the press, but he also managed to secure the support of John Gladstone, father of William Gladstone, the Victorian Prime Minister, who was MP for Liverpool and a popular figure in the city. Gladstone agreed from the outset both to support the cause and to appear at a public meeting.[110] As before, the local press welcomed Blaquiere to Liverpool, describing him as 'the celebrated traveller, and talented commentator on the moral and political condition of several portions of Europe'.[111] The *Liverpool Mercury* printed a letter from Blaquiere and offered to receive subscriptions.[112]

A week later the same newspaper published another letter from Blaquiere ('the patriotic and spirited writer') referring to developments in Cambridge, Bristol, Manchester, and Birmingham and looking forward to a substantial contribution from Liverpool.[113] According to the newspaper, a 'requisition' to the Lord Mayor to call a public meeting had already been signed by 'many most respectable gentlemen of the town, who ordinarily differ widely from each other upon political subjects'.[114] This was followed on 30 January by a long (1½ columns) editorial in favour of supporting the Greek cause largely on the grounds of supporting liberty and Christianity and opposing Russian influence in the Mediterranean.[115] Within a month, a public meeting was held which was widely reported in both Liverpool and London newspapers.[116] The Lord Mayor presided, Gladstone made the first speech, and a number of resolutions were passed. Whatever the setting, whether in March 1823 in London or in February 1824 in Liverpool, and however different the various people making the speeches in support of Greece, these speeches were remarkably similar in content. The common bond of religion and culture, the indebtedness of Europe to Greek art and literature, and a general dislike of the Holy Alliance and Russian designs were repeatedly and eloquently expressed. The appearance of the Lord Mayor and other municipal officers at the meeting, encouraged by Gladstone's own appearance, raised the occasion above party considerations. The new position of Canning was perhaps apparent in the remark of one town official: 'whilst it might be the duty of Government to

[110] Ibid. vol. vii, fo. F¹, Blaquiere to Hume, 12 Jan. 1824.
[111] *Liverpool Mercury* (16 Jan. 1824).   [112] Ibid.
[113] Ibid. (23 Jan. 1824).   [114] Ibid.   [115] Ibid. (30 Jan. 1824).
[116] See ibid. (20 Feb. 1824); *Morning Chronicle* (21 Feb. 1824).

observe neutrality in the contest, the people of this free country had but one course to pursue . . . to answer the call made on them for assistance by a free and suffering people.'[117]

By the time of the public meeting the subscription had passed £400 and by 5 March would be greater than £600. As in Manchester most of the subscriptions were small and many were for a guinea or less.[118] Although he had left Liverpool in mid-January, Blaquiere was obviously pleased with developments there. He wrote publicly to thank the local committee and reassured members that their efforts were not in conflict with the Greek loan which had by then been launched. 'Although Liverpool may have been a little tardy in declaring herself on this most sacred question,' he wrote, 'yet when she did come forward, it was done as becomes a great, liberal and enlightened community.'[119]

When Blaquiere reported to Bowring on his journey on 13 February, he had good reason to be satisfied with his considerable effort, and the achievement at Liverpool was the jewel in the crown. For this seemed to be the first city, besides London, that moved above partisan squabbling, and with the support of local officials, held not only a subscription but also a public meeting. That it managed to do so perhaps owed more to Gladstone and his friendship with Canning than to Blaquiere, but without Blaquiere no action at all might have taken place.[120] His success was obviously recognized by others and there were calls for him to go elsewhere, for example, to Glasgow: 'The population of Glasgow is a religious one but also a tory one in some measure. When however Cambridge and Liverpool and London once break the ice . . .'[121]

The significance of Blaquiere's journey does not merely lie in the unique way it has revealed the means by which such a successful campaign could be launched by a fairly obscure visitor to these various towns and cities. His use of the press, local public figures, and churchmen was handled with sufficient care and sensitivity (as well as industry) that a charitable cause which had not met with much response for two to three years could appear to require urgent attention. More importantly, Blaquiere brought to this

---

[117] *Liverpool Mercury* (20 Feb. 1824).
[118] See ibid. (20, 27 Feb., 5 Mar. 1824).   [119] Ibid. (5 Mar. 1824).
[120] See LGC papers, vol. v, fo. M³, Blaquiere to Bowring, 13 Feb. 1824.
[121] Ibid. fo. O³, J. Maxwell to Bowring, 14 Feb. 1824.

work neither a narrow ideological position nor even the views of Bentham (who was not mentioned by Blaquiere throughout the entire journey). He appealed instead to Christianity and phil-hellenism and to an Englishman's devotion to liberty, and he managed to direct these feelings towards concrete support for Greece.

Nevertheless, his success was to a degree determined by a division in society that can only be depicted as ideological in character. Yet this division did not contain clearly held patterns of ideas or beliefs that could be directly applied to the problem of Greece. Philhellenism appealed to all sections of society and to men of all parties, but older notions of order and obedience on the one hand and liberty and reform on the other determined who would support a cause which the government of the day would not. Unlike the newly developing liberalism which, however confused and in conflict, was useful in directing action, the division between Whigs and Tories served more to prevent action in the sense of establishing ideological boundaries that could only rarely be crossed, whatever the sympathies of those involved in attempting to cross them.

PART III

INTEREST

Go into the London Stock Exchange—a more respectable place than many a court—and you will see representatives from all nations gathered together for the utility of men. Here Jew, Mohammedan and Christian deal with each other as though they were all of the same faith, and only apply the word infidel to people who go bankrupt.

(Voltaire, *Letters on England*)

As for Bowring I am convinced that his only object is his personal interest, hoping to get the Management of their Loan.

(George Foresti to Thomas Gordon, 17 Jan. 1824)

12

Who Killed Lord Byron?

The commonly held view that the failure of the expedition to Greece was largely due to the misguided attempt to apply Bentham's ideas in that country has been shown to be a false one, in so far as the various liberal ideas which guided actions on that stage were not those of Bentham himself. Bentham, the theorist, was working on a different level and towards different objects from the ideologues Blaquiere and Stanhope. However, one cannot account for the desires, motives, and interests that guide human action either by theory or by ideology alone. The failure of the expedition to Greece was not simply, or even primarily, a failure of liberalism to take root in that stony soil. Without the ideological commitment of Bowring and Blaquiere, the London Greek Committee might never have been founded and no assistance of any consequence would have been forthcoming. But the roots of the failure of the expedition, even the death of Byron and the madness of Parry, may be seen in the way these founders of the Committee allowed the expedition to be organized. It was in the general arrangements, worked out in the spring and summer of 1823, prior to the departure of the expedition, that a seriously defective plan was agreed, and from that plan disaster followed with the inevitability of an ancient Greek tragedy.

1. The Drama Shifts from Spain to Greece

The Bourbon invasion of Spain early in 1823 brought down the curtain on the liberal drama that had been enacted there, leaving Blaquiere and Bowring temporarily without a theatre or an audience. They quickly turned to Greece, and on 1 March 1823, the *Morning Chronicle* announced:

We are enabled to state that the cause of the Greeks has recently been taken up by a number of individuals of distinction in this metropolis, who are now occupied with means for calling public sympathy most efficaciously into action. In a few days we expect to be able to enter more at large into the subject.

No special events had occurred to justify forming a Committee to support Greek independence in March 1823. The struggle in Greece had been continuing for nearly two years, and although Bentham, Blaquiere, and Bowring had been in contact with Adamantios Korais from early in the summer of 1821 and had received Pikkolos, his emissary, in the same year, every effort at large-scale fund-raising initiated by various sympathizers with Greece during the last two years had failed.[1] Bowring and Blaquiere were to succeed where others had not, but what stimulated their efforts was not some notable victory or defeat in Greece, but rather the failure of liberalism in Spain.[2]

There was one additional and more immediate connection with Spain: the arrival of Louriottis in Madrid to attempt to raise funds for Greece.[3] He was not well received there, and went on to London where, in the feverish financial speculation of the early 1820s, enormous foreign loans had been raised, including loans for the new states of Latin America whose independence and solvency

---

[1] See P. Kitromilides, 'Jeremy Bentham and Adamantios Korais', *Bentham Newsletter*, 9 (1985), 36 ff. See also Ch. 1 above. On early philhellenism in Britain, see Virginia Penn, 'Philhellenism in England (1821–1827)', *Slavonic Review*, 14 (1935–6), 363–71, 647–59.

[2] See above, Ch. 7. Blaquiere and Bowring were not the only ones to shift their attentions from Spain to Greece. W. H. Humphreys, who had already been in Greece with Gordon during 1821, wrote to him on 29 January 1823, hoping for some sort of military commission in Spain (Gordon papers, 1160/21/9/3; see also fo. 4, Humphreys to Gordon, 20 Feb. 1823). On 23 March, he says that he is off to Paris to learn Greek in anticipation of going there (1160/21/9/9, Humphreys to Robertson).

[3] According to A. Palma (*Greece Vindicated* (London, 1826), 6–7) Bowring (who was in Madrid) had established a Philhellenic Committee in Madrid at the end of 1821 or early in 1822 and Palma himself served as Secretary. Palma recommended Louriottis to Bowring in September 1822, and Louriottis arrived in London in February 1823. Both C. M. Woodhouse (*The Philhellenes* (London, 1969), 74) and D. Dakin (*The Greek Struggle for Independence 1821–1833* (London, 1973), 109) suggest that Blaquiere met Louriottis in Madrid and sent him to London with introductions to Bowring. No evidence can be found for these assertions, and both Blaquiere and Bowring appear to have been in London at this time. According to Thomas Gordon (*History of the Greek Revolution*, 2 vols. (Edinburgh, 1832), ii. 78), Louriottis 'reached London, where he fortunately made the acquaintance of Mr. Blaquiere, and that gentleman, whose liberal opinions are matter of publicity, introduced him to several distinguished members of the English opposition'. Bowring was equally involved in the reception of Louriottis. Bentham met him on 19 February (Colls's Diary, BL Add. MS 33563, fo. 119).

were not much more established than was the case in Greece.[4] Bowring and Blaquiere might have been wiser to confine their activities to raising a loan for Greece, but they doubtless felt that, without active efforts to rally support for the Greek cause, even a loan might fail. Furthermore, though only 31 years old, Bowring sought to establish himself as a public figure, and could see in the London Greek Committee (as in the newly established *Westminster Review*) a vehicle for greater public prominence. Blaquiere was more ideologically committed and determined to fill as soon as possible the emptiness created by the defeat of Spain.

Neither Blaquiere nor Bowring had been to Greece, and they quickly enlisted the support of several notable figures who had. One was Hobhouse, whose journey to Greece with Byron in 1809 had given him something of a reputation for knowledge of the country. Through Hobhouse, Blaquiere enlisted Byron, whom he visited in Italy when he journeyed with Louriottis to Greece to inspect the country and make arrangements for the negotiation of the loan.[5] Even more important at the time, however, was Thomas Gordon from Cairness, near Aberdeen, the early philhellene with military experience in Greece who had returned to Britain after serving with distinction under Ypsilanti in 1821.

2. Gordon's Proposal

Gordon was wealthy, educated, and a professional soldier. He served in the Scots Greys prior to taking over the large estate at

[4] See Palma, *Greece Vindicated*, 7; see also Ch. 6 above.

[5] See *Byron's Bulldog: The Letters of John Cam Hobhouse to Lord Byron*, ed. Peter W. Graham (Columbus, Oh., 1984), 326–31 (Hobhouse to Byron, 2 Mar., 29 Apr., and 6 May 1823); *Byron's Letters and Journals*, x: *'A heart for every fate'* (1822–3), ed. L. Marchand (London, 1980), 142–4, 149, 151–2 (Byron to Hobhouse, 7, 14, 17 Apr. 1823). Bowring assumed that Hobhouse was in regular communication with Byron: 'I take it that Mr. Hobhouse tells you all' (Murray archive, Box A21, Bowring to Byron, 26 Apr. 1823). Blaquiere's letters to Byron may be found in the Murray archive, and they present a different account of their relationship from that suggested by W. St Clair (*That Greece Might Still Be Free* (London, 1927), 166–7). Blaquiere not only attempted to contact Byron on his return journey, but he also sought to persuade him to delay his trip to Greece probably to co-ordinate Byron's activities with those of the Committee and possibly to avoid his becoming involved in the civil strife in Greece. There is no evidence that Blaquiere was somehow a convert who followed in Byron's footsteps, as Woodhouse (*The Philhellenes*, 61) suggests.

Cairness and embarking on travels throughout Europe and the Middle East.[6] He married a Greek-Armenian in Constantinople and knew a number of languages which would enhance his role in Greece.[7] He not only had practical experience of the Greek insurrection, but he also maintained numerous contacts in Greece and on the Continent as useful sources of information. He was an original member of the Committee, a generous contributor, and he helped with fund-raising in Scotland.[8] As early as 27 March, he proposed in a letter to Bowring that funds raised by the Committee might equip an artillery corps and a laboratory for making shells, bullets, and other materials. He offered to pay a third of the expense if the Committee raised two-thirds. At that early date and, indeed, in this very letter he linked Parry, who was already known to Bowring and Blaquiere, probably through Gordon, to his proposal.[9] Gordon's proposal was welcomed by the Committee.[10] A week later the military subcommittee was formed and the most important matter on the agenda would have been Gordon's proposal. It was not accepted immediately because at this early stage the additional funds had not yet been raised.

Gordon also prepared for the Committee various materials for its deliberations. Some of these were copies of correspondence regarding Greece written in 1822 and containing an account of the primitive state of conditions there and a frank statement about Greek atrocities.[11] The most important of these submissions was a 'Minute. With regard to the most advantageous method of applying the funds that are at the disposal of the Greek Committee.'[12] The Minute considered three options: firstly, to hand the funds to the Greek government; secondly, to raise and equip a body

[6] Margaret Chapman, 'Thomas Gordon of Cairness: The Struggle for Greek Independence', *Aberdeen University Review*, 47 (1978), 240–1, 245. See also *DNB*.

[7] Ibid. 240.

[8] See Gordon papers, 1160/21/9/10, Bowring to Gordon, 26 Mar. 1823.

[9] LGC papers, vol. i, fo. P². See also fo. J¹, Blaquiere to Bowring, 17 Mar. 1823; and Gordon papers, 1160/21/9/12, Blaquiere to Gordon, 27 Mar. 1823.

[10] The minutes of 5 April contained the following resolution: 'That the most cordial Thanks of the Committee be communicated to him, with the assurance that his liberal proposition shall be immediately taken into the consideration when the Lists of the Committee shall be completed' (LGC papers, vol. iii, fo. E, 5 Apr. 1823). Bowring wrote enthusiastically in similar terms. See Gordon papers 1160/21/9/16, Bowring to Gordon, 7 Apr. 1823.

[11] LGC papers, vol. i, fos. E⁴ ff., 24 Apr. 1823.

[12] Ibid. fo. L⁴. See Gordon papers, 1160/23/2/54, for another copy.

of European troops; and thirdly, the favoured option, to raise and equip a brigade of artillery and a group of craftsmen capable of producing bullets, shells, and rockets in a fully equipped laboratory.

The first option, giving money directly to the Greeks, was rejected, even though he admitted that it would have been the option most favoured by the Greeks themselves. 'For besides that the money would be very likely to prove an apple of discord,' Gordon wrote, 'it is scarcely to be expected that it should be turned to the best account by men who are little versed either in policy or in the art of war.'[13] This statement should have disturbed the members of the Committee who considered it. If there was not a Greek government or a group of Greeks on whom the Committee could depend for the wise and efficient use of funds, how could they conceive of rendering assistance by raising a considerable loan which the Greeks themselves would have to repay. As no one else on the Committee had the experience of Greece that Gordon possessed, his statement should have set alarm bells ringing. Perhaps the more optimistic report of the ideologically motivated Blaquiere several months later tended to blunt the sharp edge of Gordon's comment, or perhaps the Committee saw in the scheme of British Commissioners for the loan a solution to the problem of accountability.

By rejecting the first, Gordon's choice of the remaining two options depended on the amount of money to be raised by the subscription. He favoured a body of European troops, but acknowledged that the £30,000 required to equip and sustain such a force was beyond the capacity of the Committee to raise. The third option required a smaller sum of money. Like the second, it allowed for control and direction to remain in European hands and seemed to lie within the financial capacity of the Committee. Gordon believed it to be 'useful and practicable' and discussed it in some detail. It was assumed that Gordon himself would organize and lead the artillery brigade. As earlier attempts by philhellenes to assist the Greeks had failed tragically, the importance of Gordon himself serving as the leader of the brigade could not be underestimated.

Gordon was invited to the public meeting on 15 May, but he did not attend. The next day, Bowring wrote to him in a positive vein:

[13] Ibid.

You will see by the Newspapers that our meeting went off very well and I hope and trust that we shall now be able to carry your plans immediately into effect. Those who understand public matters say that the Subscription *will* succeed—about which I am most anxious. We have your name and your beneficent projects constantly before us and I have had a thousand motives to regret that so much time appeared to have been lost. However, it is so difficult to move large bodies and to form large bodies that one can hardly wonder at the delay. We should have been very much delighted to see you had that been possible.[14]

At the first meeting of the Committee after the major public meeting of 15 May, when it seemed that sufficient funds from subscriptions would be raised to fund at least part of Gordon's plan, the following resolution was approved:

That Col Gordon be informed that the amount of the Subscriptions already received will enable the Committee to adopt means for immediate assistance being afforded to the Greeks and that he be requested to come up to London at his earliest convenience in order to concert with the Committee the best manner of affording such assistance.[15]

At the same time Parry, now working both for Gordon and, on Gordon's behalf, for the Committee, purchased two artillery pieces and related equipment for £265 and prepared an estimate for £3,170 to cover for one year the costs of four non-commissioned artillery officers, five artificers, four artillery pieces and equipment, the laboratory, and various stores.[16] The estimate was probably for Gordon's contribution, that is, one-third of the total sum of approximately £10,500 to be raised, and corresponded to his original offer. Parry also prepared an estimate for the Committee for its contribution to Gordon's plan.[17] The Committee had not yet raised the required £7,000 as the public meeting had only taken place two weeks earlier. Nevertheless, £3,000 had actually been raised and Gordon was assured that 'there is little fear of getting at least seven thousand pounds'.[18] Nothing, it seemed, stood in the way of Gordon coming to London and taking charge of the expedition. Even the confused reports of the paranoid Parry, who saw threats to Gordon's proposal behind most ideas expressed at

[14] Gordon papers, 1160/21/9/26, Bowring and Parry to Gordon, 16 May 1823.
[15] LGC papers, vol. iii, fo. L, Minutes, 24 May 1823.
[16] Gordon papers, 1160/21/9/27, Parry to Gordon, 21 May 1823.
[17] Ibid. 9/30, Parry to Gordon, 25 May 1823.
[18] Ibid. 9/29, Bowring to Gordon, 24 May 1823.

various meetings, would only have served to hasten his arrival in London.[19] To emphasize his devotion to Gordon, however, he portrayed the Committee as impractical and foolish. Such continual denigration by Parry might have made Gordon wary of the whole enterprise, but Gordon did not seem to have taken Parry's reports as sound 'intelligence'. He had other sources of information in London, and his concern was less with the activities of the Committee than with the political situation in Greece.

George Foresti, the son of a former British consul at Corfu, who was then residing in London, was in fairly close contact with Gordon at this time.[20] Most of his news was about Greece, and he made clear to Gordon that conditions in Greece posed the greatest obstacles to Gordon's planned expedition. Ypsilanti and Mavrokordatos had lost power to the military chiefs, and were quarrelling with each other. Gordon would have to work with the military chiefs if he were to be successful in Greece. But as he had already criticized them publicly after the massacre at Tripolizza, he might not be able to do so. More importantly, as they did not (and could not) form a government of Greece as a whole, no invitation would be forthcoming from them to Gordon. The chiefs also distrusted European military assistance and would only use it on their own terms and for their own ends. In addition, Foresti was apprehensive of the adequacy of the reports Blaquiere would bring back from Greece, as he thought that Blaquiere would simply become the mouthpiece of Mavrokordatos and fail to understand the weak position of the Westernized Greeks. Nevertheless, he believed that the expedition should begin as soon as possible so that the Greeks, using the artillery supplied by Gordon and the Committee, could take some of the fortresses they were besieging before winter set in.[21]

[19] For Parry's 'reports' to Gordon at this time see ibid. 9/26, 16 May 1823; 9/27, 21 May; 9/30, 25 May; 9/34, 1 June; 10/18, 2 June; 9/35, 4 June; 9/40, 1 July; 9/57, Parry to Robertson, 4 Aug.; 9/59, 10 Aug.; 9/61, 28 Aug.; 9/65, Oct. 1823.

[20] The correspondence in the Gordon papers begins in January 1822. See 1160/21/ 8/1, 18 Jan. 1822; 8/11, 23 July 1822; 8/13[a-b], 7 Aug. 1822; 9/14, 28 Mar. 1822; 9/ 33[a-b], 31 May 1823; 10/2, 17 Jan. 1824; 10/20, 28 Apr. 1824.

[21] Ibid. 9/33[a], Foresti to Gordon, 31 May 1823. Foresti also mentioned the fact that Mrs Gordon had just recovered from a serious illness and suggested that she might go to Zante, where, with Foresti's help, she might rent a villa and be reasonably close to Gordon in Greece. It is not clear to what extent domestic considerations delayed or prevented Gordon from going to London and, indeed, from taking on the expedition to Greece.

Neither Foresti's assessment of conditions in Greece nor his advice would have encouraged Gordon to overcome a natural caution and move positively to lead the expedition. While he remained in Scotland, he could indicate his readiness to go without actually taking on the mantle of positive leadership until conditions in Greece changed. Gordon obviously thought that any return to Greece must be successful, and he fully intended to make a major impact in that country. He knew that conditions were not favourable for him to realize his considerable ambitions. He could not be invited by the Greek government, as no clearly established government actually existed. He was too experienced a soldier to be entirely willing to link his fortunes with those of Mavrokordatos, as Byron was to do at the end of the year. Nevertheless, plans in London were now moving forward, and Gordon was expected to make a decision.

3. Gordon's Delay and Withdrawal

At the beginning of July, Gordon further delayed his trip to London. Even Parry, who thought he was Gordon's agent in London, was taken by surprise: 'I find from Mr. Bowring's information,' he wrote to Gordon, 'that a letter from you was read to the Committee on Saturday last in which your intention of visiting London was delayed until you received further advices from Greece. I am now, sir—at a loss how to proceed without your immediate order'.[22] Gordon had obviously not thought it desirable to take Parry into his confidence. His delay was also a serious blow to Bowring's plans, as the whole expedition depended on his direction and leadership. Bowring tried to reassure him with copies of positive letters from Blaquiere about conditions in Greece and news of Byron's proposed journey.[23] Gordon finally decided to send his secretary James Robertson to London in his place to explain his position. Robertson arrived on 12 July and 'immediately commenced operations'.[24] He went to the Crown and Anchor Tavern in an unsuccessful attempt to make contact with the

---

[22] Gordon papers, 9/40, Parry to Gordon, 1 July 1823.
[23] Ibid. 9/39, Bowring to Gordon, 28 June 1823.
[24] Ibid. 9/44, Robertson to Gordon, 12 July 1823.

London Greek Committee and especially with Bowring. In a tired and despondent tone he wrote that '*it* appears never to meet and *he* appears very seldom to look near it'.[25] It seems that Bowring and most Committee members had abandoned London for the country. He did make contact with Parry and reported that 'I can only say that from Mr Parrys account—that members have all particular interests to serve and labour to promote them with tooth and nail'.[26] Nevertheless, Robertson was to see Bowring two days later on the latter's return, and he described his meeting in the next letter:

His counting house was crowded with all nations tongues and languages and from his having been in the country for some time past his table was so loaded with correspondence, that after passing a few compliments and regretting your detention, he told me that the committee would be summoned for Thursday and concluded by wishing me goodmorning and giving me a note to Col. Stanhope. I wished however to have an earlier opportunity of conversing him, and he fixed tomorrow at 11 o'clock— when I shall perhaps be able to do something, and learn what intelligence he may have from Greece, as he told me that he had received a letter from Blaquiere from Tripolizza which referred him to documents he had dispatched by the Ionian Islands.[27]

Robertson also met with a Dr Thomas, a friend of Gordon, who had news of Greece. According to Thomas, anarchy and confusion still existed in the Morea and a 'military despotism' was exercised by the chiefs. The Europeans were adrift and under the command of Petrobey, while Mavrokordatos had become disgusted with the whole enterprise. Thomas indicated to Robertson that he would try to prevent Gordon from going to Greece 'where neither honor, nor self-satisfaction are to be looked for'.[28] After discounting some-what Thomas's pessimism, he reported on a meeting with Foresti where, he noted, a better account of the Committee was received (presumably better than that which he had heard from Parry), but a similar one of conditions in Greece to that he had received from Thomas. But Foresti, unlike Gordon, saw these conditions as being

[25] Ibid. [26] Ibid.
[27] Ibid. 9/45, Robertson to Gordon, 14 July 1823.
[28] Ibid. Dr Thomas was probably the head of sanitation on Zante with whom Gordon resided when, seriously ill from fever, he left Greece in 1821. He seems to have been in London in 1823. See *W. H. Humphrey's First 'Journal of the Geeek War of Independence'*, ed. Sture Linnér (Stockholm, 1967), 72, 74, 78. It is worth noting that Robertson had also accompanied Gordon on the expedition to Greece in 1821.

ultimately promising: 'They have kicked out the Franc Greeks and the true Greeks now and will always—possess the power.'[29] For Gordon, it meant that his sought-after invitation would be further delayed.

While Robertson was attempting to see Bowring and the Committee, and was gathering information in London, he did not reveal exactly what he was in London to do. At the same time, he was writing regularly to Gordon, who was enjoying the views of 'hill, lake and open country', 'glorious snipe and redshank shooting' and not missing the 'heat, dust and smoke of London' even if 'enlivened by the oratory of Mr. Parry'. Nevertheless, he took the time to write to Robertson to provide 'a few observations for his guidance'.[30] Gordon's observations consisted of an extract from an Austrian newspaper describing the civil strife in the Morea and concluded:

Thus it appears, that the government, which invited me to return, was forcibly turned out of office, and that the Military Chiefs are masters of Greece. It is quite natural, that men born in the country, and who have been long connected with it, and who have besides run the greatest risks during the war, should have the direction of affairs, in preference to Ipsilanti, Mavrocordato, etc. etc., although these last are far more capable, and have made real pecuniary sacrifices, without desiring any undue advantages from the present confusion, which to their rivals has been a source of great gain; but whose European manners, and want of political connection with the Morea, cause them to be looked upon as strangers and adventurers. It is however unfortunate for the cause, as the *Capitanei*, brought up in the school of the Turks, and who (pour appeller chacque chose par un nom) are little better than ignorant and rapacious Barbarians, are not likely to adopt improvements from abroad, or to promote any sort of organization, whether civil or military.[31]

After reaching these conclusions, one would have thought that Gordon would have withdrawn from the expedition. But for some reason he chose to delay his decision even further. He said that he wanted to await further news from Blaquiere and to ensure that the Committee fully intended to send artillery and laboratory stores to Greece. He also repeated his offer to finance part of the expedition. These are curious remarks as he already knew about conditions in

[29] Gordon papers, 9/45, Robertson to Gordon, 14 July 1823.
[30] Ibid. 9/46, Gordon to Robertson, 14 July 1823.
[31] Ibid.

Greece and little that Blaquiere could say would change his mind. He also knew that the Committee had agreed to his proposal and only wanted his presence in London to put it into practice. Whatever strategy Gordon pursued in delaying his decision even further, he did not confide it to Robertson.

Over the next few days, Robertson wrote regularly describing his meetings and contacts. In his next letter he recounted his meeting with Bowring where he stated Gordon's views about Greece and the 'great improbability' of his returning in the present circumstances. Bowring replied that Gordon's not going 'would place the Committee in a state of great embarrassment'.[32] This reply seems to have surprised Robertson who countered by saying that no firm decisions had been made by the Committee and that only £5,000–£6,000 had been raised thus far. But Bowring was correct, for the great efforts at raising a subscription and holding the public meeting were based on the belief, formed, as we have seen, when the Committee began in March (if not before), that Gordon, a man of ability and experience, would lead and partly finance such an expedition. At this moment, Bowring was fully conscious of the extent of his dependence on Gordon. After all, Bowring himself had neither military experience nor experience of Greece. There were few people on the Committee who possessed either and very few who knew even enough about weapons and stores to call Parry's bluff—one reason, perhaps, for his extravagant view of his own abilities in relation to the Committee. If Gordon withdrew, two serious problems loomed before him. Who could organize such an expedition which required considerable military, organizational, and administrative skills? The capacity to deal with the Greeks, now engaged in civil war, other British officers, the 'operatives' like Parry and Hodges, soldiers recruited from the Continent, the innumerable problems to be overcome in loading and unloading, sailing to Greece, the problems posed by the Ionian Islands, not to mention the Turks, and to be understood in a number of languages would seem to belong to very few.

Secondly, if Gordon withdrew because of conditions in Greece, how could the Committee justify sending another expedition? Gordon was placing Bowring and the Committee in an impossible situation by on the one hand dictating what sort of expedition

---

[32] Ibid. 9/48a, Robertson to Gordon, 15 July 1823.

would be suitable for Greece, but on the other hand declining to lead it. Without Gordon the expedition consisting of artillery and laboratory stores might not have been even conceived, and Parry would probably not have been involved in it. Indeed, Gordon's withdrawal under these circumstances was more than an embarrassment; it was a disaster—one from which the Committee would never recover. Had Bowring paid full attention to the problem before him, he might have concluded that if Gordon, a man of experience, withdrew from his own scheme, that scheme might better be abandoned and the subscription devoted to other purposes. Bowring did not reach that conclusion partly because Gordon so arranged his withdrawal to make it appear as a personal decision so that the expedition would go ahead without him, and partly because the momentum of the Committee and its activities were such that to abandon the project would require a repudiation of a view of Greece that Blaquiere and Bowring had especially developed in order that the subscription and loan might succeed. In other words, Bowring and the Committee were already prisoners of their own propaganda.

Robertson's letter also contained a brief summary of Blaquiere's most recent news from Greece. Blaquiere admitted that there had been civil dissent but said that this had come to an end. He also said that the 'franc Greeks are busted'. Nevertheless, he saw no obstacle to the expedition and suggested that if Gordon brought out a ship filled with the materials to reduce the strongholds of the Turks, 'your name would be immortalized'.[33] Blaquiere's view of Greece was obviously very different from that of Gordon.

Robertson wrote again to Gordon after he met with the Committee itself two days later. To the Committee he had presented Gordon's views about Greece and his opinion that the money should be immediately appropriated. According to Robertson, all was going well at the meeting until Hobhouse entered and was quoted as saying 'with Mr. Gordons opinions or suggestions we have nought to do as he does not intend going to Greece at present'. Hobhouse then moved that Byron be appointed the agent of the Committee in Greece in conjunction with Blaquiere. The Committee, however, seems to have accepted most of Gordon's suggestions, and it resolved that £4,000 be placed at

---

[33] Gordon papers, 9/48a, Robertson to Gordon, 15 July 1823.

the immediate disposal of the military subcommittee. Apart from the outburst from Hobhouse, which in fact led to a situation of which Gordon strongly approved, the Committee seemed to remain committed to Gordon's original plan. Robertson thought the meeting was a success, and he looked forward to the meeting of the military subcommittee in several days.[34]

The summer of 1823 was an especially wet one in London, and Robertson was forced to walk through streets that had turned into a sea of mud. However, he dutifully attended the meeting of the military subcommittee, though his mind was partly on a cricket match at Lord's he hoped to attend in a few days. The military subcommittee first heard a letter from Byron to Bowring written from Italy in which Byron stated that he was sailing for Greece and that he planned to devote £8,000 or £9,000 of his own money to the Greek cause. This expression of intent seemed sufficient for the subcommittee to make him their agent in place of Gordon. But at this stage the expedition seemed curiously cut off from reality. It was being launched without securing Byron's express approval to a scheme about whose details he could only have the slightest knowledge. And in terms of the military knowledge possessed by Gordon and his authority based on previous experience, how could Byron replace Gordon? His only qualifications were his earlier trip to Greece and his willingness to go again and devote a part of his fortune to the cause. Nevertheless, once Gordon had withdrawn, for the reasons which he gave, reasons which were never challenged and were never shown to be applicable to him alone, the expedition was doomed to failure. At this decisive moment one can foresee the death of Byron, the madness of Parry, and the failure of Bowring. For if the truth was as Gordon saw it, then no expedition at that time could succeed. Byron, as a poet and philanthropist, might perhaps have imagined a grander death on the field of battle, clad in armour and helmet like an ancient Greek. But as the agent of the London Greek Committee, it was to be a squalid death from fever in the dank, wet, mosquito-infested town of Missolonghi.

The military subcommittee adopted an estimate similar to that prepared by Parry for Gordon in May: five artificers, two sergeant-majors of artillery, Mr Parry and Mr Hodges, ten pieces of light mountain artillery, a laboratory, ammunition and various stores for

---

[34] Ibid. 9/49a, 17 July 1823.

a year. The sum was £3,250 and Parry was directed to obtain
tenders for the various items. Parry himself was engaged for a year
from departure dependent, however, on his finding 'security', and
he was paid £4 a week for his services prior to departure. Gordon's
offer of assistance was welcomed, and he was asked to state how
much he would contribute.[35]

Gordon was delighted with the news from Robertson, especially
about the appointment of Byron and the decision that the
expedition would go ahead. These developments, whatever the
consequences for the people concerned, meant that Gordon could
withdraw without embarrassment and without it appearing that he
was sabotaging either the Committee or assistance for Greece.
When he received this news from Robertson, he prepared some
remarks which he asked Robertson to deliver to the Committee as
'my valediction'.[36] These provide a fair summary of his position:

I beg leave to express to the Committee, how much I am flattered by the
confidence, with which they have honoured me, and by the intention they
expressed of putting their expedition under my direction. If I decline
returning to Greece, at the present moment, it is for the following reasons.
Because, having served in that country, during the Campaign of 1821 (at
which period, I was at the head of the Staff, and enjoyed the full confidence
of the Commander in Chief, and was besides seconded by experienced
Officers,) I found that my exertions could produce no beneficial result, on
account of the strong repugnance, which the Greeks in general manifested
towards the introduction of European discipline, and tactics.

Because the late Government, which invited me to return, and all those
men with whom I was disposed to act, have been forcibly turned out of
office, and the European Officers obliged to retire in disgust, and because
the Chiefs, who now possess the power, although very zealous to promote
the honour, and independence of their country, are (I am apprehensive)
opposed to any system of military organisation. At the same time, I am as
anxious as ever, for the triumph of the cause, and disposed to make every
sacrifice, as soon as I see a probability, that my personal services can
contribute to its success. I have learned with great pleasure, that the
Committee are resolved to send out Artificers, and Laboratory stores, as
this sort of assistance, is the most important, and advantageous, that can be
given, and I must heartily concur, (as a member of the Committee,) in the

---

[35] Gordon papers, 9/50, 19 July 1823.
[36] Ibid. 9/53, Gordon to Robertson, 21 July 1823.

proposition, that the charge and direction of the expedition, be confided to Lord Byron.[37]

He also told Robertson to offer to the Committee the pieces of artillery which he had in London and to indicate that a further contribution might be made when the expedition was further advanced. 'I am quite indifferent as to any mention of my name,' he wrote with somewhat false modesty; 'neither am I anxious to give advice, where it is not wanted.'[38] In reality, he was highly pleased that he had extricated himself so painlessly from an enterprise which was clearly doomed to failure.

4. The Aftermath

It might be argued that whatever role Gordon intended to play for the Committee, neither his presence nor his absence had much effect on the failure of the expedition in Greece or on the death of Byron. Byron had offered to go to Greece in April 1823, and while he was willing to assist the Committee (largely through Hobhouse), he was not linked directly with Gordon. Furthermore, the appointment of Stanhope, also an experienced soldier, might arguably have served as a satisfactory replacement for Gordon. Nevertheless, Gordon was the ideal man for the Committee with direct military experience in Greece and detailed knowledge of the people and their languages. Byron could never replace him, and it was absurd to think that he could. Stanhope was also no substitute for Gordon. He was able to transfer his experience of India to Greece only through a narrow ideological perspective, and there is no evidence that he was any more equipped to establish an artillery brigade than was William Parry himself. Stanhope saw himself as a replacement for Blaquiere, and his role in Greece was more political than military.[39] It fell to the ill-fated Byron to inherit the military mantle from Gordon.

In fairness to Gordon, however, there is no suggestion that he intended the expedition to fail. Furthermore, he had the most to

---

[37] Ibid.   [38] Ibid.
[39] *Greece, in 1823 and 1824* (new edn., London, 1825), 1–2 (Stanhope to Bowring, 14 Sept. 1823).

lose by precipitously returning to Greece, when conditions did not
favour his own success there. As Gordon had served in Greece
before the Committee was even conceived, he clearly did not see
his own interests as identical with those of the Committee or even
with the expedition that he had largely instigated and partly
organized. Whatever the Committee might decide, he would not
go to Greece until conditions were right for Gordon.

The fault (if, in these matters, there was one) lay with the
Committee's determination to proceed with the expedition without
Gordon. Bowring's ambition to make a name for himself and
Hobhouse's devotion to his friend Byron overcame the reservations of Joseph Hume who sought at least some further guarantees
for Parry's abilities and success from Gordon.[40] But Gordon,
though recommending the incompetent Parry, skilfully avoided
committing himself to any financial guarantee for Parry's success in
undertaking the expedition. The Committee clearly needed
Gordon more than Gordon needed the Committee. Yet, if the
expedition had succeeded, Gordon would have still been well
placed to receive the invitation he sought from an established Greek
government to play a major military role against the Turks.

Throughout 1823 and 1824, when the Committee was active,
Gordon continued to play this teasing role on the fringe. When he
was approached in March 1824 to serve as one of the Commissioners for the first Greek loan, he at first was disposed to decline at
least until he received more information:

The only thing that can induce me again to leave this country, is the
prospect of honorable service in Greece: I would not go out merely as
agent for the loan, except with the hope of taking an active part in the war:
indeed in any other way, I can be of little use, for if the Greeks will not
compose their dissensions, and private feuds, at the voice of Lord Byron,
(after all the sacrifices he has made,) neither will they, although one should
rise from the dead.[41]

Gordon clearly had his eye on his own role in Greece, and would
only be willing to assist the Committee, if somehow his military
role and service as a Commissioner could be linked. But within

[40] See Ch. 10 above.
[41] LGC papers, vol. vi, fo. U³, Gordon to Blaquiere, 21 Mar. 1824. See also vol.
vii, fo. G⁴, Hume to Blaquiere, 2 Mar. 1824, where Hume favoured the
appointment of Gordon as the third Commissioner.

two weeks he apparently accepted the Commission, with the
proviso that he could remain in Britain for three or four more
months: 'it appears to me that no inconvenience will arise to the
service, since the zeal, and ability of Colonel Stanhope who is at
present acting, leave nothing to desire.'[42] Gordon's reluctance and
then delay exacerbated Blaquiere's difficulties when he arrived in
Greece at the end of April with the first instalment of the loan to
find Byron dead. Gordon was not expected for another three
months, and if Blaquiere's beliefs about the urgency of distributing
the loan were correct, Gordon's absence again proved critical. But
Gordon remained in Britain. When he learned of the death of
Byron at the end of May, he was still reluctant to depart. He wrote
to Bowring that he needed more information, though 'my own
intentions remain unchanged'.[43] Nevertheless, by mid-June he
began to express unease about his role as Commissioner and the
conditions for distributing the loan. He also requested 'some hints
respecting the line of conduct, that I shall be expected to pursue,
and the extent of my powers'.[44] By this time, two instalments of
the loan had arrived in Zante, and Blaquiere was nearly driven mad
with anxiety attempting to find means to distribute the money
without the presence of the requisite number of Commissioners
and in the face of Stanhope's opposition to any speedy distribution.
Gordon, however, continued to dither. On 20 June he wrote to
Bowring that he was willing to go to Greece now that the civil war
seemed to be over, but he wanted to await the return of Stanhope
to London and wanted another person to go with him to Greece.[45]

On 17 July, the Committee passed a resolution appointing
Hobhouse, Gordon, Lytton Bulwer, and Hamilton Browne as
Commissioners of the loan with the Commission to last as long as
any of the members stayed in Greece. Power was also given to
them to fill vacancies in their numbers with the appointments
reported to the Committee for approval.[46] Having rashly and
perhaps guiltily committed himself to go to Greece in place of
Byron whom he had so unwisely encouraged to go, Hobhouse
soon withdrew after a dispute with Hume over the terms of his

---

[42] Ibid. vol. vi, fo. P⁴, Gordon to Bowring, 5 Apr. 1824.
[43] Ibid. vol. viii, fo. L⁴, Gordon to Bowring, 20 May 1824.
[44] Ibid. vol. ix, fo. T, Gordon to Bowring, 13 June 1824.
[45] Ibid. fo. C², Gordon to Bowring, 20 June 1824.
[46] Ibid. fo. Z³.

appointment.[47] Gordon, however, remained committed to going and as late as 26 September reaffirmed his intention, though adding typically that he had been 'induced to postpone it a little'.[48] At the end of the year, Gordon journeyed as far as London looking for a letter from the Greek government supposedly in the hands of the Greek Deputies, Orlandos, Louriottis, and now Zaimēs. They, however, reported that the letter had never arrived.[49]

Gordon never led an expedition nor actually served the London Greek Committee as a Commissioner, but he went on to a distinguished military career in Greece to which he returned in 1826, bringing with him the final proceeds of the Greek loans. He remained in the service of the Greek government after the war restoring order to Roumeli in 1835 and serving as chief-of-staff in the Peloponnese.[50] He continued to live and work in Greece until he returned to Scotland shortly before his death in 1841. He was a great figure among the British philhellenes, but none the less played no small role in sealing the fate of the London Greek Committee and its most famous agent.

[47] See BL Add. MSS 36460, fos. 254 ff. and 56548, fos. 29 ff. for an account of Hobhouse's agreement to serve and subsequent withdrawal as Commissioner following the death of Byron.

[48] LGC papers, vol. x, fo. Q^3, Gordon to Hume, 26 Sept. 1824.

[49] Ibid. vol. xi, fo. K^6, Gordon to Orlandos, Zaimēs, and Louriottis, 17 Dec. 1824; fo. L^6, Orlandos, Zaimēs, and Louriottis to Gordon, 18 Dec. 1824.

[50] Margaret Chapman, 'Thomas Gordon of Cairness', 241.

13
Greek Pie

The Greek loan scandal, smouldering since early 1826, erupted in a spectacular way between October and December of that year with accusations of corrupt dealings and revelations of wrongful practices filling the newspapers almost daily. As Cobbett observed:

It is notorious, that two million eight hundred thousand pounds have been got from the bondholders, for carrying on of the Greek Cause; it is notorious, that the Greek Cause has, to all appearance, been totally ruined; it is notorious, that the Greek bonds, for which the Greek bondholders paid fifty-nine pounds each, are now worth only about twelve or thirteen pounds each; it is notorious that here has been mischief and wrong done and ruin and misery inflicted to an enormous amount; it is now notorious, that Burdett, Hobhouse, Ellice, Hume, Bowring, Rump Galloway, have been cramming their fingers into this pie.[1]

Most of the criticism was directed at various individuals, but often overlooked was the way the scandal emerged from the ideological conflicts within early liberalism that so affected the perceptions of Greece adopted by members of the London Greek Committee. Although one object of this chapter is to explore the way self-interest influenced the ideas and decisions reached by the key figures involved in the two loans, another object is to show that interest alone will not explain how and why these well-known figures acted in the manner that they did.

1. The First and Second Greek Loans

The two Greek loans were different in their objects and only the first was arranged by the London Greek Committee. Its terms and

[1] *Cobbett's Weekly Register*, 60 (1826), 366–7 (4 Nov. 1826). See also BL Add. MS 35153, fo. 240, Place to Say, 21 Nov. 1826: 'They are all to be blamed. Galloway Ricardo Hume Cochrane Burdett Hobhouse Ellice Bowring and the Greek Deputies, never surely was a matter of importance so mismanaged.'

its initial success have been discussed in Chapter 6 above, where the quarrel between the Greek Deputies, Orlandos and Louriottis, and Bowring, who, as Honorary Secretary of the Committee, had done most to arrange the loan, was noted in some detail. For Bowring, the loan meant a good deal more than a chance for public service as honorary secretary of a charitable committee. He not only sought honour and recognition for his support for Greece but he also hoped to profit from the management of the loan. He was not a man of independent wealth, Bowring & Co. was not a securely established trading company, and Bowring himself was often dismissed by others as a mere 'jobber'. But his friendship with Bentham which recently had led to his assuming the editorship of the *Westminster Review*, his involvement in liberal politics in Spain, France, and then Greece, and his other literary activities had brought him to a degree of public prominence. The Greek loan was to give him some financial security. He received a commission of £11,000 for arranging the loan and, despite his limited resources, he was able to raise the money to purchase (at a significant discount) £25,000 worth of scrip. Bowring was investing heavily in the future of Greece, not only in the time and energy he had devoted to the Greek cause but also in the return he expected from a highly speculative investment.[2] Joseph Hume, another major figure in the Committee and a Commissioner of the loan, also invested in Greek scrip to the sum of £10,000. Hume's motives were perhaps different from Bowring's. As an MP, a leading reformer, and the scourge of ministerial financial irregularities, he had already achieved public prominence; he was also not in need of money to maintain his position in public life. When his dealings were later held up to public criticism, Hume's initial investment in Greek scrip was defended as a selfless act of public leadership to inspire others to invest as well.[3] Not everyone agreed, and Francis Place referred on several occasions to his friend's inordinate love of money that blinded him to a potential conflict of interest between serving as Commissioner for the loan and being an investor in it.[4]

The first Greek loan was highly successful, but, as we have seen, it was dogged with controversy before the ink on the agreement

[2] See G. F. Bartle, 'Bowring and the Greek Loans of 1824 and 1825', *Balkan Studies*, 3 (1962), 61–74.   [3] See *Morning Chronicle* (6 Nov. 1826).
[4] See e.g. BL Add. MS 35146, fo. 51 (31 Oct. 1826), fo. 52 (4 Nov. 1826), fo. 53 (5 Nov. 1826).

was dry. The main issue between Bowring and the Greek Deputies was over who would control the loan, the Greeks who were borrowing the money or the British Commissioners who would represent the interests of the bondholders. Despite the determination of Stanhope, Bowring, and Hume, who tended to see the Greeks as somewhat inferior and not entirely to be trusted, most of the money raised by the first loan was, in fact, sent to Greece, where, after delays effected by the machinations of Stanhope, it was delivered to the Greeks with very little control exercised on behalf of the bondholders save receipts upon acceptance of delivery. Thus, while the view of Blaquiere (which coincided with that of Orlandos and Louriottis) was rejected by the leading members of the London Greek Committee, his view, in fact, prevailed, as the Greeks eventually took control of the receipts of their own loan and used the money for their own ends.

Related to the issue of who should control the loan was that of whether or not there was a single legitimate government in Greece which could take on the responsibility not only for the receipt of the loan but also for its repayment. Even before the loan was arranged, Bowring heard from Byron, Stanhope, and others of the civil strife in Greece, but as he hoped to control the payment of the money raised, he did not see this obstacle as an absolute bar to proceeding with the loan. As was shown in Chapter 12, once Gordon refused to go to Greece, because no settled government existed for him to serve, the expedition was clearly doomed to failure. The fact that an experienced man like Gordon refused to go should have alerted Bowring to the dangers of attempting to arrange a loan with a government that hardly existed. Despite his letters and strictures, it was clear in 1823 that the Greeks were more interested in getting their hands on the money than in making satisfactory arrangements for the repayment of the loan. But Bowring was both encouraged by his brand of liberalism and blinded by the propaganda he himself was generating. In addition, he had hopes of personal gain that would repay him for the time and energy he had expended. None of his hopes and all of his fears would be realized.

The second Greek loan for £2,000,000 was arranged in January and February 1825 with virtually no reference to the London Greek Committee. The terms of the loan were slightly inferior to the first and its management was confused and fragmented. Some thought that the object of the second loan would be to stabilize the first and enable it to be placed on a sound financial footing.[5] But the second was arranged between the Greek Deputies Orlandos, Louriottis, and Zaimēs and the bankers J. & S. Ricardo. Also involved in the negotiations were the MPs Edward Ellice, Sir Francis Burdett, and John Cam Hobhouse, all members of the London Greek Committee. In the personnel involved at least there was some continuity between the loans.

If the Greek Deputies had been dissatisfied with the arrangements for the first loan, they were about to find themselves in a disastrous position over the second. As most of the money raised by the first loan had been sent to Greece, and even though the bondholders had cause for concern over the prospect of repayment, the Greeks themselves had little cause for complaint. Much of £1,200,000 raised by the second loan was squandered and a good deal of it on two major projects. The first was an agreement to construct six steamboats for an expedition to be headed by the celebrated Lord Cochrane. At the time the scandal broke, approximately £160,000 had been appropriated and not one steamboat had been completed despite the fact that they had been promised by the engineer Alexander Galloway 2½ months after the agreement was signed on 17 August 1825. The second project was an agreement to build two frigates at Philadelphia for which £155,000 had been spent but neither frigate had been completed. If the first project drew Ellice, Burdett, Hobhouse, Galloway, and Cochrane into the scandal, the second revealed that the Americans could be as adept at sticking their fingers into Greek pie as the British. The one frigate that was eventually completed cost nearly three times the price of the American frigate *Brandywine*, built at the same time, though the *Brandywine* was a superior ship in every respect.[6]

2. Financial Crisis and Bowring's Defence

The failure of the second loan to produce the urgently needed money for the Greek government, when it was facing defeat at

[5] See E. Blaquiere, *Letters from Greece; with Remarks on the Treaty of Intervention*, (London, 1828), 166–7.   [6] See *The Times* (9 Nov. 1826).

Missolonghi and elsewhere, raised questions about the competence of the Greek Deputies, and Georgiou Spaniolakes was sent to London to investigate their conduct. At the same time the financial bubble burst with regard to the numerous foreign loans that had been raised during the 1820s. Cobbett, for example, was scathing not only about Greece but also about the state of the South American loans:

Not a penny will those *ever* get, who continue to hold these South American 'securities'; and not a penny *ought* they to get. They have lent their money to a set of men, who have *pawned the people and the soil* of those five countries, and enriched themselves with the plunder. I am confident, that those who keep these bonds, will never get one penny for them.[7]

In August 1826 he drew attention to the fact that more than £50 million in foreign loans, costing more than £31 million, now had a value of only £12 million.[8] The first Greek loan, launched at £59 for a £100 bond, was then at £10, and the second Greek loan, initially sold at £55 (Cobbett says £56), was then worth £11.[9] In December 1825, Hobhouse recorded in his diary the panic that finally gripped the City and the rest of the country: 'All London in an uproar' (13 December); 'the city was in the greatest possible confusion' (15 December); 'the country is now in the same uproar as the city was' (19 December).[10]

With panic in Britain, defeat in Greece, and rumours of corruption and malpractice surrounding the two Greek loans, those involved in the Greek cause began to defend themselves against various accusations and rumours which had been circulating since the early spring of 1826. Bowring himself produced an article on

[7] *Cobbett's Weekly Register*, 55 (1825), 592–3 (3 Sept. 1825).
[8] Ibid. 59 (1826), 431–2 (12 Aug. 1826). [9] Ibid.
[10] BL Add. MS 56550, fos. 38–9. Hobhouse's entries were amply confirmed in *The Times*: 'An indescribable gloom was diffused through the City yesterday morning. . . . At about eleven o'clock the alarm had reached its height, and so great was it, that men evidently felt as if all that was stable in the property of merchants or bankers was about to be involved in ruin' (13 Dec.); 'The agitation and alarm in the city have experienced yet no abatement' (14 Dec.); 'Another day of agitation and alarm has passed over in the city' (15 Dec.); 'There were no failures in the City yesterday. That negative sentence contains all the good news that we have to report respecting the money-market. The accounts of failures in the country will be still found to be sufficiently numerous' (17 Dec.). See also Boyd Hilton, *Corn, Cash, Commerce: The Economic Policies of the Tory Governments, 1815–1830* (Oxford, 1977), 202–31; Frank Griffith Dawson, *The First Latin American Debt Crisis: The City of London and the 1822–25 Loan Bubble* (New Haven, Conn., 1990).

the 'Greek Committee' published anonymously in the *Westminster Review* of July 1826.[11] It was ostensibly a reply to Count Alerino Palma whose intervention on the side of Blaquiere against Stanhope in their ideological dispute has already been discussed.[12] Palma's liberalism was closely linked to the nationalism of Blaquiere and he strongly resented attempts by the Committee to retain funds and frustrate the wishes of the Greeks themselves. It is important to emphasize that Palma's critique of the Committee over the loans was ideologically motivated, and Bowring's reply reflects this earlier debate.

In the event, Bowring spent little time in the article on Palma. His object was to draw a sharp distinction between the first and second Greek loans and to defend the Greek Committee's management of the first. He made it clear (and this was one object of the article) that the second Greek loan and the current discussions about the prudent use of the considerable sum raised by it in the purchase of the steamboats and the American frigates was wholly outside the control of the Committee, and he called upon those involved (Burdett, Hobhouse, and Ellice) to respond to public criticism, while placing the blame for the blunders on Lord Cochrane, who made the agreement with Galloway, the engineer, to build the steamships.[13] But he placed most of the blame for the failure to control the loans (first and second) on the Greek Deputies: 'He [Palma] deems that all the misfortunes have occurred in Greece because the deputies had too little control over the Greek funds. We, on the contrary, think that almost every evil is clearly and distinctly to be attributed to their having too much.'[14]

Bowring had clearly rejected Blaquiere's brand of liberalism and closely associated himself with Stanhope's. He praised Stanhope explicitly and at some length, not only for his personal qualities and achievements but for his whole approach to Greece.[15] The high moral tone, the patronizing regard for the backwardness of the

[11] 6 (1826), 113–33.

[12] See above, Ch. 9. Bowring's article in the *Westminster Review* was ostensibly a reply to Palma's *A Summary Account of the Steamboats for Lord Cochrane's Expedition* (London, 1826) (incorrectly dated by Bowring, 'Greek Committee', 113, '1820'). It is curious that Bowring's article was published in July 1826 and Palma's pamphlet was signed '2, 3 September, 1826'. See Palma, *A Summary Account*, 33, 36. Bartle, 'Bowring and the Greek Loans of 1824 and 1825', 69, seems to suggest that Bowring's reply was to Palma's *Greece Vindicated*, published in the spring of 1826.

[13] 'Greek Committee', 129.   [14] Ibid. 130.   [15] See ibid. 121–2.

Greeks, and the specific allusions to the failure of the Deputies to
ensure the best use of the funds reflected and even surpassed
Stanhope's own treatment of the Greeks. As far as the Committee
was concerned, Bowring argued that 'it will be seen that no
dilapidations or misappropriations of the *first loan* took place in this
country at least' and that 'the whole amount raised, was honestly, if
not judiciously applied'.[16] But where the funds were 'not judiciously
applied', he continued, they were under the control of the Deputies
and not under that of the London Greek Committee.

Within two months, Stanhope himself appeared again on the
Greek Committee stage, when a Mr John Robertson placed an
advertisement in the public newspapers and called a meeting of
Greek bondholders for 4 September.[17] At this meeting, Stanhope
took the chair and Bowring produced a statement of expenditure
originally supplied to the Greek Committee by Spaniolakes, who
had recently come from Greece to replace Zaimēs as the third
Deputy, and to investigate the reasons for the delays in the
completion of the steamboats and frigates and other financial
irregularities connected with the second loan. The meeting ended
with the formation of a bondholders' committee to investigate the
state of both loans with the committee consisting, among others, of
Stanhope and Bowring. Although Joseph Hume was nominated to
the committee, his absence from London at the time precluded his
serving on it. The bondholders' committee took nearly six weeks
to gather information, held approximately twenty meetings of its
own, and called another general meeting of bondholders for 23
October with Stanhope again in the chair.[18] At first only thirty
bondholders were present, but this number doubled as the meeting
progressed. Colonel Jones read the long and fairly detailed report of
the financial transactions surrounding the two loans. 'The inquiries
of your Committee have met with many obstructions and
difficulties on every side,' said the report, 'and they have been
altogether disappointed in finding that sincere co-operation which

[16] Ibid. 122.
[17] See *The Times* (5 Sept. 1826). The identity of John Robertson is not established
at the meeting. He may be the same James Robertson who was Thomas Gordon's
secretary (see Ch. 12 above). That he was not well known may be seen from the fact
that *The Times* referred to him in one article as 'Mr. Robinson'. See *The Times* (24,
25 Oct. 1826).
[18] See *The Times* (24 Oct. 1826), from which the following account has been
taken.

might have led to a complete elucidation of past transactions, and
have given efficient security for the future.' J. & S. Ricardo, it
seems, refused to recognize or to co-operate with the committee.
Louriottis and Spaniolakes did co-operate (Orlandos having
already left the country) and, with some exceptions, provided the
information requested. Nevertheless, out of the confusing figures
presented by Louriottis, a number of questions were raised about
various transactions and commissions. As for the scandal concerning the American frigates on which £156,700 had been spent and
another £50,000 was needed to fit them out, the blame was placed
squarely on the Greek Deputies:

The Committee cannot understand the motives which induced the Greek
Deputies to despatch from England a French military officer with
instructions so vague and general as would authorize so large an
expenditure, especially as it appears there would have been no difficulty in
purchasing and despatching from the ports of Europe vessels ready built
and obtainable at a moderate price; and the instructions of the Greek
Government appear to have especially directed the purchase of vessels
ready for sea. Your Committee have ascertained that many offers of
warlike vessels were really made to the Deputies, but always rejected by
them.

As for the steamboats, the committee proceeded with great caution
and reticence for fear of arousing the interest of the government
which might then act to prevent the very enterprise of preparing a
military force from going ahead. The names of Cochrane,
Galloway, and even Burdett, Hobhouse, and Ellice were not given
and whatever blame was apportioned was placed on 'the engineer',
that is Galloway, for lack of 'knowledge and experience' but not for
'dishonesty and treachery'.

The report seems to have been written by Stanhope and Bowring
who were in fact less concerned with apportioning blame, except
perhaps to suggest that the Greeks generally were incapable of
managing their own money, than with making arrangements for
the immediate future to salvage the situation. Stanhope himself
proposed four resolutions regarding the preparation of a naval force
from the funds that were still available and might be obtained from
various sources, serving under the control of a committee of five
persons to be named by the bondholders. But his proposal and the
report generally were not greeted with general approval. When he
finished speaking about the report and proposing his resolutions,

John Robertson (who had originally called the first bondholders' meeting) rose to explain why he had subsequently resigned from the bondholders' committee. His main objection was that the committee had not fully presented the facts with regard to the steamboats, and he argued that as the names of the people involved and the existence of the steamboats were well known to the government through the press, full publicity could be given to the issue with appropriate blame assigned. He then proceeded to read several letters from Orlandos and Louriottis to Hobhouse which indicated that the control over the order for the steamboats had been taken out of the hands of the Deputies and the project was being supervised by Burdett, Hobhouse, and Ellice, with the money being paid out by Ricardo. The Deputies, argued Robertson, had agreed to the purchase of five steamboats to be placed at the disposal of Lord Cochrane, but more than fourteen months later no steamboats had been produced, and the Deputies had no control at all over the arrangements. Robertson criticized Burdett, Hobhouse, and Ellice for taking on the task of supervising their construction. If the Deputies were criticized for sending a French cavalry officer (General Lallemand) to supervise the construction of the frigates in America, Robertson 'did not think that the impolicy of such a measure was greater than that of intrusting the equipment of steamboats to members of Parliament and to dealers on the Stock Exchange'. He continued:

Whether Sir F. Burdett or Mr. Hobhouse were qualified for the task which they had voluntarily undertaken, he would not pretend to decide; but that they were not inclined to execute it, was evident, from the fact that one of them had gone with his family to spend the summer in France, and that the other had gone to partake in the festivities of the coronation at Moscow.

As for Galloway, Robertson mentioned the fact that his son was working for the pasha of Egypt in Alexandria and that, with the pasha's forces involved in Greece, Galloway had an obvious reason for delaying the completion of the steamboats in the safety and well-being of his son. Nevertheless, he did not believe that Galloway had intentionally delayed the boats so as not to place his son in any peril in Egypt. He thought Galloway had displayed a lack of skill and energy, while Lord Cochrane, in choosing and instructing Galloway, had failed to manage this arrangement properly. Besides criticizing Ricardo, Robertson called attention to the way Spaniolakes was willing to co-operate with the bond-holders' committee in an investigation of the accounts of the Deputies, but he was not willing to submit his own accounts, and was about to be appointed by the Greek government with Burdett and Ricardo to a commission to audit the accounts of the two loans. Robertson condemned this arrangement as allowing those involved to audit their own accounts.

Robertson's intervention clearly meant that the meeting of the bondholders would not easily agree to the proposals set forth by Bowring and Stanhope. G. Merle then spoke and insisted that the Greek Deputies were not free of blame:

When those gentlemen first came to England, they were described as men of honour and patriotism, in the enjoyment of great wealth and influence among their own countrymen. Since that time, however, they had been found dabbling in the stocks, looking after every change in the market, taking personal bribes from the contractors of their loans, and yet, after all, coming before the bondholders with a claim to be considered as men of honour and respectability.

Merle then went on to refer to Burdett, Hobhouse, and Hume also as guilty parties. At the mention of Hume's name, Bowring quickly intervened with the remark: 'Mr. Hume, at any rate, is free from suspicion.' The remark was a significant one, as it was not only an attempt to deflect interest from wrongdoing in the administration of the first Greek loan but also served to deflect interest from Bowring's own involvement in financial dealings that were not very different from those of Hume. Bowring's own involvement had not yet been revealed although there were rumours circulating about Hume. Merle sought to have Hume's role clarified in light of the rumours. Bowring responded by talking generally about the arrangements for the first loan and he steered the debate away from any further reference to Hume's alleged offence and from any closer scrutiny of the first loan. Nevertheless, criticism of the second loan easily led to criticism of the first. A Mr. Chichester attacked the £64,000 commission taken by J. & S. Ricardo to arrange the second loan: 'It was also a matter to be regretted, that in this country of boasted independence, and in this metropolis, of whose boasted liberality they had heard so much, a commercial house should be found not ashamed to take, in the way of commission, a sum of £64,000 from a comparatively small loan raised for a state, endeavouring by the most heroic efforts to break the fetters imposed on them by the most appalling despotism.' Bowring's own commission had not yet been made public.

Another major criticism of Bowring and those involved in the first loan arose from the way he had presented his case and cast the blame for failure not on the Committee, but on the Greeks themselves. One member of the Stock Exchange pointed out:

He [Bowring] had stated that such was the instability of the Greek Government, so often had the hands in which it was invested been changed, that there was no security for any contract that might be made with it. Now he wished to ask Mr. Bowring and the Greek Committee, how long they had been acquainted with that fact? If they had long been acquainted with it, then the tirade, which they had directed against the contractors ought rather to be directed against themselves; for if they had let out the secret, which they had kept till that day, they would have prevented the money being raised at all, and by so doing would have saved the bondholders from the desperate situation in which they were now placed.

Rather than blame Ricardo and the Stock Exchange for accepting advantageous terms (if they had), he thought that the blame might lie elsewhere and not necessarily with the Greeks. Even though Bowring was in control of the meeting and no one directly pointed a finger at him, he was hardly free from criticism, and censure would not be long in coming. But at the bondholders' meeting, nothing definite was determined. Colonel Jones tried to make light of the fact that Burdett, Ellice, and Hobhouse were unfit for taking on the examination of accounts and the management of the business of the loans. His friendly, though critical, remarks about Burdett were much quoted later in the debate over the scandal:

Sir F. Burdett, of all men, was least a man of business; he knew him well, and knew that he had kept important letters in his pocket for seven months unopened. He would admit that on great public discussions Sir F. Burdett was a very able and a useful man, and so were the other gentlemen he had named; but on that to which he had alluded, they were not the proper men to be chosen. . . . Indeed, this unfitness for application to business of accounts, was the fault of the system of education adopted in our public schools—a system which, he was glad to find, would be likely to find a remedy in the establishment of the new university that had lately been so zealously taken up by the public.

The meeting ended without any satisfactory resolution, but the smouldering embers would soon spring dramatically to light.

3. *The Times* and the Attack on Hume

The reaction of *The Times* to the bondholders' meeting combined moral indignation with a teasing expectation of further revelations which served mainly to fan the flames of scandal. Of the scale of the scandal, the newspaper was certain: 'Europe certainly was never before privy to such a system of monstrous misconduct as is and will be brought to light in these Greek loans.'[19] This patent exaggeration reflected more the enthusiasm with which *The Times* took up the scandal than its actual scale. As if to confirm this perspective, the newspaper pointed its finger most at British individuals who might have profited from the loans: for example Ricardo's £64,000 commission from the second loan or the mysterious transactions not spelled out in the bondholders' report that would point the finger of scandal at Hume and Bowring. According to *The Times*: 'The Greek cause has been betrayed. It has been betrayed in England. It would have triumphed 'ere now, but for England, and the English Stock-Exchange!'[20]

The newspaper pronounced Louriottis free from scandal, and his further revelations of whose bonds were bought back by the Greek government at a price above the market were eagerly awaited. *The Times* soon took on the mantle of crusading and investigative journalism, thoroughly enjoying producing daily revelations of malpractice:

Light breaks in more and more on the dark mystery of the management of the Greek Loan. We recommend to our readers to peruse every word of the letter of the Greek Deputy [Louriottis] in to-day's *Times*. Further disclosures are in preparation, which, though we confess we are sickened and pained at the sight of them, we shall not flinch from exposing to public view.[21]

The next main revelations concerned Hume, Bowring, and a William Burton who acted largely for George Lee, secretary to the

---

[19] See *The Times* (25 Oct. 1826).   [20] Ibid. (26 Oct. 1826).
[21] Ibid. (27 Oct. 1826).

Greek Deputies.[22] According to Louriottis, the Deputies were pressed to buy back Greek scrip so that these holders would not suffer much loss when the price had declined in the summer of 1824. Hume had purchased £10,000 worth of scrip at £59 paying £5,900 for his investment. The value of the bonds dropped sixteen points and the value of his investment declined correspondingly to £4,300. The Greek Deputies agreed to pay him £4,600 for his bonds, thus limiting his loss to £1,300. When the value of the bonds increased in the autumn of 1824, Hume then applied to the Deputies to recover the £1,300 that he had lost from his investment. In addition, he was not satisfied with the £1,300 he had supposedly lost, but he wanted (and got) £54 interest from the Deputies for the period during which they had supposedly had possession of his £1,300. Hume never disputed the facts but his interpretation differed from that of Louriottis. According to Hume, he purchased the Greek loan scrip (though already a Commissioner of the loan) to encourage others to invest in the bonds and to show his confidence in their value. In the summer of 1824, he was approached by the Deputies who believed that his reluctance to agree to pay the proceeds of the first loan over to the Greeks was based on his holding the Greek scrip and his fearing its decline in value. Hume then agreed to sell his bonds (to avoid the imputation of a conflict of interest) and accepted the loss of £1,300. Nevertheless, he wanted the loss made up (plus interest) when the value of the bonds improved.[23]

Francis Place was closely involved in assisting Hume to defend himself. He recorded in his diary his surprise when he heard that Hume had purchased Greek scrip, but he argued that Hume should not have sold the scrip at a loss. When he heard that Hume had done so, and was apparently satisfied with the arrangement in spite of the loss, he thought that the matter had ended, and was surprised to learn that Hume had later recovered the sum he had lost.[24] On 4 November, Hume replied in letters in the *Morning Chronicle* and the *Morning Herald* giving his version of the story, but he also wrote to Place 'under strong feelings' requesting that Place and James Mill

---

[22] See ibid. (30 Oct. 1826).

[23] See above n. 3. For a recent account of Hume's involvement in the loan scandal, see Ronald Huch and Paul R. Ziegler, *Joseph Hume: The People's M.P.* (Philadelphia, 1985), 47 ff.

[24] BL Add. MS 35146, fo. 51, 31 Oct. 1826.

come to see him the next day.[25] Mill and Place spent four hours
discussing his position. According to Place they found Hume
'somewhat agitated', having decided to return the money (the
£1,300 recovered from the Greek Deputies plus interest).[26] In this
he was influenced by his wife, *The Times*, and the *John Bull*. At
first, Mill seemed to agree that he should return the money, but
Place argued that to return it would be to admit that he had no right
to hold it. Place noted:

Mill thought there were a considerable number *of well meaning weak minded*
persons who would be satisfied with Hume's conduct if he returned the
money, and so thought Hume. I maintained that more people would
conclude that he kept the money as long as the matter was unknown and
only paid it when he was by fear compelled to do so, and further that they
would say, knowing as we do Mr. Hume's attachment to money he would
never have paid so large a sum had he not been quite conscious that he had
no just right to hold it.[27]

Hume and Mill agreed to meet again the next day in the late
afternoon, and, in the meantime, Mill consulted the editors of the
Morning Chronicle and the *Traveller* and close colleagues such as
Henry Brougham and George Grote. All agreed that Hume should
not return the money. Place drafted a paper for Hume that might
serve as an explanation of his connection with the Greek loan.[28]
Hume followed the course of action planned by Place and Mill, and
Place recorded as early as 14 November, despite a steady attack on
Hume's character, that Hume 'is recovering his spirits'.[29]

On 6 November the *Morning Chronicle* printed a long editorial in
support of Hume. Referring to the reformer's numerous enemies
who had wrongly attempted to link him with the management of
the second loan, and to the mischievousness of *The Times* and the
Greek Deputies, the *Morning Chronicle* completely exonerated
Hume's conduct in supporting Greece and the loan. It dismissed the
charge of conflict of interest and believed Hume right to expect a
further payment once the value of the loans had increased to par.
The newspaper took the view that Hume had bought the scrip in
order that the loan should succeed and that the Deputies (fearing a

---

[25] See *Morning Chronicle* (4 Nov. 1826); see also BL Add. MS 35146, fo. 52, 4
Nov. 1826.
[26] BL Add. MS 35146, fo. 52.   [27] Ibid. fos. 52-3, 4 Nov. 1826.
[28] Ibid. fo. 53, 6 Nov. 1826.   [29] Ibid. fo. 57, 14 Nov. 1826.

possible conflict of interest) forced him to sell at a loss. Contrary to other newspapers, the *Morning Chronicle* argued that he should have been reimbursed for his loss in so far as he had been forced to sell:

Mr. Hume is not bound to apply his private fortune to the cause of the Greeks, any more than other English Gentlemen. But it is not the less true that hundreds, nay, thousands, of English Noblemen and Gentlemen, not one of whom would have either given an hour's time or a pound's value to the Greeks, will be ready to blame Mr. Hume, because he did not choose to lose his £1,300. It is, therefore, with a view to the people of England themselves that the matter acquires importance. . . . It is with reference to the people themselves, to whom any diminution of Mr. Hume's means of being useful, and not to that gentleman himself, that the affair acquires consequence. But we cannot bring ourselves to believe that the people will really be so doltish as to withdraw any part of their sympathy from their best friend, and thereby injure themselves, because that friend chose to be guided by the principle of strict justice at a time when he had an opportunity for a theatrical display of generosity.[30]

The *Morning Chronicle* could thus see that the attack on Hume was part of a larger political campaign, based on party feeling, that had been orchestrated against him by *The Times*, just as *The Times* had a year earlier used Parry's *Last Days of Lord Byron* to attack Bentham.[31] The *Morning Chronicle* kept up a running defence of Hume well into December 1826, publishing evidence of a personal vendetta between *The Times* and Hume which had begun the previous year, and quoting from numerous other newspapers which had supported Hume.[32] As the *Manchester Guardian* (2 December) put it, 'we perceive, with no little dissatisfaction—we might almost say disgust—that *The Times*, in ill-assorted conjunction with the dregs of the Tory Press on the one hand, and with Mr. Cobbett on the other, continues to bespatter Mr. Hume with abuse'.[33]

In Hume's case, at least, the attack led by *The Times* was based on ideological differences which the scandal enabled the newspaper to exploit. Many felt that Hume should not have taken the £1,300 from the Deputies nor asked for the £54 interest. His friends seemed well aware of his avarice, and both they and Hume himself knew that he was in the wrong, however strong the mitigating

---

[30] *Morning Chronicle* (6 Nov. 1826).　　　　[31] See Ch. 10 above.
[32] See *Morning Chronicle* (8, 9, 11, 28 Nov., 2, 5 Dec. 1826).
[33] Quoted in ibid. (5 Dec. 1826).

circumstances.[34] Curiously, there is no evidence (besides conjecture) that Hume had attempted to hold up the loan or delay payments, because of his fear of losing his investment in the Greek bonds. Like Stanhope, Hume had experience of India and tended to regard the Greeks as inferiors not wholly to be trusted. The kind of liberalism to which Hume subscribed was sufficiently prevalent that many of those who organized the first Greek loan, including Stanhope, Bowring, and Hume, were in agreement in their attempt to direct the Greeks towards better government and a good use of the loan. As the Greek Deputies became dissatisfied with this ideological position and with the corresponding arrangements, which did not sufficiently allow for the nationalist aspirations of the Greeks to direct their own destiny, for good or ill, they turned away from men like Hume to organize the second loan directly with J. & S. Ricardo. The case against Hume, if there was one, had more to do with liberalism and less with Greek pie.

4. Hobhouse Fights Back

Although Hume and Bowring may have lost most from the Greek loan scandal, they were not alone. But where they were seen as thieves, others were considered bunglers. Hobhouse returned to London from holiday in France to find both himself and Burdett under constant attack in the press for their failure to control expenditure on the steamboats. His brother Henry Hobhouse had already briefed him, drawing a sharp distinction between Ellice, Hume, and Bowring who were 'specifically charged with selfish sacrifices of the Greek nation' and Hobhouse and Burdett who had only received 'some funny strictures on your habits and fitness for business in the Executive line'.[35] Never the less, Hobhouse realized that he had to defend himself and set out to demonstrate that he and Burdett had no authority over the funds or arrangements for the steamboats. On 12 November he called on Place where he heard 'all the charges made against Burdett and myself for neglecting our duty to Greece. Even he [Place] thought us culpable.'[36] Hobhouse

---

[34] See e.g. BL Add. MS 56550, fo. 113, Hobhouse's Diary, 13 Nov. 1826.
[35] BL Add. MS 36463, fo. 16, Henry to John C. Hobhouse, 7 Nov. 1826.
[36] BL Add. MS 56550, fo. 112, 12 Nov. 1826.

gathered his documents together until he was certain that he had a case, and went to see key figures involved in the scandal. On 13 November he called on Stanhope, who had, after all, chaired the meeting that had criticized him. According to Hobhouse, 'He [Stanhope] spoke very fair to me and agreed in the propriety of all I had done. I then talked to him about his own conduct and he told me he had been blamed for taking Burdett's part and mine.'[37]

Like Stanhope, Hobhouse had no respect for the Greek Deputies and was especially upset by the way *The Times* took the side of Louriottis against the Ricardos.[38] As for Ellice, he noted: 'His letters on the Greek business have done him no good—though he attempted to [do] his best for that cause.'[39] Both Hobhouse and Burdett felt they were being unfairly criticized not for what they had done but for what they had not done and had no power to do. When he showed his case to Brougham 'by appointment' at King's Bench, Brougham supported Hobhouse's position and suggested that 'Stanhope ought to do Burdett and me justice by retracting his assertions at the meeting of bondholders.'[40] Hobhouse thus clearly established that he and Burdett were not responsible for the expenditure of funds on the steamships, and made this clear in various meetings, including one with Ricardo:

on Ricardo saying that Burdett, Ellice and I were a Committee for seeing the £157,000 properly expended towards fitting out Cochrane's expedition— I contradicted him flatly and Stanhope supported me. I told Ricardo he was wrong. I showed Ricardo how the matter really stood and produced the documents. He asked me if I had not frequently come to the meetings at his house—certainly, but not with any duty to perform—merely because I was a friend to Greece and had been asked to come. I complained of the efforts I had made being quoted in proof that I ought to have made more. Spanilachi, confessed I was right,—that without seeing the papers he knew what we must have undertaken to do—namely to guarantee for Cochrane's services no more. We parted amicably.[41]

It was by then clearly established that, once Burdett and Hobhouse had made Cochrane the leader of the steamboat expedition, their formal role was at an end, and it was Cochrane who made the

---

[37] Ibid. 13 Nov. 1826.   [38] Ibid. fo. 113, 13 Nov. 1826.
[39] Ibid. 14 Nov. 1826.   [40] Ibid. fo. 116, 24 Nov. 1826.
[41] Ibid. fos. 117–18, 2 Dec. 1826.

agreement with Galloway to build the steamboats, for which Ricardo supplied the funds on behalf of the Greek Deputies.[42]

5. Bowring and the Greek Loan Scandal

Bowring's position reveals more strongly some of the ideological problems of early liberalism. Unlike Hume or, for that matter, Hobhouse and Burdett, who are clearly recognizable as reformers in an older, traditional mode, Bowring was, so to speak, a 'new

---

[42] For a summary of Hobhouse's view of the scandal, see Finlay papers, British School of Archaeology at Athens, E. 9 (P.8.11), fo. 9, Hobhouse to Hastings, 12 Dec. 1826: 'The worthy ex-deputies Orlando and Luriottis finding their rogueries discovered resolved to create an explosion themselves in the noise and smoke of which their own misconduct might have had some chance of being concealed and remaining unpunished. So they suborned one Count Palma to write a pamphlet abusing Sir F. Burdett, myself, Mr. Ellice, and Messrs Ricardo—and imputing all the delay of Cocherane's expedition to us. Burdett and I were out of England— Ellice and Ricardo scorned to answer such lax nonsense—The newspapers (Times particularly) took to abusing us—Stanhope and Bowring encouraged a fellow called Robinson to call a meeting of bondholders who appointed a Committee–who drew up a report full of all sorts of lies and according to which it appeared that we (B and E and I) had undertaken all kinds of duties and then neglected them—unluckily, however, for your Mr Bowring, in the course of the enquiry it appeared that he had been fingering some cash not quite his own—Mr Hume also had been at some sport of that sort but not so bad by any means—more imprudence than any thing else—In an instant the public quitted us whom they had worried enough and fell tooth and nail upon Hume and Bowring—Such was the state of things when I came back to England on 12th November and such is the state of things now. Sir F. Burdett and myself have been silent under all these atrocious calumnies which indeed by this time are almost forgotten—we have privately convinced Stanhope etc. that they were wrong—but we have said nothing publicly—You know the truth—therefore I need not call to your mind how little I can be charged either with undertaking or neglecting any duties—Yet even your name has been quoted as giving evidence and complaining against us—The truth begins to be known and the Greek government itself has shown its opinions by ap[p]ointing Burdett, Spaniolacki, and Ricardo auditors of the late deputies accounts—. The wretched Luriottis has, however, dispatched the needy Blaquiere to Greece to intrigue against Spaniolacki and set aside Burdett's commission—This commission has produced nothing as yet but John Smith MP and Barnett the banker have been requested to act for Sir Francis—If they do so—the ex-deputies will appear in their true light—Should ambassador Blaquiere come across you, you will know how to treat the emissary of so honorable an employer—I think Luriottis' conduct to me, whose door was open to him night and day and who did all I could—little enough but still all I could—for him and his country, as black an instance of ingratitude as I ever heard of— However, I shall not retire from the post in which I happen to find myself—but still continue to do my best for the cause.'

man', one difficult to define except perhaps in negative or conflicting terms. He was not a philosopher like Bentham, but he sought assiduously to use philosophical ideas for political ends. Though lacking the independence conferred by wealth which was at that time useful for an active career as a reformer, he was politically active and frequently mentioned in the press in connection with support for liberal causes abroad. Though much inclined to use strongly moralistic language, perhaps due to the influence of his religious background, he earned his living as a 'jobber' in the City. The one strand in his life did not fit easily with the other.

When the Greek loan scandal erupted, Bowring had already worked out his strategy. He defended the London Greek Committee and the handling of the first loan, while criticizing the conduct of the Greek Deputies and the general management of the second loan. As we have seen, he was vulnerable on three issues: firstly, the acceptance of the commission of £11,000 for his role in arranging the first loan; secondly, his selling his scrip to the Greek Deputies when its value fell and then wanting it returned to him when it rose; and thirdly, his arrangement of the loan when he knew that there was no settled government in Greece with which to negotiate its repayment. Although the commission of £11,000 was small when compared with the £64,000 taken by Ricardo a year later, there were many who thought that those who were crusading on behalf of the suffering and desperate Greeks should not profit from their misery. Bowring's view was perfectly reasonable but not widely shared. He had worked tirelessly for the Greeks for several years and had taken on the heaviest burden of organizing and running the Committee. Without Bowring it is doubtful that any committee for the assistance of the Greeks would have been launched. His commission was in his opinion merely a small reward for his efforts. Nevertheless, such a reward was not known until it was revealed by Louriottis. Bowring did not mention his commission in his defence of the Greek Committee.[43] Nor was it brought out in the report of the Greek bondholders, though the report included a figure of £25,746 9s. 2d. under the heading 'Commission on loan, and Shipments to Greece'.[44] If

---

[43] See 'Greek Committee', 113–33. There was some comment on Bowring's commission at the time the loan was arranged. See Guilford papers, Kent County Archives, U471 C75, Foresti to Guilford, 24 Feb. 1824.

[44] *The Times* (24 Oct. 1826).

Bowring was so confident about the acceptability of his commission, one wonders why this was not listed in a straightforward
manner in the accounts. Nevertheless, in comparison with Ricardo's
massive commission for simply putting through the financial
transaction, Bowring eventually appeared somewhat virtuous, and
the main public reaction concerned his sale of Greek scrip back to
the Deputies, another transaction not made public prior to its
revelation by Louriottis in *The Times*.[45] Bowring had purchased
£25,000 of the scrip at £59, costing him £14,750 when all payments
were made. When the value of the stock fell and he was unable to
meet the payments, he tried to persuade the Deputies to lend him
£5,000 on the security of the scrip on which he had paid
approximately £7,500. The Deputies refused to authorize the loan,
but eventually in late September 1824 they agreed to the purchase
of the scrip at a price of £49. When the value of the stock increased
in November, Bowring applied to the Deputies to have his stock
returned on the repayment of the sum received, plus interest, and
the Deputies were surprised in so far as they had thought that they
had purchased the stock from Bowring. Finally, to end the matter,
they passed the decision to Hume and Ellice who arranged that
Bowring should receive the scrip back, even though he had
technically sold it to the Greek government.

The details of this complex transaction emerged only gradually
with Bowring at first denying that he had agreed to sell his scrip to
the Deputies. When a letter was published in which he clearly
indicated his agreement to such a sale, he said that he had no
recollection of the letter due to his absorption at the time 'when a
heavy family sorrow occupied all my thoughts, at a time when the
mind is hardly answerable for its own acts'.[46] Thus, in his view, his
request for the return of the scrip was not a move to obtain bonds
he had already sold and gain an advantage by re-selling them at a
higher price, but one to regain possession of the scrip on which he
had only borrowed money.

Bowring's actions were portrayed by *The Times* and elsewhere as
crude speculation and selfish opportunism, based on an obvious
conflict of interest. Bowring replied by calling attention to this
great service on behalf of the Greeks and to the fact that, unlike
other transactions, the Greeks had lost no money from his

[45] See *The Times* (30 Oct. 1826). See also ibid. (1 Nov. 1826).
[46] *The Times* (6 Nov. 1826); see also ibid. (3, 4 Nov. 1826).

arrangements. Nevertheless, he found few friends to support him. If the *Morning Chronicle* devoted its columns to major support for Hume, it was less enthusiastic in its efforts for Bowring, though it published Bowring's replies to the accusations of Louriottis in *The Times*.[47] In a curious way the attack on Bowring himself was somewhat muted as if his behaviour was what might be expected from a 'jobber' in the City. Francis Place recorded in his diary:

Advised Mr. Hume very strongly to avoid mixing himself in any way with either Ellice or Bowring, both of whom are jobbers and [word obliterated] as indeed the letters and papers in Mr. Hume's hands prove, altho I wanted no proof beyond my own knowledge of the men and their conduct on particular occasions.[48]

This approach seemed to hurt Bowring even more, as he did not regard himself simply as a 'jobber'. He was especially sensitive to the rumours circulating about him, and thought Place had instigated one concerning his relationship with Bentham.[49]

The Times saw in Bowring's plight an opportunity to attack Bentham and even published a poem, 'The Ghost of Miltiades', which began:

> The Ghost of Miltiades came at night,
> And he stood by the bed of the Benthamite,

whom he roused, as a lover of liberty, to support the Greek cause. The Benthamite promptly went off to the Stock Exchange to speculate in Greek scrip. Finally, when fed up with his machinations, the ghost of Miltiades,

> Gave a Parthian kick to the Benthamite
> Which sent him, whimpering, off to Jerry—[50]

Cobbett likewise linked the scandal and Bowring with Bentham as in this passage:

Here is a great public wrong done: great wrong to the English bondholders: and, I am very well convinced that the law, imperfect as Mr. Bowring's great friend Jerry Bentham, thinks it, is not so slack twisted as

[47] See *Morning Chronicle* (7 Nov. 1826). See also ibid. (4, 6 Nov. 1826).
[48] BL Add. MS 35146, fo. 53, 5 Nov. 1826.
[49] See ibid. fo. 56, 8, 11 Nov. 1826. The rumour concerned Bowring owing Bentham £3,000.
[50] *The Times* (8 Nov. 1826).

to be unable to hold fishes like these. In short, if I were a bond-holder, I would prosecute the whole of them tomorrow.[51]

Of all those involved in the scandal, Bowring probably suffered and lost the most. He seemed to be surrounded by enemies: besides those ideologically opposed to him, like *The Times*, there were also those, like Place and Mill, who resented his closeness with Bentham. Place, for example, recorded this meeting and conversation with the radical politician Joseph Parkes, at the time of the scandal:

In the evening Mr. Joseph Parkes much interesting conversation respecting Mr. Bentham his connection with Bowring and the state and preservation of his M.S. Mr. Parkes as well as every one else who is really a friend to Mr. Bentham, regrets that he should be so much as he is under the control and management of Bowring, but this seems at present to be unav[o]idable. Bowring gives much of his time to him, dines with him, and takes him out with him now and then, and for this Bentham undoubtedly owes something to Bowring. Bowring also panders to him, is his toad eater, and can therefore command him, and as something of the sort is necessary to Mr. Bentham's comfort, to deprive him of Bowring without substituting some one in his stead would if it could be done, make him unhappy.[52]

If *The Times* and Cobbett were ideologically motivated, it might also be argued that Place and those who agreed with him were also unable to see clearly due to ideological considerations. They saw Bowring as an opportunist, a toady, and a 'jobber'; what they failed to see was Bowring as the new liberal, suffering as much for his public views as for his private vices. His commission and speculative involvement in the Greek loan were, in his own view, perfectly compatible with great service for the Greek cause. Without Bowring, as we have noted at several points, these vast sums would probably never have been raised for Greece or, at least, not at the time when they were most needed. It is arguable, therefore, that Bowring suffered for his beliefs and not just for his sins. His main belief was in the close relationship between unrestricted trade and commerce and moral and political progress, a belief which would become a mainstay of liberalism in the nineteenth century. In organizing the Committee and in negotiating the loan, Bowring was demonstrating his faith in this

[51] *Cobbett's Weekly Register*, 60 (1826), 483–4 (18 Nov. 1826).
[52] BL Add. MS 35146, fo. 58, 19 Nov. 1826.

relationship. But not everyone shared his vision. Within a year
Bowring wrote to Hobhouse:

The tempests have been long blowing about me and I am wrecked at last.
Having got rewarded for laborious exertions by obloquy and penury (the
loss of *all*) I have now with half a dozen little ones, to start anew in life. I
have for the present taken up my abode with Mr. Bentham—whose
delicacy and kindness are something more than paternal.[53]

Bowring was writing to obtain support from Hobhouse for an
appointment to a Chair in English Literature at the newly
established University of London. Bentham was his main backer,
but he met opposition on the Council from many, including Mill
and Brougham.[54] In part, opposition to Bowring was based on a
reaction to the Greek loan scandal, but there were other reasons
connected with the other candidates for the post. However
successful Bowring became later in life, he certainly felt now that
he was a martyr for a cause he so emphatically advanced but
without much public understanding of his motives and achievements.

The Greek loan scandal did not end with the various revelations
in the autumn and winter of 1826 but drifted on, with bondholders
receiving no settlement for more than sixty years. The key figures,
especially Hume, Bowring, and Ellice, suffered diminished reputa-
tions, but all seem to have recovered fairly quickly to continue their
political and business careers. Nevertheless, in the whole saga of
the Greek loans, there were no winners, and the losers were those
who tried hardest to serve the cause of Greece. Did they fail because
of individual greed, dishonesty, and incompetence? Or were they
somehow blind to political and economic realities both in Greece
and Britain? No final answer can be given to these questions, and
perhaps both should be answered affirmatively. Still, it has been
argued here that greed and incompetence alone do not allow one to
account for the Greek loan saga, for the expectations surrounding it
and the problems which it failed to overcome emerged from the
ideological context within which the various decisions regarding
the loan were taken. That context was the meeting of an

---

[53] BL Add. MS 36464, fo. 64, Bowring to Hobhouse, 4 Oct. 1827.
[54] See U. C. Brougham MSS 26,000–1,26,003. Bentham to Brougham, 13, 20
Sept. 1827, 1 Jan. 1828; see also Chester New, *The Life of Henry Brougham to 1830*
(Oxford, 1961), 333–5.

authoritarian British liberalism with Greek nationalism, which rendered the former ineffectual and the latter self-destructive. Beneath this context was another: the more traditional division between Whigs and Tories which tended to direct debate about Greece along predictable lines. *The Times*, Cobbett, and many others saw 'Greek Pie' as simply another chance to score a few points against the radical and reforming opposition they had already attacked on numerous occasions. They could not see new political ideas at work in the context of Greece.

14

Conclusion: Liberalism, Nationalism, and the Study of Political Ideas

1. Varieties of Liberalism

'Liberalism' and 'liberal' are protean terms especially among historians of political ideas. Even when non-political senses of 'liberal' and 'liberality' (meaning generous and freely giving) are excluded, many scholars subscribe to the view that there is more than one 'liberalism' and numerous ways of being 'liberal'.[1] Where there is an attempt to discern a single liberal tradition, even in Britain, there is little agreement over what its main features are and which writers best represent its principles.[2] One can sympathize with David Manning when he writes: 'It simply will not do to attempt to characterize liberalism by taking the work of Locke, Mill, or Green as representing the essential teaching of the tradition.'[3] But other attempts at characterization are often even less illuminating. Nor do various lists of so-called 'liberal' writers provide much assistance, although the objects of the editors in making the selections are not difficult to discern.[4] The so-called

[1] See e.g. M. Cranston, *Freedom: A New Analysis* (London, 1953), 65–113; L. Siedentop, 'Two Liberal Traditions', in A. Ryan (ed.), *The Idea of Freedom* (Oxford, 1979), 153–74; Nancy Rosenblum, *Another Liberalism: Romanticism and the Reconstruction of Liberal Thought* (Cambridge, Mass., 1987); J. Gray, *Liberalisms: Essays in Political Philosophy* (London, 1989).

[2] See F. Rosen, 'Bentham and Mill on Liberty and Justice', in G. Feaver and F. Rosen (eds.), *Lives, Liberties, and the Public Good* (London, 1987), 136.

[3] D. J. Manning, *Liberalism* (London, 1976), 13.

[4] See J. Plamenatz (ed.), *Readings from Liberal Writers, English and French* (London, 1965), which includes Locke, Montesquieu, Rousseau, Burke, Constant, Mill, Acton, Tawney, Voltaire, Diderot, Bentham, Milton, Hume, Chenier, Tocqueville, etc.; A. Bullock and M. Schock (eds.), *The Liberal Tradition from Fox to Keynes* (London, 1956), which contains excerpts from Fox, Sheridan, Earl Grey, Russell, Lansdowne, Byron, Macaulay, Smith, Bentham, Ricardo, J. S. Mill, Cobden, Bright, Joseph Hume, Palmerston, Acton, Gladstone, Green, Spencer, Hobson, Hobhouse, Samuel, Lloyd George, Keynes, etc.

liberal tradition from the seventeenth century is largely the creation
of a Marxist or neo-Marxist conception of ideology or part of a
reaction to it. As Laski wrote: 'New material conditions, in short,
gave birth to new social relationships; and, in terms of these, a new
philosophy was evolved to afford a rational justification for the
new world which had come into being. This new philosophy was
liberalism.'[5]

For Laski, liberalism was the ideology that justified bourgeois
capitalism, and this view has animated much discussion of
liberalism, with greater or lesser sophistication, to the present day.[6]
The argument presented here differs from this view in two
important respects. Firstly, it is based on a distinction between
philosophy or theory on the one hand and ideology on the other, a
distinction which is not as clearly made in Marxism, where a
historical conception of truth tends to reduce past philosophy to
ideology. On this view, thinkers like Locke, Smith, and Bentham
are bourgeois ideologists whose *theoretical* contributions can only
be seen to the extent that they do or do not transcend these
ideological constraints in foreshadowing socialism or in embodying socialist principles. No distinction can be made, as has been
made here, between Bentham as a theorist of constitutional liberty
within a utilitarian philosophy and Bentham as a liberal icon used
by those committed more to political action than to the pursuit of
truth. In making this distinction, it is possible to overcome some of
the reservations recorded by scholars as to whether or not Bentham
was a liberal at all.[7] These reservations have arisen largely because
the conflation of theory and ideology has prevented a due
appreciation of theory. There is no conflict between utilitarianism
and liberalism, because one is a philosophical system and the other
a political doctrine.[8] Utilitarians may or may not also be liberals;
Bentham himself was not a liberal during part of his life.
Nevertheless, it has been argued here that at the heart of Bentham's
utilitarianism and especially his theory of constitutional govern-

---

[5] H. Laski, *The Rise of European Liberalism* (London, 1936), 12.

[6] See e.g. C. B. Macpherson, *The Political Theory of Possessive Individualism*
(Oxford, 1962); Macpherson, *The Life and Times of Liberal Democracy* (Oxford,
1977).

[7] See. E. Halévy, *The Growth of Philosophic Radicalism*, trans. Mary Morris
(London, 1928), 74, 375–6; A. Arblaster, *The Rise and Decline of Western Liberalism*
(Oxford, 1984), 350–2; Manning, *Liberalism*, 29–30.

[8] This problem has been specifically raised in Arblaster, *Rise and Decline*, 350.

ment is a major role for liberty.[9] The place of liberty in Bentham's philosophical system has been partly obscured because this issue has been confused with that of whether or not Bentham was a liberal. Bentham's constitutional theory, freed from the constraints of ideological interpretation, can be more usefully explored in the context of theories of constitutional liberty from Locke and Montesquieu, through Blackstone and Delolme, and forward to a writer like John Rawls. This context represents the level of discourse on which the theory was presented. The philosophical context is appropriate to the enterprise, and seems more fruitful than (say) Halévy's attempt to interpret Bentham's political and constitutional ideas in terms of Bentham's rejection of a Whig/liberal tradition as embodied in Montesquieu and his replacement of it with an authoritarian doctrine taken from the utilitarianism of Helvetius. Halévy's approach uses liberalism in a way that brings confusion both to an account of Bentham's philosophy and to his role in the development of liberal ideology.[10]

Secondly, the distinction between theory and ideology has led here to a focus of attention on liberalism as an *active* doctrine more closely related to practice than appears in numerous conceptions of liberalism.[11] Within interpretations inspired by Marxism, ideology and philosophy are regarded somewhat passively as reflecting material conditions and not particularly as a force in the world directing political action. This passive view of ideology not only underestimates its active role, but also tends to locate the fullest expression of ideology, as we have seen, within philosophical systems, as these best reflect the development of productive forces. However, the belief that ideology can be best understood through the writings of philosophers is not confined to Marxists. Manning suggests that liberalism as an ideology can be found in Mill, Tocqueville, and Hobhouse in a deeper form than in politicians like Gladstone, Cavour, and Theirs.[12] Whatever the merits of these examples, it has been argued here that liberalism is best understood not in terms of Bentham and Byron, but through writers like

[9] See Rosen, 'Bentham and Mill on Liberty and Justice', 121 ff.; and Ch. 2 above.
[10] See Halévy, *The Growth of Philosophic Radicalism*, 74, 375–6. See also F. Rosen, 'Elie Halévy and Bentham's Authoritarian Liberalism', *Enlightenment and Dissent*, 6 (1987), 59–76, where Halévy's interpretation is considered at greater length.
[11] For this active sense of ideology see e.g. J. Hamburger, *Intellectuals in Politics: John Stuart Mill and the Philosophic Radicals* (New Haven, Conn., 1965), 1.
[12] Manning, *Liberalism*, 11–12.

Stanhope and Blaquiere. It is their grasp of ideology that makes them both effective in directing action and partially blind in grasping what action is appropriate to take. Neither Bentham nor Byron, though often used by ideologists, and even celebrated later as ideologists, was very effective at this level, largely because neither the philosopher nor the poet was able to dwell happily in that twilight world where certainty of conviction and the determination to go ahead were more important than clarity of vision and depth of understanding.

Though these remarks amount to a partial disparagement of ideology in comparison with either philosophy or poetry, there is no intention to suggest here that ideology is less important or less effective in politics. At the level of politics, the liberalism of Blaquiere and Stanhope was perfectly understandable and coherent, though the two men subscribed to conflicting brands of liberalism and neither clearly understood Bentham's philosophy. But when it came to directing action in a coherent manner, only Blaquiere, Stanhope, and perhaps Bowring possessed coherent and relevant ideologies.

2. Liberalism and the 1820s

The view of ideology advanced here has led to a conception of liberalism much closer to practice than appears in the writings of many historians of ideas. The introduction of the political term 'liberal' into English from the Spanish 'liberales', and the association of men like Bowring and Blaquiere with the development of liberalism in Spain, make the 1820s especially appropriate for an exploration of a self-conscious liberal ideology. Nevertheless, it is important to proceed with caution, as any attempt to distinguish clearly among Whig, radical, and liberal in the 1820s is fraught with difficulty. Most historians would agree that to speak of liberalism as a party or in terms of a coherent political creed in the 1820s would present a misleading picture of the ideology in this period. Nevertheless, even at the risk of anachronism, many scholars have sought to write about liberalism in a variety of contexts. Thus, Brent discusses the 'Liberal Anglicans' (some of whom signed the Cambridge Address); Davis distinguishes between 'old' and 'new'

Unitarians (with Bowring as an example of the new unitarianism) and refers to the new Unitarians as 'Liberals' after 1830; and Gordon uses the term 'Tory liberalism' to refer to the introduction of a degree of *laissez-faire* into British trade in the Liverpool administration of the 1820s.[13] In these examples, 'Liberal' is used in different ways, but they share the sense that there were developments taking place in the 1820s in Britain that were progressive in nature, related to later developments in liberalism as an ideology, but could not be wholly understood in terms of such existing categories as 'Tory', 'Whig' or 'radical'.

The most difficult distinction to draw at this time is between 'radical' and 'liberal', and especially between 'radical Whig' and 'liberal'. For the most part no such distinction was drawn. It has been suggested here that liberals, like Bowring, Blaquiere, and Stanhope, tended to draw together traditional Whigs and their radical critics into a common cause as they tended to minimize the divisive issue of electoral reform at home in favour of an emphasis on free trade, a free press, educational opportunity, and other liberties in foreign states. The three men mentioned above seem to stand apart from the radicalism (say) of Francis Place who was mainly, though by no means exclusively, concerned with extending the suffrage and radical consciousness to and beyond the middle classes. But even here there are no clear distinctions, and when Stanhope wrote that he had been a liberal in politics all his life, he was looking backwards from the 1850s when it made more sense to talk of liberalism as a political creed. This lack of clarity about liberalism may be seen in the writings of John Stuart Mill. He wrote about 'liberalism' as early as 1831, but used it as a general term meaning 'individualism'.[14] In the 1830s and 1840s he was

[13] R. Brent, *Liberal Anglican Politics: Whiggery, Religion, and Reform, 1830–1841* (Oxford, 1987), pp. xii, 144 ff., 187–8; Richard W. Davis, *Dissent in Politics, 1780–1830: The Political Life of William Smith, M.P.* (London, 1971), 206–7 and n., 251; Barry Gordon, *Economic Doctrine and Tory Liberalism, 1824–1830* (London, 1979). See also J. E. Cookson, *The Friends of Peace: Anti-War Liberalism in England, 1793–1815* (Cambridge, 1982); Boyd Hilton, *Corn, Cash, Commerce: The Economic Policies of the Tory Governments, 1815–1830* (Oxford, 1977), 303 ff.; Bernard Semmel, *Liberalism and Naval Strategy: Ideology, Interest and Sea Power during the Pax Britannica* (Boston, 1986); W. Thomas, *The Philosophic Radicals: Nine Studies in Theory and Practice, 1817–1841* (Oxford, 1979), 165; E. Halévy, *A History of the English People*, trans. E. I. Watkin, 6 vols. (London, 1961), ii: *The Liberal Awakening (1815–1830)*, 81 n.

[14] *The Earlier Letters of John Stuart Mill*, ed. F. Mineka, 2 vols. (Toronto, 1963) (*Collected Works of John Stuart Mill*, vols. xii and xiii), xii. 84.

envisaging the formation of a liberal party from Philosophic Radicalism.[15] But in the 1850s and 1860s, he could look back and see the whole radical movement, including his father and Francis Place, in terms of the development of liberalism.[16] In various periods, then, with liberalism evolving as a creed and a distinct party, the formative, early period was being recast in light of later developments.

3. Liberal Ideology, Nationalism, and Empire

If it makes sense at all to talk of liberalism as an ideology in the 1820s, related to and overlapping with Whig and radical doctrines, how might this early liberalism be characterized? What do Stanhope's emphasis on a free press, Bowring's interest in free trade, and Blaquiere's belief in the virtue of national self-determination have in common? We do not see in these beliefs any particular emphasis on such ideas as a balanced constitution, civil liberty, a restricted suffrage, and rights to property, though some aspects of what might be called these 'Whig' doctrines would clearly underpin the liberal ideas expressed here. Nor do we see much regard for an extensive or universal suffrage, a highly regarded doctrine of radical reformers, though such a notion is not foreign to these liberal doctrines. Furthermore, free trade, a free press, an emphasis on education, and national self-determination might be accepted by Whigs, radicals, and even some Tories. What these ideas have in common, besides a regard for liberty in one form or another, is how they are formulated as ideological precepts. In the hands of Stanhope, Blaquiere, and Bowring, they become principles as part of a programme, precepts for immediate action. They provide answers to difficult questions, not by the profundity of the answer but by the way the answer provides a certain path to present action and a vision of the future. On the face

[15] See John Stuart Mill, *Essays on England, Ireland, and the Empire*, ed. J. M. Robson (Toronto, 1982) (*Collected Works of John Stuart Mill*, vol. vi), 342–3, 389, 449–51, 467 ff.
[16] See John Stuart Mill, *Newspaper Writings*, ed. Ann Robson and J. M. Robson, 4 vols. (Toronto, 1986) (*Collected Works of John Stuart Mill*, vols. xxii–xxv), xxv. 1262 ff.

of it, Stanhope looks absurd marching around Greece setting up printing presses, newspapers, and Lancasterian schools, but what makes Stanhope's ideas and actions intelligible is that they provide a clear answer to the question—what should be done for Greece?— that makes certain assumptions about present needs and points clearly and directly to a desirable future condition.

So long as people believe that such institutions as a free press and widespread education are important aspects of European civilization and that Greece should aspire to this condition, then marching around Greece promoting such institutions and practices, however eccentric given the occasion, is not unintelligible. Stanhope had considerable support for the application of his brand of liberalism to Greece, largely because underlying his actions were coherent and widely shared ideas about civilization, progress, and liberty. These underlying assumptions were widely shared, because they evolved not only in the context of British political thought generally, but also in the context of empire and especially of India.[17]

On several occasions we have noted links in terms of people and ideas between the British experience of ruling India and the development of liberal ideas. This connection has hardly been explored, but the example of Stanhope provides one important corrective to the influential views of Eric Stokes in *The English Utilitarians and India*.[18] Stokes has argued that the utilitarians (and especially James Mill) formed a sect apart from 'the main stream of English Liberal opinion', and introduced into India an authoritarian form of liberalism at variance with this liberal mainstream.[19] I have argued that prior to the developments chronicled by Stokes, Stanhope had exported from India to Greece an authoritarian liberalism which he had developed in India without much influence from Bentham or Mill. Stokes sees Benthamite utilitarianism as authoritarian largely because he has adopted Halévy's interpretation of Bentham's so-called liberalism.[20] If we reject this aspect of Halévy's interpretation of Philosophic Radicalism by distinguishing clearly between utilitarian philosophy and liberal ideology, it is possible to see the British experience in India and in other colonies itself as the possible source of the view that certain practices and

[17] Stanhope is an interesting example of the evolution from Whig, to radical, to liberal. Born into an aristocratic Whig family, he developed radical ideas on such themes as flogging in the army, slavery, and liberty of the press, but later in life saw his development in terms of liberalism.

[18] Oxford, 1959.   [19] Ibid. 58.   [20] Ibid. 324 (n. F).

institutions ought to be imposed in certain societies for their own good, whether or not the leaders or the people wanted them. Stanhope took radical/liberal ideas and would have imposed them in Greece as part of a considered view of how to encourage progress and civilization in that country. He is authoritarian in Greece, because of his experience in India.

It is generally believed that there was no conflict between early liberalism and nationalism, and that nationalism posed a major problem for liberalism only later in the century.[21] Indeed, liberal support for the Greek struggle for independence has been taken as evidence for the absence of conflict between the two ideas.[22] Although the setting for this conflict of ideas within the London Greek Committee was an unusual one, the fact of the conflict is indisputable, and significantly, as we have seen, British opinion was almost wholly opposed to the nationalistic sentiments expressed by Blaquiere, the Greek Deputies, and other philhellenes. Some have interpreted this opposition to Greek nationalism in terms of the self-interest of the holders of the Greek scrip. It has been contended that Bowring and others opposed Greek aspirations in order to guard their investments. But I have argued that the Greek loan scandal can only be fully understood as a development of one form of liberal ideology which opposed giving the money directly to the Greeks because of the rejection of these nationalistic sentiments. If Hume and Bowring were *only* concerned with their own personal advantage, they might very well not have supported the Greek cause or the Greek loan at all, given the information about conditions in Greece that they possessed. That they did so seemed to them a logical next step for those committed to the spread of liberal ideas, once Spain had fallen, and it was their brand of liberalism that provided the conviction that they could proceed with the expedition and loan despite the fact that the Greeks were on the brink of civil war, and there was no established government in the country. So long as they felt that they could control the loan and expedition and direct the 'inferior' Greeks (recall Stanhope's implacable hostility to 'Prince' Mavrokordatos who did not fit the paradigm[23]) by making satisfactory arrangements for payment and

---

[21] See Arblaster, *Rise and Decline*, 262; K. Minogue, *Nationalism* (London, 1967), 133–8.
[22] See Arblaster, *Rise and Decline*, 262.   [23] See above, Ch. 8.

repayment of the loan, they proceeded; when even such control seemed impossible (as it did to Stanhope in Greece), they tried to keep the money in their own hands. Such decisions flowed directly from their conviction as liberals, with personal interest only important for grasping the complexity of mixed motives that always lie behind human action.

The response of Blaquiere and other foreign philhellenes who did not reject the nationalist aspirations of the Greeks was incredulity in the face of what seemed to them a wholly irrational policy. Did not the Greeks borrow the money? Should they not use it for purposes of their own design in order to win a war that they themselves must fight? Why loan them the money with full knowledge of conditions in Greece, and then not give it to them when they needed it most? The answers to these questions only become intelligible when it is appreciated that the liberalism adopted by Stanhope, Hume, Bowring, and others, nurtured in the context of India and exported to Greece, decisively rejected the validity of the aspirations of the Greeks themselves for self-determination. Put simply, they did not believe that the Greeks knew what was best for them. The conflict over nationalism thus emerges early as a conflict that threatened to undermine liberalism as an ideology potentially universal in application and that continued to bedevil it from its inception.

4. Bentham and Liberalism

In this book, Bentham's philosophical theory has been contrasted with the ideological doctrines concerned with Greece. On several occasions in later chapters Bentham has been depicted as a liberal icon—an image to be used by emerging liberalism to advance its doctrines. The use of this term is not meant to minimize Bentham's importance to liberal ideology. One need not be an admirer of Bentham to recognize that he was, as a student of Constant has written, 'the most famous and influential liberal of the age'.[24] The contrast between Bentham's theory and liberal ideology is intended to emphasize that Bentham's main intention with regard to Greece was not to advance the cause of liberalism, but to relate his theory,

[24] G. H. Dodge, *Benjamin Constant's Philosophy of Liberalism: A Study in Politics and Religion* (Chapel Hill, NC, 1980), 5–6.

through various codes, to practice; this endeavour had little to do with liberalism as an ideology. It may be thought that this approach to Bentham's theory is too self-consciously Platonic, and that, as stressed by Collini, Winch, and Burrow, 'Bentham seems more at home with a neighbouring group of Law Lords than in a fitting-room dominated by busts of Plato and Aristotle.'[25] To fit Bentham out with such grand 'philosophical finery' may seem an extreme response to those who would see the London Greek Committee as simply applying, through Stanhope, Blaquiere, and Bowring, Bentham's ideas to Greece.[26] One might also argue that the problem with these followers was that they were mere vulgarizers and not true disciples and, consequently, still leave Bentham off the grand philosophic pedestal.

It has been argued here, however, that Bentham's constitutional theory can only be understood in the context of the development of theory, especially from Montesquieu but also from Hume and other thinkers. In making this argument in Chapters 2–4 above it is intended that ideological debate regarding Greece will be interpreted in light of or, perhaps, separate from this achievement in theory, if only to avoid the reverse move of interpreting Bentham's theory in light of ideological developments in liberalism and radicalism.[27] This latter move tends to occur when Bentham is taken from his philosophic pedestal so that, as in the view of Winch, the importance of Bentham to the development of political science or philosophical politics in the nineteenth century is his involvement in the ideological debate between 'Philosophic Whigs' and 'Philo-sophic Radicals'.[28] Although, as Winch rightly points out, some Whig opinion was uneasy about Bentham's writing even before he became a radical, this uneasiness seems to stem from an inability to understand the subtlety of his thought beneath the complex and stilted prose style. Real opposition developed after Bentham openly declared ideologically radical views in 1817, but even here the Whig critique of his advocacy of universal suffrage and representative democracy was made by Whigs who none the less accepted the importance of his philosophical work in jurisprudence and in other

[25] S. Collini, D. Winch, and J. Burrow, *That Noble Science of Politics: A Study in Nineteenth Century Intellectual History* (Cambridge, 1983), 9–10.
[26] See ibid. 9.
[27] See e.g. G. H. Sabine, *A History of Political Theory* (3rd edn., London, 1963), 669–700.
[28] Collini, Winch, and Burrow, *That Noble Science of Politics*, 93–126.

spheres. Macaulay's attack on James Mill in 1829, as I have argued elsewhere, was not an attack on Bentham, however much the attack may have hurt Bentham because of his association with Mill and radicalism.[29] In the same manner, though Stanhope was not a disciple of Bentham, Bentham has suffered from the widespread belief that Stanhope was bringing his ideas to Greece. In both cases Bentham has suffered because of a confusion of theory and ideology.

It is possible to write a history of the Greek struggle for independence, as Douglas Dakin has done, without mentioning Bentham at all.[30] Bentham did not actually influence events in any direct sense, and Dakin may be justified in ignoring him. Nevertheless, it is not possible to write such a history without discussing Blaquiere, Bowring, and Stanhope, who did influence events, and Dakin gives them due attention. What Dakin has done is to distinguish implicitly and perhaps unconsciously between ideology and philosophy. Bentham's writings for Greece do not stand in the same relation to events in Greece as do those (say) of Blaquiere and Stanhope. He offered his writings to Greece as he did 'for the use of All Nations and All Governments professing Liberal Opinions'.[31] But he also offered his code to nations and governments that did not profess liberal opinions.[32] His constitutional writings were especially suited, however, for states that did adopt principles of government such as universal suffrage, representative democracy, freedom of speech, widespread publicity and access to information, equal access to protection by the law, freedom to enter and leave the country, access to government posts based on ability, and so forth. Yet, few states that had adopted liberal principles, such as the United States, could conceivably adopt Bentham's proposals—not because they were incoherent, but because they were frankly visionary or utopian.[33] This is not, of

---

[29] See F. Rosen, *Jeremy Bentham and Representative Democracy* (Oxford, 1983) 168–82.

[30] See Douglas Dakin, *The Greek Struggle for Independence 1821–1833* (London, 1973).

[31] J. Bentham, *Constitutional Code*, i, ed. F. Rosen and J. H. Burns (Oxford, 1983) (*CW*), 1.

[32] See 'Securities against Misrule' in *Securities against Misrule and Other Constitutional Writings for Tripoli and Greece*, ed. T. P. Schofield (Oxford, 1990), (*CW*), 23–141. See also *Constitutional Code*, i (*CW*), p. xl.

[33] Referring to his proposals for an educated civil service chosen by competitive examination and other constitutional reforms, Bentham wrote: 'In the meantime, to

course, to deny that many ideas Bentham supported have been adopted by modern states since his day. But for Bentham they were conceived and developed as part of a philosophical theory of constitutional liberty and their appropriateness was their utility and not necessarily their immediate acceptability. Bentham was more concerned, as a philosopher, with the validity of his arguments and the truth of his assertions than with whether or not his codes and schemes were adopted, although he would also have been pleased if they were in fact implemented. As a lawgiver, Bentham was in his lifetime conspicuously unsuccessful, and it is doubtful that he could have survived so much rejection of his ideas if he were not mainly concerned with their truth rather than with their actual adoption by states.

Bentham's writings and activities to advance the Greek cause, as discussed in Chapters 5 and 6, were also unsuccessful. His intervention in the negotiations over the first Greek loan is an excellent example. His proposal for four Commissioners was distinctive in the way it was derived from a theory of interests and not in its acceptability to the parties concerned. It was an excellent solution to a difficult problem, but was none the less unacceptable because neither party could grasp the philosophical insight involved in the solution, and Bowring could not even see its value as a solution to the ideological problem. Without developing a general theory of the problems posed for philosophical politics when it comes into contact with ideological politics, it is sufficient here simply to acknowledge and appreciate that these different levels of discourse actually exist.[34]

5. Byron's Liberalism

Although a full account of Byron's political thought is beyond the scope of this book, it is hoped that this study will provide some

those who have the faculty of extracting amusement from dry matter, it may serve as a second Utopia, adapted to the circumstances of the age. Of the original romance, it may, however, be seen to be—not so much a continuation as the converse. In the Utopia of the sixteenth century, effects present themselves without any appropriate causes; in this of the nineteenth century, appropriate causes are presented waiting for their effects' (Bowring, v. 278).

[34] See Duncan Forbes, *Hume's Philosophical Politics* (Cambridge, 1975).

important correctives to commonly held views, especially about Byron and Bentham, and some guide-lines as to how such an account might be written. Like Bentham, Byron became a liberal icon whose importance to liberalism was not entirely related to his actions in Greece where he was a most moderate reformer, hardly an enthusiast for Greek self-determination, and a victim of both the expedition that failed him and his own need to prove his worth to a society that would not condone his behaviour. This is not to deny that Byron, as Crane Brinton has claimed, 'was one of those who did most to make nationalism the religion of the last century'.[35] But this achievement was not really Byron's, though he, like others, favoured Greek independence. While in his poetry strong national-istic sentiments may have been expressed, in his politics, he was a curious mixture of aristocratic Whig, radical reformer, and earnest liberal. Nor was he hostile to Bentham, to whom, of the various people discussed here, he stands closest both in political doctrine and in belonging primarily to a realm of political discourse apart from ideology. In their search for truth (albeit truth of different sorts) both Bentham and Byron are distinguished from the liberal activists and both are treated somewhat similarly by the wider public—either as eccentrics not entirely to be trusted or as liberal icons of great political significance.

Byron has been linked with 'romantic liberalism', a phrase so far not used in this study.[36] It does not refer to a specific doctrine or set of doctrines, except that its roots are European and its appeal was especially to the young. As for Byron's appeal to the young, there is plenty of evidence in the London Greek Committee archive to suggest that, had Bowring not actively discouraged such a move, a small army of philhellenic volunteers might have been easily collected to join Byron in Greece. 'I should particularly wish to join my Lord Byron,' wrote John Freme to Bowring in September 1823, when Byron's involvement in the expedition was widely publicized. 'Please mention the speediest way of doing it or should you hear of any young men and who are embarking in the same cause I shall be happy in joining them.'[37] Others, who had

---

[35] *The Political Ideas of the English Romanticists* (Ann Arbor, Mich., 1966), 154.
[36] See e.g. John Vincent, *The Formation of the British Liberal Party 1857–1868* (2nd edn., Hassocks, 1976), pp. xiv–xv.
[37] LGC papers, vol. iii, fo. L¹, Freme to Bowring, 11 Sept. 1823; see also fo. Z¹, Bowring to Freme, 22 Sept. 1823.

obviously never travelled abroad, wrote at length to Bowring, including one whose 'only ambition is to be a soldier of liberty', who intended to walk across the Alps in winter, averaging thirty miles a day on foot, to Ancona where he might obtain a passage to Greece.[38] Macaulay also noticed the popularity of Byron among the young, but thought 'this affectation' had disappeared by the end of the 1820s.[39]

Byron's liberalism is a more difficult and complex matter. There is no doubt that he was 'a great spiritual force with European liberals in the nineteenth century'.[40] Yet such an assessment is nearly always qualified. Malcolm Kelsall has rightly emphasized the importance of the Whig patrician tradition in the formation of Byron's views. But to write that 'his Philhellenism . . . derives from a patrician education which saw events in the Peloponnese as if they were a continuation of classical antiquity, and from the usual Whig support for national liberation movements whether in the American colonies, Italy, or Greece', is to oversimplify the complex world of Whig, radical, and liberal in the 1820s.[41] Byron was clearly associated with liberalism at this time and perhaps more so than most. Although Hazlitt saw Byron's liberalism as full of contradiction between his 'haughty and aristocratic' genius and his advocacy of equality, he did not doubt that 'in his politics' Byron was 'a *liberal*', even if he called it 'Lord Byron's preposterous *liberalism*'.[42] Byron's involvement with Leigh Hunt in the publication of the *Liberal* in 1822–3 might also appear to fix Byron as a liberal, except that Leigh Hunt's preface to the first number does not clearly state that the review was meant to form the vanguard of a liberal doctrine.[43] Hunt endorsed the older notion of liberal knowledge and learning, but seemed more ambivalent about

---

[38] Ibid. vol. iv, fo. U[1], Cowie to Bowring, 11 Nov. 1823. See also vol. iii, fo. J[1], Marshall to London Greek Committee, 20 Sept. 1823; vol. vi, fos. U, W, Macguire to Bowring, 24, 31 Jan. 1824; vol. v, fos. B[4]–C[4], Macguire to Bowring, 6, 21 Feb. 1824; vol. vi, fo. K[2], Stokes to Bowring, 16 Mar. 1824; vol. vi, fo. C[5], Child to Bowring, 13 Apr. 1825.

[39] See T. B. Macaulay, 'Moore's Life of Lord Byron', in *The Complete Works of Lord Macaulay*, 12 vols. (London, 1898), vii. 568–9.

[40] R. W. Harris, *Romanticism and the Social Order 1780–1830* (London, 1969), 344.

[41] M. Kelsall, *Byron's Politics* (Brighton, 1987), 195.

[42] William Hazlitt, *The Spirit of the Age*, ed. E. D. Mackerness (London, 1969), 115–16, 125.

[43] Cf. William H. Marshall, *Byron, Shelley, Hunt and the Liberal* (Philadelphia, 1960), 82 ff.

liberalism in a political sense, especially as the review was intended to be more of a literary journal and not overtly political.[44]

Nevertheless, Byron was a liberal in the sense of his being opposed to the European system of 'legitimacy' and in favour of the extension of liberty to states under the yoke of the Holy Alliance. His perspective was clearly European and not simply British; he did not see the Greeks as inferiors as did other Whigs and radicals who dominated the London Greek Committee. However, Byron did not identify overly with Blaquiere whose version of liberalism exhibited strong support for national self-determination. Nor did he follow Stanhope in abandoning Mavrokordatos in seeking to impose, through Odysseus, a 'suitable' government on to the Greeks. But if Stanhope and Blaquiere represent the two strands of early liberalism we have been studying and Byron, clearly a liberal, cannot be associated with either of these, is there yet a third strand of liberalism in existence at this time? It would be tempting to follow other scholars and refer to this strand as 'romantic liberalism', and such a label is useful up to a point. But it fails to emphasize that Byron, like Bentham, was an icon of liberalism, both in the 1820s and to later generations. This view of Byron accommodates not only the way he appeared to others and was used by them, but also the fact that in his politics he was closer to a Whig tradition of constitutional liberty and did not actively embrace an ideological position that might properly be called liberal*ism*. This link with Bentham is an important one, for it extends both to their ideas and to the status of these ideas. Both emerge in the 1820s from a Whig tradition of constitutional liberty with a strong commitment to a radical critique of Whig politics generally. Both look for the acceptance of their ideas abroad and are attracted to the states of the Mediterranean basin. Both offer their services but neither has much direct influence with Byron never to see action in Greece and Bentham never to see his codes adopted there. Both are important to an emerging liberalism in the 1820s, though neither does much to effect the emergence of the doctrine.

Blaquiere and Stanhope were more important in the context of Greece. Yet they have for the most part been forgotten, and Bentham and Byron have not. This essay cannot explain why this

---

[44] See 'Preface', *Liberal*, 1 (1822), pp. viii–ix.

omission should have taken place in the development of liberal ideology. It can only point to what has happened and suggest that a full understanding involves metaphysics more than history. It involves an understanding of the relationships of ideas to action, of ideas to truth, and of appearance to reality. If the history of political ideas provides a unique way to attempt to understand these relationships in context, it does not provide an explanation of what these relationships are. Nor can it be expected to do so, though it can be expected to acknowledge that an understanding of the complexity of these relationships is at the heart of any history of political thought worthy of the name.

Appendix I: Early Membership of the London Greek Committee

Beaumont, Barber
Bennet, Hon. H. G., MP
Bentham, Jeremy
Burdett, Sir F., Bt., MP
Campbell, Robert
Coke, T. W., MP
Dacre, Right Hon. Lord
Davies, Col., MP
Ebrington, Lord, MP
Ellice, Edward, MP
Elphinstone, Sir H., Col. of
  Engineers
Elton, C. A., of Clifton
Erskine, Right Hon. Lord
Evans, W., MP
Gilchrist, J. B.
Gordon, T., of Cairness
Hamilton, Lord A., MP
Henry, J.
Hobhouse, J. C., MP
Hume, Joseph, MP
Hutchinson, Hon. C. H., MP
Kinnaird, Hon. Douglas
Lambton, J. G., MP
Lennard, T. B., MP
Long, Gen.

Macaulay, Zachariah
M'Crie, Dr
Mackintosh, Sir James, MP
Mavrogordato, J.
Maxwell, J., MP
Moore, Thomas
Parkes, Samuel
Paxton, Sir W., Bt., MP
Philips, George, MP
Ralli, N.
Ricardo, D., MP
Rice, T. S., MP
Rogers, Samuel
Rumbold, C., MP
Russell, Lord J., MP
Scarlett, James, MP
Schinas, D.
Smith, John, MP
Smith, W., MP
Taylor, Richard
Turnbull, W.
Weatherstone, G.
Wilks, John
Williams, J., MP
Wilson, Sir R., MP

John Bowring, Hon. Secretary

Source: *Morning Chronicle* (29 Mar. 1823).

Appendix II: Full Membership of the London Greek Committee

Barker, E. H.
Barratt, S. M., MP
Beaumont, Barber
Bennett, Hon. H. G., MP
Bentham, Jeremy
Boddington, Samuel
Brougham, Henry, MP
Burdett, Sir Francis, Bt., MP
Byron, Right Hon. Lord
Campbell, Robert
Campbell, Thomas
Chaloner, Robert, MP
Chatfield, Dr
Christie, John
Clark, Revd Dr Adam
Coke, T. W., MP
Crompton, S., MP
Dacre, Right Hon. Lord
Davies, Col., MP
Dundas, Hon. Capt. George
Ebrington, Lord, MP
Ellice, Edward, MP
Elphinstone, Col. Sir Howard
Elton, C. A., of Clifton
Erskine, Lord
Evans, William, MP
Fitzwilliam, Right Hon. Lord
Gilchrist, J. B.
Gordon, Thomas, of Cairness
Hamilton, Lord A., MP
Henry, J.
Heron, Sir Robert
Hobhouse, J. C., MP
Hume, Joseph, MP
Hutchinson, Hon. C. H., MP

Jones, Col.
Kinnaird, Hon. Douglas
Knight, H. G.
Lambton, J. G., MP
Lawrence, Hon. Sir Robert
Lempriere, Dr, of Sheldon
Lennard, T. B., MP
Long, Gen.
Macaulay, Zachariah
M'Crie, Revd Dr
Mackintosh, Sir James, MP
Maclean, Dr
Mavrogordato, J.
Maxwell, J.
Milton, Lord, MP
Monck, J. B., MP
Moore, Thomas
Nugent, Lord, MP
Ord, William, MP
Parkes, Samuel
Parr, Revd Dr, of Hatton
Paul, Sir T. D., Bt.
Paxton, Sir W.
Philips, George, MP
Pierce, H.
Ralli, N.
Ricardo, D., MP
Rice, T. S., MP
Rogers, Samuel
Rumbold, Charles, MP
Russell, Lord J., MP
Scarlett, James, MP
Schinas, D.
Smith, John, MP
Smith, William, MP

Sondes, Right Hon. Lord
Stanhope, Hon. Col.
Sykes, D., MP
Taylor, Richard
Titchfield, Marq. of
Tulk, Henry
Turnbull, William

Weatherstone, Gen.
Whitmore, W. W., MP
Wilks, John
Williams, J., MP
Williams, W., MP
Wilson, Sir Robert, MP
Wood, Matthew, MP

Hon. Secretary: John Bowring

Source: E. S. De Beer and Walter Seton, 'Byroniana: The Archives of the London Greek Committee', *Nineteenth Century*, 100 (1926), 398 n.

Appendix III: Major Subscriptions to the London Greek Committee

(References to various cities are to subscriptions collected there and remitted to the London Committee.)

Subscriptions of £200 and over:

City of London

Fishmongers Co.

Liverpool

Manchester

Cambridge

Brighton

Sir F. Burdett, Bt., MP

Earl Fitzwilliam

Subscriptions of £100 and over:

Duke of Bedford

John Smith, MP

T. W. Beaumont

Earl Grosvenor

Duke of Gloucester

W. J. Denison

Lord Sondes

Lord Milton, MP

Subscriptions of £40 and over:

Marq. of Titchfield, MP

Lord John Russell, MP

J. Mavrogordato

N. Ralli

Marq. of Lansdowne

T. P. Winter

Aberdeen

Duke of Grafton

Yarmouth

Sir W. W. Pepys, Bt.

Francis Barnard & Son

Nottingham

J. Marshall

Bath

Rickards, Mackintosh & Co.

G. Haldimand

W. Haldimand

Joshua Grigby

Subscriptions of £20 and over:

T. W. Coke, MP

Leicester Stanhope

J. C. Hobhouse, MP

John Wilks

W. Wilberforce, MP

John Maxwell, MP

C. B. Sheridan

William Evans, MP

Edward Ellice, MP

Jeremy Bentham

William Beaumont

James Barnett

James Alexander

Sir George Robinson

G. Philips, MP

Lord A. Hamilton, MP

David Ricardo, MP

Lieut.-Gen. Long

Visc. Glenorchy, MP

Lord Dacre

Sir J. D. Paul, Bt.,
  and R. Snow

John Christie

Col. Davies, MP

Earl of Carysfort

Sir Henry Bunbury

Charles Henderson

Samuel Sharwood

Hon. Gen. Robert Taylor

Earl of Hardwicke

William Williams

S. Henning

C. B. Cockerell

Sir Thomas Dyke Acland,
  Bt., MP

John Heath

J. Fuller

R. Wilson

Sir R. Vyvyan, Bt.

L. White, MP

Marq. of Sligo

Williams, Williams, Burgess
  & Williams

Ralph Leycester

William Strutt

G. B. Strutt

J. Strutt

Earl of Aberdeen

Revd E. Elliott

Lord Carrington

George Smith, MP

S. G. Smith

S. Boddington

Charles Morris

A. L. Prevost

Revd Thomas Gisborne

J. Hawkins

J. G. Lambton, MP

Gen. George Roberts

S. Shore

William Fairlie

Lord W. Bentinck

Sir F. W. Wood, Bt.

J. Gurry

R. Ashe

Lady Ruthven

C. C. Western, MP

Col. James Young

M. B. Lister

Revd Thomas Gosset

Messrs Loughnan, Son,
  & O'Brien

Source: *Morning Chronicle* (19, 26 May, 9, 23 June, 18 July, 5 Aug., 1, 29
Sept., 30 Oct. 1823, 26 Jan., 15 Mar. 1824).

Bibliography

(Note: This bibliography is confined to manuscript collections and works cited in the text and notes.)

MANUSCRIPTS

Aberdeen University Library: Gordon papers.
Benaki Museum, Athens: General archives; Mavrokordatos papers.
Bibliothèque Publique et Universitaire, Geneva: Dumont papers.
Bodleian Library, Oxford: Barker correspondence.
British Library: Bentham papers; Broughton papers; Place papers.
British School of Archaeology at Athens: Finlay and Hastings papers.
Centre for Neo-Hellenic Research, National Research Foundation, Athens: Louriottis papers.
ELIA, Athens: Archeio Spiridon Tricoupi.
General State Archives: Copybooks, Orlandos and Louriottis correspondence; Mavrokordatos papers; Stanhope papers, K. 121.
John Murray (Publishers) Ltd.: General archive.
Kent County Record Office, Maidstone: Guilford papers.
National Library of Greece, Athens: London Greek Committee papers.
Public Record Office, London: Colonial Office papers.
University College London: Bentham letters and manuscripts; Brougham papers.

NEWSPAPERS

Bath and Cheltenham Gazette
Bath Chronicle
Bristol Gazette
Calcutta Journal
Cobbett's Weekly Register
Courier
Examiner
Globe and Traveller
Greco telegrapho

Hampshire Telegraph and Sussex Chronicle
Hellenika chronika
Liberal
Liverpool Mercury
Manchester Guardian
Mechanics' Magazine
Morning Chronicle
Southampton County Chronicle and Isle of Wight Journal
The Times

BOOKS AND ARTICLES

ALLEN, W., The Life of William Allen with Selections from His Correspondence, 3 vols. (London, 1846).
ARBLASTER, A., The Rise and Decline of Western Liberalism (Oxford, 1984).
ARISTOTLE, Politics, trans. H. Rackham (Loeb Classical Library) (London, 1967).
BAHMUELLER, C. F., The National Charity Company: Jeremy Bentham's Silent Revolution (Berkeley, Calif., 1981).
BARKER, E. H., A Letter Addressed to the Rev. T. S. Hughes (Southampton, 1822).
BARTLE, G. F., 'Bowring and the Greek Loans of 1824 and 1825', Balkan Studies, 3 (1962), 61–74.
—— 'The Greek Boys at Borough Road during the War of Independence', Journal of Educational Administration and History, 20 (1988), 1–11.
—— 'The Political Career of Sir John Bowring (1792–1872) between 1820 and 1849', (MA thesis, London University, 1959).
BAUMGARDT, D., Bentham and the Ethics of Today (Princeton, NJ, 1952).
BEARCE, G., British Attitudes towards India, 1784–1858 (Oxford, 1961).
BELCHEM, J., 'Orator' Hunt: Henry Hunt and English Working-Class Radicalism (Oxford, 1985).
BENTHAM, J., The Collected Works of Jeremy Bentham, ed. J. H. Burns (1961–79), J. R. Dinwiddy (1977–83), F. Rosen (1983–) (in progress):
—— Chrestomathia, ed. M. J. Smith and W. H. Burston (Oxford, 1983).
—— A Comment on the Commentaries and A Fragment on Government, ed. J. H. Burns and H. L. A. Hart (London, 1977).
—— Constitutional Code, i, ed. F. Rosen and J. H. Burns (Oxford, 1983).
—— Correspondence, i and ii (1752–80), ed. T. L. S. Sprigge (London, 1968).
—— Correspondence, iii (1781–8), ed. I. Christie (London, 1971).
—— Correspondence, iv and v (1788–97), ed. A. Taylor Milne (London, 1981).

—— *Correspondence*, vi (1798–1801), ed. J. R. Dinwiddy (Oxford, 1984).

—— *Correspondence*, vii (1802–8), ed. J. R. Dinwiddy (Oxford, 1988).

—— *Correspondence*, viii (1809–16), ed. S. R. Conway (Oxford, 1988).

—— *Correspondence*, ix (1817–20), ed. S. R. Conway (Oxford, 1989).

—— *Deontology, Together with A Table of the Springs of Action and Article on Utilitarianism*, ed. A. Goldworth (Oxford, 1983).

—— *First Principles Preparatory to Constitutional Code*, ed. T. P. Schofield (Oxford, 1989).

—— *An Introduction to the Principles of Morals and Legislation*, ed. J. H. Burns and H. L. A. Hart (London, 1970).

—— *Of Laws in General*, ed. H. L. A. Hart (London, 1970).

—— *Securities against Misrule and Other Constitutional Writings for Tripoli and Greece*, ed. T. P. Schofield (Oxford, 1990).

—— *A Fragment on Government*, ed. F. C. Montague (Oxford, 1891).

—— *The Iberian Correspondence of Jeremy Bentham*, ed. P. Schwartz, 2 vols. (London and Madrid, 1979).

—— *Traités de législation, civile et pénale*, ed. E. Dumont, 3 vols. (Paris, 1802).

—— *The Works of Jeremy Bentham*, ed. J. Bowring, 11 vols. (Edinburgh, 1838–43).

BLACKSTONE, W., *Commentaries on the Laws of England*, 4 vols. (Oxford, 1765–9).

BLAMIRES, C., 'Étienne Dumont: Genevan Apostle of Utility', *Utilitas*, 2 (1990), 55–70.

BLAQUIERE, E., *The Greek Revolution* (London, 1824).

—— *An Historical Review of the Spanish Revolution* (London, 1822).

—— *Letters from Greece; with Remarks on the Treaty of Intervention* (London, 1828).

—— *Letters from the Mediterranean*, 2 vols. (London, 1813).

—— *Narrative of a Second Visit to Greece* (London, 1825).

—— *Report on the Present State of the Greek Confederation* (London, 1823).

BORALEVI, LEA CAMPOS, *Bentham and the Oppressed* (Berlin, 1984).

BOWRING, J., *The Autobiographical Recollections of Sir John Bowring*, ed. L. B. Bowring (London, 1877).

—— *Details of the Arrest, Imprisonment and Liberation, of an Englishman, by the Bourbon Government of France* (London, 1823).

—— 'Greek Committee', *Westminster Review*, 6 (1826), 113–33.

—— *Observations on the State of Religion and Literature in Spain, made during a Journey through the Peninsula in 1819* (London, 1819).

BRENT, R., *Liberal Anglican Politics: Whiggery, Religion, and Reform, 1830–1841* (Oxford, 1987).

BRINTON, C., *The Political Ideas of the English Romanticists* (Ann Arbor, Mich., 1966).

BUCKINGHAM, JOHN SILK, 'Greece in 1823 and 1824', *Oriental Herald and Colonial Review*, 3 (1824), 334–40.
—— 'Tyrannical Conduct of the Austrian Authorities towards the Honourable Leicester Stanhope', *Oriental Herald and Colonial Review*, 5 (1825), 437–41.

BULLOCK, A., and SCHOCK, M. (eds.), *The Liberal Tradition from Fox to Keynes* (London, 1956).

BULWER, H. LYTTON, *An Autumn in Greece* (London, 1826).

BURNS, J. H., 'Bentham and Blackstone: A Lifetime's Dialectic', *Utilitas*, 1 (1989), 22–40.
—— 'Bentham and the French Revolution', *Transactions of the Royal Historical Society*, 5th Series, 16 (1966), 95–114.

BURROW, J. W., *Whigs and Liberals: Continuity and Change in English Political Thought* (Oxford, 1988).

BURSTON, W. H., *James Mill on Philosophy and Education* (London, 1973).

BYRON, GEORGE GORDON, LORD, *Byron's Letters and Journals*, ed. L. Marchand, 12 vols. (London, 1973–82: x: *'A heart for every fate'* (1822–3) (London, 1980); xi: *'For Freedom's battle'* (1823–4) (London, 1981).

CHAPMAN, MARGARET, 'Thomas Gordon of Cairness: The Struggle for Greek Independence', *Aberdeen University Review*, 47 (1978), 238–48.

COLLINI, S., WINCH, D., and BURROW, J., *That Noble Science of Politics: A Study in Nineteenth Century Intellectual History* (Cambridge, 1983).

CONWAY, S. R., 'Bentham and the Nineteenth Century Revolution in Government', in R. Bellamy (ed.), *Victorian Liberalism* (London, 1990), 71–90.

COOKSON, J. E., *The Friends of Peace: Anti-War Liberalism in England, 1793–1815* (Cambridge, 1982).

CRANSTON, M., *Freedom: A New Analysis* (London, 1953).

CROMPTON, L., *Byron and Greek Love: Homophobia in 19th-Century England* (London, 1985).

DAKIN, D., *British and American Philhellenes during the War of Greek Independence, 1821–1833* (Thessaloniki, 1955).
—— *The Greek Struggle for Independence 1821–1833* (London, 1973).

DALLEGGIO, E., *Les Philhellènes et la guerre de l'indépendance* (Athens, 1949).

DAVIS, RICHARD W., *Dissent in Politics, 1780–1830: The Political Life of William Smith, MP* (London, 1971).

DAWSON, FRANK GRIFFITH, *The First Latin American Debt Crisis: The City of London and the 1822–25 Loan Bubble* (New Haven, Conn., 1990).

DE BEER, E. S., and SETON, WALTER, 'Byroniana: The Archives of the London Greek Committee', *Nineteenth Century*, 100 (1926), 396–412.

DELOLME, JEAN LOUIS, *The Constitution of England; or, An Account of the English Government* (London, 1775).

DICKINSON, H. T., *Liberty and Property: Political Ideology in Eighteenth-Century Britain* (London, 1977).

DIMARAS, ALEXIS, 'Foreign, and Particularly English, Influences on Educational Policies in Greece during the War of Independence and Their Development under Capodistrias, 1821–31' (Ph.D. thesis, London University, 1973).

—— 'The Other British Philhellenes', in Richard Clogg (ed.), *The Struggle for Greek Independence* (London, 1973), 200–23.

DINWIDDY, J. R., 'Bentham and the Early Nineteenth Century', *Bentham Newsletter*, 8 (1984), 15–33.

—— 'Bentham's Transition to Political Radicalism, 1809–10', *Journal of the History of Ideas*, 36 (1975), 683–700.

—— 'The Early Nineteenth-Century Campaign against Flogging in the Army', *English Historical Review*, 97 (1982), 308–31.

—— 'Early Nineteenth-Century Reactions to Benthamism', *Transactions of the Royal Historical Society*, 5th Series, 34 (1984), 47–69.

—— *From Luddism to the First Reform Bill: Reform in England 1810–1832* (Oxford, 1986).

DODGE, G. H., *Benjamin Constant's Philosophy of Liberalism: A Study in Politics and Religion* (Chapel Hill, NC, 1980).

DROULIA, L., *Philhellénisme: Ouvrages inspirés par la guerre de l'indépendance grecque 1821–1833* (Athens, 1974).

DUBE, D. A., 'The Theme of Acquisitiveness in Bentham's Political Thought' (Ph.D. thesis, London University, 1989).

ELLIOTT, E. B., *Appeal from the Greek Committee to the British Public in General, and Especially to the Friends of Religion* (London, 1823).

EMERSON, J., 'Journal of a Residence among the Greeks in 1825', in *A Picture of Greece in 1825: As Exhibited in the Personal Narratives of James Emerson, Esq., Count Pecchio, and W. H. Humphreys, Esq.*, 2 vols. (London, 1826).

FLETCHER, F. T. H., *Montesquieu and English Politics* (London, 1939).

FOOT, M., *The Politics of Paradise: A Vindication of Byron* (London, 1988).

FORBES, DUNCAN, *Hume's Philosophical Politics* (Cambridge, 1975).

FRANCIS, J., *Chronicles and Characters of the Stock Exchange* (London, 1855).

GAMBA, P., *A Narrative of Lord Byron's Last Journey to Greece* (London, 1825).

GOBBI, C., 'Edward Blaquière: Agente del liberalismo', *Cuadernos hispano-americanos*, 350 (1979), 306–25.

GORDON, BARRY, *Economic Doctrine and Tory Liberalism, 1824–1830* (London, 1979).

GORDON, THOMAS, *History of the Greek Revolution*, 2 vols. (Edinburgh, 1832).

GRAY, J., *Liberalisms: Essays in Political Philosophy* (London, 1989).

GREEN, P. J., *Sketches of the War in Greece* (London, 1827).

GRIFFITHS, P., *The British Impact on India* (London, 1952).

HALÉVY, E., *La Formation du Radicalisme Philosophique*, 3 vols. (Paris, 1901–4). trans. Mary Morris as *The Growth of Philosophic Radicalism* (London, 1928).

—— *A History of the English People*, trans. E. I. Watkin, 6 vols. (London, 1961).

—— *Thomas Hodgskin*, trans. A. J. Taylor (London, 1956).

HAMBURGER, J., *Intellectuals in Politics: John Stuart Mill and the Philosophic Radicals* (New Haven, Conn., 1965).

HAMILTON, A., JAY, J., and MADISON, J., *The Federalist* (New York, n.d.) (The Modern Library Edition).

HARRIS, R. W., *Romanticism and the Social Order 1780–1830* (London, 1969).

HARRISON, R., *Bentham* (The Arguments of the Philosophers) (London, 1983).

HART, H. L. A., *The Concept of Law* (Oxford, 1961).

—— *Essays on Bentham: Studies in Jurisprudence and Political Theory* (Oxford, 1982).

HAZLITT, W., *The Spirit of the Age; or, Contemporary Portraits,* ed. E. D. Mackerness (London, 1969).

HEY, R., *Happiness and Rights: A Dissertation upon Several Subjects Relative to the Rights of Man and His Happiness* (York, 1792).

—— *Observations on the Nature of Civil Liberty, and the Principles of Government* (London, 1776).

HILTON, BOYD, *Corn, Cash, Commerce: The Economic Policies of the Tory Governments, 1815–1830* (Oxford, 1977).

HINDE, WENDY, *George Canning* (London, 1973).

HOBBES, T., *Leviathan* (Oxford, 1962).

HOBHOUSE, J. C., *Byron's Bulldog: The Letters of John Cam Hobhouse to Lord Byron,* ed. Peter W. Graham (Columbus, Oh., 1984).

HODGSKIN, T., *An Essay on Naval Discipline* (London, 1813).

—— *Labour Defended against the Claims of Capital* (London, 1825).

—— *Travels in the North of Germany* (Edinburgh, 1820).

HOLYOAKE, GEORGE JACOB, *Sixty Years of an Agitator's Life*, 2 vols. (London, 1892).

HOUGHTON, WALTER E. (ed.), *Wellesley Index to Victorian Periodicals 1824–1900*, 4 vols. (Toronto, 1966–87).

HUCH, RONALD, and ZIEGLER, PAUL R., *Joseph Hume: The People's MP* (Philadelphia, 1985).

HUGHES, T. S., *An Address to the People of England in the Cause of the Greeks, Occasioned by the Late Inhuman Massacres in the Isle of Scio* (London, 1822).

HUME, DAVID, *Essays: Moral, Political, and Literary*, ed. E. F. Miller (Liberty Classics Edition) (Indianapolis, 1985).

—— *The History of England from the Invasion of Julius Caesar to the Revolution in 1688*, 6 vols. (Liberty Classics Edition) (Indianapolis, 1983).

HUME, L. J., *Bentham and Bureaucracy* (Cambridge, 1981).
—— 'Preparations for Civil War in Tripoli in the 1820s: Ali Karamanli, Hassuna D'Ghies and Jeremy Bentham', *Journal of African History*, 21 (1980), 311–22.

HUMPHREYS, W. H., 'Journal of a Visit to Greece', *A Picture of Greece in 1825: As Exhibited in the Personal Narratives of James Emerson, Esq., Count Pecchio, and W. H. Humphreys, Esq.*, 2 vols. (London, 1826).
—— *W. H. Humphreys' First 'Journal of the Greek War of Independence'*, ed. Sture Linnér (Stockholm, 1967).

INGHAM, K., *Reformers in India, 1793–1833* (Cambridge, 1956).

JAMES, M. H., 'Bentham's Democratic Theory at the Time of the French Revolution', *Bentham Newsletter*, 10 (1986), 5–16.

KEDOURIE, E., *Nationalism* (rev. edn., New York, 1961).

KELLY, P. J., *Utilitarianism and Distributive Justice: Jeremy Bentham and the Civil Law* (Oxford, 1990).

KELLY, T., *George Birkbeck: Pioneer of Adult Education* (Liverpool, 1957).
—— *Radical Tailor: The Life and Work of Francis Place (1771–1854)* (London, 1972).

KELSALL, MALCOLM, *Byron's Politics* (Brighton, 1987).

KENNEDY, J., *Conversations on Religion with Lord Byron and Others* (London, 1830).

KING, S. T., 'James Silk Buckingham 1786–1855: Social and Political Reformer' (MA thesis, London University, 1933).

KITROMILIDES, P., 'Jeremy Bentham and Adamantios Korais', *Bentham Newsletter*, 9 (1985), 34–48.
—— 'Tradition, Enlightenment, and Revolution: Ideological Change in Eighteenth and Nineteenth Century Greece' (Ph.D. thesis, Harvard University, 1978).

KORAIS, A., *Sēmeiōsis eis to prosōrinon politeuma tēs Ellados tou 1822 etous*, ed. Th. P. Volides (Athens, 1933).

LASKI, H., *The Rise of European Liberalism* (London, 1936).

LIEBERMAN, D., *The Province of Legislation Determined: Legal Theory in Eighteenth-Century Britain* (Cambridge, 1989).

LIGNADĒ, ANASTASIOU D., *To Proton Daneion tēs Anexartēsias* [The First Loan of Independence] (Athens, 1970).

LIND, J., *Three Letters to Dr. Price . . .* (London, 1776).

LIVELY, J., and REES, J. (eds.), *Utilitarian Logic and Politics* (Oxford, 1978).

LOCKE, J., *An Essay Concerning Human Understanding*, ed. A. C. Fraser, 2 vols. (New York, 1959).
—— *Two Treatises of Government*, ed. P. Laslett (Cambridge, 1963).

LOCKHART, J. G., 'Parry's Last Days of Lord Byron', *Blackwood's Edinburgh Magazine*, 18 (1825), 137–55.

LONG, DOUGLAS G., *Bentham on Liberty: Jeremy Bentham's Idea of Liberty in Relation to His Utilitarianism* (Toronto, 1977).

LOWENTHAL, E., *The Ricardian Socialists* (New York, 1911).

MACAULAY, T. B., 'Moore's Life of Lord Byron', *The Complete Works of Lord Macaulay*, 12 vols. (London, 1898), vii. 528–69.

MACPHERSON, C. B., *The Life and Times of Liberal Democracy* (Oxford, 1977).

—— *The Political Theory of Possessive Individualism* (Oxford, 1962).

MANNING, D. J., *Liberalism* (London, 1976).

MARCHAND, L., *Byron: A Biography*, 3 vols. (London, 1957).

—— *Byron: A Portrait* (London, 1971).

MARSHALL, WILLIAM H., *Byron, Shelley, Hunt and the Liberal* (Philadelphia, 1960).

MILES, DUDLEY, *Francis Place: The Life of a Remarkable Radical 1771–1854* (Brighton, 1988).

MILL, J. S., *The Collected Works of John Stuart Mill*, ed. J. M. Robson, *et al.*: vi: *Essays on England, Ireland, and the Empire*, ed. J. M. Robson (Toronto, 1982); xii–xiii: *The Earlier Letters of John Stuart Mill*, ed. F. Mineka (Toronto, 1963); xix: *Essays on Politics and Society*, ed. J. M. Robson (Toronto, 1977); xxii–xxv: *Newspaper Writings*, ed. Ann and J. M. Robson (Toronto, 1986).

MILLINGEN, J., *Memoirs of the Affairs of Greece* (London, 1831).

MINOGUE, K., *Nationalism* (London, 1967).

MONTESQUIEU, BARON DE, *De l'esprit des lois*, *Œuvres complètes* (Paris, 1964).

MOORE, DORIS LANGLEY, *The Late Lord Byron: Posthumous Dramas* (London, 1961).

—— *Lord Byron: Accounts Rendered* (London, 1974).

NEW, CHESTER, *The Life of Henry Brougham to 1830* (Oxford, 1961).

NICOLSON, HAROLD, *Byron: The Last Journey, April 1823–April 1824* (new edn., London, 1948).

PALEY, W., *The Principles of Moral and Political Philosophy* (London, 1785).

—— *The Works of William Paley, D.D.*, 5 vols. (London, 1819).

PALMA, ALERINO, *Greece Vindicated* (London, 1826).

—— *A Summary Account of the Steamboats for Lord Cochrane's Expedition* (London, 1826).

PANANTI, Signor F., *Narrative of a Residence in Algiers*, ed. E. Blaquiere (London, 1818).

PARRY, WILLIAM, *The Last Days of Lord Byron* (London, 1825).

PATEMAN, CAROLE, *Participation and Democratic Theory* (Cambridge, 1970).

PECCHIO, Count G., *Anecdotes of the Spanish and Portuguese Revolutions*, ed. E. Blaquiere (London, 1823).

—— *Semi-serious Observations of an Italian Exile, during his Residence in England* (London, 1823).

—— 'A Visit to Greece in the Spring of 1825', *A Picture of Greece in 1825: As Exhibited in the Personal Narratives of James Emerson, Esq., Count Pecchio, and W. H. Humphreys, Esq.*, 2 vols. (London, 1826).

PENN, VIRGINIA, 'Philhellenism in England (1821–1827)', *Slavonic Review*, 14 (1935–6), 363–71, 647–60.

—— 'Philhellenism in Europe, 1821–1828', *Slavonic Review*, 16 (1937–8), 638–53.

PHILIPS, C. H., *The East India Company, 1784–1834* (London, 1949).

PLAMENATZ, J. (ed.), *Readings from Liberal Writers, English and French* (London, 1965).

PLATO, *Republic*, trans. P. Shorey (Loeb Classical Library), 2 vols. (London, 1963).

POCOCK, J. G. A., *Virtue, Commerce, and History: Essays on Political Thought and History, Chiefly in the Eighteenth Century* (Cambridge, 1985).

POLYCHRONIADES, K., *Remarks on the Present State of Turkey, Considered in Its Commercial and Political Relation with England* (London, 1821).

POSTEMA, G. J., *Bentham and the Common Law Tradition* (Oxford, 1986).

PRICE, R., *Additional Observations on the Nature and Value of Civil Liberty* (London, 1777).

—— *Observations on the Nature of Civil Liberty, the Principles of Government, and the Justice and Policy of the War with America* (London, 1776).

PRIESTLEY, J., *An Essay on the First Principles of Government; and on the Nature of Political, Civil, and Religious Liberty* (London, 1768).

The Provisional Constitution of Greece (London, 1823).

PRYME, G., *Autobiographic Recollections of George Pryme, Esq. M.A.*, edited by His Daughter [A. Bayne] (Cambridge, 1870).

QUENNELL, PETER, *Byron: The Years of Fame* (Harmondsworth, 1954).

RAFFENEL, C. D., *Histoire des événemens de la Grèce* (Paris, 1822).

ROSEN, F., 'Bentham and Mill on Liberty and Justice', in G. Feaver and F. Rosen (eds.), *Lives, Liberties, and the Public Good* (London, 1987), 121–38.

—— 'Bentham's Letters and Manuscripts in Greece', *Bentham Newsletter*, 5 (1981), 55–8.

—— 'Elie Halévy and Bentham's Authoritarian Liberalism', *Enlightenment and Dissent*, 6 (1987), 59–76.

—— *Jeremy Bentham and Representative Democracy: A Study of the Constitutional Code* (Oxford, 1983).

—— 'A Note on Bentham and Korais', *Bentham Newsletter*, 9 (1985), 49–50.

ROSENBLUM, NANCY, *Another Liberalism: Romanticism and the Reconstruction of Liberal Thought* (Cambridge, Mass., 1987).

SABINE, G. H., *A History of Political Theory* (3rd edn., London, 1963).

ST CLAIR, WILLIAM, 'Postscript to *The Last Days of Lord Byron*', *Keats–Shelley Journal*, 19 (1970), 4–7.

—— *That Greece Might Still Be Free: The Philhellenes in the War of Independence* (London, 1972).

Schwartz, P., 'Bentham's Influence in Spain, Portugal, and Latin America', *Bentham Newsletter*, 1 (1978), 34–5.

Semmel, Bernard, *Liberalism and Naval Strategy: Ideology, Interest and Sea Power during the Pax Britannica* (Boston, 1986).

Semple, Janet, 'Jeremy Bentham's Panopticon Prison' (Ph.D. thesis, London University, 1990).

Shackleton, R., *Montesquieu* (Oxford, 1961).

Sheppard, F. H. W. (ed.), *Survey of London*, xxxvii (London, 1973).

Siedentop, L., 'Two Liberal Traditions', in A. Ryan (ed.), *The Idea of Freedom* (Oxford, 1979), 153–74.

Spear, P., *The Nabobs: A Study of the Social Life of the English in Eighteenth-Century India* (London, 1932).

Stanhope, L., *The Earl of Harrington on the Maine-Law; on the Law of Libel, as Opposed to the Declaration of Truth and the Defence of Character; and Other Subjects* (Derby and London, 1858).

—— *Greece, in 1823 and 1824; being a Series of Letters, and Other Documents, on the Greek Revolution, Written during a Visit to that Country* (new edn., London, 1825).

—— 'Letter of the Hon. Leicester Stanhope to the Editor of Blackwood's Magazine', *Oriental Herald and Colonial Review*, 7 (1825), 113–16.

—— *The Military Commentator; or, Thoughts upon the Construction of the Military Code of England, Contrasted with that of the Codes of Other Nations; Together with Remarks upon the Administration of that Code, Particularly with Regard to Military Flogging* (London, 1813).

—— *Sketch of the History and Influence of the Press in British India* (London, 1823).

Stokes, E., *The English Utilitarians and India* (Oxford, 1959).

Tarlton, C. D., 'The Overlooked Strategy of Bentham's *Fragment on Government*', *Political Studies*, 20 (1972), 397–406.

Temperley, H. V., *The Foreign Policy of George Canning, 1822–1827* (London, 1925).

Thomas, D. O., *The Honest Mind: The Thought and Work of Richard Price* (Oxford, 1977).

Thomas, William, *The Philosophic Radicals: Nine Studies in Theory and Practice, 1817–1841* (Oxford, 1979).

Thompson, E. P., *The Making of the English Working Class* (Harmondsworth, 1968).

Thompson, N. W., *The People's Science: The Popular Political Economy of Exploitation and Crisis 1816–34* (Cambridge, 1984).

Tocqueville, Alexis de, *Recollections*, ed. J. P. Mayer and A. P. Kerr, trans. G. Lawrence (London, 1970).

Triantaphyllopoulos, K., 'Ypomnima tou Bentham peri tou prōtou ellēnikou politeumatos kai anekdotoi apantēseis tou Bouleutikou', *Praktika tēs Akadēmias Athēnon*, 37 (1962), 80–7.

TULLY, J. (ed.), *Meaning and Context: Quentin Skinner and His Critics* (Cambridge, 1988).

VILE, M. J. C., *Constitutionalism and the Separation of Powers* (Oxford, 1967).

VINCENT, JOHN, *The Formation of the British Liberal Party 1857–1868* (2nd edn., Hassocks, 1976).

VOLTAIRE, *Letters on England*, trans. L. Tancock (Harmondsworth, 1986).

WADDINGTON, G., *A Visit to Greece in 1823 and 1824* (2nd edn., London, 1825).

WICKWAR, W. H., *The Struggle for the Freedom of the Press 1819–1832* (London, 1928).

WOODHOUSE, C. M., *The Philhellenes* (London, 1969).

ZEGGER, R. E., *John Cam Hobhouse: A Political Life 1819–1852* (Columbia, Mo., 1973).

ZEPOS, PAN J., 'Jeremy Bentham and the Greek Independence', *Proceedings of the British Academy*, 62 (1976), 293–305.

Index